The late Victorian army

Manchester History of the British Army
Ian F. W. Beckett *general editor*
There has been no multi-volume history of the British army for over sixty years and this series of volumes is intended to fill that gap, drawing together the new social, economic and political scholarship that has become integrated with more traditional campaign history. The new nine-volume history of the British army will include the most recent academic research to address such subjects as organisation, training, the recruitment of officers and men, conditions of service and the relationship of the army with society and state. The history will be contributed by leading authorities in each period of the army's development and will be an invaluable guide for undergraduates and postgraduates, as well as academics and specialists in military history. The volumes will also appeal to the wider readership interested in military affairs.

Also in the series:

Ian F. W. Beckett *The amateur military tradition, 1558–1945*

The late Victorian army
1868–1902

Edward M. Spiers

Manchester University Press
Manchester and New York
Distributed exclusively in the USA and Canada by St. Martin's Press

Copyright © Edward M. Spiers 1992

Published by Manchester University Press
Oxford Road, Manchester M13 9PL, UK
and Room 400, 175 Fifth Avenue, New York, NY 10010, USA

Distributed exclusively in the USA and Canada
by St. Martin's Press, Inc., 175 Fifth Avenue, New York,
NY 10010, USA

British Library Cataloguing-in-Publication Data
A catalogue record for this book is available from the British Library

Library of Congress Cataloging-in-Publication Data
Spiers, Edward M.
    The late Victorian army, 1868–1902 / Edward M. Spiers.
        p.   cm.—(Manchester history of the British army)
    Includes bibliographical references (p.   ) and index.
    ISBN 0–7190–2659–8
    1. Great Britain—History, Military—19th century. 2. Great
Britain—History—Victoria, 1837–1901. 3. Great Britain. Army—
History—19th century. I. Title. II. Series.
DA560.S65   1992
941.081—dc20   91–33282

ISBN 0 7190 2659 8 *hardback*

Photoset in Linotron Sabon
by Northern Phototypesetting Company Limited, Bolton

Printed in Great Britain
by Redwood Press Ltd, Melksham

Contents

Tables

Illustrations

'They belong to the First Coldstream Guards, but don't look it': the garrison of No. 29 blockhouse during the Second

Preface

When Ian Beckett invited me to write a volume in a multi-volume series, to be known as the Manchester History of the British Army, I accepted with alacrity. I relished the opportunity of contributing to a series which would demonstrate the transformation of writing about British military history over the past generation. This has been particularly evident in writing about the late Victorian period, where there has been a profusion of publications – books, articles and doctoral dissertations – over the past thirty years. Much of this phenomenon derives from the stimulus provided by the scholarship and teaching of Professor Brian Bond. His pioneering writings in the 1960s and 1970s, along with those of Jay Luvaas and W.S. Hamer, indicated that writing in this area could transcend the limits of biographies, campaign studies, and regimental histories. Moreover, as scholars followed in their wake over the next two decades, they have unearthed more and more collections of private papers or have benefited from those which have recently been placed in the national repositories. There is now a vast array of material, published and unpublished, in this field.

It is now possible to review many aspects of military history in this period, to place the army in a broader social and political context, to assess its response to changes in technology and tactics, and to evaluate its utility as an instrument of imperialism. During the last quarter of the nineteenth century the army faced an expanding range of commitments at home and overseas but had to undertake them, or plan to do so, within significant constraints. These constraints included the structural organisation created by the Cardwell reforms, the parsimony of successive governments, the dependence upon voluntary recruiting, and the failure to create a General Staff.

All these factors impinged upon the functioning and effectiveness of the late Victorian army, constraining the scope of its peacetime training, its mobilisation planning, and the state of its combat readiness. How the army coped in these circumstances, both in peace and war, warrants analysis, as does the manner in which it lobbied for more resources and pressed for political guidance about its strategic priorities. Just as important was the way in which successive governments responded to the increasing strains and even bitterness which became a feature of civil–military relations, and to the pressures for further reform from within the military, Parliament and the press.

Cardwell had sought to alleviate some of the strains in the military system by enhancing the appeal of service life and broadening the base of recruitment. In promoting his reforms, he raised expectations that his measures might bring about a major change in the army's social composition. This change never materialised, and the reasons for the failure will become apparent from an analysis of the social composition of the officers and other ranks, the nature of their life-style, and their education, training and promotion prospects. Recruiting remained an intractable problem throughout this period, despite the considerable popularity of the army as an instrument of imperialism. The depth of the army's appeal was reflected in plays, songs and exhibitions, in battle painting, fiction, and paramilitary activities, and in reporting during the 'golden age' of the war correspondent. The central paradox remains and has to be addressed, namely why was a military career held in such low esteem while the army's achievements overseas were popularly acclaimed?

Undoubtedly this popularity derived partly from the army's ability to respond to the many demands of colonial campaigning, to overcome a number of ferocious enemies, and to preserve or expand the Empire. As many of these wars were first and foremost wars against nature, involving arduous expeditions over difficult terrain in debilitating climates, the army placed a premium upon meeting its logistical requirements. In making these provisions, field commanders and their staffs had to rely partly upon improvisation, partly upon the support services (some of which were extensively reorganised in this period), and partly upon the assistance of civilian auxiliaries. Commanders had the advantage of extensive experience in small colonial warfare, but this was a mixed blessing. Forced to adapt to the peculiar circumstances of each campaign, they sometimes had to fight in formations rendered obsolete by modern weapons, refining their tactics and their notions of command and staff-work accordingly. They lacked the experience of fighting in a large-scale war, and had never encountered an enemy which was armed and proficient in the use of smokeless, small-calibre, long-range magazine rifles. Although the army had rearmed with these weapons in the late 1880s and 1890s, and had begun to modify its tactics in the light of them, the significance of the new weapons was still disputed, especially by the cavalry and artillery, training was severely restricted outside Aldershot, and the potential impact of the weapons not fully appreciated.

Hence the Second South African War proved a decisive test as the army encountered a well-armed and highly mobile adversary, capable of inflicting humiliating defeats upon it and of conducting a resourceful guerilla campaign. Although the army eventually prevailed, the war proved more protracted, more costly and more controversial than anyone had expected. It raised a multitude of questions about the adequacy of the army's pre-war preparations and its performance in the field. It occasioned a heated debate among contemporaries about the 'lessons' of the war, prompted the War Office to embark upon the process of army reform, and fuelled a debate among future historians about the British military performance. As the historiographical debate indicates, the military triumph raised more questions than it answered; it bequeathed an uncertain legacy which was only turned to the army's advantage by a shrewd and adroit politician, Richard Burdon Haldane, and by his capable military advisers.

Edward M. Spiers
1 September 1991

Acknowledgements

I should like to acknowledge my gratitude to several colleagues who have assisted me in the preparation of this work. I am particularly grateful to Dr Ian Beckett, the academic editor of the series, who proffered the original invitation to write the volume and who cheerfully and helpfully advised me whenever I sought his assistance. I am indebted, too, to the support and encouragement of Professor David Dilks, School of History, University of Leeds, and of Professor Brian Bond, Department of War Studies, King's College, London. I appreciate, finally, the endeavours of the staff of Manchester University Press to publish the book as expeditiously as possible, especially the contribution of Jane Carpenter.

I should like to acknowledge my indebtedness to Her Majesty the Queen for her gracious permission to use materials from the Royal Archives at Windsor Castle. I am also grateful for the permission of the Controller of Her Majesty's Stationery Office to make references from Crown-copyright records in the Public Record Office. I further appreciate the generosity of the following for enabling me to consult and, where requested, to reproduce material from archives in their possession and/or copyright: namely, Earl Haig, Dr Roger Stearn, the Army Museums Ogilby Trust, the Black Watch Archive, the Trustees of the British Library Board, the Centre for Kentish Studies, Kent Record Office, Hove Reference Library, the India Office Library, the King's Own Scottish Borderers Museum, the Trustees of the Liddell Hart Centre for Military Archives, King's College London, the Ministry of Defence Whitehall Library, the National Army Museum, the National Library of Scotland, Queen Mary and Westfield College, University of London, the Scottish Record Office, the Worcestershire and Sherwood Foresters Regimental Museum.

I am grateful for the assistance of several librarians and their staffs, including Ms Sheila de Bellaigue (Registrar, Royal Archives), Dr Peter Boyden and Miss Clare Wright (Department of Archives, Photographs, Film and Sound, National Army Museum), Mr Brian Murphy (Queen Mary and Westfield College), Mr M.M. Chapman (Head of Reader Services, Ministry of Defence Whitehall Library), Colonel (Retd.) the Honourable W.D. Arbuthnott, MBE (the Black Watch Archive), Mr Derek Law (Liddell Hart Centre for Military Archives), Major (Retd.) R.A. Creamer (the Worcestershire and Sherwood Foresters Regimental Museum), and Lieutenant-Colonel (Retd.) D.C.R. Ward (King's Own Scottish Borderers Regimental Museum). I also appreciate the assistance of the staffs at the British Library, the Public Record Office, the National Library of Scotland, and the inter-library loan section of Leeds University Library.

I am extremely grateful to the British Academy for a grant from the Small Grants Research Fund in the Humanities which enabled me to undertake research for this publication. I acknowledge, too, my appreciation of a small grant from the University of Leeds Research Fund.

Finally, I must express my sincere gratitude to Fiona, Robert and Amanda, who have endured the preparation of this volume. They have borne the domestic strains with tolerance and humour, and Fiona has proffered invaluable support not only in proof-reading but also in mastering the word-processor.

1

The Cardwell reforms

As Secretary of State for War (1868–74), Edward T. Cardwell was responsible for the comprehensive reform of the administration and organisation of the late Victorian army. He terminated the so-called 'dual government' of the army, by establishing a statutory distribution of duties within the War Office and by formally subordinating all administrative officers, including the Field-Marshal Commanding-in-Chief, to the Secretary of State. He introduced short service enlistment, facilitating the formation and growth of a new army reserve. He abolished purchase. He localized the home army, basing battalions in specific territorial districts and affiliating them with local auxiliary forces. These achievements earned the unstinting praise of his private secretary and hagiographer, Sir Robert Biddulph: 'a system,' argued Biddulph, 'was introduced, where no system could be said to have existed before.'[1] More recent research has emphasised the limitations of Cardwell's reforms, and has indicated a degree of continuity between his endeavours and the proposals of previous Ministers, notably Lord Grey and Sidney Herbert.[2] Yet if Cardwell's reforms hardly constituted a turning point in the history of the army, they represented the outcome of an immense political undertaking and established the parameters within which the army would operate for the remainder of the century.

Born in 1813, the son of a Liverpool merchant, Cardwell was educated at Winchester and Balliol College, Oxford. Graduating with a double first, he was called to the bar in 1838 but quickly took an interest in politics. In 1842 he entered Parliament as a free-trade Conservative and a firm supporter of Sir Robert Peel. Following the repeal of the Corn Laws, he became a prominent Peelite before joining Lord Aberdeen's coalition government in 1852. Highly competent in financial and administrative matters, he assisted William E. Gladstone in preparing his budgets and rose through a series of ministerial appointments to become Colonial Secretary (1864–66). In the general election of 1868, he vigorously and successfully defended his Oxford seat, and, as the condition of the army was neither a contentious nor a prominent electoral issue, he only mentioned it on a few occasions. He asserted that the next government should withdraw troops from the colonies and should seek enhanced efficiency and reduce military expenditure.[3]

Although the Liberals under Gladstone's leadership swept into office with a majority of some 100 seats, they suffered one significant casualty, namely the loss of their military spokesman, the Marquess of Hartington. Cardwell had never previously displayed any interest in military matters and had not participated in the purchase debates of the 1860s. Lord John Russell had considered him for the War Office in October 1865 – a prospect which hardly delighted Cardwell, who confided in Henry Bruce Austin. The latter noted that Cardwell 'dwelt much upon his horror or the War Office: he will fight hard to escape it'.[4] In December 1868, however, the War Office seemed the most likely possibility by which Cardwell could attain a senior cabinet post. He made a bid for office by sending a memorandum, entitled 'The Army', to Gladstone. He devoted two-thirds of the document to War Office administration, revealing his knowledge of the evidence submitted to a Select Committee on this subject some eight years previously. Thereafter he mentioned issues like the appointment and promotion of officers, recruiting and retirement, without making any specific proposals. The new government, he argued, could not adopt 'a merely passive attitude' towards these matters but had to undertake a 'thorough investigation of them'.[5]

For Gladstone, Cardwell possessed several advantages as a prospective Secretary of State for War. His old Peelite ally had proved himself in office. He had deftly handled financial problems and had gained useful experience as Colonial Secretary. If not an impressive orator, he was a competent parliamentarian and still held a seat in the House of Commons. He had never promoted any contentious army reforms and had not, thereby, incurred the displeasure of the Queen and her cousin, the Duke of Cambridge, who was the Field-Marshal Commanding-in-Chief. Having dreaded the appointment of John Bright as Secretary of State,[6] the Duke could only welcome the choice of Cardwell. Above all, Gladstone knew that Cardwell shared his own concern about retrenchment in military expenditure. He duly appointed Cardwell as Secretary of State for War.

On entering office, Cardwell's immediate task was to prepare the Army Estimates, which were due for presentation in the following March. Within a month, he completed proposals which fully met the Premier's desire for significant reductions in military expenditure. As Cardwell explained in a letter, dated 9 January 1869, he proposed to reduce the army abroad from 50,00 to 26,000 men. He advocated the reorganisation of the Militia by placing it under the discipline of the War Office, with an establishment of half-pay regular officers and periods of training with the army. He hoped to improve the Volunteers by removing inefficient corps and by training the remainder more frequently with the Militia and regulars. Cardwell did not anticipate that the colonial reductions – the most important of these measures – would encounter much opposition, as successive governments had promoted a policy of colonial self-reliance. The withdrawal of forces from distant stations would not only save money but would also permit the reorganisation of the home army. Protracted periods of overseas service, he maintained, had discouraged enlistment from 'the more respectable portions of the population' and had thwarted any attempt to reduce the period of enlistment. Short service, he claimed, was necessary to realise further economies and to enhance military efficiency by ensuring that the army only contained soldiers 'in the prime of life'. It would enable a reserve to be formed from the ex-regulars in the civil population and would slash the pension vote by nearly £1,500,000.[7] Gladstone applauded: 'It is really like seeing a little daylight after all these years, and a return to reason from what has been anything except reason.'[8]

Cardwell implemented his retrenchment programme in a phased process over the two estimates for 1869–70 and 1870–71. He secured cumulative savings of £2,330,800 by withdrawing 25,709 men from colonial service, by cutting £641,370 from the stores vote, and by reducing the size of infantry battalion cadres to 560 other ranks (later reduced to 520 other ranks) apart from the ten larger units at the top of the roster for overseas service. Cardwell marginally increased the size of the home army (retaining 86,225 men at home instead of 84,077 men in 1868–69) and deployed them in a larger number of smaller formations – 105 batteries, nineteen cavalry regiments and sixty-eight infantry battalions (as compared with ninety-seven batteries, sixteen regiments and forty-six battalions in 1868–69). While he claimed that this was a nucleus at home which could be rapidly expanded in case of emergency, the Duke of Cambridge was not impressed. The Duke deprecated the removal of so many forces from colonial stations, the abandonment of some overseas garrisons, and the reduction in the size of the cadre establishments. He particularly disliked the small size of the infantry battalions, as these units, after the deduction of raw recruits, would number about 300 men – 'a very sorry account for a Regiment of Infantry which may be called upon for service in Ireland, or for any other special duty'. He feared that the remaining overseas battalions would become even less effective as soon as disease and dissipation began to take their toll. Finally, he noted that the proposed Reserve could only be used on the outbreak of war: 'in times of emergency or anxiety short of war, we can do nothing but recruit up, and we may have difficulty in obtaining them'.[9]

Cardwell's reductions, however, were overwhelmingly popular. Some Radicals derided the paucity of the savings, but his cabinet colleagues and a vast bi-partisan majority were supportive. Although some Conservatives echoed the criticisms of *The United Service Gazette* and *The Naval and Military Gazette* about the scale of the reductions, most Conservatives welcomed the policy of colonial retrenchment. *The Times* was delighted. The savings over two years, it stated, had 'an eloquence to which nothing need be added'; the reorganisation would ensure that the army was not 'frittered away in Colonial Garrisons but massed at home, where it may learn the art of war, and not merely the details of drill and the routine of barrack life'.[10]

The House of Commons also responded favourably to Cardwell's first reform – the reorganisation of the War Office. As Cardwell had indicated in his memorandum of 3 December 1868, he shared the view of Sir James Graham that the administration of the War Office was chaotic. The problem, argued Cardwell, derived from the hasty reorganisation of army administration in the wake of the Crimean War. The amalgamation of thirteen separate military departments had left the Secretary of State for War as the Minister responsible for the efficiency of the army and for its civil administration, but an exemption in his patent had left matters of command, discipline, appointments and promotion with the Duke of Cambridge (the *de facto* Commander-in-Chief who held office at the pleasure of the

Crown, the *de jure* Commander-in-Chief). Although the Duke had conceded that the supreme control of the army rested with the Secretary of State, the maintenance of two distinct departments, each with its own separate headquarters (the Horse Guards and the War Office) and overlapping responsibilities, created the impression of two distinct departments. The system had produced a costly and cumbersome bureaucracy, with double establishments monitoring each other and duplicating the transaction of business.[11] It reflected, too, the continuing influence of Queen Victoria as she staunchly supported her first cousin, the Duke of Cambridge. She wished to preserve the army's special connection with the Crown, to maintain the role of the Duke as a 'non-political' Commander-in-Chief with responsibility for command, discipline, promotion and appointments, and to prevent any diminution of his status and authority.[12]

A committee, chaired by Lord Northbrook, reviewed the vexed issues of constitutional control and administrative reform. It recommended that the Secretary of State should be formally confirmed as the responsible Minister, that all departments should be designated as subordinate to him, and that the new unified administration should be consolidated by housing the offices in one building. It proposed, too, that the new department, under the general authority of the Secretary of State for War, should contain three divisions: Military, Supply and Finance. The Commander-in-Chief, heading the Military Division with a greatly reduced staff, would remain as the principal military adviser. He would be responsible for discipline, training, recruiting, education, promotion, appointments, the Reserve forces, the Chaplain-General and the Army Medical Departments and the newly created Topographical Department. The Control or Supply Department would be administered by another officer, subsequently known as the Surveyor-General of the Ordnance. He would be responsible for supply and transport, clothing, fortifications, military contracts and the manufacture of ordnance and stores. A Financial Secretary would be responsible for the preparation of the estimates, accounts and auditing. Finally, the committee recommended that the heads of the Supply and Finance Departments should be eligible for election as Members of Parliament, so easing the parliamentary burdens of the Secretary of State.[13]

The Duke of Cambridge stubbornly resisted these proposals, especially the move from the Horse Guards to the War Office in Pall

Mall. This move, he asserted, would undermine his position as representative of the sovereign's powers and diminish his status within the army. Although the Queen, alarmed by any possible curtailment of her prerogative powers, supported the Duke, he eventually succumbed. Unable to challenge the constitutional propriety of the proposed changes, he still secured some concessions from Cardwell. Once esconced in Pall Mall, the Duke was allowed to address his letters from the 'Horse Guards, Pall Mall'. He successfully blocked any redesignation of his post as Chief of Staff and preserved the post of Quartermaster-General, which the Northbrook Committee had wished to merge with the Adjutant-General's office.[14]

Cardwell had never wished to erode the status and authority of the Duke of Cambridge but had never accepted that there was any 'dual government' of the army, even in theory. He was merely seeking a ratification of his own constitutional responsibility as a basis for rationalizing the administrative machinery. He did not seek additional powers of patronage and fully accepted that all matters of command, discipline, appointment and promotion should be conducted on a non-political basis. He deprecated personal attacks on the Duke by Radical Members of Parliament, appreciating that he needed the co-operation of the Duke as well as the new Surveyor-General of the Ordnance (Sir Henry Storks) and the Financial Secretary (the Hon. J.C. Vivian in 1870, followed in 1871 by Henry Campbell, later known as Henry Campbell-Bannerman). These administrative assistants were supposed to intercede between the sub-departments and the Secretary of State, so relieving him of all but the most important questions. They were to inherit many of the responsibilities which had hitherto been concentrated in the War Office. The Duke of Cambridge also gained additional responsibilities for the Medical, Education and Chaplain-General's Departments, as well as the new Topographical Department. Moreover, by confirming his support for the non-political basis of command and discipline, while emphasising the constitutional supremacy of the Secretary of State, Cardwell ensured a cordial parliamentary reception for his War Office Bill in February 1870. It passed into law four months later.[15]

The War Office Act did not remove the likelihood of friction recurring between the Secretary of State and the Commander-in-Chief. It probably ensured that business was conducted more expeditiously than hitherto, that some duplication of labour was modified, and that the appearance of 'dual government' was removed. However useful, these changes could not in themselves produce a more effective or supportive administrative arrangement. The Duke of Cambridge remained an immensely powerful figure. Bolstered by his royal connections, unlimited tenure of office, and enhanced departmental responsibilities, he was Cardwell's principal military adviser and the military head of the army. His official status, resentment at the subordination of his office, and known opposition to many of Cardwell's policies on military expenditure, short service, localisation and the abolition of purchase inhibited his subordinates from advising the Secretary of State directly. Above all, the Duke, if appalled by Cardwell's procedures or initiatives, could seek to thwart them by appealing for royal support. Cardwell, nonetheless, had important powers of initiative. He could consult the Duke's subordinates informally, and, as the sole decision-maker, could choose to consult the Duke as and when he saw fit. After several protests from the Duke, who sometimes learned of major policy initiatives from the military press, Cardwell instituted weekly meetings in a War Office Council. Although he claimed that he wished to increase the 'weight and influence' of the Duke's opinion, Cardwell was probably more concerned to reduce unnecessary misunderstandings and encourage the Duke's co-operation.[16]

Yet Cardwell harboured few, if any, illusions about the Duke of Cambridge. Aware of his implacable hostility to army reform, Cardwell looked elsewhere for positive assistance and technical guidance. He found staunch support from Lord Northbrook, his Under-Secretary of State, and from his civil servants. Northbrook received invaluable briefings, especially on the issue of purchase, from Lieutenant Evelyn Baring and Major George Colley. Major-General Sir George Balfour and Brigadier John Adye also proffered useful memoranda and minutes on the purchase question, while Major-General Patrick MacDougall, as chairman of the Localisation Committee, provided active support for this reform. Finally, Cardwell received support, if not in the gestation of his reforms then in their subsequent promotion, from Lieutenant-Colonel Garnet (later Field-Marshal Lord) Wolseley. The latter's career had just begun to flourish after the publication of his *Soldier's Pocket Book* (1869) and his first independent command (the Red River Expedition of 1870). Although he only entered the War Office as Deputy

Assistant Adjutant-General in May 1871, and so hardly contributed to the conception of Cardwell's reforms, Wolseley firmly endorsed the regimental reorganisation and advocated further reforms of military education and training. Frequently thwarted by the Duke of Cambridge, Wolseley turned increasingly to the press to promote his ideas, so establishing his reputation as a military reformer. Cardwell profited from the assistance of military specialists and from the divisions among the military to secure his domination of the War Office.[17]

Reorganising the home army was the primary task of Cardwell and his advisers. The army had a wide range of duties. It had to provide for home defence against external attack, a priority emphasised by the periodic fears of a French invasion. It had to provide drafts and reliefs for garrisons in India, where British military commitments had increased in the wake of the Mutiny, and for garrisons in widely scattered colonies. It had to be able to send expeditionary forces to small colonial conflicts and to intervene, if necessary, on the Continent. Finally, it had to furnish support for the civil power, especially in Ireland, where Fenian disturbances had recently occurred. In numbers and in organisation, the army was ill-equipped to respond to all these demands or even to some of them.

The reduction of the colonial garrisons paved the way for further reform. It fostered colonial self-reliance, concentrated forces at home, and reduced the prospect of protracted periods of overseas service for new recruits. It facilitated, too, the introduction of short service enlistments – a reform which had often been advocated as a palliative for recruiting. In his Army Enlistment Bill of 1870, Cardwell proposed to keep the initial term of engagement for the infantry at twelve years, with the first six years to be spent with the Colours and the remainder in the Reserve. He reserved the right of the War Office to reduce the first period of Colours service for home-based regiments to three years, if recruitment permitted. He emphasised that these terms would only apply to the infantry of the line and not to the cavalry or the artillery in the first instance. Denying any 'revolutionary' intent, he indicated that the provisions of the Bill would not replace the existing mode of enlistment but merely supplement it with the option of short service. He aimed, thereby, to form a Reserve, to reduce the pension list, and to induce, if possible, a better class of man to enter the army. As these proposals received a largely favourable reception from the press and Parliament, the Bill passed without a division.[18]

The Army Enlistment Act (1870) established a highly flexible system of short service enlistment. The soldiers of every corps could still extend their service with the Colours to twenty-one years, but it was expected that most infantrymen would choose to pass out of the army at the end of the minimum period. This period could and would be varied according to the policies of the War Office and the Treasury (as financial savings could be made by prematurely passing men into the Reserve, where they received only 4*d* a day). The War Office gradually extended shorter terms of enlistment to the other arms (altering the cavalry terms in 1874 to eight years with the Colours and four years in the Reserve, but permitting the three regiments of Household Cavalry to serve for twelve years in the Colours without any Reserve service). Nevertheless, during the 1870s a quarter of the infantry enlistment, including the noncommissioned officers, extended their service to twelve years with the Colours and one half the artillery recruits undertook long service.[19]

Creating a Reserve, originally expected to number 60,000 men, was the principal objective of introducing short service. The Reserve was not intended to be a reserve *per se*, but simply a means by which the small peacetime cadres could be brought up to their war establishments during a period of national emergency. As the Duke of Cambridge realised, this concept had two basic flaws. First, it was essentially a long-term proposition which would materialise slowly. Soldiers would not enter the Reserve until 1876, and, even then, would not join in the numbers anticipated because of re-enlistments in India and the high rate of wastage through desertion, purchase of discharge and the discharge of servicemen with bad characters. Secondly, the Reserve could not meet the requirements of small colonial conflicts, an all too frequent occurrence which would require the rapid formation of expeditionary forces.[20] Sir Garnet Wolseley would regularly respond to such emergencies in the 1870s and 1880s by 'raiding' different battalions for experienced men, a practice which contradicted the essence of regimental *esprit de corps* and became a topic of heated controversy within the army. Despite these shortcomings, and the reluctance of successive governments to meet the costs of regularly drilling the reservists as the military authorities demanded, a substantial Reserve emerged over the next few decades. In 1884 it was bolstered by a Supplemental Reserve, involving an extra four years' supplementary Reserve service. By the end of the century, the Reserve numbered some 80,000 men.

By withdrawing colonial garrisons and shortening the period of Colour service, Cardwell had hoped to attract a better quality of recruit and to reduce the wastage from desertion and other offences. He consistently endeavoured to enhance the appeal of military service. In 1869 he confirmed restrictions upon flogging in the peacetime army and, two years later, prohibited the branding of deserters. His administration extensively reformed the recruiting service. It abolished enlistment bounties and instructed recruiting officers to remove their offices from public houses and to refrain from enlisting men with bad characters. It entitled any recruit who could prove that he had been misled on enlistment to be given a free discharge, with the recruiter bearing the expenses. Finally, it prohibited soldiers from re-engaging once they had left the service. In short, the War Office tried to modify the elements of fraud, deception and dissipation associated with the recruiting process.[21] Yet neither these measures nor the introduction of short service proved a panacea for the recruiting problem. The rate of pay (1s 2d) remained unattractive, many ex-soldiers found difficulty in securing civilian employment, and military service had a lowly status and limited appeal.

However frustrating, the recruiting dilemma paled by comparison with Cardwell's other difficulties in March 1870. As part of his reductions, he had proposed to abolish the ranks of cornet and ensign and to appoint all new officers at the rank of lieutenant, thereby reducing the number of subalterns per battalion from twenty to fourteen. He envisaged that the ten senior lieutenants should remain with the ten companies of each battalion, and that the four supernumeraries, holding the same rank, should cover for any vacancies caused by sickness or leave. As junior officers, the four supernumeraries would receive an ensign's pay. Officers who had already purchased their commissions as an ensign or cornet would be compensated at the regulation rate, costing a total sum of £509,500. In effect, Cardwell proposed to modify, albeit marginally, the extent of the purchase system.

The purchasing of commissions was probably the greatest anomaly of the late Victorian army. A centuries-old practice, it enabled officers to purchase their commission and promotion to the rank of lieutenant-colonel (or captain in the Foot Guards). It had been extensively examined by Royal Commissions and Select Committees and had been the subject of numerous debates in the House of Commons. Criticism had focused not merely upon the concept itself but also upon its abuses (the unofficial payments which facilitated exchanges between regiments and the over-regulation payments by which younger officers induced their senior colleagues to retire). The system had ensured a relatively rapid rate of promotion for those officers who could buy their advancement, and it had sustained the interdependence of the army with the upper social classes, so underpinning the political compliance of the officers and preventing them from becoming an isolated and exclusive caste. It had proved economical, too; purchase had obviated the need for increased rates of pay or for the provision of proper pensions, while its complete abolition would prove extremely expensive in compensatory payments. Its defects, though, had become ever more apparent; it had clearly restricted the sources of officer recruitment, created powerful vested interests within the purchase regiments, inhibited the reform of the purchase and non-purchase forces, and, above all, hindered the development of professional attitudes within the army.

Cardwell had not anticipated any difficulties with his limited proposal. On the one hand, it complemented the policy already endorsed by the House of Commons, of retaining cadres but reducing their peacetime establishments. On the other hand, the idea derived from a suggestion of his Conservative predecessor, Sir John Pakington, a known defender of the purchase system. Indeed, the scheme had been approved by Disraeli's cabinet and had received royal endorsement just before the Conservatives lost office. Moreover, the plan was not intended as the first step towards the abolition of the purchase system. Although Cardwell deplored the purchase system, he evinced little enthusiasm for the cause of abolition. On 23 November 1869 he had discussed with the Duke of Cambridge whether selection should begin with the rank of captain or major, but, after the Duke's reply, in which he stressed the difficulties of selection and the immense cost of reform at a time when 'rigid economy' was being 'enforced on every Department of State', Cardwell had not pressed him further. In presenting his proposal before Parliament, Cardwell insisted that this was a limited and modest measure which would only diminish the ultimate cost of abolishing purchase 'if ever it is wound up'.[22]

Cardwell had completely misjudged the mood of the House. He

encountered widespread opposition. From the Radical benches, he was criticised for failing to tackle the root of the problem, the purchase system itself, and, from the opposition back benches, Conservatives protested that he had not provided for the repayment of over-regulation sums. Cardwell now faced a real dilemma. Although over-regulation sums had become a standard feature of the peacetime army (when the supply of officers exceeded the demand for their services), they were illegal. As the cabinet would not countenance their repayment, and as the supporters of purchase would not relent (on 10 March, Colonel C.W. White requested a postponement of the Bill until officers in the purchase regiments could have an 'opportunity of meeting and deliberating'),[23] Cardwell withdrew his measure. He announced that a Royal Commission, headed by Sir George Grey, would investigate the issue of over-regulation payments.

The Royal Commission completed its deliberations promptly. In June 1870 it reported unanimously in favour of the officers' claims for official recognition of over-regulation payments. Officers were justified, it concluded, in inferring that over-regulation payment

> though contrary to the letter of the law, it was not seriously disapproved, and that they might continue it without the fear of incurring the penalties of the law or the displeasure of the military authorities . . . there has been a tacit acquiescence in the practice, amounting, in our opinion, to a virtual recognition of it by civil and military departments and authorities.[24]

The law officers of the Crown, having read this report, agreed that the government could not prevent over-regulation payments under existing legal statutes. As a consequence, Cardwell realised that he had only two options. He could either legalise the payment of over-regulation sums and abort his reforms, particularly the amalgamation of the purchase officers of the regular army with the non-purchase officers of the Reserve forces, or eliminate an illegal practice by abolishing purchase altogether. During the summer of 1870, he conferred with Lord Northbrook and concluded that he had to abolish purchase and pay compensation for the over-regulation prices as the Royal Commission recommended.[25]

Administrative considerations dominated Cardwell's thinking. He had never been a doctrinaire abolitionist and could never have reconciled such a commitment with his preference for military economy. Had he wished to alter the class composition of the army, he would have had to raise the rates of pay of officers considerably and possibly impose restrictions upon their extravagant life-style. During the subsequent debates on the purchase Bill, he specifically denied that he was advocating reform for class reasons. 'It is a libel upon the old aristocracy,' he declared, 'to say that they are ever behindhand in any race which is run in an open arena, and in which ability and industry are the only qualities which can insure success.'[26]

When he was planning his legislative strategy during the summer and autumn of 1870, he was undoubtedly aware that the outbreak of the Franco–Prussian War had had a profound impact upon influential sections of British opinion. The use of Prussia's reserves and the professionalism of her officer corps had occasioned unfavourable comparisons with the state of the British army in many newspapers. Initially, Cardwell sought to turn this criticism to his own advantage. In reply to questions about whether Britain could secure the neutrality of Belgium (as she was obliged to do under the Treaty of London, 1839), Cardwell conceded that the peacetime army could not even send an expeditionary force of 20,000 men. On 2 August 1870, he sought and received from Parliament a supplemental vote of another 20,000 men. He also believed that the war might facilitate the quest for reform. 'The great events on the Continent,' he wrote in October 1870, 'seem to have given rise to a great feeling in this country which may make the question of army organisation a less hopeless one than it has been hitherto.'[27]

Even so, Cardwell's reforms were not determined by the Prussian successes. He did not believe that Britain could slavishly follow the Prussian model because their military systems reflected the fundamental differences between the two countries. Prussian military planning had profited from conscription, a lack of colonial responsibilities, the proximity of a dangerous neighbour, and a smaller proportion of workers engaged in industry than in the United Kingdom. Cardwell had to base his reforms on very different assumptions, and his critical decision – to abolish purchase – was almost certainly taken before the decisive Prussian victories.[28]

Cardwell soon learnt of the depth of opposition to his proposals and the difficulties of reform. When he forewarned Gladstone and the Duke of Cambridge, he found that neither was enthusiastic. In defending the *status quo*, the Duke urged Cardwell

to see what the Prussians have done with their officers – all gentlemen and *not one* from the ranks; the French all from the ranks. Let us keep our old class of officers only giving them a lot more opportunity of instruction and we shall do wisely and well . . . .[29]

The Prime Minister was circumspect, too. He advised Cardwell to make 'a full and careful study of the whole Prussian system of officering', exhorting him to refrain from action until he had formulated an alternative system. Gladstone feared that Cardwell was being too ambitious and too hasty at a time when the 'public mind' was 'excited and unbalanced in no small degree'.[30] Cardwell was not easily dissuaded. He maintained that his scheme was not too ambitious, and that the government had to prepare a 'comprehensive scheme' for the next session of Parliament. He recommended that the abolition of purchase should be linked to new requirements for the education of officers, improved training of recruits, the removal of the discipline of the Militia from the Lords-Lieutenant, and the combination of regular and auxiliary forces under one command. Only by such a scheme, he suggested, could the government keep pace with public expectations.[31]

The scheme still had to be costed. In the hope of minimising the ultimate expenditure, both Cardwell and Gladstone tried to restrict the principles of repayment. Cardwell initially proposed that officers should only be compensated for half the over-regulation price of their commissions. Gladstone recommended that an officer should not be compensated for a commission which he had not purchased. Lord Northbrook, however, feared that any compensation of officers on terms less generous than those which they might obtain by selling their commissions on the open market would be deemed unfair in principle and would risk parliamentary defeat. Having discussed the matter with George Glyn, the Liberal chief whip, Northbrook advised that the Liberal Party was not 'disposed to pare down' the compensation. 'There is hardly a member of Parliament,' he warned, 'who has not some relative personally interested in the Purchase system.'[32] Cardwell eventually agreed. He accepted that officers should be fully compensated on a basis similar to that which they might expect from their entitlement to sell their commissions. The net cost of the compensation would be approximately £8,000,000.

Cardwell, at Gladstone's behest, was equally concerned to prepare a new system of appointments, promotion and retirement. He took advice from Lord Northbrook, Hugh Childers, then First Lord of the

Admiralty, Captain J.C. Vivian, the Financial Secretary, and some individual officers, including Major George Colley, who submitted a plan for the appointment of candidates to first commissions, and Sir William Mansfield, the Commander-in-Chief in Ireland, who produced with Northbrook a critique of another proposal on promotions which could have produced an illicit form of purchase. Although Cardwell greatly welcomed this specialist assistance, he became increasingly aware of his own limitations and pressed Gladstone to secure a parliamentary seat for a senior military officer who could defend the government's proposals with authority and technical expertise. Eventually Sir Henry Storks, the Surveyor-General, did secure a seat from which he could proffer Cardwell parliamentary support. Meanwhile, the protracted War Office discussions failed to produce a scheme for appointments, promotion and retirement before the Army Regulation Bill was presented to Parliament on 16 February 1871. Ultimately new regulations would be drafted by Mansfield, and, once agreed with minor revisions by the Duke of Cambridge, they would form the basis of the Royal Warrant of 30 October 1871.[33]

The Army Regulation Bill aroused little interest outside the House of Commons. During the three weeks between Cardwell's introductory speech and the first debate on the second reading, there was only one letter on the Bill printed in *The Times*. There were few public meetings in support of abolition, and the Liberal press reported widespread indifference towards the measure in the provinces, especially after the termination of hostilities on the Continent on 1 March. By 25 May 1871 the House of Commons had still not received any petitions in support of abolition. By early July, Cardwell admitted that 'the breeze of popular enthusiasm has died away during the contest'.[34]

Within the House of Commons, the Bill experienced a difficult passage. As soon as the second reading debate began on 6 March, the extent and passion of the opposition became apparent. Led by a group of mainly retired army officers, known as 'the Colonels', the critics defended the *status quo*, denounced the cost of abolition, and contested the efficacy of any system of examination and selection. They deplored the government's proposal to limit the number of officers who could retire each year and receive compensation, and dreaded lest the army become subordinated politically. Several Liberals joined the chorus of criticism, protesting about the cost of abolition and the propriety of compensating officers for over-regulation payments. Although some well known opponents of purchase, such as George Otto Trevelyan, applauded the Bill, opponents were more conspicuous in the chamber and a division was only avoided by a somewhat ambiguous speech by Benjamin Disraeli, the Conservative leader. He qualified his dislike of the Bill by refraining from any defence of the purchase system *per se*. Unwilling to divide the House over the principle of abolition – at a time when the 'eyes of Europe are on England reorganising her Army' – he mollified his own supporters by arguing that they could examine the Bill in detail, and possibly amend it, in committee.[35]

Thwarted on the second reading, the Colonels resumed their filibustering in committee. They repeatedly tried to delay proceedings, and then sought to challenge nearly every clause of the Bill during the thirteen occasions (between 8 May and 19 June) when it was discussed in committee. Colonel the Hon. Augustus Anson led the tenacious resistance, sometimes with Radical support. The opponents met with increasing success, steadily reducing the government's majority until it numbered a mere sixteen votes on 25 May. At this stage Gladstone was willing to compromise but Cardwell remained obdurate. He contended that

There sits below the gangway on our side a plutocracy, – who have no real objection to Purchase, – and are in truth more interested in its maintenance than the gentlemen opposite. They use popular arguments like young Mr Seeley, & they say in private that they want something *more* for the money involved; that something being the removal of the Duke of Cambridge: – while in truth they wish to purchase an aristocratic position for personal connections, who would never obtain it otherwise.[36]

These critics never represented a potential majority. By imposing firmer party discipline, the government brought in more apathetic Members to secure a majority of fifty-eight votes on the third reading (13 July 1871).

Facing an even more formidable hurdle in the House of Lords, the government sought the active support of the Duke of Cambridge. Cardwell reminded him that his tenure of office had not been limited to five years because the government had expected his open and cordial assistance on all matters of military policy. Although the Duke protested that he should have 'no politics' and should not participate in political discussion, Cardwell and Gladstone insisted that he should speak. He duly obliged but his intervention, which was noncommittal and inaudible in parts of the chamber, had little impact. The Bill provoked strong partisan feelings and was defeated on the second reading by twenty-five votes.[37] Having anticipated defeat, the cabinet had resolved on 15 July to terminate purchase, if necessary, by the issue of a Royal Warrant. It could do so because the purchase of commissions was prohibited under the terms of the Brokerage Act of 1809 other than in regulations published, or to be published, by the Crown. Unwilling to continue tolerating the illegality of over-regulation payments, the cabinet resolved to abolish purchase without further debate and to defy the predictable protests from Conservatives in the press and Parliament. It feared that another year's prevarication might impair the discipline of the army, especially if promotion ground to a halt, with officers refusing to make over-regulation payments without a guarantee that Parliament would approve compensation in 1872. Reluctant to let matters drift or to risk another parliamentary defeat, the cabinet authorised abolition by Royal Warrant, which the Queen signed on 20 July 1871. The purchase, sale and exchange of commissions were duly cancelled from 1 November 1871.[38]

Abolition neither altered the social composition of the officer corps nor infused the army with a new professional spirit. Cardwell, unlike some advocates of reform, had never anticipated that social change would automatically follow abolition. Unwilling to improve the pay of officers or to impose sumptuary controls upon regimental expenditure, he could not prevent regiments from finding the bulk of their officers from candidates with acceptable social pedigrees and adequate private incomes. He had hoped, though, that terminating purchase would alter attitudes within the profession, especially if merit became the criterion of promotion. The Duke of Cambridge had never agreed. Despite the new emphasis upon competitive examinations for entry, he was still 'the arbiter of the fitness of any gentleman for a commission' and was only willing to supervise promotion on the principle of seniority tempered by selection.[39] Although Cardwell knew of the Duke's reservations, he had refrained from pressing his own views upon the Commander-in-Chief or from limiting his tenure of office. He preferred to avoid a constitutional clash with the Crown and to retain the services of the Duke during the period of transition from a purchase to a post-purchase army. Cardwell almost certainly realised that his professional hopes would remain largely rhetorical, but he still sought abolition as a prerequisite for further reform.

The abolition of purchase enabled Cardwell to proceed with the fusion of the regular, auxiliary and reserve forces. On 22 February 1872, he introduced his Localisation Bill in the House of Commons, proposing to divide the country into sixty-six territorial districts, each of which would contain a brigade depot. Two line battalions, two Militia infantry battalions and a certain quota of Volunteers would be based in each district. One of the regular battalions was to be based at home while the other served abroad, but each was to retain two companies at the depot centre, which would serve as a training base for new recruits as well as a centre for the payment, training and discipline of reservists.

The fostering of local connections, argued Cardwell, would develop 'ties of kindred and of locality', with the aim of attracting 'a better class of men and a greater number than now present themselves'. The localisation would also induce men from the Militia to enter the army and would improve the morale and efficiency of the auxiliary forces (the Volunteer Corps, once placed under the command of their district lieutenant-colonels, would be required to attend brigade instruction once a year, receive a small allowance for doing so, and become liable to forfeit their capitation grant if less than half their enrolled strength attended). Cardwell requested that Parliament should authorise the expenditure of £3,500,000 to construct twenty-six new stations and to convert the other forty, which were currently occupied by regular units. By this expenditure, he concluded, the State would be maximising its investment in the regular and auxiliary forces and would be buttressing the national defences.[40]

The Bill was in fact a compromise. It did not amalgamate the two infantry battalions into double battalions – as was already the case with the first twenty-five regiments of the line – but left the remaining battalions as independent units. Although the Duke of Cambridge had initially professed his approval of fusing the linked battalions, he found that senior officers were unanimously opposed to the idea. They feared that the loss of their traditional battalion numbers and facings would jeopardise *esprit de corps*. So the Duke required that the Localisation Committee, chaired by Major-General Patrick MacDougall, should accept that linked regiments must remain as 'separate Corps for the Officers' but be 'made to act as much as possible in mutual support'.[41]

Based on these recommendations, the Localisation Bill was accorded a largely favourable reception. It met most of the criticisms which had been voiced during the Franco–Prussian War, namely that the regular and auxiliary forces should be linked and localised, and that more stringent training conditions should be imposed on the Volunteers. In fact the final report of the Localisation Committee had distinguished between its proposal and the Prussian model, and may have reflected the recent Canadian experience of two of the committee's five members – MacDougall and Wolseley – neither of whom was particularly impressed with the Prussian achievements. During his Canadian service, MacDougall had reorganised the Canadian Militia in 1866 by amalgamating its battalions with regular units into district-based brigades. The Bill was duly welcomed by Conservatives, and encountered only rearguard opposition from Radicals, appalled by the cost of the proposal and its purportedly militaristic overtones. These protests had little effect; the Bill was approved on 29 July 1872 by 170 votes to 24. [42]

The Localisation Act represented the consummation of Cardwell's reforms. In theory it instituted a system whereby one of the two linked battalions was based at home while the other served abroad. Each battalion was to have two companies at the depot centre, where recruits received their initial training. Thereafter these recruits passed into the battalion serving in Britain, which provided drafts for the overseas battalion and which would ultimately replace it. The authorised size of the home units varied from 520 to 820 rank and file, depending on their place on the roster for overseas service. The whole system depended upon the maintenance of a balance between the battalions at home and abroad: in 1872, there were seventy battalions at home and seventy-one abroad (the 79th, renamed the Queen's Own Cameron Highlanders in 1881, was not linked to a second battalion until 1897).

In practice localisation evolved both slowly and imperfectly. The establishment of the local depots proved extremely slow, with only forty formed by 1874. Many line battalions rarely visited their nominal locality and officers were not freely transferred between their affiliated battalions. More significantly, successive governments never maintained the essential parity between battalions at home and abroad. For financial reasons, Cardwell had had to assume that colonial commitments were unlikely to increase, and so that it was unnecessary to retain a surplus of additional battalions at home to meet colonial emergencies. The short-lived Ashanti War (1873–74) seemed to vindicate these arrangements, but, when a much more formidable challenge occurred in the Zulu War (1879), the whole system was thrown out of balance. By February 1879 there were eighty-two battalions abroad and only fifty-nine at home.

Home-based battalions, already burdened by the increased turn-over of men caused by short service enlistments, suffered as a consequence. Even in peacetime they struggled to supply the necessary reliefs for foreign service and to provide sufficient men for the Reserve. The demands of small colonial wars merely compounded the strain, particularly the periodic need to form expeditionary forces. These forces often included home battalions, bolstered by volunteers from other regiments, or, more rarely, by reservists called out in circumstances short of a national emergency.[43] Such expedients, which appalled military conservatives, worried about the depleted condition of the home battalions and the erosion of regimental *esprit de corps*, merely emphasised that the reforms had failed to solve the recruiting problems of the late Victorian army.

Short service, localisation and various changes in recruiting practices had all been intended to improve recruiting. Cardwell had hoped that the battalions, by forming 'ties of kindred and of locality', could reverse the decline of enlistment from rural areas, attract a better class of man, and swell the recruiting intake. He was too optimistic. Admittedly, localisation enabled recruiting drives to reach areas which had hitherto been relatively neglected, and, in 1874, local districts supplied 83·8 per cent of the recruits (special recruiting districts, centred upon large urban areas, supplied the remainder). But localisation could not redress the effects of rural depopulation: by 1898, only 63.3 per cent of the total intake was recruited locally.[44] As the home battalions shrank in size, recruiting standards were lowered to maintain establishments. Many recruits were too young or too physically inadequate to undertake active service or colonial duty, even when fully trained. Their presence as 'ineffectives' simply diminished the fighting potential of the home-based battalions, so ensuring that units earmarked for service in expeditionary forces had to take volunteers from other regiments. Although the number of recruits substantially increased during the last two decades of the century, enabling the formation of a Reserve of 80,000 men by 1899, neither short service nor localisation redressed the qualitative deficiencies. A soldier's pay remained low, a military career had limited appeal, and genuine short service never really existed: as a consequence, during a period of imperial expansion, it proved difficult to meet the manpower needs of the army through voluntary enlistment.[45]

Nevertheless, localisation served purposes other than improved recruitment. It enlarged the basic unit of army organisation from the battalion to a regiment of two battalions, and it enhanced the auxiliary forces by enabling them to train periodically with the regulars or to camp at the brigade depot. It also stimulated the growth of regimental spirit, by fostering local and county connections. Some regiments, like the 27th Foot (later the Royal Inniskilling Fusiliers), already had strong local attachments, but many others, especially those which became English county regiments, undoubtedly prospered from their new status. As the abolition of purchase had placed a premium upon loyalty *to* the regiment and upon service *within* the regiment as the basis of a military career, the regiments clearly benefited. Embodying many features which appealed to the upper middle-class Victorian – an ancient lineage, county status, royal connections (in many cases), and a degree of separate autonomy, with the added attractions of mess life and abundant sporting opportunities – the regiment came to resemble, in John Keegan's phrase, a 'large, comfortable Victorian county family'.[46]

Localisation encouraged Cardwell to expand the military manoeuvres which he began in 1871. Subsequent manoeuvres in 1872 and 1873 were considerably larger; they proved immensely popular, attracting sizeable crowds (some 150,000 spectators attended the Cannock Chase manoeuvres of 1873), and permitted closer relations between the regulars and the auxiliary forces. Yet these benefits were somewhat attenuated. Localisation fulfilled neither the requirements of strategic planning nor the need for training in large-scale military formations. Geared primarily to the purposes of recruiting, it accentuated the dispersal of battalions throughout the country, so augmenting the costs of holding military manoeuvres. Indeed, economic constraints curtailed the scale of subsequent manoeuvres, and, after 1875, prevented the holding of any large-scale manoeuvres until 1898. Home-based battalions never really trained in larger bodies as army corps, and so, whenever expeditionary forces were despatched as army corps, these were principally administrative and not tactical formations.

Many of these shortcomings would not become fully apparent until Cardwell left office. He had anticipated some of them, particularly the difficulty of meeting the recruiting requirements of short service enlistments. Having recruited less than half the requisite number of men in 1873, he abandoned any hope of introducing three-year terms of service and conceded that only a substantial increase of pay could attract sufficient recruits from a relatively buoyant labour market.[47] Increasing military expenditure was not politically possible during his last few years in office, and Cardwell was repeatedly pressed by Gladstone and Robert Lowe, the Chancellor of the Exchequer, to reduce the Army Estimates. He only managed to block such demands in the estimates for 1874. In these circumstances, he fully realised that increasing the pay of officers and men was beyond the realm of practical politics.

Throughout his term of office, Cardwell had always acted in a prudent and realistic manner. In pursuing the priorities of economy and efficiency, he had recognised that he would have to work within a limited period of time and within the constraints of contemporary politics. He had, nonetheless, implemented reforms which would serve as the army's structural bedrock over the next quarter of a century. His biographer extolled this achievement as permitting the country to maintain the voluntary system of enlistment and an acceptable volume of military expenditure while meeting the strategic needs of a European and an imperial power. Successive cabinets, both Conservative and Liberal, endorsed this view, as did Printing House Square, some officers like Wolseley, MacDougall and Adye, and senior departmental officials, including Sir Ralph Thompson, Sir Arthur (later Lord) Haliburton and Sir Ralph Knox — the Permanent Under-Secretaries of State from 1878 to 1901. This consensus reflected the broad measure of support which most of his reforms had enjoyed initially.

Cardwell had ensured this support by adopting ideas either launched by his predecessors (colonial withdrawal, forming a Reserve and abolishing the ranks of cornet and ensign), or advocated by previous reformers (short service), or currently in vogue on account of Prussian military triumphs (localisation). Having embodied these ideas in legislative proposals, he provided the leadership to carry them through the parliamentary process. He displayed rare gifts of political courage, tenacity and perseverence in pressing for the abolition of purchase as the prerequisite for further reforms.

He constructed a military system which was administratively convenient, reasonably inexpensive to maintain, and capable of further refinement without wholesale reorganisation (as undertaken by Hugh Childers in 1881 when he fused the linked battalions). Finally, Cardwell bequeathed a military structure which, despite the criticisms of the Duke of Cambridge and many senior officers, still enabled the army to perform efficiently in many small colonial wars and to accumulate a sizeable Reserve by the end of the century.

His five years in office exhausted Cardwell physically and mentally. After the general election of 1874 he sought and received a peerage, effectively withdrawing from active politics. His legislative achievements were substantial, but the shortcomings of his reforms became increasingly apparent over the next twenty-five years. The strains imposed by the failure to preserve a parity of battalions at home and abroad, coupled with the persistence of the recruiting problem and the burden of repeatedly despatching expeditionary forces to small colonial conflicts, proved considerable. Ultimately, these problems derived from a failure to assess Britain's strategic requirements, or to establish her military priorities, or to organise the army on any basis of likely military needs. The home army lacked any surplus capacity for the formation of expeditionary forces. It neither trained regularly in large-scale military formations nor possessed mobilisation plans which would enable it to fight in a major war in Europe. Cardwell had not only neglected this dimension of planning but had also promised or predicted immense changes from reforms which were intrinsically limited. Unfortunately this optimism permeated his devoted body of admirers, who proved reluctant to consider anything other than minor changes to his legislative achievements over the next twenty-five years. As a consequence, the debate over army reform largely stagnated.

Notes

1 Sir R. Biddulph, *Lord Cardwell at the War Office: A History of his Administration, 1868–1874* (John Murray; London, 1904), p.229.

2 B.J. Bond, 'The Effect of the Cardwell Reforms on Army Organisation 1874–1904', *Journal of the Royal United Services Institution*, Vol.CV (1960), pp.515–24; A.V. Tucker, 'Army and Society in England 1870–1900: A Reassessment of the Cardwell Reforms', *Journal of British Studies*, Vol.2 (May 1963), pp.110–41; H. Strachan, *Wellington's Legacy: The Reform of the British Army 1830–54* (Manchester University Press; Manchester, 1984), pp.219, 262 and 'Lord Grey and Imperial Defence' in

I.F.W. Beckett and J. Gooch (eds.), *Politicians and Defence: Studies in the Formulation of British Defence Policy 1845–1970* (Manchester University Press; Manchester, 1981), pp.19–20.

3   *Oxford Chronicle and Berks & Bucks Gazette*, 27 June 1868, p.6 and 5 September 1868, p.2; E.M. Spiers, *The Army and Society 1815–1914* (Longman; London, 1980), p.177; A. Bruce, 'Edward Cardwell and the Abolition of Purchase' in Beckett and Gooch (eds.), *Politicians and Defence*, pp.25–6.

4   Letter, 18 November 1865, *Letters of the Rt. Hon. Henry Austin Bruce G.C.B., Lord Aberdeen of Duffryn*, 2 Vols. (private; Oxford, 1902), Vol.1, p.232.

5   Biddulph, *Lord Cardwell at the War Office*, pp.249–54.

6   Earl Granville to W.E. Gladstone, 2 August 1868, Gladstone Mss., B[ritish] L[ibrary] Add. Mss. 44,165, f.170.

7   E.T. Cardwell to Gladstone, 9 January 1869, Gladstone Mss., B.L. Add. Mss. 44,119, ff.21–3.

8   Gladstone to Cardwell, 11 January 1869, Cardwell Mss., P[ublic] R[ecord] O[ffice], 30/48/6, f.32.

9   Duke of Cambridge to Cardwell, 2 January 1870, Cardwell Mss., PRO, 30/48/13, ff.3–4, 3 August 1869 and 14 December 1869 in Col. W. Verner, *The Military Life of H.R.H. George Duke of Cambridge*, 2 Vols. (John Murray; London, 1905), Vol.1, pp.394–9; *Parliamentary Deb*ates, Third Ser[ies], Vol.194 (11 March 1869), cols.1111–40, Vol.199 (3 March 1870), cols.1159–90 and Vol.214 (27 February 1873), col.859.

10   *The Times*, 4 March 1870, p.9; see also *Parl. Deb.*, Third Ser., Vol.194 (11 March 1869), cols.1112 and 1164; *United Service Gazette*, 5 March 1870, p.4; *Naval and Military Gazette*, 1 January 1870, p.6; *Parl. Deb.*, Third Ser., Vol.199 (3 March 1870), cols.1206–8, 1229–30.

11   *Reports of a Committee appointed to inquire into the Arrangements in Force for the Conduct of Business in the Army Departments*, hereafter referred to as the *Northbrook Reports*, C. 54 (1870), XII, pp.ix–x; Biddulph, *Lord Cardwell at the War Office*, pp.50–1, 249–51; H. Gordon, *The War Office* (Putnam; London, 1935), pp.53–7; O. Wheeler, *The War Office: Past and Present* (Methuen; London, 1914), pp.175–6, 183–6.

12   Cardwell to Gladstone, 16 January 1870, Gladstone Mss., B.L. Add. Mss. 44,119, ff.91–2; Queen Victoria to Gladstone, 3 October 1871, Cardwell Mss., PRO, 30/48/3, f.184.

13   *Northbrook Reports*, pp.x–xxiv.

14   Cambridge to Cardwell, 21 November, 5 and 27 December 1869, Cambridge Mss., R[oyal] A[rchives], E/1/6158, 6173, 6189; Queen Victoria to Cardwell, 22 December 1869, Cardwell Mss., PRO, 30/48/1, f.88.

15   Cardwell to Gladstone, 27 February 1869, Gladstone Mss., B.L. Add. Mss. 44,119, f.51; Cardwell to Queen Victoria, 3 March 1869, Cardwell Mss., PRO, 30/48/1, f.200; *Parl. Deb.*, Third Ser., Vol.199 (15 February 1870), cols.390–405; Gordon, *The War Office*, pp.53–5.

16   Bruce, 'Edward Cardwell and the Abolition of Purchase', pp.30–1; Cardwell to Cambridge, 12 April 1870, quoted in Verner, *The Military Life of H.R.H. George Duke of Cambridge*, Vol.1, p.428.

17 Lord Northbrook to Cardwell, 26 October, 31 October and 23 November 1870, Cardwell Mss., PRO, 30/48/19, ff.141–4, 146, 151; A. Preston (ed.), *The South African War Diaries of Sir Garnet Wolseley 1875* (A.A. Balkema; Cape Town, 1971), pp.57–60; Biddulph, *Lord Cardwell at the War Office*, pp.214, 221; W.S. Hamer, *The British Army: Civil–Military Relations 1885–1905* (Clarendon Press; Oxford, 1970), pp.18, 28–9; T.F. Gallagher, 'Cardwellian Mysteries; The Fate of the British Army Regulation Bill, 1871', *Historical Journal*, Vol.18 (1975), pp.327–48.

18 *Parl. Deb.*, Third Ser., Vol.199 (3 March 1870), cols.1175–7; Vol.201 (16 May 1870), cols.787–90; Vol.203 (18 July 1870), cols.444–7; *Pall Mall Gazette*, 4 March 1870, p.4 and 17 May 1870, pp.1–2; *The Times*, 4 March 1870, p.9.

19 B.J. Bond, 'The Introduction and Operation of Short Service and Localisation in the British Army, 1868–1892', unpublished M.A. thesis (University of London, 1962), pp.92–3; Marquess of Anglesey, *A History of the British Cavalry 1816–1919*, 4 Vols. (Leo Cooper; London, 1973–86), Vol.3, pp.31–2.

20 Cambridge to Cardwell, 11 January 1870, Cardwell Mss., PRO, 30/48/13, f.17; *Parl. Deb.*, Third Ser., Vol.203 (26 July 1870), col.938; Bond, 'The Introduction and Operation of Short Service and Localisation in the British Army, 1868–1892', pp.166–8; Biddulph, *Lord Cardwell at the War Office*, p.58.

21 Cardwell to Gladstone, 9 January 1869, Cardwell Mss., PRO, 30/48/6, f.30; A.R. Skelley, *The Victorian Army at Home* (Croom Helm; London, 1977), pp.147–52, 243–7, 253; Spiers, *The Army and Society*, pp.183–5.

22 *Parl. Deb.*, Third Ser., Vol.199 (3 March 1870), cols.1172–4; Cambridge to Cardwell, 24 November 1869, Cardwell Mss., PRO, 30/48/12, ff.150–1; A.P.C. Bruce, *The Purchase System in the British Army, 1660–1871* (Royal Historical Society; London, 1980), pp.119–20.

23 *Parl. Deb.*, Third Ser., Vol.199 (3 March 1870), cols.1205–6, 1231 and (10 March 1870), col.1629; 'Cabinet memorandum', 5 March 1870, Gladstone Mss., B.L. Add. Mss. 44,638, f.33; Gallagher, 'Cardwellian Mysteries', pp.330–1.

24 *Report of the Commissioners appointed to Inquire into Over-regulation Payments on Promotion in the Army*, C. 201 (1870), XII, pp.xxiv–xxv.

25 Cardwell, 'Military Organisation', n.d. but probably October 1870, and Cardwell to Gladstone, 5 October 1870, Gladstone Mss., B.L. Add. Mss. 44,615, f.33 and 44,119, f.155; Northbrook to Cardwell, 8 July 1872, Cardwell Mss., PRO, 30/48/21, f.12; for an assessment of how far the War Office advisers may have influenced Cardwell, compare Gallagher, 'Cardwellian Mysteries', pp.332–4 with Spiers, *The Army and Society*, pp.189–90.

26 *Parl. Deb.*, Third Ser., Vol.205 (16 March 1871), col.137. See also N.H. Moses, 'Edward Cardwell's Abolition of the Purchase System in the British Army, 1868–1874: A Study in Administrative and Legislative Processes', unpublished Ph.D. thesis (University of London, 1969), pp.110–12.

27 Cardwell, 'Military Organisation', f.33; *Parl. Deb.*, Third Ser., Vol.203 (2 August 1870), cols.1440–63; *The Times*, 17 October 1870, p.9; *The Manchester Guardian*, 17 October 1870, p.3; *The Saturday Review*, 27 August and 17 October 1870, pp.225–6 and 512–13.

28 Cardwell to Gladstone, 22 September 1870, Gladstone Mss., B.L. Add. Mss. 44,119, ff.151–2; Moses, 'Edward Cardwell's Abolition of the Purchase System', pp.113–14; T.F. Gallagher, 'British Military Thinking and the Coming of the Franco–Prussian War', *Military Affairs*, Vol.39 (1975), pp.19–22.

29 Cambridge to Cardwell, 30 September 1870, Cardwell Mss., PRO, 30/48/14, ff.190–1.

30 Gladstone to Cardwell, 23 September, 8 and 14 October 1870, Cardwell Mss., PRO, 30/48/7, ff.136, 142–3, 146–7.

31 Cardwell to Gladstone, 10 October 1870, Cardwell Mss., PRO, 30/48/7, ff.155–6.

32 Northbrook to Cardwell, 30 September and 26 October 1870, Cardwell Mss., PRO, 30/48/19, ff.96–8 and 141; Bruce, *The Purchase System in the British Army*, pp.125–6.

33 *Proposed method of appointments, promotion and retirements after the abolition of purchase*, Gladstone Mss., B.L. Add. Mss. 44,617, ff.67–8; Bruce, *The Purchase System in the British Army*, pp.126–8; Cardwell to Gladstone, 17 November 1870 and 3 January 1871, Gladstone Mss., B.L. Add. Mss. 44,119, ff.173–4 and 191–2; Northbrook to Cardwell, 23 November and 23 December 1870, Cardwell Mss., PRO, 30/48/19, ff.146 and 157–8; S. Childers, *The Life and Correspondence of the Rt Hon Hugh C.E. Childers, 1827–1896*, 2 Vols. (John Murray; London, 1901), Vol.1, pp.187–8.

34 *The Times*, 18 February 1871, p.8; *The Manchester Guardian*, 24 May 1871, pp.4–5; *North British Mail*, 19 July 1871, p.4; *The Birmingham Daily Mail*, 20 June 1871, p.4; *Parl. Deb.*, Third Ser., Vol.206 (25 May 1871), col.1303; Cardwell to Sir H. Ponsonby, 3 July 1871, Cardwell Mss., PRO, 30/48/2, f.108; Moses, 'Edward Cardwell's Abolition of the Purchase System', pp.186–7; Gallagher, 'Cardwellian Mysteries', p.342.

35 *Parl. Deb.*, Third Ser., Vol.204 (6 March 1871), cols.1397–8, 1403–4, 1411–12 (9 March 1871), col.1725; Vol.205 (16 March 1871), col.122 (17 March 1871), cols.240–4.

36 Cardwell to Gladstone, 28 May 1871, Gladstone Mss., B.L. Add. Mss. 44,119, f.243.

37 Cardwell to Cambridge, 3 and 4 June 1871, and Cambridge to Cardwell, 3 June 1871, Cardwell Mss., PRO, 30/48/15, ff.181–2, 195–7 and 185–9; *Parl. Deb.*, Third Ser., Vol.207 (14 July 1871), cols.1690–7 (17 July 1871), cols.1867–70.

38 *Royal Warrant, dated 20 July 1871, to cancel and determine all Regulations authorising the Purchase or Sale or Exchange for Money of Commissions in the Army, from 1 November 1871*, C. 417 (1871), XXXIX; Cardwell, 'memorandum', 18 July 1871, Cardwell Mss., PRO, 30/48/8, ff.103–8; Moses, 'Edward Cardwell's Abolition of the Purchase System', pp.343–7.

39   *Parl. Deb.*, Third Ser., Vol.216 (20 June 1873), col.1218; Bruce, *The Purchase System in the British Army*, pp.159, 163–5.

40   *Parl. Deb.*, Third Ser., Vol.209 (22 February 1872), cols.893–906.

41   Cambridge to Cardwell, 17 May 1872, Cardwell Mss., PRO, 30/48/16, f.52 and Cambridge, 'memorandum', n.d., reproduced in Biddulph, *Lord Cardwell at the War Office*, pp.167–9.

42   *Parl. Deb.*, Third Ser., Vol.212 (15 July 1872), col.1210 (23 July 1872), cols.1644 and 1650; Vol.213 (29 July 1872), col.104; J. Luvaas, *The Education of An Army: British Military Thought, 1815–1940* (Cassell; London, 1964), pp.120–1.

43   *Report of a Committee of General and other Officers of the Army on Army Reorganisation*, hereafter referred to as the *Airey Report*, C. 2791 (1881), XXI, pp.3–4, 10, 369–400. See also *Report of the Committee on Certain Questions Relative to the Militia and the Present Brigade Depot Systems*, C. 1654 (1877), XVIII, pp.iii–v.

44   *General Annual Returns of the British Army . . .*, C. 1323 (1875), XLIII, p.16 and C. 9426 (1899), LIII, p.16; *Reports of the Inspector-General of Recruiting*, C. 5953 (1890), XIX, p.7 and C. 3169 (1882), XVI, p.1; *Parl. Deb.*, Third Ser., Vol.209 (22 February 1872), col.901 and Cardwell to Queen Victoria, 18 December 1871, Cardwell Mss., PRO, 30/48/3, ff.250–1.

45   *Airey Report*, pp.10–11; Skelley, *The Victorian Army at Home*, p.254; Bruce, 'Edward Cardwell and the Abolition of Purchase', p.34; Spiers, *The Army and Society*, pp.38–9.

46   J. Keegan, 'Regimental Ideology' in G. Best and A. Wheatcroft (eds.), *War, Economy and the Military Mind* (Croom Helm; London, 1976), pp.9–11; D. Weston, 'The Army: Mother, Sister and Mistress: the British Regiment' in M. Edmonds (ed.), *The Defence Equation: British Military Systems Policy, Planning and Performance* (Brassey's; London, 1986), pp.142–3; Regimental Historical Records Committee, *The Royal Inniskilling Fusiliers* (Constable; London, 1928), p.340.

47   Cardwell to Gladstone, 20 December 1873 and 'Memorandum', 3 January 1874, Gladstone Mss., B.L. Add. Mss. 44,120, ff.192–3 and 197.

2

The War Office

Theoretically, the reorganization of the War Office, based on the proposals adumbrated by Lord Northbrook's committee, had simplified the system of military administration and subordinated it to a single head, the Secretary of State for War. The constitutional issue and any lingering doubts about dual control had supposedly been settled. As the Hartington Commission later observed, 'The complete responsibility to Parliament and the country of the Secretary of State, for the discipline as well as for the Administration of the Army, must now be accepted as definitely established.'[1] The War Office had absorbed the administrative functions hitherto exercised at the Horse Guards. It had also been divided into three great departments – the Military Department under the Officer Commanding-in-Chief, the Supply or Ordnance Department under the Surveyor-General of the Ordnance, and the Financial Department under the Financial Secretary. All matters other than those connected with the personnel, finance, supplies, transport and equipment of the regular army were administered by a central department under the Secretary of State. By removing the Duke of Cambridge from the Horse Guards, and by delineating clear areas of administrative remit, the War Office bureaucracy had been co-ordinated under the control of the Secretary of State. Over the next thirty years, almost every aspect of this reorganisation would be questioned as the shortcomings of the War Office Act (1870) became increasingly apparent.

Although the military leadership never formally challenged the constitutional relationship, their complaints about it remained a recurrent source of irritation for several Secretaries of State. The allegiance and loyalty of the army to the Crown persisted, as did a recognition that appointments and discipline ultimately derived from royal authority (albeit an authority exercised by the Secretary of State for War upon the recommendations of his military advisers). The royal connection pervaded the army; it was reflected in ceremonial, medals (the much coveted Victoria Cross), and the military service of members of the royal family. Queen Victoria retained a 'special feeling' for the army, which was not merely a personal interest but also a legacy of Prince Albert's involvement. She instinctively favoured the pre-Cardwellian army, with which the Prince had been connected. She feared, too, lest any changes of policy should curtail her prerogative powers, especially her right to communicate direct with the Officer Commanding-in-Chief. Finally, she staunchly supported her cousin, the Duke of Cambridge, whom she appointed as her personal *aide-de-camp* in November 1882. Five years later, she marked his completion of fifty years' service in the army by appointing him Commander-in-Chief by patent. The Duke regularly corresponded with the Queen, appealing to her whenever he wished to block, modify or delay the proposals of various Secretaries of State.[2]

The Queen was limited in what she could accomplish. She was obliged constitutionally to accept the advice of her Minister but could exercise influence and occasionally delay a governmental proposal. Although she enabled the Duke of Cambridge to remain in office for far longer than many politicians desired, she failed to have her son, the Duke of Connaught, succeed him as Commander-in-Chief. Secretaries of State could never ignore her interventions. Even in 1899 when the Queen referred to Lord Wolseley, then the Commander-in-Chief, as the 'Executive Chief of the Army', Lord Lansdowne, the Secretary of State, had to correct this misunderstanding of the Commander-in-Chief's authority which had been amended four years earlier. 'As she listens to soldiers rather than to Ministers,' noted Viscount Esher, a royal *confidant*, 'the task of the Secretary of State for War is never easy.'[3]

During his long tenure of office, which did not terminate until 31 October 1895, the Duke of Cambridge compounded these difficulties. He feared any further encroachments upon his authority or diminution of his responsibilities. When Hugh Childers as Secretary of State for War (1880–82) required him to desist from writing letters under the title 'Horse Guards War Office', an outraged Duke replied that the *command* of the army rests with the Commander-in-Chief, as representing the Sovereign; the Secretary of State is the high political official who controls all army matters and represents the Department, for which he is fully responsible in Parliament. But he certainly does not command the Army.

As a consequence, argued the Duke, his letters and orders had to have some 'individuality' and any change of procedure had to be approved by the Queen.[4] Childers gave way over the designation but felt that he should pronounce emphatically upon the constitutional question. In a speech to his constituents at Pontefract, he declared that

No act of discipline can be exercised, no appointment or promotion can be made, no troops can be moved, no payments can be made, without the approval, expressed or implied, of the Secretary of State. To say that the Secretary of State has no controlling power in such matters, when he is responsible to Parliament for any improper exercise of the Queen's prerogative in regard to them, is manifestly absurd.[5]

The constitutional issue was more a reflection than the source of the differences between the Duke and successive Secretaries of State. At bottom, the Duke profoundly resented the interference of civilians in professional and technical matters, especially when such interference had produced the linked battalions, short service and the abolition of purchase. His ill-concealed indignation undoubtedly encouraged some officers to believe that the reforms of 1870–72 could be reversed. Indeed, after the difficulties encountered in the Second Afghan and Zulu Wars, the Horse Guards requested that a committee should be formed to inquire into the functioning of the army organisation. Approved by the Earl of Beaconsfield's government in 1879, this committee of officers under the presidency of Lord Airey, the former Adjutant-General (1870–76), moved beyond its remit to review the entire Cardwellian system. It proposed an extension of the length of Colours service and the unlinking of battalions. Only printed a few days before the dissolution of Parliament in the spring of 1880, this report was immediately set aside by Childers as the incoming Liberal Secretary of State. He resolved instead to implement the Cardwellian system in its entirety. He brought the cavalry and artillery fully into the short service system, marginally extended the period of Colours service at home from six to seven years, and amalgamated the two linked battalions of line with two Militia battalions into one territorial regiment. The Duke of Cambridge deplored this territorialisation as it involved the loss of historic regimental numbers and facings on uniforms and thereby eroded *esprit de corps*. Although he failed to thwart these reforms in the short term, he sustained his criticisms over many years, so narrowing the scope of the military debate. By extolling the virtues of the old army, by repeatedly opposing the Cardwellian system, and by hiding behind non-existent constitutional privileges, he kept attention 'upon domestic political issues and away from the broader considerations of military policy and imperial defence'. As W.S. Hamer observed, 'a dead horse was being whipped with a vengeance'.[6]

The Secretary of State was rarely able to wrest the initiative. He carried an immense burden of duties and responsibilities. As a member of the cabinet and a Member of Parliament, he had to attend meetings and debates, present papers, deliver speeches, and answer parliamentary questions. During the parliamentary session of 1887–88, the Commons sat until 2.30 a.m. on an average of four out of five 'parliamentary days' for eight months, involving 485 divisions which each member of cabinet was expected to attend. In addition, the Minister would be regularly engaged in parliamentary or departmental committees, or in the War Council, or in giving interviews.[7] He was responsible to Parliament for the supply, equipment, and preparedness of the army, for the conduct of wars and military expeditions, and for political questions like the abolition of purchase or legislative issues like the Discipline Act. He had to make judgements upon peculiarly technical questions like cannon, small arms and ammunition, fortifications, the Commissariat, and the management of stores and factories. These were not only highly complex matters but they also involved millions of pounds of public revenue. The Minister, finally, was responsible for presenting the Army Estimates and for regulating the expenditure of public money, which, by the mid-1880s, totalled some £16,000,000 to £18,000,000 annually.

Secretaries of State struggled to perform these tasks. As political appointees, they often had limited and uncertain tenures of office. During the 1880s there were six Secretaries of State for War, and only two of Cardwell's eleven successors, Edward Stanhope and Lord Lansdowne, emulated his feat of spending more than five years in office (Appendix 1). Under such circumstances, it was rarely possible to develop new policy initiatives in office. Moreover, of these twelve Ministers, only Colonel Frederick A. Stanley had any military experience (and even that was a mere seven years serving in the Grenadier Guards before retiring as a lieutenant – he would later become an honorary colonel of the Royal Lancashire Militia). So when Secretaries of State had to pass judgement upon highly technical issues, for which they lacked either the knowledge or the experience, they were under pressure to heed the views of military experts who might not appreciate the financial or political implications of their advice. Should Ministers rely upon their advisers, they risked subsequent criticism for decisions which were not their own; should they act independently, as Childers did in insisting upon the retention of the breech action and so delaying the introduction of the magazine rifle, they risked being criticised for ill-informed civilian interference.[8]

In trying to discharge these duties satisfactorily, Secretaries of State could expect little assistance from the cabinet. As a collective body, concerned with a multitude of domestic, foreign and financial issues, it depended upon the specialist advice of the responsible Minister. It possessed neither the detailed knowledge nor any alternative source of information to pass judgement on military matters. Nevertheless, it was concerned with questions of policy and would consider the political and financial implications of any military issue which came before it. Of particular importance were the draft annual estimates, which might reach the cabinet with or without the prior agreement of the War Office and the Treasury. Whenever the cabinet needed to appease the recurrent clamour for retrenchment in Parliament, it regularly sought economies from Vote 12 (military stores), the 'most elastic part' of the Army Estimates.[9] The cabinet also had the right to intervene in the execution of policy (as it did when it terminated the First Boer War after the British defeat at Majuba Hill in 1881), and, occasionally, it might be embarrassed by a commanding officer who exceeded the bounds of prescribed policy (as Major-General Gordon did when he refused to leave Khartoum in 1884–85). In either circumstance, the legacy was likely to involve bitter recriminations between the civil and military authorities.

Within the War Office itself, the Secretary of State faced further difficulties. The War Office Act had left him dependent upon the Commander-in-Chief as his principal military adviser. This was too onerous a burden for the Commander-in-Chief, who had to undertake a wide array of duties. He was not only the sole adviser on questions of military policy, organisation and preparations for war, but he was also administratively responsible for recruiting, appointments, promotion, discipline, education and training, and held executive, command and inspection responsibilities for the forces in Great Britain. This highly centralised system diminished the sense of responsibility of the subordinate heads of department, and, in the absence of a General Staff, lacked a central organising department able to collect and co-ordinate information, to make plans of military operations, and to proffer advice upon all matters of organisation and the preparation of the army for war. The Duke of Cambridge, having blocked the creation of a Chief of Staff, had accepted the formation of a War Office Council in 1870. The Secretary of State periodically presided over this body, which met in a desultory manner. It became preoccupied with minutiae and its members were not required to come to any decisions. Like the other departmental committees, which co-ordinated aspects of defence, mobilisation and ordnance without reference to a broad strategic analysis (that a General Staff might have provided), the council was hardly an answer to the consultative limitations of the War Office.

Compounding these difficulties were the weaknesses in the office of the Secretary of State's principal civilian adviser, the Surveyor-General of the Ordnance. Expected to advise on the highly complex matters of supply, transport, equipment and ordnance, the Surveyor-General was supposed to be a senior military officer who could answer questions in Parliament. He was meant thereby to relieve the Secretary of State of a considerable burden in the area of his greatest ignorance. He had to manage the departments of supply, manufacture and ordnance and to exercise 'a strict control' over expenditure on all supplies and stores. He had under him the Director of Artillery and Stores, the Director of Supplies and Transport, the Director of Clothing, the Director of Contracts and the Inspector-General of Fortifications, as well as the controllers in each military district responsible to their respective major-generals.

Major-General Sir Henry Storks, the former Controller-in-Chief, was the first Surveyor-General. He possessed all the necessary qualifications. A veteran of the Crimean War, he was a senior and distinguished officer. A former Lord High Commissioner of the Ionian Islands, he was a Privy Councillor, and, after his ministerial appointment, gained a seat in the House of Commons. Despite these personal credentials, senior officers deeply resented the system of control, especially the tendency of controllers to interfere in the military activities of their districts. When Lord Eustace Cecil succeeded Sir Henry, he and Gathorne Hardy, the Secretary of State for War, used their 'best endeavours to abolish the word 'control' as soon as possible'.[10] Moreover, the military authorities insisted that all Commissariat appointments should be made from military men, claiming that soldiers on active service would not respect these officers if they were civilians. This demand was eventually acceded to, so depriving the Director of Supplies and Transport of any control over the promotion of his officers and placing his personnel under the Military Department.

These challenges succeeded because the office of Surveyor-General was steadily devalued. When the Conservatives entered office in 1874, Disraeli ignored the qualifications expected by the Northbrook Committee and appointed Lord Eustace Cecil in an act of patronage. Lord Eustace Cecil had very limited military experience, having left the army in 1863 with the rank of captain and lieutenant-colonel after twelve years' service in the 43rd Light Infantry and the Coldstream Guards. His successor, Lieutenant-General Sir John Adye, possessed the appropriate military background but lacked a seat in the House of Commons. All subsequent Surveyor-Generals were simply political appointees. As the Royal Commission, headed by Sir James Fitzjames Stephen, concluded in 1887,

out of seven persons who have held the office in the course of upwards of 16 years, three were never soldiers, one left the army as a subaltern and two only, namely, Sir H. Storks and Sir John Adye, possessed the qualifications which were in the mind of those who originally established the office.[11]

The consequences of this rapid turnover of office-holders, who rarely had the necessary qualifications, were profound. The Secretary of State lacked an experienced adviser, and the Surveyor-General became little more than a parliamentary mouthpiece for his departmental subordinates. The Directors of Artillery, Contracts, Clothing, Supplies and Transport and the Inspector-General of Fortifications became increasingly dominant; the Hon. Stafford Northcote, Surveyor-General (August 1886 to December 1887), admitted that he had to be guided by his professional experts, and that he discharged his parliamentary duties on the advice of his subordinates.[12] The departmental heads, however, were primarily concerned with their own departments and not with the Ordnance as a whole. They began to by-pass the Surveyor-General, either appealing from his decisions to the Secretary of State or even pre-empting his decisions by seeking a judgement from the Secretary of State before the Surveyor-General knew that any appeal had been made. In effect, the system had lamentably failed to fulfil the aims of the Northbrook Committee. It did not relieve the Secretary of State of many of his burdens as he still had to consider the demands of the various departmental heads, and as he lacked an experienced parliamentary spokesman. The Surveyor-General of the Ordnance, argued Lord Eustace Cecil, had become 'a fifth wheel to the coach'.[13]

Underpinning many of these problems was the vexed issue of financial control, including the methods of preparing the annual estimates and of determining their size. The process began in early November each year, when the Financial Secretary produced a draft estimate based on the establishments and expenditure of the previous year. He was officially responsible for preparing an estimate of the pay of the army, for collecting the requests of all the departments, and for compiling a general estimate which incorporated the votes on stores and the manufacturing departments prepared by the Surveyor-General of the Ordnance. Assisted by the Auditor of the Army and the Accountant-General, both civilians like his other assistants, the Financial Secretary conducted a financial review of the proposals from the other departments but could not veto them. In fact, the military usually submitted their demands after prior consultation, on an unofficial basis, with the Secretary of State. Once the draft estimate was completed, the Secretary of State normally summoned a meeting with the Financial Secretary, the Surveyor General and their assistants to review it. The subsequent discussion commonly produced 'a considerable curtailment of the amount provided',[14] although the draft total usually reflected an increase upon the estimates of the previous year.

Thereafter the Secretary of State entered into discussions with the Chancellor of the Exchequer. Any differences between them would be settled in the cabinet, and, in the absence of any change of policy requiring an increase of appropriations, the sum granted to the War Office was normally much lower than the sum requested. The Secretary of State, assisted by the departments responsible for the expenditure, would then have to reduce the estimates. Their room for manoeuvre was limited, as the estimate was divided into separate 'votes', such as 'stores', 'supplies', 'pay and personnel', most of which were fixed charges determined by Act of Parliament. These fixed charges could not be altered except by another Act of Parliament, and the money appropriated for specific purposes could not be transferred to other votes (unless a permanent regulation was established, with Treasury approval, to cover all future transfers of a similar nature). Only two votes, Vote 1 (the number of men on the establishment) and Vote 12 (stores) were readily manipulated, and Vote 12 normally bore the brunt of the reductions. Once reduced to the approved amount, the estimate was taken to the Treasury for approval before it was submitted to Parliament in the middle of March.

This system had numerous shortcomings. The degree of financial control within the War Office was utterly inadequate. The Surveyor-General had to assess the demands of his subordinates, especially those of the Director of Artillery, without any financial assistance. During the 1880s, when the turnover of office-holders became more rapid (five were appointed in six years), and when civilians tended to be appointed without any prior knowledge of the office, the Surveyor-General could hardly scrutinise the requests properly. As he prepared the estimates for, and subsequently administered the expenditure of, about 45 to 50 per cent of the annual estimates (that is, by the mid-1880s), his limitations had profound repercussions throughout the process. The Royal Commission, chaired by Sir Matthew Ridley, observed that

if the Financial Secretary of the War Office, and his chief adviser, the Accountant-General of the Army, were put into their proper positions . . . as financially responsible for the whole of Army expenditure, the Secretary of State would have a real grasp and control, which he does not now possess, over both estimates and votes.[15]

The process also set soldiers against civilians. The military heads of department were primarily concerned with their own sectional interests, and not with the Army Estimates as a whole. They regularly sought to protect these interests by inflating their original demands in the hope of offsetting the effects of the anticipated reductions. Aware of this practice, the Secretary of State and his advisers were in an acute dilemma. They could neither scrutinise all the demands effectively, especially those relating to stores, ordnance and supplies, nor, on many occasions, justify them in the national interest. All too often they simply had to reduce the excessive demands within the overall limits imposed by the cabinet. Arbitrary economies, in short, took precedence over any criteria of military efficiency or the requirements of national security.

Whether the outcome was cost-effective was highly doubtful. As the Stephen Commission rightly noted, the cabinet and Treasury were more concerned 'with cutting down demands than with ascertaining their wisdom'. The process had produced 'not an answer to the question, How can the best articles of the kind required be most economically produced? but a conflict between the demands urged by a variety of conflicting claimants, and the absolute decision of an authority . . .'. The upshot, it concluded, was far from beneficial: 'extravagance controlled by stinginess is not likely to result either in economy or efficiency'.[16]

Ultimately the system of financial control left the soldiers without any sense of responsibility for the efficiency of the service. The Military Department refrained from making proposals which it regarded as necessary but which it anticipated the government would reject. Even so, the Duke of Cambridge frequently found that his more modest requests were still reduced by the civilian councils from which he was excluded. Unable to present his demands before Parliament, the Duke refused to accept any responsibility for the actual estimates, as they had left the army, in his opinion, seriously undermanned, ill-equipped and poorly quartered. He even refused to proffer a statement on how the 'many deficiencies' could be corrected, as he knew that there was not any government which would fund the requirements.[17]

As the shortcomings of the Cardwell reorganisation became increasingly apparent, the demands for War Office reform revived. Some favoured replacing the Commander-in-Chief as the principal adviser to the Secretary of State with a council of advisers analogous to the Board of Admiralty.[18] Others feared that a council would produce confusion, delays, and a lack of co-ordination; they suggested that a more powerful officer should head the army, with greater administrative and financial responsibility and with a remit to pronounce authoritatively upon the requirements of national defence. Wolseley favoured one variant of this option, while some of the leading civilian advocates of army reform, Spenser Wilkinson and Sir Charles Dilke, favoured another.[19]

Wolseley and his military followers faced several difficulties in promoting War Office reform. Although they agreed with the Duke of Cambridge that the military should have more financial responsibility, and that the supply functions should be wrested from civilian control, they did not wish to bolster the Duke's administrative position. Wolseley doubted that the army could ever be efficient or 'in good order' until the Duke left office.[20] He therefore favoured the Duke's removal, but expected the government to replace him with an even more powerful Commander-in-Chief. Moreover, in pressing for more financial responsibility, Wolseley and his acolytes were challenging the whole basis of financial control established by the Order-in-Council of 23 June 1870. Sir Redvers Buller, when Adjutant-General, criticised the requirement that the Financial Secretary should advise on questions of army expenditure (as established under the reforms of 1888). The military, he contended, should be responsible for military expenditure, and the Finance Department should simply audit completed expenditure. This proposal, argued Sir Arthur Haliburton, was 'merely the thin end of a wedge to divide up the office in accordance with that theory of organisation'.[21]

Nevertheless, the reformers had an unprecedented opportunity to advance their cause in the late 1880s and 1890s. The Second Afghan and Zulu Wars, followed by the Egyptian campaigns of 1882 and 1884–85, had exposed the malfunctioning of the Cardwell system. Dissatisfaction mounted as successive governments failed to pay for the additions which would have restored the balance of linked battalions, and as the rapid turnover of Secretaries of State and Surveyor-Generals frustrated any continuity of administrative policy. Indeed, by 1885, Britain's military resources seemed all too stretched when a war scare erupted as Russian forces advanced towards Afghanistan. As the supply and transport services had incurred criticisms during the Egyptian campaign, a Royal Commission, headed by Sir James Fitzjames Stephen, was appointed to investigate. Although the commissioners were specifically instructed by the Secretary of State to confine their inquiries to the supply services, they resolved to examine all aspects of army administration. They provided thereby an excellent platform for those who wished to criticise the War Office system.

The report of the Stephen Commission, which was issued on 16 May 1887, reflected many of these concerns. The commissioners began by reviewing the history of army administration from the pre-Crimean period to the reports of Lord Northbrook's Committee

and the Orders-in-Council of 1870. They emphasised that the process of reform had concentrated enormous powers and duties upon
the Secretary of State, who was normally a civilian with limited
technical knowledge and a precarious tenure of office. In these
circumstances, they doubted that any single person could perform all
his duties satisfactorily, a shortcoming which also applied, *mutatis
mutandis*, to the Surveyor-General of the Ordnance. Both the Secretary of State and the Surveyor-General, they argued, were unduly
dependent upon their subordinates, so weakening the system, under-
mining all real responsibility, and effectively preventing 'the public
from knowing for what purpose their money is raised or how it is
applied'. They concluded that the present system lacked either a
definite object or an efficient head; it had no proper organised
method of dealing with the technical questions which arose from the
construction or purchase of warlike stores.[22]

In their recommendations the commissioners were equally
forthright. They advocated the formation of a commission of
eminent men, independent of any particular government, which
should pronounce annually upon the nation's military requirements
and so establish definite standards for manpower, horses, stores,
ordnance, vehicles and all other forms of military equipment. These
would be annual standards of what should exist and what actually
existed, so informing Parliament and the public of the actual state of
military preparedness. The commissioners recommended, too, that
the Ordnance Department should be separated altogether from the
department of the Secretary of State for War. They suggested that the
department should be placed under a Master-General of the
Ordnance, a military officer of great eminence, who should have a
seat in the Lords or Commons and hold office, independent of
government, for a period of seven years. The Master-General would
be charged with preparing and publishing an annual statement of
what he regarded as necessary for his department. The Secretary of
State would still present estimates before Parliament, but Parliament
would be able to consider both his presentations and those of his
advisers, and to perceive 'where the difference between them lay, and
what are the matters which must be foregone for the sake of
economy'.[23]

Although these proposals were never acted upon, as they threatened the essence of civilian control, the Stephen report was still a
valuable source of information. It highlighted many of the admini-

strative problems of the War Office (apart from the role of the Commander-in-Chief). It emphasised that the army, though constitutionally controlled, was far from efficient, and that party political control had compounded the difficulties of addressing some of the crucial questions of national security. Above all, it drew attention to the degree of military frustration over the process of financial control. Indeed, it endorsed Wolseley's contention that the recurrent search for economies had gravely impaired the efficiency of the army, and that experts should apprise Parliament about 'the military requirements of the Empire'. It was 'the greatest misfortune', he argued, 'that our military requirements have never been inquired into – have never been tabulated and laid down'.[24]

Civil administration, nonetheless, had its defenders, including a Select Committee, chaired by Lord Morley, which reported in July 1887. It had investigated the army's manufacturing departments, following complaints by Wolseley about the munitions with which his forces had been equipped in Egypt, particularly defective cartridges and swords and bayonets that bent.[25] The committee duly examined the organisation of the government factories and the process by which estimates and appropriations accounts were presented to Parliament. It identified three principal deficiencies: a lack of co-operation between the factories, the quinquennial changes of their chief officers, and the system of inspection by which factory officials had to inspect the quality of articles manufactured by their own factories and articles of a similar nature purchased from private firms. It recommended that the activities of the factories should be co-ordinated under a Superintendent of Ordnance Factories, who would head the design and drawing office and act as the sole channel of communication between the War Office and the manufacturing departments. It advocated a greater permanence in the tenure of factory superintendents and the creation of an inspection system which would be independent of the manufacturing process and headed by an Inspector-General of Warlike Stores. He would be responsible for the inspection and testing of all stores and weapons. Finally, the committee stipulated that design and inspection should be military tasks, while manufacture should remain a civilian undertaking.[26]

Although the Morley Committee favoured the creation of new military appointments – both the proposed Superintendent of Ordnance Factories and the Inspector-General of Warlike Stores – it did not propose that the manufacturing departments should be transferred from civil to military control. Fundamentally, it concentrated upon the organisation and the procedures of the factories at a level where political considerations hardly intruded. It also reviewed the work of civilians who were highly qualified by virtue of their education and experience to supervise the manufacturing process. By keeping within this remit, the Morley Committee came to different conclusions from those reached by the Stephen Commission. It actually emphasised that there should be more civilian administrators, including a Chief Mechanical Engineer with a staff of civilian subordinates, and that they should have more authority over the manufacturing departments.[27]

Another Royal Commission on Civil Establishments, chaired by Sir Matthew Ridley, issued its report in September 1887. The commissioners defended the existing system of civilian administration from the criticism 'in some quarters' that it has led 'to extravagance and want of efficiency'. They maintained that, constitutionally, both the Secretary of State for War and the First Lord of the Admiralty had to be 'high Parliamentary officers, holding cabinet office, and owing their position to political and not merely professional qualifications'. They rejected any reforms which might divide the responsibility for the expenditure on the army and navy. They insisted that

It is no doubt necessary that the highest professional skill should be at the disposal of these responsible Ministers to advise upon military and naval questions, but if such advice and its sufficient continuity is provided for, there is, we believe, no insuperable difficulty in reconciling Parliamentary headship and control with a completely adequate maintenance of the defensive forces of the country.[28]

This pronouncement, though impeccable from a constitutional perspective, hardly addressed the question which had troubled the Stephen Commission, namely the differing criteria by which the politicians and soldiers had evaluated issues of national security. Even so, the Ridley Commission recognised that the civilian Ministers were probably not receiving the best professional advice from the existing system. Like the Stephen Commission, it acknowledged that the Surveyor-General had become greatly overburdened, and that the office had failed to develop as the Northbrook Committee had intended. It learnt from Wolseley that an internal War Office committee, known as the Committee on Lines of Communication for an Army, favoured the complete reorganisation of the Surveyor-General's department, with the military assuming responsibility for supplies, transport and the lines of communication. The Ridley Commission recommended that future Surveyors-General should be military officers 'of high standing and experience', appointed for a fixed term of five to seven years, and that they should not be Members of Parliament.[29]

Confronted with this extensive range of criticism, Edward Stanhope, the Secretary of State for War, decided to reorganise the War Office. Although he was unwilling to enhance the powers of the military advisers by creating the council proposed by the Stephen Commission, Stanhope accepted that their administrative authority should be extended. He resolved to abolish the office of Surveyor-General of the Ordnance and to unify all the principal departments, apart from finance and manufacture, under the Commander-in-Chief. Confirmed in the Order-in-Council of 21 February 1888, this reorganisation transferred Supply and Transport to the jurisdiction of the Quartermaster-General and placed the Inspector-General of Fortifications and the Director of Artillery within the Military Department.[30]

The reorganisation of 1888 undoubtedly simplified the administrative process. It clearly divided responsibility between the soldiers and the civilians. Henceforth the Commander-in-Chief became responsible for all matters pertaining to the personnel and *matériel* of the army, including the auxiliary forces, as well as the collection of intelligence and the construction and maintenance of fortifications. The Financial Secretary became responsible for reviewing all proposed expenditure, including any proposals for new expenditure or the redistribution of allotted funds, for compiling the estimates, and for examining the accounts. He also assumed control of the manufacturing departments, including the Clothing Department. In short, the reorganisation established the control of the Commander-in-Chief over supply and operations, so imparting a degree of co-ordination to the military system hitherto lacking. Finally, it established that the Financial Secretary should act as the adviser to the Secretary of State on all questions of army expenditure.

Yet the reorganisation did not enhance the individual responsibility of the subordinate officers. Although the Director of Artillery, the Quartermaster-General and the Inspector-General of Fortifications administered large spending departments, they were not directly responsible to the Secretary of State but to the Commander-in-Chief. If the Secretary of State wished to consult these officers, he could only do so informally. The Duke of Cambridge remained the only responsible adviser on military matters, but he still lacked a proper staff department and now had his considerable executive, command and administrative burdens augmented by responsibility for supply and transport and for preparing the whole of the annual estimates. Unifying the military administration had simply produced an excessive centralisation of responsibility, a lack of adequate consultative procedures, and a diminished sense of responsibility among the subordinate heads of department.

The reforms, too, had exacerbated the problems associated with financial control. As Stanhope stated in a memorandum explaining the Army Estimates of 1888, the control of the Financial Secretary had been extended to all branches of the War Office. The reorganisation, he added, would enable 'the military authorities . . . to take a comprehensive view of the whole condition of the military resources of the country, of our requirements, and of the means available for meeting them. All the threads are in their own hands.'[31] William St John Brodrick, the Financial Secretary, clarified this expectation in a speech at Guildford on 1 February 1888. Henceforth, he declared, 'the entire responsibility for the efficiency of the Army as regards men and material and for the defence of the country had been placed in military hands'.[32] Both the Duke of Cambridge and Wolseley were incensed by these statements. So long as the civilian authorities retained financial control, the military advisers could not, in their view, be responsible for an army which was undermanned and ill-equipped. Profoundly concerned about the unsatisfactory defences at home and abroad, they attributed these deficiencies to estimates which had been recurrently trimmed to meet the political priorities of successive governments. Accordingly, they refused to accept responsibility for inadequate defences.

As concern about the nation's defences had already been voiced by Lord Charles Beresford after his resignation from the Board of Admiralty in January 1888, and would be exacerbated by another invasion scare in the following spring, the military quickly pressed their case. Addressing the Select Committee on the Army Estimates on 24 April 1888, the Duke of Cambridge stated that 'whoever has the purse strings has the power . . . . I am not responsible until you choose to show what I asked for, and what that other more powerful element than myself has reduced'.[33] Wolseley, speaking more intemperately at a private dinner in honour of Sir John Pender, denounced party government as 'the curse of modern England'. All incoming Ministers, he asserted, tried to make 'claptrap' reputations by cutting down the service estimates.[34] These widely publicised remarks infuriated Stanhope and earned a parliamentary rebuke from Lord Salisbury, the Prime Minister. On 14 May, Wolseley defended himself in the House of Lords. He denied that his remarks had been directed at the Secretary of State personally or at the military policy of the present government, but he insisted that the army and navy were neither properly organised nor fully equipped, and that they could not guarantee the safety of the capital (a popular anxiety in view of the contemporary invasion scare).[35]

On the following day the government sought to defuse the debate. It announced the formation of another Royal Commission, headed by Lord Hartington, to investigate the army and navy departments and their relations with the Treasury. By narrowly defining the terms of reference, the government precluded examination of such issues as the adequacy of the stores or the quality of the ordnance or the number of home battalions. By appointing three former Secretaries of State for War (Lord Hartington, W.H. Smith and Henry Campbell-Bannerman) to serve on the commission, it clearly wished to ensure an endorsement of the principle of civilian control. In short, it was not prepared to investigate the questions raised by the Stephen report or to approve the kind of inquiry which the Duke of Cambridge and Wolseley had requested.

The Hartington Commission began its hearings in 1888 and issued its report, without any minutes of evidence, in two parts – the first on 10 July 1889 and the second on 11 February 1890. It found a complete lack of regular communication between the army and navy, and the absence of any planning which took into account the plans and requirements of the other service. It proposed that a defence committee, composed of soldiers, sailors and cabinet Ministers, should authoritatively decide upon questions of defence policy, including the requirements of the two services, in accordance with a plan of imperial defence, and consider the estimates of the services before they were submitted to cabinet. It also favoured abolishing the office of Commander-in-Chief, after the Duke's retirement, and the substitution of a War Office Council as the principal source of advice to the Secretary of State for War. Under the presidency of the Secretary of State, the council would include the Parliamentary and Permanent Under-Secretaries, the Financial Secretary, and five senior military officers who would be responsible to the Secretary of State for the efficient administration of their departments. These officers would include the Adjutant-General, the Quartermaster-General, the Director of Artillery, the Inspector-General of Fortifications and a Chief of the Staff.

Undoubtedly the proposed creation of a Chief of the Staff was the most radical of the commission's recommendations. He would be appointed for five years and would head a 'central organising department' drawn from the Intelligence Division and those officers in the Adjutant-General's department who dealt with mobilisation planning and the defence of the United Kingdom. The Chief of the Staff would advise the Secretary of State on general military policy, consult the First Lord of the Admiralty on inter-service questions, and present an annual report to the Secretary of State on the military requirements of the Empire. 'Freed from all executive duties', a Chief of the Staff would be responsible for 'preparing plans of military operations, collecting and co-ordinating information of all kinds, and generally tendering advice upon all matters of organisation and the preparation of the army for war'.[36]

Although the Hartington report would have a long-term significance as a basis for the future reorganisation within the War Office, its immediate impact was negligible. The Queen, still harbouring hopes that the Duke of Connaught would succeed her cousin as Commander-in-Chief, was firmly opposed. Neither the Duke of Cambridge nor Wolseley favoured the appointment of a Chief of Staff other than as an officer responsible to the Commander-in-Chief. Facing royal opposition and the determination of the Duke to remain in office, the government settled for the creation of a War Office Council from May 1890, with the Commander-in-Chief as the first military member. Stanhope baulked at any further compromise. When the Duke of Cambridge and Sir Redvers Buller, who succeeded Wolseley as Adjutant-General in 1890, suggested that the Adjutant-General's title should be changed to 'Chief of the Staff and Adjutant-General' to the Commander-in-Chief, Stanhope replied that the cabinet would not countenance this deception of the public. Their proposal, he added, would totally contradict the recommendation of the Hartington Commission that the Chief of Staff should advise the Secretary of State and not the Commander-in-

Chief.[37]

Even so, the new War Office Council was an emasculated version of the Hartington concept. The Secretary of State's powers of initiative and his responsibility were carefully preserved (no item could be raised in discussion without his prior approval). Only the decisions of the Secretary of State, after hearing the opinions of the council, were recorded (and not the whole discussion, as recommended by the Hartington Commission). All decisions, and hence the responsibility, would be the Secretary of State's alone, and not, as in the Board of Admiralty, those of the council as a body. The military officials lacked any sense of equality as they appeared in the presence of the Commander-in-Chief. Finally, the Secretary of State could use the council as and when he saw fit. During 1891, Stanhope's last full year in office, it met on only eleven occasions; it met on eight occasions in 1892, seven in 1893, four in 1894, and not at all in the first half of 1895 before Lord Rosebery's resignation.[38]

Campbell-Bannerman, who succeeded Stanhope as Secretary of State for War in August 1892, was more interested in trimming the estimates than in administrative reform. He had formally dissented from the Hartington report over the proposed creation of a Chief of Staff. Britain, he argued, differed fundamentally from those Continental countries which were constantly concerned about the military preparations of their neighbours and did not need a 'general military policy'. The new department, he feared, might be tempted 'to create such a field for itself'. He suspected, too, that the role of the Chief of Staff as an 'intimate and confidential adviser of the Minister upon all great military questions' would undermine the War Office Council, in which all members were supposed to discuss matters in perfect equality and so proffer frank and independent advice to the civilian Minister. The Chief of Staff, he argued, would soon be seen as 'separate from and superior to his colleagues', so reproducing 'most of the disadvantages' of the office he replaced. Similarly, he deprecated the form of War Office Council established in May 1890, claiming that the military members would be overawed by the Commander-in-Chief. Once in office he rarely summoned the council, preferring to leave the business of the War Office to the various departments and the administration of the army to the civil servants, whom he held in high regard.[39]

As a staunch Cardwellian and an advocate of strict financial control, he was always willing to defend the *status quo* against criticism from parliamentary reformers. Administratively, he was only interested in enhancing civilian control, and, in the autumn of 1894, had his civil servants, headed by Sir Ralph Thompson, examine the issue. By the end of May 1895 they had produced a modified version of the Hartington proposals, involving a reduction in the authority of the Commander-in-Chief by vesting his powers of patronage in an Army Board. This board, composed of the principal military advisers, would also be responsible for all military proposals in the annual estimates. Its military members would have direct and equal access to the Secretary of State, and, if they differed with the Commander-in-Chief, the Secretary of State could arbitrate between them.

This proposal could not be implemented until the Duke of Cambridge, now seventy-six years of age, was eased out of office. In view of the Duke's determined recalcitrance, this was a highly delicate undertaking which depended ultimately upon mollifying the Queen. When she was assured that the Duke's resignation would not preclude the future appointment of the Duke of Connaught as Commander-in-Chief, she reluctantly concurred. Nevertheless, it still required extensive lobbying throughout May and June before the government was able to announce the proposed changes on 21 June 1895 and the Duke's intention to retire.[40] Ironically, on the same day, Brodrick introduced a motion in the Commons to reduce the salary of the Secretary of State for War because of the inadequate reserves of small arms ammunition and the risks it implied for national security. The government lost the vote by 132 to 125, and decided to resign three days later. Lord Salisbury agreed to form a new government, and, after offering the War Office to Joseph Chamberlain, appointed Lord Lansdowne as the new Secretary of State for War.

The Conservative government exploited the opportunity caused by the Duke's imminent retirement. On 19 August it announced that Wolseley would be appointed as the new Commander-in-Chief, and, one week later, indicated how his office would be altered as part of more extensive reforms. Lord Lansdowne explained that the Commander-in-Chief would assume the duties of a Chief of Staff, by taking direct control of the Intelligence and Mobilisation Departments. He would still be the 'principal adviser of the Secretary of State on all military questions', but Campbell-Bannerman's Army Board would be established to discuss matters referred to it by the Secretary of State and those questions which affected more than one department. The Accountant-General would attend the board, not as a member, but as a financial adviser. The War Office Council, composed of civilian and military members, with its discussions recorded, could discuss the political and financial aspects of questions already examined in purely professional terms by the Army Board.

These proposals were eventually amplified in the Order-in-Council of 21 November 1895. The Commander-in-Chief was charged with the 'general supervision' of the military departments of the War Office, and with the preparation and maintenance of schemes of offensive and defensive operations. The Adjutant-General, Quartermaster-General, Inspector-General of Fortifications and the Inspector-General of the Ordnance were made directly responsible to the Secretary of State. These four officers under the presidency of the Commander-in-Chief would comprise the Army Board, to report upon promotions above the rank of major, staff appointments above the rank of lieutenant-colonel, proposals for the estimates, and any other questions referred to it by the Secretary of State. The Financial Secretary retained his authority in financial matters. He was charged with reviewing expenditure proposed for the annual estimates and any proposals for new expenditure or the redistribution of allotted sums, with the task of compiling the estimates, and with the auditing and accounting of the approved expenditure. In short, he advised the Secretary of State on 'all questions of Army expenditure'.[41]

These reforms hardly transformed the War Office. The council functioned much as its predecessor had done. Lord Lansdowne, who summoned meetings and determined the agenda, used the council as a purely consultative body. Any decisions based on the advice given remained his alone. Lord Wolseley, despite a significant loss of authority, dominated the military members in the proceedings of the council. Although minutes of the discussions were supposed to be kept, it seems that only the decisions were recorded. The meetings were held on a desultory and infrequent basis; Sir Henry Brackenbury, who became Director-General of the Ordnance in February 1899, could not recall more than half a dozen meetings of the council between the time of his appointment and Lord Lansdowne's departure from office in November 1900.[42]

The Army Board, under Wolseley's presidency, met irregularly but quite frequently in the autumn and winter months when the estimates were under discussion. Apart from its reports upon promotions and staff appointments, the board lacked any power of initiative other than in its proposals for the estimates (and could only consider other matters if they were referred to it by the Secretary of State). The board's specific role in the preparation of the estimates represented the first direct involvement of the military in the process. Once the Secretary of State had received proposals from the heads of the military departments for any new or increased expenditure, he could refer these requests to the board for its consideration. The board was then required to indicate the relative importance of these proposals for the army, to state which of them they would recommend for insertion in the estimates, and to indicate whether any economies could be made in the existing expenditure. The Accountant-General was specifically required to assist this process by supplying the board with calculations or information on the cost of the various proposals. The Secretary of State could then decide which of the proposals should be included, and this decision would form the basis for preparing the estimates in their final form.

Sir Ralph Knox, the Accountant-General and later Permanent Under-Secretary, realised that the military profoundly disliked the new procedures. On 26 November 1896, he informed Campbell-Bannerman that he was 'seldom summoned' to the Army Board:

The soldiers don't like it, because they have to face one another & argue out their ideas instead of attempting to push them through independently, and they don't like my presence, because it makes them consider the financial aspect of affairs and also lets me know the differences of opinion.[43]

Although these resentments persisted over the next three years, Knox observed that the board's machinery had begun to work more effectively: 'S[ecretary] of S[tate] seems satisfied but the soldiers can't bear it much preferring to paddle their course in their own way if they can. However matters are going with great smoothness, though with much fuss which I try to keep down'. More generally, though, Knox feared that the military might try to undermine civilian influence in the War Office. He feared that

The soldiers are most restive, and I imagine are determined to make a long pull, a strong pull & a pull together to get rid of anything like an independent financial control in the Dep[artmen]t and Lord L[ansdowne] is so weak and Mr W[yndham] so sympathising that I fear we shall go to the wall.[44]

Personal animosities and resentments were largely responsible for this rapid deterioration in civil–military relations. The mutual dislike of Sir Redvers Buller and Sir Arthur Haliburton persisted until the former left in 1897 to take over the command at Aldershot. Wolseley never fully accepted the terms of the Order-in-Council of 21 November 1895. As a former Quartermaster-General and Adjutant-General who had laboured under the dominating influence of the Duke of Cambridge, he resented that his own authority as Commander-in-Chief had been curtailed. He particularly deprecated the separation of responsibility for discipline and training (in the Adjutant-General's department) from his own command. He chafed at the ambiguity of the term 'general supervision', which left him responsible for the efficiency of the military departments without having full authority over them. He never accepted that his principal subordinates should have direct access to the Secretary of State; indeed, he undermined the spirit of the 1895 regulations by requiring that these subordinates should send their correspondence to the Secretary of State through his own office.[45]

Endowed with nominal responsibility but limited power, Wolseley became increasingly bitter. Privately, he disparaged the control of the army by ignorant politicians, such as Lord Lansdowne, and their civilian officials. 'I am working hard,' he informed his wife, 'but it is difficult to lead my little man of small mind and undecided views. He does so look like a cross between a French dancing master & a Jewess.'[46] Publicly, he continued to criticise the Order-in-Council of 21 November 1895, describing its defects in a memorandum to the Prime Minister on his retirement. The Commander-in-Chief, he argued, had become a 'fifth wheel to a coach', lacking either the supreme control of the Secretary of State or the administrative functions conferred on his subordinates. The present system had eroded the basis of military efficiency and should be rescinded. Lord Lansdowne retorted that the former centralisation of administrative responsibilities in the Commander-in-Chief had meant that a large part of these duties were perforce unperformed. He emphasised that the Order-in-Council had strengthened the powers of the Commander-in-Chief by comparison with the draft prepared by Campbell-Bannerman (which had not made any reference to powers of 'general supervision'). He also noted that had Wolseley fulfilled all the planning duties of a Chief of Staff which had been allocated to him, he could not have given anything other than 'general supervision' to the other military departments. Wolseley, however, had always disparaged the concept of a Chief of the Staff. He believed that it had been promoted within the Hartington Commission by an embittered Brackenbury, who had no hope of becoming Commander-in-Chief but who had accumulated experience as head of the Intelligence Division which would have served him admirably as a future Chief of the Staff. In 1897 Wolseley had also succumbed to a serious illness from which he never fully recovered. He suffered periodic lapses of memory thereafter, visited the War Office much less frequently, and so enabled his critics to charge that the man and not the office had failed the army.[47]

Undoubtedly the appalling personal relationships and the departmental rivalries widened the rift between the soldiers and the civilians in the War Office. The rift reflected the reluctance of successive governments either to determine the requirements of imperial and national defence in advance of a crisis or to let their military advisers publicise their own assessment of these requirements. Faced with recurrent military protests, governments firmly defended their constitutional authority, enhanced their techniques of financial control, and weakened the military by imposing a system of 'divide and rule'. As a consequence the War Office languished, with senior officials engrossed in a mass of routine work, governed by a vast body of minute regulations. Lacking sufficient time, these officials could not concentrate on 'matters of policy' and 'questions of great importance'. Hamer aptly concluded that as long as governments operated upon a formula of 'decision by crisis', the training and preparation of the army for war was bound to suffer.[48]

Notes

1 *Preliminary and Further Reports (with Appendices) of the Royal Commissioners appointed to Enquire into the Civil and Professional Administration of the Naval and Military Departments and the Relation of those Departments to each other and to the Treasury*, hereafter referred to as the *Hartington Report*, C. 5979 (1890), XIX, p.xxiv.

2 Tucker, 'Army and Society in England 1870–1900', pp.121–2; F. Hardie, *The Political Influence of Queen Victoria, 1861–1901* (Oxford University Press; London, 1935), p.178; Hamer, *The British Army*, pp.35–7.

3 Lord Esher, journal, 15 November 1900, M.V. Brett (ed.), *Journals and Letters of Reginald Viscount Esher*, 4 Vols. (Ivor Nicholson & Watson; London, 1934–38), Vol.1, p.269; G. St Aubyn, *The Royal George* (Con-

stable; London, 1963), pp.204–7; Tucker, 'Army and Society in England 1870–1900', pp.121–2; Hardie, *The Political Influence of Queen Victoria*, pp.181–2.

4 Cambridge to Childers, 7 August 1881, Childers, *The Life and Correspondence of the Right Hon. Hugh C.E. Childers*, p.52.

5 *Ibid.*, p.57.

6 Hamer, *The British Army*, p.39; *Airey Report*, pp.44–5; Childers to Queen Victoria, 20 November 1880, Childers, *The Life and Correspondence of the Right Hon. Hugh C.E. Childers*, pp.39–42.

7 W. St J. Brodrick, 'Edward Stanhope', *National Review*, Vol.22 (February 1894), pp.844–5; I.F.W. Beckett, 'Edward Stanhope at the War Office, 1887–92', *Journal of Strategic Studies*, Vol.5 (June 1982), pp.278–307.

8 *Report of the Royal Commission appointed to inquire into the System under which Patterns of warlike Stores are adopted and the Stores obtained and passed for Her Majesty's Service*, hereafter referred to as the *Stephen Report*, C. 5062 (1887), XV, pp.ix and xvi; Hamer, *The British Army*, pp.45–6.

9 *Stephen Report*, p.xiv.

10 Lord Eustace Cecil, q.5546 evidence appended to the *First Report of the Royal Commission appointed to inquire into the Civil Establishments of the different Offices of State at home and abroad with minutes of evidence, appendix, etc.*, hereafter referred to as the *Ridley Report*, C. 5226 (1887), XIX, p.207; G. Hardy, diary, 5 August 1874, N.E. Johnson (ed.), *The Diary of Gathorne Hardy, later Lord Cranbrook, 1886–1892: Political Selections* (Clarendon Press; Oxford, 1981), p.217.

11 *Stephen Report*, p.xi.

12 Hon. H.S. Northcote, qs.1490–4 and Sir J. Adye, qs.5028–32 evidence appended to the *Stephen Report*, pp.56 and 188.

13 Cecil, qs.5546–51 evidence appended to the *Ridley Report*, p.207.

14 W.H. Smith, q.35 evidence appended to the *Stephen Report*, p.2; Hamer, *The British Army*, pp.62–3; Viscount Wolseley, q.6095 evidence appended to the *Fourth Report from the Select Committee on Army Estimates*, C. 269 (1888), IX, p.135; *Ridley Report*, p.xxii.

15 *Ridley Report*, p.ix; *Stephen Report*, pp.xii–xiv and Northcote, qs.1537–8 evidence appended to the *Stephen Report*, p.58; *First Report from the Select Committee on Army and Navy Estimates*, C. 216 (1887), VIII, pp.2–4 and R. Knox, qs.3503–5 evidence appended to this report, pp.227–8; Hamer, *The British Army*, pp.63–4.

16 *Stephen Report*, p.xiii; Wolseley, *q.2303 evidence appended to the Ridley Report*, p.86.

17 Cambridge, qs.1832–3, 1850, 1861–3, 1954–6, 1994–2010 evidence appended to the *Second Report from the Select Committee on Army and Navy Estimates*, C. 212 (1888), VIII, pp.34, 36–7, 46–7, 52–4; Wolseley, qs.6099–102 evidence appended to the *Fourth Report from the Select Committee on Army and Navy Estimates*, p.136.

18 Sir G. Chesney, 'The Army as a Public Department', *Nineteenth Century*, Vol.XXX (July 1891), pp.7–25; 'The Reconstructed War Office'

and 'The War Office : Outside Departments', *Blackwood's Edinburgh Magazine*, Vol.142 (October 1887), pp.567–82 and Vol.143 (January 1888), pp.128–48.

19   Wolseley, q.6095 evidence appended to the *Fourth Report from the Select Committee on Army and Navy Estimates*, p.135; Sir C. Dilke and S. Wilkinson, *Imperial Defence* (Constable; London, 1892), pp.208–22.

20   Wolseley to Lady Wolseley, 24 November 1884 and 28 August 1890, Wolseley Mss., Hove Reference Library, W/P 13/31 and 19/20.

21   Sir A. Haliburton to H. Campbell-Bannerman, 12 December 1892, Campbell-Bannerman Mss., B.L. Add. Mss. 41,218, ff.221–2.

22   *Stephen Report*, pp.viii–xii, xxxvi, civ.

23   *Ibid.*, pp.xxxviii–xxxix, civ–cv.

24   *Ibid.*, pp.xli–xliii, quoting Wolseley's evidence qs.2640–60.

25   Sir F. Maurice and Sir G. Arthur, *The Life of Lord Wolseley* (Heinemann; London, 1924), pp.227–8.

26   *Report of the Committee appointed to inquire into the Organisation and Administration of the Manufacturing Departments of the Army; with minutes of evidence, appendix and index*, hereafter referred to as the *Morley Report*, C. 5116 (1887), XIV, pp.xiv, xviii, xxvi–xxvii.

27   *Ibid.*, p.xxvi.

28   *Ridley Report*, pp.vi–vii.

29   *Ibid.*, p.ix and Wolseley, qs.2225–34 evidence appended to the *Ridley Report*, pp.82–3.

30   *Order in Council relative to the War Department with a Statement of the Duties Assigned to Certain Officers under such Orders*, C. 5304 (1888), LXVII, pp.3–5; Hamer, *The British Army*, pp.129–30.

31   *Memorandum of the Secretary of State relating to the Army Estimates, 1888–9*, C. 5303 (1888), LXVI, p.4.

32   *The Times*, 2 February 1888, p.8.

33   Cambridge, q.2010, see also qs.1843–51, 1944–2003 evidence appended to the *Second Report from the Select Committee on Army Estimates*, pp.35–6, 45–54; Wolseley to Cambridge, 8 February 1888, Cambridge Mss., RA, E/1/12098; Lady Geraldine Somerset's diary, 2 May 1888, St Aubyn, *The Royal George*, pp.279–80.

34   Maurice and Arthur, *The Life of Lord Wolseley*, pp.238–9.

35   E. Stanhope to Cambridge, 26 and 28 April 1888 and Cambridge to Stanhope, 27 April 1888, Cambridge Mss., RA, E/1/12181, 12184 and 12182; *Parl. Deb.*, Third Ser., Vol.326 (11 May 1888), cols.1–7 and (14 May 1888), cols.90–102. On the invasion scare, see Gen. Sir E. Hamley, 'The Defencelessness of London' and H.M. Hozier, 'Our Actual Military Strength', *Nineteenth Century*, Vol.23 (May and June 1886), pp.633–40 and 799–808.

36   *Hartington Report*, pp.xxii–xxiii; see also pp.vi–viii, xxvi–xxvii.

37   Stanhope to Cambridge, 6 June 1890; Cambridge to Stanhope, 3 June 1890 and Sir R. Buller to Cambridge, 20 September 1890, Cambridge Mss., RA, E/1/12607, 12605 and 12653; *Parl. Deb.*, Third Ser., Vol.346 (3 July 1890), cols.767–9; Queen Victoria to Sir H. Ponsonby, 20 March 1890, Ponsonby to Cambridge, 25 March 1890; Cambridge to Ponsonby, 10 April

1890, G.E. Buckle (ed.), *Letters of Queen Victoria*, 3rd Series (John Murray; London, 1930–32), Vol.1, pp.582–4, 589, 594–5; B.J. Bond, 'The Retirement of the Duke of Cambridge', *Journal of the RUSI*, Vol.106 (November 1961), pp.544–53.

38   Lord Lansdowne, 'Changes Consequent upon Retirement of His Royal Highness the Duke of Cambridge', 12 August 1895, PRO, CAB 37/40/41; Sir R.H. Knox, qs.1153–7, *Minutes of Evidence before the Royal Commission on the War in South Africa*, hereafter referred to as the *Elgin Report*, Cd. 1790 (1904), XL, p.54; Lansdowne, q.21471 evidence appended to the *Elgin Report*, Cd. 1791 (1904), XLI, p.533.

39   *Hartington Report*, pp.xxix–xxxi; *Parl. Deb.*, Third Ser., Vol.346 (4 July 1890), cols.876–7; Hamer, *The British Army*, p.152; J. Wilson, *CB: A Life of Sir Henry Campbell-Bannerman* (Constable; London, 1973), p.171.

40   J. Wilson, *CB*, pp.190–201; Queen Victoria to Cambridge, 19 May 1895 and Cambridge to Queen Victoria, 20 May 1895, *Letters of Queen Victoria*, 3rd series, Vol.2, pp.512–13.

41   *Order-in-Council, 21 November 1895* and *Memorandum showing the Duties of the Principal Officers and Departments of the War Office and Details of Procedure under the Order in Council dated 21st November 1895*, C. 7987 (1896), LI; Knox, qs.1135–7 evidence appended to the *Elgin Report*, Cd. 1790 (1904), XL, p.53; Hamer, *The British Army*, pp.165–7.

42   Knox, q.1408 and Sir H. Brackenbury, q.1574 evidence appended to the *Elgin Report*, Cd. 1790 (1904), XL, pp.64 and 72; Brodrick, qs.21595–6 evidence appended to the *Elgin Report*, Cd. 1791 (1904), XLI, pp.539–40; *Parl. Deb.*, Fourth Ser., Vol.306 (26 August 1895), cols.773–4.

43   Knox to Campbell-Bannerman, 26 December 1896, Campbell-Bannerman Mss., B.L. Add. Mss. 41,221, f.241.

44   Knox to Campbell-Bannerman, 18 October 1899, Campbell-Bannerman Mss., B.L. Add. Mss. 41,221, ff.261–2. See also Knox, qs.1140–51 evidence appended to the *Elgin Report*, Cd. 1790 (1904), XL, pp.53–4; *Memorandum showing the Duties of the Principal Officers and Departments of the War Office and Details of Office Procedure under the Order in Council dated 21st November 1895*, paras. 16–19.

45   O. Wheeler, *The War Office Past and Present*, pp.256–7; Wolseley to Sir J. Ardagh, 4 October 1895, Ardagh Mss., PRO 30/40/2 and Wolseley to Buller, 3 October 1895, Buller Mss., PRO, WO 132/5.

46   Wolseley to Lady Wolseley, 4 July 1899, Wolseley Mss., W/P 28/35; see also Wolseley to Lady Wolseley, 14 July 1898, 6 October 1898, 9 November 1898, 13 July 1899 and 6 September 1899, Wolseley Mss., W/P 27/49, 96, 104 and W/P 28/40, 50; Wolseley to Ardagh, 23 September 1899, Ardagh Mss., PRO 30/40/3.

47   *Memorandum by Field-Marshal Viscount Wolseley, addressed to the Marquis of Salisbury, relative to the working of the Order in Council of 21st November 1895* and 'Minute by the Marquis of Lansdowne on Lord Wolseley's Memorandum', Cd. 512 (1901), XXXIX, pp.2–9; Brodrick to Lord Roberts, 20 December 1900, Roberts Mss., N[ational] A[rmy] M[useum], 7101–23–13–13; Lord G. Hamilton, *Parliamentary Reminiscences and Reflections*, 2 Vols. (John Murray; London, 1916–22),

Vol.2, pp.293–4; Buller to Campbell-Bannerman, 5 January 1899, Campbell-Bannerman Mss., B.L. Add Mss.. 41,212, f.230.

48   Hamer, *The British Army*, p.172. See also *Report of the Committee appointed to enquire into War Office Organisation*, Cd. 580 (1901), XL, p.2.

3

The organisation of the army

During the last third of the nineteenth century, the Victorian army was repeatedly involved in colonial warfare. Every year, apart from 1883, its forces saw active service in campaigns of conquest or annexation, in actions to suppress insurrection and lawlessness within the Empire, or in punitive expeditions (Appendix 2). In these campaigns the army had to battle against the forces of nature, often marching immense distances over difficult terrain in debilitating climates, before it encountered enemies like the Maoris, Ashanti, Afghans, Zulus, Boers and Dervishes who differed greatly in their tactics, weaponry and fighting qualities. The army struggled periodically, and suffered notable defeats at Isandhlwana (22 January 1879), Maiwand (27 July 1880) and Majuba Hill (27 February 1881), but it generally excelled in this form of warfare. Successes derived from a combination of factors, including the organisation and discipline of the British forces, the close attention paid to supply and transport arrangements, and the resourcefulness of commanders such as Wolseley, Sir Frederick (later Lord) Roberts and Horatio Herbert (later Lord) Kitchener.

Initially the late Victorian army lacked any plan for mobilising its home-based forces. Despite the example of Prussian mobilisation in 1870, the War Office had failed to prepare effectively. Neither the mobilisation plan of 1875, envisaging an army of eight corps, nor Childers's scheme for a single army corps, which could be sent abroad without disturbing the normal relief of overseas garrisons, proved more than paper proposals. As neither provided for the necessary stores, supporting units or the proper proportion between the various arms, they were quickly abandoned. Only in 1886 was a systematic analysis of the existing forces undertaken, by Major-

General Henry Brackenbury, the head of the Intelligence Branch
(later Director of Military Intelligence). In three reports he asserted
that the existing forces could provide sufficient men for all home and
colonial garrisons, and form two army corps of regular troops, with
a cavalry division and lines of communication. Wolseley, then
Adjutant-General, pressed these recommendations upon W.H.
Smith, the Secretary of State for War. The latter duly appointed a
committee of two, Sir Ralph Thompson and Brackenbury, to review
the proposals. In December 1886, they confirmed that two army
corps, with the appropriate supporting forces, should become the
standard for mobilisation.

Edward Stanhope, who succeeded Smith as Secretary of State for
War in January 1887, realised that Brackenbury's proposals could
be attained without any substantial increase of men or expenditure.
In his estimates for 1887–88, he endorsed the two army corps
standard and indicated how he planned to reorganise the home-
based forces to realise the requisite proportion between the various
arms. He proposed that each battalion should be marginally cut, and
that the surplus artillery batteries (beyond the eight horse artillery
and twenty-four field artillery batteries required for the two army
corps) should be removed by converting three horse artillery
batteries into field artillery batteries and by reducing the others (one
of those due for conversion was saved after parliamentary protest).
He used these savings to increase the number of Royal Engineers and
other support forces.[1]

Wolseley maintained, nonetheless, that the army should have a
definitive statement of the purposes for which it existed. Senior
officers had sought such a statement since the early 1870s, and, after
the invasion scare of May 1888, Sir John Colomb and the Duke of
Cambridge reiterated this demand. Wolseley, having suggested a list
of priorities in January 1888, repeated his proposal in the following
June. In his reply (see the memorandum, Appendix 3), Stanhope
virtually duplicated Wolseley's order of priorities, only insisting that
a standard of two army corps (and not the three requested by
Wolseley) should meet all domestic and expeditionary requirements.
He placed aid to the civil power as his first priority, the garrisoning of
India and the colonies as second and third, home defence as fourth,
and the 'improbable' employment of two army corps in a European
war as a final task – a ranking which has been criticised as
anachronistic and irrelevant to the needs of imperial defence. In

effect, the memorandum reflected current concerns about aid to the civil power (troops had been employed in the Welsh 'Tithe War', the Scottish 'Crofters' Land War' and the 'Bloody Sunday' riot in Trafalgar Square, November 1887), and about home defence after the recent invasion scares. It also set a feasible goal for mobilisation planning, one which was ultimately met in the successful mobilisation of the army between October 1899 and January 1900.[2]

The size, deployment and composition of the army varied considerably over the last thirty years of Victoria's reign. When Cardwell entered office, the regular army had already been falling steadily from an average strength of 222,839 all ranks in 1862 to 196,900 all ranks in 1868. Under his policies, and those of his immediate successor, it fell still further to 184,433 all ranks in 1876 before rising again to a peak of 225,027 all ranks in 1898. Cardwell cut the proportion of officers and men who were serving abroad from 53·8 per cent in 1869 to 47·6 per cent in 1874. It remained at less than 50 per cent until the late 1870s, when the tide of colonial campaigning and imperial expansion carried the proportion of officers and men serving abroad back to 54·4 per cent in 1898. The proportion of 'teeth' arms remained fairly constant. On 1 January 1869, 9 per cent served in the cavalry, 16·9 per cent in the artillery and 66·2 per cent in the infantry. The support corps included 2·6 per cent serving in the Royal Engineers, 0·9 per cent in the military train (transport), 0·5 per cent in the Army Hospital Corps and 0·5 per cent in the Commissariat Staff Corps and the Military Store Staff Corps (with other logistical and supporting tasks being performed by men seconded from the fighting arms). On 1 January 1899, 8·4 per cent served in the cavalry, 17 per cent in the artillery and 64·1 per cent in the infantry. A slightly higher proportion of men supported the front-line in the Royal Engineers (3·4 per cent), the Army Service Corps (1·6 per cent), the Royal Army Medical Corps (1·6 per cent), the Army Ordnance Corps (0·6 per cent), and the Army Pay Corps (0·3 per cent).[3]

The nominal strength of the regular army concealed palpable weaknesses in the quality and fighting capacity of the home-based forces. The Localisation Committee had sought to minimise this problem by proposing that eighteen infantry battalions should be maintained at 820 other ranks, eighteen at 700 and thirty-five at 520, so retaining 45,560 men at home. Within one year of the linked battalion system being introduced, the home establishments had fallen to four battalions at 820, eleven at 600 and fifty-five at 520, or a total of 38,480 men. Battalion establishments fluctuated there-after, but, by 1877–78, there were only eighteen battalions at 740 and forty-six at 520, or 37,240 men at home. Each home-based battalion had to furnish an annual quota of drafts for its linked battalion overseas, train recruits, and employ men in daily fatigue duties or as officers' servants, cooks, clerks, bandsmen and regimental tradesmen. As the Duke of Cambridge claimed, a battalion of 600 men would only have 400 left after supplying its annual quota of drafts and from 400 men it would 'never have 200 men on Parade'.[4]

Successive governments compounded these problems by failing to maintain a parity between the battalions at home and abroad (initially in 1874 and from 1876 onwards). The overseas surplus became quite pronounced; of the 141 battalions deployed in each year from 1888 to 1896 (and of the 142 battalions in 1897), there was an average surplus overseas of twelve battalions or more per annum. By sending trained men overseas or into the Reserve, the home-based battalions became, in Wolseley's phrase, 'squeezed lemons': none of them, as Buller and the Duke of Cambridge agreed, was fit to go to war.[5] Their training suffered, particularly at company level in the weaker battalions. If reduced to 200 men fit or available for training, the eight companies of each battalion might have to train in twelve or thirteen files (a file had a front-rank man and a rear rank man).

The numerical, if not necessarily the effective, strength of the home battalions was further reduced by a War Office regulation in 1881, which precluded any men from serving overseas until they had reached the age of twenty or had completed one year of service. This complicated the task of responding to colonial crises, as Parliament would not mobilise the Reserve, in part or in whole, except in a national emergency (as in 1878, 1882 and 1885). Small expeditionary forces could only be formed by reducing colonial garrisons, by employing Indian forces (both British and native) outside the Indian subcontinent, and by calling upon volunteers from various home-based units or from unmarried reservists (as in 1879, 1881, 1884 and 1885). In 1898, Parliament approved an Act which offered a small remuneration to 5,000 reservists if they voluntarily rendered themselves liable for twelve months' service in any expeditionary force. Though quite inadequate in scale, this was a belated recognition of the problems which small colonial warfare had posed.[6]

Originally, neither the artillery nor the cavalry had been affected by short service and localisation. Shorter terms of service (seven years in the Colours, followed by five years in the Reserve) were gradually extended to these arms, excluding the Household Cavalry, and these terms or three years in the Colours and nine years in the Reserve were offered to the Guards and Royal Engineers. Territorial localisation was more difficult to introduce because the artillery and cavalry enlisted recruits for general service, and both sought smaller numbers of men who could perform specialist duties (as gunners and drivers in the horse and field artillery and as troopers who had to care for horses and horse equipment in the cavalry). Yet these arms, like the infantry of the line, had to supply drafts for units deployed overseas. Of the twenty-eight cavalry regiments, excluding the Household Cavalry, there were never less than six or more than nine regiments in India (and often one or sometimes as many as four regiments in Africa). Nearly half the horse and field artillery batteries served in India while the other half remained at home. The garrison artillery batteries were divided in roughly equal numbers between the stations at home, in India, and in the colonies. Finally, the artillery and cavalry had to provide the appropriate level of support for any expeditionary force despatched from the United Kingdom.[7]

In 1881 the War Office established committees to consider whether localisation could be extended to the artillery and cavalry. The artillery committee, under the presidency of Lord Morley, accepted that artillery recruiting, which had experienced some difficulties in the 1870s, might benefit from localisation. It emphasised, though, that localisation could not be implemented as thoroughly as it had been in the infantry because the tactical artillery unit – the battery – was so much smaller than the battalion. The committee believed that a close affiliation between the Royal and Militia Artillery could foster local connections and associations and thereby boost recruiting. It proposed that eleven territorial divisions, each based on a depot, should be established nationally, and that the garrison artillery should be transformed into eleven brigades to form part of each division. The eleven depots were to serve as headquarters for the regiments of Militia artillery, to receive recruits for all branches of regular artillery (other than the horse artillery which retained its own depots at Woolwich), and to undertake the preliminary training of gunners and drivers for the four brigades of field artillery. Implemented by Order 72 of 1882, these reforms incurred the wrath of many battery majors in the field artillery. They protested about the dislocation caused by the loss of their former depots and about the inadequate training of their recruits. Endorsed by senior officers, these protests prompted a further reorganisation on 1 January 1884, whereby each field artillery brigade was given a depot to receive and train its recruits and to provide drafts for overseas service. The general order stated that all drafts for horse, field and garrison batteries overseas should come from the depots, and not from the batteries at home. In practice, the home-based batteries still made up any deficiency in the annual supply of drafts from the depots. They were also unable to take the field without transfers from other units. Batteries were classified on three different establishments – '1st Army Corps', '2nd Army Corps' and those of 'low strength' with four and not six guns – but even those on a '1st Army Corps' establishment contained a large number of recruits and men who were medically unfit or ineligible for foreign service. Transfers, therefore, were essential between the different units and the different branches of the Royal Artillery Regiment.[8]

Transferring officers, though, posed acute problems for the garrison batteries, whose establishments of subalterns had been reduced from three to two in 1872. As the supply of officers from Woolwich failed to replenish all the regimental vacancies, and as the mounted branches were generally kept up to strength, the garrison batteries languished below their reduced establishments. They suffered from a constant turnover of officers and had little *esprit de corps*. The better officers were often discontented and restless until they could be transferred to the smarter, mounted branches, which had more opportunities for active service and for earning promotion (other than in the mountain batteries). The garrison units endured a greater proportion of foreign service than the horse or field artillery, and were dispersed in isolated stations which had little to commend them whether at home or overseas. The coastal postings, as Colonel Goodeve acknowledged, were often particularly bleak and bereft of mess life: his single batteries at Picklecombe and Staddon in Plymouth Sound were 'virtually cut off from the rest of the world'.[9] Many artillery officers disliked not only these postings but also the fortress duties. Whereas mounted officers were primarily concerned with the tactics of moving, emplacing and firing guns for maximum effect, garrison officers had a myriad of more mundane tasks. They had to handle much more varied equipment, including extremely heavy guns of up to 100 tons (see Chapter 9), and had to understand the mechanics of manipulating them, with some knowledge of hydraulics, pneumatics and electricity. In addition they had to know about methods of attacking and defending fortresses, the coastal defence of harbours, and combined operations with the Royal Engineers. As these duties lacked the appeal of the mounted service, the 'cream' of the gunners gravitated towards the horse and field artillery, leaving the 'residue' with the garrison batteries.[10]

When a Select Committee, chaired by Lord Harris, investigated this issue in 1887–88, it found opinion sharply divided. Some artillery officers, supported by Wolseley, favoured separating the dismounted from the mounted branches and giving the former the inducements of better pay and a separate promotion structure; others, supported by the Duke of Cambridge, claimed that the exchange of officers benefited each branch, and that separation would create administrative difficulties. As these divisions found reflection within the Harris Committee, it issued a compromise report, advocating some concentration of garrison artillery batteries in the winter months, the institution of auxiliary schools of instruction, the withdrawal of obsolete armaments, and an increase of 2s a day in garrison pay. As this merely postponed a decision without greatly enhancing the appeal of the garrison artillery, a War Office committee, chaired by Major-General G.H. Marshall, reconsidered separation after the Duke had retired. Eventually the War Office authorities decided not to split the Royal Regiment of Artillery but to organise it into two separate corps. Under Army Order 96 of June 1899, officers who joined either corps from 1 June 1899 would not be eligible for transfer to the other corps without their consent.[11]

Cavalry regiments, like artillery batteries, had to seek volunteers from other regiments or from fit reservists before they could serve abroad. The cavalry was divided into three classes – heavy, medium and light – in accordance with the size and weight of the horses and riders. The five regiments of heavy cavalry, excluding the 4th and 5th Dragoon Guards, which were converted to medium cavalry in 1888, did not take their turn of foreign service (although they sometimes served on expeditionary forces, notably in the Egyptian campaign of 1882). The remaining twenty-six, both medium (dragoon guards and lancers) and light (hussars), served in rotation at home and abroad, and several of the home regiments remained on a higher establishment, supposedly ready to go to India or anywhere else

whenever required. In 1891 the seven regiments on a higher establishment should have taken the field with 4,100 troopers but their
effective strength was considerably less than their numbers suggested. After deducting 956 recruits and the men who were medically
unfit, they could only have mustered 2,954 men.[12]

In 1882 a committee, chaired by General Wardlaw, reported upon
the problem of sustaining the increased flow of recruits required by
short service enlistments. It recognised that the traditional depots
could only cope with the larger numbers if their establishments were
raised from eighty-five to 135, and if the increased cost was offset by
reducing the establishments of the home-based regiments. The committee preferred to dispense with the depots and 'brigade' or affiliate
regiments in groups of three (the two home-based regiments would
supply drafts for the third affiliated regiment serving in India). The
Duke of Cambridge deplored this suggestion, claiming that it would
lead to 'the gradual destruction by amalgamation of *two-thirds* of
the Cavalry Regiments of the Army'.[13] The proposal was shelved, a
decision almost certainly facilitated by the buoyancy of cavalry
recruiting (even under short service, the cavalry at home and abroad
numbered 17,157 in 1891 – only 130 short of its establishment).
Nevertheless, the costs and inefficiency of depot recruiting persisted.
The depots possessed neither adequate facilities nor sufficient horses
nor a full complement of drill instructors. After their ten-month
period of training, any recruits, who had enlisted at the age of
eighteen, languished without anything to do until they departed for
India at the age of twenty. Eventually, in 1897, the depots were
abolished and 'brigading' was introduced to supply drafts more
efficiently for the overseas regiments. The establishments of home-
based regiments were marginally increased (from 603 other ranks in
the hussar regiments to 668), but not sufficiently to obviate the
dependence upon volunteers and reservists in the formation of
expeditionary forces.[14]

Improvisation was even more apparent in the deployment of
mounted infantry units. The mounted infantry were men who fought
on foot with the rifle and bayonet but who rode on horses, ponies,
camels, carts and even bicycles. Originally raised on an *ad hoc* basis
during active service, mounted infantry detachments provided close
infantry support for cavalry and horse artillery, or, in the absence of
the cavalry, undertook scouting, flanking and outpost duties for the
infantry. In the Gordon Relief Expedition they rode camels in the

Desert Column, and in several campaigns operated as counter-guerilla forces against mobile adversaries. In 1888, when the War Office found itself unable either to augment the cavalry or to reorganise its regimental structure, it established the first mounted infantry school at Aldershot as a relatively inexpensive alternative. It issued a provisional handbook on mounted infantry duties in 1889 but never formed a permanent mounted infantry corps. Men were selected from their infantry battalions to be trained at Aldershot, and, after completing their ten week period of training, returned to their own battalions where they could form, if needed, mounted infantry sections (one subaltern and thirty-five men). If grouped in fours, these sections comprised a mounted infantry company, and four companies, once amalgamated, could act often independently as a mounted infantry battalion.[15]

Underlying the difficulties of constructing expeditionary forces were even more problems in military planning and field command. Under the War Office Act (1870), once the cabinet had approved a military operation, the Secretary of State for War became politically responsible for it. In the planning of a campaign, any Secretary of State might have to collaborate with the First Lord of the Admiralty, the Colonial Secretary and the Secretary of State for India. The outcome largely depended upon the vigour of individual Ministers and of the rapport between them. There was neither an institution nor an interdepartmental staff to facilitate their co-operation, and even the creation of a defence committee of the cabinet in 1895 hardly redressed this shortcoming. Arthur Balfour, its founder, was too engrossed in the leadership of the House of Commons to develop it. Lord Salisbury, the Prime Minister, was uninterested, and the committee, which lacked a permanent secretariat, suffered from the absence of key Ministers, including the Foreign Secretary and the military leadership. Accordingly, it barely participated in the management of the Second Boer War or in promoting co-ordination between the two services.[16]

Military planning was further hampered by the lack of a General Staff, which could collect and analyse information, prepare mobilisation plans and supervise their implementation, co-ordinate policy with that of the Royal Navy, and select qualified officers for the headquarters staff in the field. Whenever a crisis arose, the appointed field commander had to improvise in his preparatory planning, choice of staff, and logistical and transport arrangements.

Wolseley and Roberts flourished in this highly personalised and pragmatic mode of campaigning, but they aroused controversy by relying upon favoured 'rings' of personally selected officers. Both commanders maintained that the peculiar demands of small colonial warfare justified their policies. Whether fighting in the tropical rain forests of west Africa or in the mountains of the North West Frontier, British forces could not anticipate that they would always operate in textbook formations. During the Ashanti expedition, Wolseley described how 'the fight resolves itself into knots of men led by officers – the result depends upon the manner in which those officers do their work'.[17] Nearly thirty years later, in the wake of the Second Boer War, Roberts argued that commanding officers could exert little control over widely dispersed fighting: they were 'obliged to leave the command of companies to the captains, while the captains have to trust in a great measure to their subalterns and section leaders'.[18]

Wolseley also believed that selection had to be applied, because the army lacked many general officers who were fit for field command. In assembling his staff for the Ashanti expedition, he chose Red River veterans, officers who had distinguished themselves in battle, and others who had shown promise at home, particularly in the Staff College. His 'ring' included Lieutenant-Colonel (later General Sir) John McNeill, VC, Lieutenant-Colonel (later Field-Marshal Sir) Evelyn Wood, VC, Major (later Major-General Sir) George Colley, Major (later General Sir) George Greaves, Captain (later General Sir) Redvers Buller, VC, Captain (later Lieutenant-General Sir) William Butler, Captain (later General Sir) Henry Brackenbury and Captain (later Major) Robert Home. By selecting so many able and talented officers for this and for subsequent campaigns, Wolseley established, at least initially, some cohesion and continuity among his staff. He enabled these officers to gain war experience, public recognition and rapid promotion. He assiduously advanced their claims: 'not one of them,' he boasted in December 1884, 'would have been where he is at this moment in the Army List if I had not fought hard with HRH for their advancement.'[19]

The 'rings' accentuated the divisions and rivalries within the service, particularly between the army at home and the British army in India. Even at home where the successes of the Wolseley 'ring' could hardly be gainsaid (at least in the period 1873–82, when Wolseley earned the sobriquet 'our only soldier' from Disraeli and 'all Sir Garnet' became a synonym for efficiency), the apparent exclusiveness of the 'ring' hardly endeared it to outsiders. The Duke of Cambridge repeatedly asserted that Wolseley, by relying upon this group, had depressed morale generally, had deviated from the principle of seniority, and, in his selection for the Gordon Relief Expedition, had failed to bring on any new men.[20] The last of these charges was exaggerated, as the 'ring' was never a compact and totally exclusive group. Wolseley had to rearrange his staff periodically because some men were unavailable for active service and others had died (Major Home) or been killed in action (Major-General Colley). Yet he still chose many veterans of the 'ring' for the Sudan and found difficulty in employing so many officers who had now risen to senior rank in one expedition. Strong-willed and self-opinionated, they proved reluctant to heed local or outside opinion in their logistical planning. In preferring the Nile to the Suakin–Berber route, they discounted the advice of the Intelligence Branch, the military authorities in Cairo, the Admiralty Intelligence Department, the Inspector-General of Fortifications, Sir Andrew Clarke, and his gifted protégé, Major George Sydenham Clarke. The 'ring' also fell out among themselves, with the rifts tending to widen as the expedition foundered. Wolseley ruefully observed,

never was there a force in the field that was less of a happy family: every one seemed to desire his own hand & to think solely of himself whilst he hated and ridiculed his neighbour. The Sudan campaign has been a horrible fiasco – how could it be otherwise in these circumstances?[21]

As a field commander, Wolseley had always enjoyed a large measure of independence not only in his selection of officers but also in his choice of men. He favoured the formation of elite corps, drawing upon volunteers and strong companies from the home-based battalions, and, when Parliament called out the Reserve, upon unmarried reservists. In justifying his choice for the Ashanti expedition, he maintained that only strong and steady volunteers could withstand the rigours of a tropical climate and cope with the peculiar rigours of bush warfare. During the Zulu War, he lavished praise upon the fitness, reliability and morale of his short service soldiers (a view firmly disputed by Lord Chelmsford) and commended the reservists after their service in Egypt and the Sudan. An army without a reserve, he argued, would be a 'theatrical army like the army we had before the Crimean War'.[22] These views enraged the Duke of

Cambridge. He fiercely deprecated Wolseley's penchant for creaming volunteers from the home-based forces because it undermined regimental *esprit de corps*. He remained extremely sceptical about the short service soldier, claiming that the older man was fitter, more robust and more reliable on active service. He never altered his belief that the home army should not be sacrificed to the Reserve, and periodically reminded Wolseley of the virtues of traditional drill and the achievements of the old army.[23]

Underpinning these disagreements were more profound resentments, laced with personal rancour. The Duke, like several senior officers, including Lord Napier of Magdala, believed that Wolseley had an exaggerated reputation as a commander, and that he had advanced his career by manipulating the press, by advocating reform, and by his connections with Radical politicians. They regarded many of his speeches as arrogant, self-serving and insubordinate. The Duke of Cambridge desperately tried to block Wolseley's career, both his hope of becoming Commander-in-Chief in India and his appointment as Adjutant-General. Although the Duke would periodically applaud Wolseley's achievements, particularly the victory at Tel-el-Kebir (13 September 1882), his administrative competence (once he became Adjutant-General), and his support in trying to dilute the civilian control of the War Office,[24] relations between them never really improved.

Wolseley despised the Duke for his brief service in the Crimea, believing that he had proved cowardly and had lost control at the battles of the Alma and Inkerman. He maintained that the Duke, and many of his staff, were totally ignorant of modern warfare, and that they had prevented the army from becoming militarily efficient. He knew that the Duke had tried to block his advancement and had never concealed his dislike of him. The Queen, wrote Wolseley in March 1880,

naturally adopts HRH views and because he hates the modern views I hold on military subjects, she assumes that I am the radical he paints me to be. I detest Radicals: men of Mr Gladstone's stamp are abhorrent to every instinct within me . . . .[25]

By 30 August 1890, having failed to secure an Indian command, Wolseley reflected

I spent yesterday at Aldershot with HRH. I felt so weary of his 'bosh' on all military subjects that I rather chuckled at the thought that much as I dislike going to Ireland, I shall at least be removed from the unreal humbug of military life under the Duke of Cambridge. It is too hard upon England that our Army should be kept back in efficiency, because we have a Royal Duke at its head.[26]

In spite of their differences about the duties and nature of command, Wolseley and the Duke of Cambridge agreed that the inculcation and maintenance of discipline were of paramount importance. Maintaining discipline was intended to enforce the instant and unhesitating obedience to orders, to sustain morale during moments of acute stress (in actions such as Rorke's Drift), and to ensure the normal functioning of the army. Military law, as a consequence, encompassed a much wider range of rules and regulations than the criminal law, covering matters of dress and appearance as well as the conduct and duties of the rank and file. Strictly enforced, these rules served not only to punish any deviant behaviour but also to prevent agitation from within the ranks and to forge a disciplined mass from a collection of individual soldiers. Drill, argued Brigadier-General J.H.A. MacDonald, was enforced 'in a hundred minute little points' until the ranks 'responded to the word of command as the machine answers to the pressing of the button'.[27] This emphasis, which produced impressive spectacles on regimental field days, and often proved effective in combat against untrained native armies, left little scope for individual initiative. Accordingly the army sometimes struggled when it encountered an adversary, like the Boer, who was resourceful, mobile, and adept at irregular warfare.

Military law was embodied in two codes, the Mutiny Act and the Articles of War (Queen's Regulations had no statutory authority). The Mutiny Act derived from the original Mutiny Act passed by Parliament in 1689, which enabled the government to punish any officer or soldier for mutiny or desertion. Normally re-enacted on an annual basis by Parliament, the Mutiny Act had grown from its original ten sections to 110 clauses, some of which overlapped with the 192 clauses of the Articles of War. The latter, which were issued under the royal prerogative, had statutory effect, confirmed by Parliament. The major offences included mutiny, desertion, insubordination, fraudulent enlistment, absence without leave, drunkenness, disgraceful conduct and quitting or sleeping on post. A separate military judicial system tried crimes committed under these categories. Regimental courts-martial, convened by regimental commanding officers, dealt with crimes within specific regiments: in

1867 they accounted for 71 per cent of the 23,535 courts-martial. District courts-martial, normally convened by the general commanding a district, tried some 28 per cent of the cases, and general courts-martial, with a president appointed by the General Commanding-in-Chief or the general officer in command at home or abroad, tried the remainder. Only a general court-martial could try a commissioned officer or pass the sentence of death or penal servitude. Military courts could also try soldiers for civil crimes, but, if civilian courts were reasonably accessible, they would usually try the most serious offences – treason, murder, manslaughter or rape.[28]

The simplification of military law was eagerly sought. In 1869 a Royal Commission on courts-martial took evidence from leading military and legal authorities, including the Duke of Cambridge and two former Judge Advocate-Generals, all of whom criticised the existing law as confused, uncertain and difficult to interpret. The commissioners strongly recommended that military law should be simplified, and that a textbook on military law and laws of evidence should be prepared for the instruction of officers and the use of courts-martial. Although parliamentary counsel produced a draft Army Discipline Bill in 1871, the death of a Judge Advocate-General, Parliament's preoccupation with the Cardwell reforms, and a change of government (which required the appointment of another Judge Advocate-General) delayed proceedings. Eventually a revised draft Bill was presented to, and approved by, a parliamentary Select Committee in 1878. In the following year Parliament approved the Army Discipline and Regulation Act, which consolidated the Mutiny Act and the Articles of War. In 1881 this was repealed and re-enacted as the Army Act, which was brought into operation each year, and for one year at a time, by the Army (Annual) Act.[29]

In the process of consolidating military law, important changes were introduced. The Courts-Martial Commission claimed that the frequency of regimental courts-martial had diminished the dread of them among the rank and file. As the crimes of being 'drunk on duty under arms' and of being 'habitually drunk' accounted for almost 55 per cent of those tried by regimental courts-martial, the commission proposed that fines for drunkenness should be introduced. It also recommended that the powers of summary imprisonment possessed by commanding officers should be increased from seven to twenty-one days. The government duly approved fines for drunkenness (usually 2s 6d for a first offence up to a maximum of 10s for habitual drunkenness), but refused to expand the summary powers of commanding officers. When another Select Committee, investigating the effects of the short service system in 1878, reiterated the case for expanding the summary powers of commanding officers, the proposal was incorporated in the Army Discipline and Regulation Bill of 1879. Parliamentary protests, however, ensured that the seven-day limit was restored (except in cases of absence without leave, when twenty-one days were accepted). Parliamentary opposition was not overcome until 1893, when the proposal was reintroduced, based on the recommendation of a War Office Committee, composed of Lord Sandhurst (the Under-Secretary of State), Sir Redvers Buller (the Adjutant-General) and James Cornelius O'Dowd (the Deputy Judge Advocate-General).[30]

Disciplinary practices were altered, too. Capital punishment was rarely enforced (only thirty-seven men were executed between 1865 and 1898), but it remained as the ultimate punishment. It covered the four capital offences still retained in the criminal law, and could be enforced for various offences committed on active service, including treachery, cowardice, shamefully casting away arms or abandoning a post, mutiny, desertion, and striking a superior officer in the execution of his office. In 1868 branding was still used to mark certain prisoners (using the tattoos 'BC' for bad character or 'D' for desertion). Military spokesmen had defended branding as an effective means of preventing fraudulent re-enlistment and of protecting the public from criminals, but sections of the press and Parliament deplored the practice as barbaric, demeaning, and an impediment to recruiting. The Courts-Martial Commission had accepted the necessity of branding as long as the army used bounties to attract recruits, without seeking character references. If the recruiting system could be reformed, argued the commission, all justification for branding would cease to exist. Cardwell accepted this logic; after he had terminated recruiting bounties in 1870, he abolished branding in 1871.[31]

Military flogging proved even more controversial than branding. It aroused fierce debates in the press and Parliament, especially at a time when the criminal law was being steadily amended by reducing the number of capital offences and by mitigating the severity of the punishments. After the death of Private Robert Slim from flogging in 1867, Parliament amended the Mutiny Act the following year: henceforth only category II soldiers (those labelled as 'bad characters') could be flogged in peacetime for mutiny, aggravated insubordination and disgraceful conduct. In war, all soldiers could be flogged for those crimes and for desertion, drunkenness on duty or on the line of march, and misbehaviour or neglect of duty in the field or on board ship. During the 1870s flogging was sparingly employed until 1879, when its extensive use in Zululand provoked parliamentary protests. Many Liberals, led by Gladstone and the Marquess of Hartington, denounced flogging as degrading and ineffective, a deterrent to recruiting, and an anachronism which most European armies had abolished. Colonel Stanley and some military Members of Parliament mounted a rearguard action. They depicted flogging as a necessary deterrent for a volunteer army, which recruited from the lowest levels of society, and insisted that it could not be replaced on active service. As they failed to convince not only the opposition but also some Conservative Members, Stanley reluctantly agreed to halve the number of lashes to twenty-five. Flogging was effectively doomed. When the Liberals returned to office, Childers swept aside the despairing pleas of the Duke of Cambridge, Chelmsford and Wolseley, and abolished flogging in 1881.[32]

He approved rules for summary punishment to replace flogging in the field. These included imprisoning offenders for up to three months, keeping them in fixed positions for limited periods of time, and employing them in hard labour. Imprisonment became the main punishment in the peacetime army, with the army mirroring the trend in civil sentencing towards the imposition of shorter sentences. Men serving short sentences were confined to barracks in cells or provost prisons with punishment drill, and those serving longer terms were incarcerated in separate military prisons. Imposed for their retributive and purportedly deterrent aspects, these sentences, or at least the shorter ones, recognised some possibility of rehabilitation. In 1881 the War Office decided to remove habitual offenders from military prisons in order that they should serve the remainder of their sentences in public prisons prior to being ignominiously discharged. Military prisons were thereby able to emulate civilian practice and ease the severity of their regimes. There were improvements in prison diet, less frequent punishments, an easing of regulations, and the introduction of school and industrial work. By 1896 a reformed system was operational. Nevertheless, the principles of retribution and deterrence remained paramount, and they may have had some effect, as the incidence of crime diminished sharply (the number of courts-martial fell from 14,290 in 1872 to 9,676 in 1898, the number of fines for drunkenness nearly halved from 51,501 in 1872 to 26,243 in 1898, and the number of minor punishments awarded by commanding officers dropped from 249,179 in 1872 to 217,236 in 1898).[33] Throughout this period crime remained a major problem, but military discipline, if less severe, proved flexible and reasonably effective.

On active service the army was not merely disciplined but was also supported in an increasingly systematic manner. The Corps of Royal Engineers provided the principal support, but in many respects it was much more than a supporting arm. Engineers now commanded expeditionary forces. Sir Robert Napier earned a peerage for his command of the Abyssinian expedition (1867–68); Sir Charles Warren commanded the Bechuanaland Field Force (1884–85), Sir Gerald Graham, VC, commanded forces in eastern Sudan and in Suakin (1884 and 1885), and Kitchener commanded the Anglo–Egyptian army in the Second Sudan War and later the British forces in the Second Boer War. Moreover, many of the campaigns could be described as 'engineer wars' inasmuch as natural obstacles – climate, topography or distance – had to be overcome before the expeditionary force could confront the enemy. In the Ashanti War (1873–74) the engineers, assisted by native labourers, had to cut a road through a dense jungle, construct fortified stations along the road, bridge numerous streams and rivers, erect a telegraph line, and cut paths in front of the final assault. During the Second Sudan War, Kitchener entrusted the task of constructing some 385 miles of railway to the engineers and their native labourers under the command of Lieutenant Percy Girouard. In the Second Boer War the engineers were just as prominent, constructing 3,700 miles of barbed wire fencing and other obstacles, guarded by 8,000 blockhouses, to limit the commandos' freedom of movement. Finally, engineers recurrently distinguished themselves as a fourth fighting arm: Colonel Anthony Durnford died heroically at Isandhlwana and Lieutenant John Chard earned a Victoria Cross for his command of the defences at Rorke's Drift (22–3 January 1879).

Engineers normally operated in companies. One field company, numbering 200 all ranks in 1893, supported a division with another or sometimes several (as in Wolseley's army of 1882) and a field park acting as corps troops. Specialised companies (survey, railway or fortress) were required in particular campaigns and so were pontoon troops, balloon sections, and telegraph troops or sections from the telegraph battalion. Their numbers and specialisations expanded as the corps exploited the military potential of new technology (like the telegraph, railways and the balloon), responded to alarms about the state of home and colonial fortifications, and undertook a vast array of survey, photographic and boundary commission work in different parts of the Empire. The corps was heavily committed in the construction of new barracks under the terms of the Military Forces Localisation Act (1872), and in the erection of permanent accommodation, including the new station at Tidworth, under the Barracks Act (1890) and the Military Works Acts (1897 and 1899). Lacking sufficient numbers to undertake all its tasks in peace and war, the corps was augmented by Stanhope when he endorsed the mobilisation plans of Brackenbury. The estimates of 1887–88 provided for an additional three field companies of engineers to facilitate the mobilisation of two army corps and their lines of communication.[34]

Brackenbury's proposals provided a standard which would benefit all the supporting arms. Some lacked sufficient men and horses, but others, notably the supply and transport services, still languished after some twenty years of abortive reforms. In 1867 a Select Committee, chaired by Lord Strathnairn, had criticised the fragmentary nature of the services of supply and conveyance. It had proposed that the Commissariat, the military train, and the barrack, purveyor's and military store departments should be brought together in a Control Department under a military officer. As the Commander-in-Chief in Ireland had also requested that all supply services should be co-ordinated during the Fenian troubles, Sir John Pakington, Cardwell's predecessor, established a Control Department, with controllers in each district, headed by a Controller-in-Chief (Sir Henry Storks). He placed this department under the Secretary of State for War. The Northbrook report recommended that Control should encompass the ordnance services, but agreed that it should remain under a civilian official (later known as the Surveyor-General of the Ordnance). These reforms enhanced civilian control, preserved the civilian status of the former Commissariat officers, who largely commanded the Army Service Corps created on 12 November 1869, and transferred transport from the military, so inhibiting any recurrence of the combatant airs which the military train had occasionally exhibited on active service.[35]

The Control system aroused vehement opposition from within the army, not least over the tendency of the controllers to interfere in the military activities of the districts, and over their right to receive orders direct from the general in command and from no other officer. General Sir Percy Herbert led the protests in the House of Commons, which eventually prompted Gathorne Hardy to abolish Control in 1876. The united Commissariat and Transport was designated a separate corps and renamed the Commissariat and Transport Staff five years later. It had to find officers from the regiments of the line for periods of service of at least five years (with possible extensions to ten years before the officers returned to their regiments). Designed to build up a reserve, the staff failed dismally, as subalterns shunned a body which was bereft of prospects of permanent employment or promotion. By November 1887 the Commissariat and Transport Staff could supply only 113 of the 224 officers required to mobilise two army corps.[36]

The paucity of officers posed problems on active service. As the Commissariat was already fully stretched to meet its peacetime duties, it frequently had to seek assistance from the line on colonial campaigns. Commanding officers not only pressed officers into Commissariat service but also improvised their own transport arrangements, thereby exacerbating the civil–military tensions between the departmental and combatant officers. In his invasion of Zululand, Lieutenant-General Frederic A. Thesiger (later Lord Chelmsford) deployed his 16,800 men in three widely separated columns (with two more held in reserve) and formed a column transport system which was partially independent of supply. He assured the Secretary of State that 'I shall be very glad to return to the normal system when I feel the Commissariat department is able, from its own numerical strength, to carry on the executive duties of transport as well as those of supply'.[37] Wolseley was even more rigorous in his militarisation of the support services. When he arrived in South Africa in 1879, he appointed seven staff officers to serve with the various lines of communication (under the command of Major-General Sir Henry Clifford) and made all commissaries responsible to them. In his Egyptian and Sudanese campaigns, Wolseley relied heavily upon regimental transport and, in 1884, used a separate company of officers and men to handle the camel transport under his own director of transport, Lieutenant-Colonel Furse.[38]

The Commissariat, though heavily criticised, generally sustained the flow of rations and medical supplies on active service, often across terrain bereft of roads and bridges and sometimes afflicted by drought. If it undertook these missions with inexperienced officers and men, the consequences were frequently costly. Transport animals suffered severely from neglect; in Zululand, animal husbandry was so poor that Chelmsford eventually had to purchase or hire over 27,000 oxen and 5,000 mules to support his movements. Similar problems plagued the Gordon Relief Expedition because few officers or men knew how to ride, load, feed or water camels and so hundreds broke down or died in support of the Desert Column. Inexperience was also apparent in some of the purchasing methods (so driving up the costs of the Zulu campaign), and in underestimating the number of camels needed for the Sudanese expedition. After its struggles in several campaigns, and the revelation that it could not support Brackenbury's army corps, the Commissariat and Transport Staff was replaced by a new military force, the Army Service Corps. Created by Buller, and constituted by a Royal Warrant on 11 December 1888, the Corps had its pay, promotions and pensions fixed on a par with the Royal Engineers. Henceforth it offered specialised training and career opportunities for incoming officers, whether direct entrants or recruited from the line. Initially, most of its officers transferred from the former Commissariat, but recruiting improved until the corps numbered 4,098 all ranks by 1 October 1899, with another 2,690 men in the Reserve.[39]

The army medical services were also transformed during the late Victorian period. Ever since the Crimean War they had undergone extensive reforms, including the creation of an Army Medical School and the Army Hospital Corps, as well as the construction of two new general hospitals at Netley near Southampton and at Woolwich. The regimental system persisted, nonetheless, with all medical officers, other than those attached to the hospitals at Netley and Woolwich, assigned to specific regiments and regimental hospitals. They depended thereby upon their respective commanding officers for the size, equipment and efficiency of their unit's medical services. This scattered dispersal of the army's medical capacity inhibited peacetime training and preparation for active service. It relied on many small, and sometimes ill-equipped, hospitals in which the medical officers could neither experience a sufficiently wide range of illnesses and injuries nor establish uniform methods of treating the

sick.
The administrative reforms of 1873 were intended to remedy these failings. They replaced regimental hospitals by larger station hospitals, combining staff and facilities whenever two or more units were quartered together. They removed medical officers from regimental control (except, initially, those attached to the Household troops), and assigned them to either of the two general hospitals or to station hospitals. The Army Medical Department assumed responsibility for the station hospitals and for the command, training and discipline of the Army Hospital Corps (AHC). In short, the reforms aimed to create better facilities, establish uniform methods of treatment, and prepare the service more effectively for active service.[40]

Personally, if not professionally, medical officers disliked the loss of their regimental attachments. They complained bitterly in the medical press about their inadequate pay and loss of regimental privileges. As this agitation coincided with an alarming drop in applications to enter the service (whereas thirty-seven candidates had competed for twenty-one vacancies in 1868, only nineteen applied for forty vacancies in 1878), a War Office committee was appointed to investigate the department. It recommended that the rates of pay, retirement gratuities and pensions should be increased, that the relative rank of senior surgeon-majors and junior surgeons should be raised, and that medical officers should be eligible for honours and awards on a scale applicable to combatants. Finally, it suggested that the department should be considered for elevation in status, with the addition of the prefix 'Royal'.[41]

Although the government increased the rates of medical pay in 1879, it set aside the issues of rank and status. In fact, the War Office tried to rid itself of this contentious issue by abolishing relative rank and by substituting a classified schedule to regulate the allowances of all army and departmental officers (the Royal Warrant of December 1886). However, this merely rekindled the departmental agitation, which found expression in the medical press and Parliament. Medical spokesmen deplored the loss of military rank (as retained by officers in the Commissariat, Ordnance, Pay and Chaplains' Departments), the categorisation of medical officers as noncombatants (when they shared the dangers of front-line service, unlike many officers of the Pay and Commissariat Departments), and the failure to award them honours or sick leave allowances on a par with combatants. After stoutly defending the warrant of 1886, as it had not diminished the pay of medical officers, Stanhope eventually accepted that a Select Committee should investigate the issue. This committee, supported by Sir Andrew Clarke, the President of the Royal College of Physicians, argued that relative army rank in the form of composite titles should be restored. In 1891, Stanhope approved the award of composite titles; and, seven years later, the War Office conceded that the whole department, including the Army Hospital Corps, should be reconstituted as the Royal Army Medical Corps.[42]

Despite these changes in professional status, the organisation of medical assistance in the field remained largely unaffected. It was based on three separate lines: a medical officer attached to every corps in the field and bearer companies as the first line, movable field hospitals as the second, and stationary field hospitals on the lines of communication and base hospitals constituting the third. The three lines reflected the guiding principle that disabled soldiers should be passed as rapidly as possible from the front through the field hospitals to the rear, so as not to encumber the fighting line. Accordingly, front-line medical officers simply treated trivial cases of sickness and rendered emergency aid until a bearer company arrived. A bearer company (213 all ranks) was attached to each division and to the corps troops. It rendered assistance to the wounded, collected and removed them to dressing stations and thence to field hospitals. Normally twelve field hospitals, each capable of accommodating 200 patients, supported an army corps. They had to move with the fighting line and so passed the wounded from the bearer companies back to the stationary hospitals in the rear (only retaining those who might recover quickly or might suffer from immediate removal). The stationary hospitals treated the wounded or prepared them for return to England. Thirteen stationary hospitals were normally attached to an army corps but a smaller number sufficed if the base was near the sea or relatively close to the area of operations.

The effectiveness of this organisation depended ultimately upon the discipline, training and competence of the medical personnel. Tested in the Egyptian expedition of 1882, the hospital staff were found wanting in many respects. A Select Committee, investigating the Army Hospital Services, reported that the noncommissioned officers and men of the AHC had received inadequate peacetime training, and that this was reflected in their inadequate nursing and care of the wounded. The committee emphasised that the men had not been properly supervised, and had been overworked in fatigue duties outside their hospitals. Although it praised the standard of medical care (as reflected in the low death rate among the invalided men and in the absence of pyaemia and other diseases in the hospitals), the committee concluded that 'the nursing, feeding, and hospital administration generally left much to be desired . . .'.[43] It recommended improvements in training and an expansion of the female nursing service. Hitherto, female nursing had been confined to the two general hospitals at Netley and Woolwich, involving about a dozen nurses. Civilian lobbyists, including Florence Nightingale, Viscountess Strangford, the Order of St John of Jerusalem and the National Society for Aid to the Sick and Wounded, had repeatedly pressed for the employment of female nurses in wartime. They had had some success; seven nurses accompanied the forces to South Africa in 1879 and another thirty-five served in Egypt and the Sudan between 1882 and 1885. The War Office, acting upon the Army Hospital Services report, issued new regulations in 1885, extending the female nursing service to all hospitals with over 100 beds (and, in 1893, it rescinded the 100 bed restriction). Nevertheless, the expansion of the Army Nursing Service was extremely modest (in 1890 there were sixty army sisters working in sixteen hospitals and in 1898 only seventy-two); an Army Nursing Reserve was not established until March 1897. This limited role reflected not only the doubts of some members of the Army Medical Department about the value of female nursing, but also the priorities of the service. Long-term nursing of the sick had a lower priority than the emergency treatment and removal of the wounded from the battlefield. Whereas medical orderlies, who might have to work under fire, gained combatant status, army sisters were left without officer status. They lacked any authority over the orderlies, and their role in training orderlies (as prescribed in the 1885 regulations) became increasingly perfunctory. Less than half the nurses who joined the service in 1893 completed three years' service, a lack of commitment which possibly derived from the loneliness of the work and the restrictions and limitations imposed on their nursing. The medical services remained predominantly a male preserve, with 3,707 of all ranks serving in the Royal Army Medical Corps on 1 October 1899 and another 1,009 men in the Reserve.[44]

The Military Store Staff Corps had had the responsibility for the provision, holding and issue of all warlike stores and equipment, other than rations and animals. It had been incorporated within the Control Department, but, when the latter was dissolved in 1876, it re-emerged as the Ordnance Store Department. Whereas the officers who had handled the clerical work served in this body, the rank and file remained in the original Army Service Corps until it was abolished in 1881. Thereafter the other ranks served in the Ordnance Store Corps, which rapidly expanded in size as detachments were posted to various foreign stations. By 1892 its establishment had risen to 857 (compared with 400 in the 1870s), and, in the following year, its organisation was streamlined for the purposes of mobilisation. The five companies were re-formed into ten, each fifty strong, supported by a depot at Woolwich. Over the next two years the corps absorbed the Corps of Armourers and the Armament Artificers, emerging as the Army Ordnance Corps with an establishment of 1,311 men in 1896. *Esprit de corps* hardly improved, as the department of officers was divided from the corps of other ranks, and as the corps was dispersed in small fragments among the bases at home and overseas.[45]

On active service Ordnance supplied ammunition to the rear areas, whereupon ammunition columns supplied by the Royal Artillery brought the reserves of artillery and small arms ammunition to the fighting units. Formal provision had been made for such columns in the mobilisation planning of 1875, but these plans had lacked any substance. The plans of Brackenbury were more specific, indicating that sixteen field artillery batteries had to be converted into ammunition columns to support two army corps. Stanhope acted upon these proposals when he recommended that three horse artillery batteries should be converted into field artillery batteries to bring the home establishment up to the requisite number.[46]

The other services reorganised in the wake of Brackenbury's mobilisation planning included the Pay Corps and the Remount Department. In 1888 the regimental paymasters were replaced by the creation of an Army Pay Corps under the control of the Quartermaster-General. The corps appointed station paymasters to service the requirements of several regiments, that is, providing the money for company officers to pay their men, receiving accounts from these officers, and accounting for the disbursements to the Accountant-General. The Army Pay Corps was extremely small (numbering 209 officers and 615 clerks on the eve of the Second Boer

War) and lacked any reserve to call upon. As Queen's Regulations stated that only twenty pay officers should accompany an army corps on active service, the Pay Corps was liable to be stretched in a major war.[47]

The Quartermaster-General also assumed responsibility over the Army Remount Department, created in 1887. Thereafter, instead of individual commanding officers buying horses for the cavalry and artillery, the new department set one standard for the quality, price, and age of the horses which it would purchase. Headed by the Inspector-General of Remounts, the department employed three assistant inspectors, based in London, Woolwich and Dublin, 130 noncommissioned officers and men, and five veterinary surgeons in the annual task of purchasing some 2,200 horses for the whole of the home army. During a mobilisation, the department would have to provide the requisite remounts – an undertaking facilitated by the passage of the National Defence Act (1888). By this Act the government acquired the right to requisition all horses and means of transport in the country in time of national danger or whenever the Militia was mobilised. Owners of the right type of horse were asked to register a percentage of their horses voluntarily, whereupon the Remount Department classified these horses and signed contracts for the supply of a certain number within forty-eight hours of a national emergency being declared. By 1896–97, over 14,500 horses were registered (10,000 of which were draft horses); at that time, the cavalry division required 3,720 horses to mobilise its eight regiments.[48]

The comprehensive range of support services was completed by the Veterinary Department, the Provost Service, whose detachments of military mounted and foot police were formally divided with their own promotion rosters in 1885,[49] and the Chaplains' Department, which continued its post-Crimean expansion, with Wesleyans gaining capitation grants in 1881 on the same terms as Anglicans, Presbyterians and Roman Catholics and the Jews gaining their first chaplain in 1892.[50] Many years of campaign experience, in short, had enabled the army to identify and cater for those aspects of organisation, support and discipline without which it would have foundered as a fighting force. Supported by the Royal Navy (not merely in transport but also in securing bridgeheads, coastal bombardments, riverine support and in combined operations), the army undertook missions in many different parts of the world. As a small force, it had to be flexible, efficient and economical; it had to adapt and develop appropriate methods to operate in small colonial wars. Even so, its military effectiveness ultimately depnded upon the qualities and training of its officers and men.

Notes

1 *Memorandum of the Secretary of State relating to the Army Estimates, 1887–8*, C. 4985 (1887), L, pp.8–13; *Elgin Report*, Cd. 1790 (1904), XL, pp.247–8; *Parl. Deb.*, Third Ser., Vol.312 (14 March 1887), cols.254–80, 290–2, 298–301; Vol.313 (14 April 1887), cols.884–5; Maj.-Gen. Sir C.E. Callwell and Maj.-Gen. Sir J. Headlam, *The History of the Royal Artillery*, 3 Vols. (Royal Artillery Institution; London, 1931–40), Vol.1, pp.96–8.

2 Wolseley, minute, 9 January 1888 and to the Permanent Under-Secretary, 8 June 1888; Stanhope, minute, 8 December 1888, PRO, WO 33/48, A 120, A126, A148a; Beckett, 'Edward Stanhope at the War Office, 1887–92', p.299; Preston (ed.), *The South African Diaries of Sir Garnet Wolseley 1875*, pp.66–9; J. Gooch, *The Plans of War* (Routledge & Kegan Paul; London, 1974), p.12; H. Bailes, 'Patterns of Thought in the late Victorian Army', *Journal of Strategic Studies*, Vol.4 (March 1981), pp.29–45.

3 *General Annual Returns of the British Army . . .*, C. 2731 (1880), XLII, pp.8–9 and C. 9426 (1899), LIII, pp.8–9.

4 Cambridge to Col. F.A. Stanley, 29 January 1879, Cambridge Mss., RA, E/1/8518 and Cambridge to the Marquess of Hartington, 22 December 1882; Verner, *The Military Life of HRH George, Duke of Cambridge*, Vol.2, pp.303–4; Sir C. Ellice, q.3026 evidence appended to the *Airey Report*, p.280.

5 Wolseley, q.4380, Buller, qs.18 and 52, Cambridge, q.2014 evidence appended to the *Report of the Committee on the Terms and Conditions of Service in the Army*, hereafter referred to as the *Wantage Report*, C. 6582 (1892), XIX, pp.154, 2, 4, 72; *Airey Report*, p.10; Lansdowne, 'Outlines of Army Proposals', 2 December 1897, PRO, CAB 37/45, pp.7–8.

6 H. Bailes, 'Technology and Imperialism: a Case Study of the Victorian Army in Africa', *Victorian Studies*, Vol.24 (1980), pp.82–104; B.J. Bond (ed.), *Victorian Military Campaigns* (Hutchinson; London, 1967), pp.6–7; *Wantage Report*, Appendix XXVIII, p.533; *Parl. Deb.*, Third Ser., Vol.259 (3 March 1881), cols.198–9.

7 *Ibid.*, col.201; Col. J.C. Russell, q.12583 evidence appended to the *Wantage Report*, p.429; *Report of the Committee on the Organisation of the Royal Artillery, with minutes and appendices*, hereafter referred to as the *Harris Report*, C. 5491 (1888), XXV, p.vi; Anglesey, *A History of the British Cavalry 1816–1919*, Vol.3, pp.49–50, 122, 430–1; Callwell and Headlam, *The History of the Royal Artillery*, Vol.1, pp.113–14; *Report of the Committee on Artillery Localisation*, C. 3168 (1882), XVI, p.3.

8 *Ibid.*, pp.4–6; *Harris Report*, Appendix J, p.261; Maj.-Gen. E. Markham, qs.12751, 12762 and 12774–5 evidence appended to the the *Wantage*

Report, pp.437–8; Callwell and Headlam, *The History of the Royal Artillery*, Vol.1, pp.87–8, 92–3.

9 Lt.-Col. H.H. Goodeve, q.2938 and see also Maj.-Gen. H.J. Alderson, q.996 and Col. C.C. Trench, qs.1715–16 evidence appended to the *Harris Report*, pp.121, 41 and 70.

10 Trench, qs.1853–4 and 1704–5, 1711, Wolseley, q.144, Maj.-Gen. W.H. Goodenough, qs.836–7, Col. C.B. Brackenbury, q.1275 and Col. S.J. Nicholson, qs.1,646–8 evidence appended to the *Harris Report*, pp.74, 69–70, 7, 33, 54 and 67.

11 *Harris Report*, pp.ix–x; 'The Royal Regiment of Artillery', *Edinburgh Review*, Vol.169 (January 1889), pp.242–76; Callwell and Headlam, *The History of the Royal Artillery*, Vol.1, pp.130–1.

12 Maj.-Gen. J.K. Fraser, qs.12946–52 evidence appended to the *Wantage Report*, p.448.

13 Cambridge to Hartington, 22 December 1882, Verner, *The Military Life of HRH George, Duke of Cambridge*, Vol.2, p.305; *Report of the Cavalry Organisation Committee*, hereafter referred to as the *Wardlaw Report*, C. 3167 (1882), XVI, pp.3–5, 7.

14 Fraser, qs.12829, 12832–6, 12942 evidence appended to the *Wantage Report*, pp.442 and 448; Anglesey, *A History of the British Cavalry 1816–1919*, Vol.3, pp.122–6.

15 Lt.-Col. A.J. Godley, qs.20021, 20063, 20089, 20124 evidence appended to the *Elgin Report*, Cd. 1791 (1904), XLI, pp.435, 437–9; Lt.-Gen. W.H. Goodenough and Lt.-Col. J.C. Dalton, *The Army Book for the British Empire* (HMSO; London, 1893), pp.172–7; S.D. Badsey, 'Fire and Sword: The British Army and the *Arme Blanche* Controversy 1871–1921', unpublished Ph.D. thesis (University of Cambridge, 1981), p.97.

16 F.A. Johnson, *Defence by Committee* (Oxford University Press; London, 1960), pp.34–42; Bond (ed.), *Victorian Military Campaigns*, pp.13–14.

17 Wolseley to Cambridge, 24 and 15 October 1873, Cambridge Mss., RA, E/1/7217 and 7207.

18 Roberts, q.10333 evidence appended to the *Elgin Report*, Cd. 1790 (1904), XL, p.436.

19 Wolseley to Lady Wolseley, 27 December 1884, Wolseley Mss., W/P 13/38; Wolseley to Cambridge, 11 December 1884, Cambridge Mss., RA, E/1/10980; Wolseley to Cambridge, 18 July 1879, Verner, *The Military Life of HRH George, Duke of Cambridge*, Vol.2, p.162; L. Maxwell, *The Ashanti Ring, Sir Garnet Wolseley's Campaigns 1870–1882* (Leo Cooper; London, 1985), p.16.

20 Cambridge to Wolseley, 12 August and 12 November 1879 and 14 November 1884, Cambridge Mss., RA, E/1/8851, 8938a and 10955.

21 Wolseley to Lady Wolseley, 20 May 1885, Wolseley Mss., W/P 14/13; Wolseley to Cambridge, 11 December 1884 and 4 April 1885, Cambridge Mss., RA, E/1/10980 and 11123; A. Preston (ed.), *In Relief of Gordon* (Hutchinson; London, 1967), pp.xx–xxi, xxix–xxxi; J. Symons, *England's Pride: The Story of the Gordon Relief Expedition* (H. Hamilton;

London, 1965), pp.65–72.
22   Wolseley, q.4675 evidence appended to the *Wantage Report*, p.167; Wolseley to Cambridge, 3 September, 15 and 24 October 1873; 18 July, 20 August and 1 December 1879, Cambridge Mss., RA, E/1/7191, 7207, 7217, 8807, 8859a and 8966. See also the *Airey Report*, including the evidence of Lord Chelmsford, qs.4701–5, pp.16–18 and 398.
23   Cambridge to Sir R. Airey, 25 August and 25 November 1873; and to Wolseley, 26 August 1879, 19 and 26 September 1884, 2 January 1885, 8 and 12 December 1887, Cambridge Mss., RA, E/1/7184 and 7250; 8864a, 10901, 10915, 11001, 12014 and 12019; Cambridge, q.2064 evidence appended to the *Wantage Report*, p.75.
24   Cambridge to Airey, 17 November 1873, to Sir E. Johnson, 18 July 1879, and to Queen Victoria, 10 November 1881, Cambridge Mss., RA, E/1/7243, 8806, 9829; St Aubyn, *The Royal George*, pp.178, 200, 202, 211 and 215; Lt.-Col. H.D. Napier (ed.), *Letters of Field-Marshal Lord Napier of Magdala* (Simpkin Marshall; London, 1936), pp.69–70, 99–100.
25   Wolseley to Lady Wolseley, 20 March 1880, 24 November 1884, 15 January and 27 February 1885, 1 February 1887, and to his mother, 4 August 1879, Wolseley Mss., W/P 9/15, 13/31, 14/1 and 14/6, 16/17, and 163/5; Preston (ed.), *The South African Diaries of Sir Garnet Wolseley 1875*, pp.212–13.
26   Wolseley to Lady Wolseley, 30 August 1890, Wolseley Mss., W/P 19/21.
27   Brig.-Gen. J.H.A. MacDonald, *Fifty Years of It* (Blackwood; Edinburgh, 1909), pp.75–6.
28   *Manual of Military Law* (HMSO; London, 1899), pp.19–31, 107; *Second Report of the Commissioners appointed to inquire into the Constitution and Practice of Courts-Martial in the Army, and the present System of Punishment for Military Offences*, hereafter referred to as the *Courts-Martial Report*, C. 4114–1 (1868–69), XII, pp.iii–v; *Parl. Deb.*, Third Ser., Vol.243 (27 February 1879), cols.1911–14; J. Stuart-Smith, 'Military Law: its history, administration and practice', *Law Quarterly Review*, Vol.85 (October 1969), p.479.
29   *Courts-Martial Report*, pp.vi–vii, x–xi; *Report from the Select Committee on Mutiny and Marine Mutiny Acts; together with the proceedings of the Committee, minutes of evidence, and appendix*, C. 316 (1878), X, pp.iii–vii; *Parl. Deb.*, Third Ser., Vol.243 (27 February 1879), cols. 1912–14.
30   *Courts-Martial Report*, p.viii; *Report of the Committee appointed by the Secretary of State for War to consider the Conditions of a Soldier's Service, as affected by the Introduction of the Short Service System, and other Matters in connection therewith 1878*, hereafter referred to as the *Short Service Report*, C. 2817 (1881), XX, p.12; *Parl. Deb.*, Third Ser. Vol.243 (27 February 1879), cols.1917–18; Vol.245 (7 April 1879), cols.489–90, 495–6; Vol.247 (20 June 1879), cols.332–55; *Parl. Deb.*, Fourth Ser., Vol.11 (20 April 1893), cols.748–53 (24 April 1893), cols.1010–13.
31   *Manual of Military Law*, pp.318–45; *General Annual Returns of the*

British Army . . ., C. 1323 (1875), XLIII, p.40; C. 6196 (1890), XLIII, p.56; C. 9426 (1899), LIII, p.58; Skelley, *The Victorian Army at Home*, pp.145, 147; *Courts-Martial Report*, pp.ix–x; R.L. Blanco, 'Attempts to Abolish Branding and Flogging in the Army of Victorian England before 1881', *Journal of the Society of Army Historical Research*, Vol.46 (autumn 1968), pp.137–45.

32 *Parl. Deb.*, Third Ser., Vol.247 (17 June 1879), cols.41–74; Vol.248 (17 July 1879), cols.634–70; Vol.251 (11 March 1880), cols.847–54; Vol.260 (7 April 1881), cols.853–4; 'Abolition of Flogging', PRO, WO 32/6045, p.7; Stanley to Cambridge, 17 June 1879 and Cambridge to Sir D. Stewart, 17 June 1881, Cambridge Mss., RA, E/1/8733 and 9654; Skelley, *The Victorian Army at Home*, pp.147–52.

33 *Ibid.*, pp.152–6; *Manual of Military Law*, pp.760–1; *Reports on the Discipline and Management of the Military Prisons . . .*, C. 398 (1900), XLII, pp.37–9; and C. 9416 (1899), XLIII, p.18; *Parl. Deb.*, Fourth Ser., Vol.71 (8 May 1899), cols.18–21; *General Annual Returns of the British Army . . .*, C. 1323 (1875), XLIII, pp.40–1; C. 6196 (1890), XLIII, pp.53, 58; C. 9426 (1899), LIII, pp.50, 54, 59.

34 *Memorandum of the Secretary of State relating to the Army Estimates, 1887–8*, C. 4985 (1887), L, p.13; W. Porter and C.M. Watson, *History of the Corps of Royal Engineers*, 3 Vols. (Longmans; London, 1889–1915), Vol.2, pp.150–1 and Vol.3, pp.21, 37–8, 67, 126, 159–67; Lt.-Col. E.W.C. Sandes, *The Royal Engineers in Egypt and the Sudan* (Institute of Royal Engineers; Chatham, 1937), p.238; Goodenough and Dalton, *The Army Book for the British Empire*, p.252.

35 *Report of a Committee appointed by the Secretary of State for War to enquire into the Administration of the Transport and Supply Departments of the Army*, C. 3848 (1867), XV, pp.xi, xxiii–xxvii; Bailes, 'Technology and Imperialism', p.90; Parl. Deb., Third Ser., Vol.190 (20 February 1868), col.986; *Northbrook Second Report*, p.vi; J.W. Fortescue, *The Royal Army Service Corps: A History of Transport and Supply in the British Army*, 2 Vols. (Cambridge University Press; Cambridge, 1930–31), Vol.1, pp.183–7.

36 *Ibid.*, Vol.1, p.213; *Parl. Deb.*, Vol.212 (22 July 1872), cols.1550–2; Maj.-Gen. A. Forbes, *A History of the Army Ordnance Services*, 3 Vols. (Medici Society; London, 1929), Vol.2, pp.12–13.

37 Lt.-Gen. F.A. Thesiger to Stanley, 11 November 1878, *Correspondence Relative to Military Affairs in Natal and the Transvaal*, C. 2234 (1878–79), LIV, p.29; Lt.-Col. C.R. Shervinton, 'On Army Transport', *Journal of the RUSI*, Vol.XXV (1882), pp.182–3; Bailes, 'Technology and Imperialism', pp.91–2.

38 Wolseley to Stanley, 30 July 1879, *Further Correspondence Respecting the Affairs of South Africa*, C. 2482 (1880), L, pp.94–6; Fortescue, *The Royal Army Service Corps*, Vol.1, pp.200–7; Bailes, 'Technology and Imperialism', pp.100–2.

39 *Ibid.*, pp.97, 101; F. Emery, *Marching over Africa* (Hodder & Stoughton; London, 1986), pp.141–2, 146–52; D.R. Morris, *The Washing of the Spears* (Sphere; London, 1968), p.319; H. Keown-Boyd, *A Good*

Dusting (Leo Cooper; London, 1986), pp.41, 43, 47; Shervinton, 'On Army Transport', pp.180–1; Fortescue, *The Royal Army Service Corps*, Vol.1, pp.205, 213–14; *Elgin Report*, p.109.

40   *Report of a Committee appointed by the Secretary of State for War, to inquire into the Organisation of the Army Hospital Corps, Hospital Management and Nursing in the Field, and the Sea Transport of Sick and Wounded, together with minutes of evidence, appendix and index,* hereafter referred to as the *Army Hospital Corps Report,* C. 3607 (1883), XVI, p.vii; 'Special Reports on the Working of the Mixed Regimental and Station Hospital System', PRO, WO 33/33; Skelley, *The Victorian Army at Home*, pp.42, 46, 49–50.

41   *Report of the Committee appointed by the Secretary of State to enquire into the Causes which tend to prevent sufficient eligible Candidates from coming forward for the Army Medical Department,* C. 2200 (1878–9), XLIV, pp.3–5, 9–11.

42   *Parl. Deb.*, Third Ser., Vol.310 (15 February 1887), col.1559; Vol.314 (12 May 1887), col.1662; Vol.320 (5 September 1887), cols.1141–2; Vol.345 (19 June 1890), cols.1371–2; Vol.356 (28 July 1891), col.558; *Report of the Committee appointed to enquire into the Pay, Status, and Conditions of Service of Medical Officers of the Army and Navy,* C. 5810 (1889), XVII, pp.3, 5–7; *Letter, dated 17th January 1891, from Sir Andrew Clark, Bart., M.D., FRS, to the Secretary of State for War . . .,* C. 6282 (1890–91), L, pp.3–6 and *Further Correspondence relative to the Status of Medical Officers of the Army,* C. 6312 (1890–91), L, pp.3–9.

43   *Army Hospital Corps Report,* pp.vii–xi, xix–xxv.

44   *Ibid.*, pp.xxix–xxx, xl; A. Summers, *Angels and Citizens: British Women as Military Nurses 1854–1914* (Routledge & Kegan Paul; London, 1988), pp.97–9, 106–9, 154–6, 166; *Elgin Report*, p.102.

45   Forbes, *A History of the Army Ordnance Services*, Vol.2, pp.151–61.

46   Callwell and Headlam, *The History of the Royal Artillery*, Vol.1, pp.54–5, 73, 96–7.

47   *Elgin Report*, pp.122–3.

48   Anglesey, *A History of the British Cavalry 1816–1919*, Vol.3, pp.389–91.

49   A. Vaughan Knight, *The History of the Office of the Provost Marshal and the Corps of Military Police* (Gale & Polden; Aldershot, 1943), p.60.

50   Brig. the Rt. Hon. Sir John Smyth, *In This Sign Conquer* (A.R. Mowbray; London, 1968), pp.xviii–xix; O. Anderson, 'The Growth of Christian Militarism in mid-Victorian Britain', *English Historical Review*, Vol.LXXXVI, (January 1971), pp.46–72.

4

Officers

In abolishing purchase, Cardwell had undoubtedly removed the greatest anomaly of the late Victorian army, but he had also disrupted the process by which officers secured their commissions, promotions and retirements. The Royal Warrant of 30 October 1871 had not fully addressed this problem; it had only stipulated that every subsequent appointment to a lieutenant-colonelcy or to a majority should be vacated after a period of five years (a provision which would not have any effect before November 1876). Meanwhile the rate of promotion had already begun to slow down (whereas in 1871 there were 737 infantry officers who had served for more than the average periods in their respective ranks – two years eight months to become a lieutenant, nine years to become a captain, eighteen years eleven months to become a major and twenty-three years six months to become a lieutenant-colonel – by 1 July 1875 there were 1,100 officers in a similar position). If this trend continued, War Office actuaries reckoned that officers would take an average of nearly seven years longer to reach the rank of captain (when they would be over thirty-five years of age), attain a majority at forty-nine years, and a lieutenant-colonelcy at fifty-three years and six months.[1] As this stagnation was bound to depress the morale of officers and the efficiency of the service, a radical reform of the terms of service became a prime concern of the military authorities.

In 1875 a Royal Commission, chaired by Lord Penzance, examined the issue of army promotion. It recognised that the present difficulties derived from the inequality of officers in successive ranks. Since a battalion of the line in 1875 contained one lieutenant-colonel, two majors, eleven captains and eighteen subalterns, the promotion prospects of the twenty-nine junior officers, particularly in peacetime, were fairly bleak. Although a reorganisation of the ranks might have mitigated the scale of the problem, the commission was precluded from considering any change of the regimental structure. It had to find a method of securing the retirement of large numbers of junior officers – the process which had sustained the flow of promotion in the purchase army (in the last ten years of the purchase system, 1,051 captains and 1,623 subalterns had sold out of the army).

The commission considered initially whether lessons could be learned from the experience of the non-purchase corps, the Royal Artillery and the Royal Engineers. It found that only a few of their officers had retired without a pension or a gratuity over the past twenty years (an average of about six per annum in the Artillery and one and a half per annum in the Engineers), and only officers above the rank of captain had been eligible for pensions. To sustain the flow of promotion, the non-purchase corps had relied upon several expedients, such as increasing their establishments, proffering additional pensions, altering the regimental organisation, creating vacancies in the lower ranks (by a special and temporary vote) and creating supernumerary officers, who were kept on full pay but who were not required by the service. By these measures, the Royal Artillery had ensured that its senior major had twenty-five and a half years' service, the senior captain about twenty years' service, and the senior lieutenant thirteen years. The commission was not impressed. Like a previous Select Committee, it regarded this 'combination of contrivances' as 'complicated, uncertain in its operation, based on no sure principle, and inadequate for its purpose'.[2]

Accordingly, the commission favoured improving the inducements to retire for junior as well as for senior officers. It advocated the offer of pensions or gratuities, varying with rank and length of service, and the introduction of compulsory retirement if the voluntary process failed to produce the requisite number of vacancies. It proposed that infantry officers might be allowed to retire voluntarily *from the army*, with a gratuity, after eight years' service; a major might be allowed to retire voluntarily *from the army* before completing twenty-three years' service; and a lieutenant-colonel might be allowed to retire, with a pension, before completing twenty-seven years' service. A captain would be entitled to retire permanently *from his regiment* after fifteen but not more than twenty years' service on half pay, provided that he remained eligible for military service until the age of forty-five, whereupon he would receive a step of honorary rank. After twenty years' service, an officer, if not promoted to the rank of major, could either retire *from the army*, with a pension and a step of honorary rank, or retire *from the regiment* with half pay and the possibility of employment outside the regiment, and the option of retiring at any time thereafter *from the army* with a pension and the step of honorary rank. After twenty-seven years' service (and either seven years' service as a major or five years in regimental command) senior officers would also be entitled to retire *from the regiment* or *from the army*, and this formula was applied to all branches of the service, albeit with some differences in the lengths of service and the pensions provided.

The commission proposed even more generous terms for the majority of officers who had obtained their commissions before the abolition of purchase. As these officers had entered the army without any prospect of compulsory retirement, the commission recognised that they would have to be compensated over and above their present retirement rights, which included the purchase and over-regulation value of their commissions. So purchase captains, who would have to retire after completing twenty-five years' service, would receive annuities ranging from £240 to £259 depending on their length of service. These sums would exceed their full pay of £211 and would represent a capital value of £3,200 (compared with their retirement rights of £2,400), while for those who had already completed twenty-five years' service or more the annuity could range as high as £311, accompanied by a step of honorary rank and a widow's pension. Finally, the commission sought to create more vacancies above the level of regimental command. Hitherto, all lieutenant-colonels, after their five years in command, automatically became full colonels and were eligible to succeed to the fixed establishment of general officers. The commission proposed that all general officers should retire at the age of seventy, and that the list of colonels should be split into two parts, Indian and British, so removing the preponderance of Indian colonels who had been promoted under quite different terms from the Indian Staff Corps. Any colonel, who had not been promoted to major-general by the age of fifty-five could retire with a pension of £420 and a step of honorary rank.[3]

As these proposals, which were approved by the Conservative government, were bound to prove extremely expensive, the next Liberal administration sought further economies. Childers warned the House of Commons that the annual pension bill might become £900,000 for the 4,500 captains who retired at the age of forty, unless the regimental system was modified.[4] In his regimental reorganisation of 1881, he proposed to introduce double companies in each infantry battalion, so reducing the number of junior officers, while doubling the number of field officers (majors and lieutenant-colonels). At the same time he approved a tightening of the terms of retirement. Henceforth lieutenants and captains, if not promoted, would have to retire at forty on £200 a year, forfeiting £10 for every year's service less than twenty; a major had to retire at forty-eight on £250 or £300 a year 'according to service'; a lieutenant-colonel and colonel at fifty-five on £365 and £420 respectively; a major-general at sixty-two on £700; and a lieutenant-general and general at sixty-seven on £850 and £1,000 respectively. Although the compulsory terms were to be inflexible, the authorities retained their discretion about accepting voluntary retirements. The terms for the latter were also marginally tightened: after twelve years' service a lieutenant or captain could retire with a gratuity of £1,200 and a major, after twenty years' service, could retire with a pension of £250 a year.[5]

By introducing these measures, Childers had hoped that the system would become more economical and more efficient, but, as double companies were never created in the infantry regiments, his hopes were thwarted. In fact, the proportion of seniors, including general officers, to juniors worsened from nearly one to two in 1884 to about one to three ten years later. The pension bill also grew from about £737,00 in 1884 to some £1,000,000 in 1894. Nevertheless, the reforms worked reasonably as a means of sustaining the flow of promotions in the post-purchase army. If abolition had terminated the 'gadfly careerism' by which officers had frequently transferred between regiments in the quest for promotion, the new reforms preserved promotion by seniority *within the regiment*. This usually kept the lieutenant-colonelcy in the regiment itself, while the threat of passing over the incompetent stimulated a degree of enthusiasm and effort among younger officers. The reforms also mitigated any lingering sense of grievance over promotion prospects among serving officers, and so diminished a potentially contentious issue which could have undermined the appeal of service life. By 1877 this appeal was flourishing, with nearly 900 applicants for some 100 cadetships at the Royal Military College, Sandhurst.[6]

Abolishing purchase had little impact upon the social composition of the late Victorian officers. Throughout this period the senior officers were largely composed of men who had gained their commissions before abolition. If these officers are compared with the senior officers in 1914, many of whom only entered the army in the 1870s and 1880s, there is little change in their social composition (Table 1). In each of the years analysed, there is a preponderant degree of self-recruitment and a substantial contribution from the landed aristocracy. This did not mean that the army had fossilised as a static or caste-like body. During the nineteenth century the landed interest was a relatively open group; as some old-established families lost their fortunes and vacated their estates, newcomers, having made their money in industry, commerce or speculation, moved on to the land. Often seeking a more elusive commodity than profits and power, these newcomers frequently sought recognition of their respectability and entrée into the activities and gatherings of county society. Military service was one method by which an aspirant or his descendants might seek the approval of local society.

Table 1   *The social composition of senior officers in 1868, 1899 and 1914, expressed in percentage terms*

| | Colonels | | | Generals | | |
Social background	1868	1899	1914	1868	1899	1914
Peerage and						
baronetage	13	12	7	14	12	10
Gentry	28	26	26	33	29	32
Armed services	18	23	23	23	19	25
Clergy	8	12	14	6	9	6
Professional	5	9	12	5	7	6
Others	12	13	15	7	18	18
'Don't know'	16	5	3	12	6	3
Total (%)	100	100	100	100	100	100
Total number	206	129	118	177	113	116

Notes: The names of officers, excluding those who had retired or were in receipt of half-pay, were obtained from the relevant Army Lists. For 1899 and 1914, the senior officers include all field-marshals, generals, lieutenant-generals and major-generals on the active list, and a random sample of one-third of each list of active colonels. Since the numbers are much larger in 1868, the random sample includes one-half of the field-marshals, generals, lieutenant-generals and major-generals, and one-quarter of the active colonels and lieutenant-colonels. For a methodological note on the sources consulted in the process of compiling Tables 1 and 2, see Appendix 4.

Military service could confirm social status because it had already become a traditional and highly regarded career for the sons of many landed families. In their memoirs, army officers frequently cited the influence of family tradition as a source of career motivation, albeit one which was sustained in different ways by different families. In many families it was a wholly positive influence, with both parents and children willing to perpetuate a military connection often stretching back over several generations. Officers like Wolseley, Sir Hubert Gough, Sir Ian Hamilton and Sir Horace Smith-Dorrien appear to have gladly followed in the distinguished military traditions of their respective families.[7] Occasionally, sons had to struggle to sustain the family tradition; Roberts had to overcome the fears of his father, General Abraham Roberts, that he would encounter financial hardship by entering the army, while Sir John French (later the Earl of Ypres), who was an orphan, had to persuade his elder sisters that he should join the fighting services (the navy originally, as he could enter it four or five years earlier than the army).[8] Where there were conflicting family traditions (for example, naval on the father's side and military on the mother's) reasons of estate management sometimes prevailed. Both parents dissuaded the Earl of Dundonald from following his father's career, since the family had suffered losses of property from its menfolk being so much at sea, and hence the earldom would be better preserved by a military head of the family.[9] Finally, some sons may have meekly acquiesced in maintaining the family tradition. As Lord Wavell candidly recalled,

I never felt any special inclination to a military career, but it would have taken more independence of character than I possessed at the time, to avoid it. Nearly all my relations were military. I had been brought up amongst soldiers; and my father, while professing to give me complete liberty of choice was determined that I should be a soldier. I had no particular bent towards any other profession, and took the line of least resistance.[10]

Diversity was equally apparent in the career motivation of those who entered the army from non-service backgrounds. Some pursued a military career in spite of their parents, overcoming a bias either in favour of a civilian profession or against a military career. John Ardagh, the son of a clergyman, took an honours degree at Trinity College Dublin, winning a prize in Hebrew, before he became fascinated with the artillery experiments of a neighbour and decided to enter the Royal Engineers. Several others, including Robert Baden-Powell, Edmund Allenby and Henry McMahon, tried to fulfil the career expectations of their parents but found them too demanding: failure in university or Indian Civil Service examinations left the army as the only profession within reach of their academic attainments. Winston Churchill never even tried to fulfil his father's expectations; he simply persuaded the latter to let him indulge his military predilections, as he was 'not clever enough to go the Bar'.[11] Conversely, there were many parents, particularly among those who had moved on to the land, who positively encouraged their sons to embark on a military career, even a short one, to fulfil the obligations of public service and gain the acceptance of county society. As Gwyn Harries-Jenkins argues, service in a fashionable regiment could be used as a means of 'confirming' an aspired social status.[12]

What these patterns of career motivation reflected was not so much the salience of parental influence (undoubtedly there were other factors which were as important, if not more so, in particular cases), but the relative lack of career opportunities for the sons of self-assigned gentlemen. If neither the Church nor the professions nor the civil service appealed or were practical propositions, the prospects could be extremely limited, especially for younger sons. As Wavell observed,

it was quite natural that some of those who failed for the Indian Civil Service should turn to the Army for a career; in fact, other openings were limited, for commercial business was not in those days considered a suitable occupation for a gentleman.[13]

When coupled with the element of tradition within military families, this artificial restriction preserved the relative homogeneity of the social intake.

Compounding this degree of homogeneity was the connection between the army and the land (see Table 2). The county communities, particularly in Scotland, Ireland and the south of England (Table 3), remained a primary source of officer recruitment. Within their confines, an uncomplicated patriotism and sense of duty flourished alongside an unbridled passion for field sports. Hunting and shooting were obviously relevant to the military activities of a pre-technological army, but they were also forms of recreation which officers zealously pursued during their ample periods of leave. Even on active service, if the opportunities arose, officers readily indulged their passion for field sports, sometimes to supplement their stocks of food, but often to relieve the boredom of campaigning and

Table 2 *The rural/urban background of the senior officers in 1868, 1899 and 1914, expressed in percentage terms*

Provenance	Colonels			Generals		
	1868	*1899*	*1914*	*1868*	*1899*	*1914*
Estates, farms, villages under 1,000 pop.	59	38	46	62	40	43
Villages and towns 1,000–5,000	9	25	19	4	22	22
Total rural (%)	68	63	65	66	62	65
Towns in excess of 5,000 pop.	28	29	26	29	30	27
Abroad	4	8	9	5	8	8
Total (%)	100	100	100	100	100	100
Total number	137	107	87	141	91	91

to keep fit. In his diary of the Second Boer War, Lieutenant Edward Longueville, Coldstream Guards, records a prodigious slaughter of fowl, buck, antelope and Cape buffalo when he was based at Naauwport, regular hunting with the Cape foxhounds at Wynberg, and 140 days of polo in South Africa: 'what with polo three days a week, and hunting three days, and a shoot on Sundays, I managed to keep myself pretty fit.'[14] By offering abundant opportunities for field sports and polo the army undoubtedly enhanced its appeal for those who had been brought up to relish these pastimes.

This social exclusivity was further preserved by substantial recruitment from the rapidly expanding public school sector. During the South African War some 62 per cent of regular officers came from public schools, with 41 per cent from the ten great public schools and 11 per cent from Eton alone.[15] Several public schools had 'army classes' and cadet corps, and specialised in training boys for admission to the military colleges (Sandhurst for the infantry and cavalry, and Woolwich for the artillery and engineers). Their success rate was variable, as many boys still had to attend crammers before they could pass their entrance examinations for Sandhurst and Woolwich (while those who failed often sought regular commissions through the 'back door' of the Militia). A public school education, nonetheless, was deemed invaluable because of the qualities of character which the schools were thought to develop. These included the training of the mind in the classical tradition, with its emphasis upon order, authority and discipline, and the training of the body

Table 3   *The regional background of senior officers in 1868, 1899 and 1914, expressed in percentage terms*

	Colonels			Generals		
Region	*1868*	*1899*	*1914*	*1868*	*1899*	*1914*
Wales	4	5	1	—	2	4
Scotland	12	12	8	13	12	17
Ireland	21	21	7	17	16	13
North of England	4	6	13	8	4	7
West Midlands	5	6	4	8	6	1
East Midlands	4	5	1	5	2	2
South Midlands	4	3	8	6	6	4
London	8	9	9	11	12	7
East Anglia	1	1	6	3	8	8
Home Counties	12	7	18	10	9	9
South and south-west	21	17	16	14	15	20
Abroad	4	8	9	5	8	8
Total (%)	100	100	100	100	100	100
Total number	137	107	87	141	91	91

Note: The regions were grouped in the following manner:

North of England	Cumberland, Westmorland, Lancashire, Durham, Yorkshire, Northumberland
East Anglia	Norfolk, Suffolk, Essex
Home Counties	Kent, Sussex, Middlesex, Surrey
South and south-west	Cornwall, Devon, Somerset, Dorset, Hampshire, Berkshire, Wiltshire and Gloucestershire
East Midlands	Lincolnshire, Nottinghamshire, Leicestershire, Rutland, Huntingdonshire, Northamptonshire
West Midlands	Cheshire, Derbyshire, Warwickshire, Shropshire, Staffordshire, Worcestershire, Herefordshire, Monmouthshire
South Midlands	Bedfordshire, Hertfordshire, Buckinghamshire, Oxfordshire, Cambridgeshire

If the South of England is considered as encompassing East Anglia, London, South Midlands, Home Counties and South and south-west, the proportions of officers coming from this area were as follows:

	Colonels			Generals		
	1868	1899	1914	1868	1899	1914
South of England	46	37	57	44	50	48

and spirit through the cult of team games. If boys played rugby and cricket, it was widely assumed that they would develop not only the physical attributes of health, strength, co-ordination and quickness of eye – all essential military requirements – but also moral virtues like self-discipline and team spirit – qualities which could be transferred into regimental service. Above all, as Geoffrey Best argues, the public schools were thought to inculcate loyalty, which 'began with loyalty to your house . . . and rose through loyalty to your school (a paradigm of the nation) to loyalty to your country, faith and leaders'.[16] Boys possessing such attributes were readily welcomed as potential officers.

Whether these boys would benefit from a specifically military education thereafter, prior to entering the army, was recurrently debated. In the 1860s a series of riots at Sandhurst and Woolwich, and parliamentary complaints about the cost of maintaining two military colleges, prompted the formation of a Royal Commission on Military Education, chaired by the Earl de Grey and Ripon (who was succeeded after six months by Lord Dufferin). It learnt from numerous witnesses about the disillusion and pervasive idleness at Sandhurst, attributed by many to the 10 per cent of cadets who were either Queen's Cadets (the sons of officers who had died on active service and left their families in impecunious circumstances) or Indian Cadets (the sons of Indian military or civil servants who had been nominated by the Secretary of State for India). As these cadets were guaranteed commissions once they had passed the qualifying examination for Sandhurst, they had no incentive to study. Witnesses also criticised the lack of tutorial supervision and the military content of the curriculum; some argued that parents, appalled by the reputation of Sandhurst, preferred to seek direct commissions for their sons in order to avoid the college. The commission, though highly critical of Sandhurst, neither wished to abolish it nor to amalgamate it with the more academically rigorous Royal Military Academy, Woolwich (where the cadets, having entered by open competition, spent two and a half years in professional study, with mathematics as the predominant subject, before graduating in a competitive examination with the incentive that those placed highest on the list could enter the Royal Engineers). The commission felt that prospective officers for the cavalry, Guards and line should receive some professional instruction, and so recommended reforms of the staffing, discipline, and entry requirements, with all admissions to be determined by open competition in which the candidates could sit papers in Latin and Greek.[17]

The value of these proposals was not immediately tested, as the abolition of purchase placed the whole future of Sandhurst in doubt.

Once the War Office had instituted a series of half-yearly examinations from which the successful candidates could gain their commissions direct, Sandhurst seemed superfluous. After the last batch of cadets had passed out of the college in December 1870, Sandhurst was used for a variety of purposes, including the provision of a year's course for 'Gentlemen Students' (commissioned sub-lieutenants who were still waiting for their regimental postings) from 1871 to 1873, courses for newly gazetted officers from 1873 to 1874, and finally courses for all 'students' who were waiting for their commissions, other than the six who passed at the top of the examination list. Only in 1877 did the college resume the teaching of Gentlemen Cadets, but the establishments continued to vary over the next decade, reflecting the incidence of ministerial economies, reorganisations and war scares (for example, all cadets were gazetted during the Russian scare of 1878).

By 1889 the establishment of 360 was divided into six companies of cadets. An establishment of fifty horses was authorised for the purposes of instruction, and the course had a duration of one year or two terms. In September 1892 a three-term system was introduced, with 120 cadets being admitted every half-year. Five years later the teaching of French and German was reintroduced, and, by the end of the century, the curriculum was quite extensive. It included military engineering, military topography, tactics, military administration, military law, languages (French or German), military history and geography, and military exercises (drill, riding and gymnastics).

If spared the bewildering changes of Sandhurst, the Royal Military Academy still experienced many administrative alterations. In 1870 the Civil Service Commissioners took over the conduct of the academy's entrance examination, and Sir Lintorn Simmons, who had been appointed Lieutenant Governor of the academy in 1869, became the academy's first resident Governor in the following year, with unlimited powers of rustication and expulsion. Discipline apparently improved, but the quarters remained fairly cramped as the establishment continued to grow, numbering 280 cadets by 1888. The length of course was reduced to two years in 1878, and a bifurcation system was gradually introduced in the 1890s, whereby the cadets in their second year were divided into an Engineers division and an Artillery division. Whereas the sappers concentrated on mathematics, fortification and compulsory landscape drawing, with only a little artillery, the gunners concentrated on artillery instead of mathematics, studied a little fortification and took landscape drawing as a voluntary subject. If this removed an element of unnecessary instruction, it also removed the chief incentive of a commission in the Royal Engineers at the end of the second year. Henceforth cadets, having entered their division after the first year examinations, only had to get sufficient marks to qualify for a commission at the end of their second year.[18]

After receiving their commissions all Engineer officers, including a small proportion from the Royal Military College at Kingston, Canada, were sent to the School of Military Engineering at Chatham, where they underwent a further course of education lasting for about two years. Artillery officers, after receiving their commissions, had to attend a short course of instruction in the School of Gunnery at Shoeburyness, which lasted from six weeks to two months. During their service as lieutenants or captains, artillery officers could also volunteer for, or be ordered to attend, the long course of gunnery at Shoeburyness. Military education, in short, did not cease when officers graduated from Woolwich.[19]

Those who entered the service academies represented a highly exclusive group, drawn overwhelmingly from propertied, professional and military service backgrounds. Indeed they probably over-represented the traditional sources of officer supply. Both institutions reserved free places for the orphaned sons of officers who had died on active service, leaving their families 'in reduced circumstances', and offered reduced fees for the sons of officers.[20] Those who passed through the college had varying memories of it. Repington and Churchill relished being free of hated school subjects, and revelled in the military topics, the outdoor activities, and the abundant opportunities for sporting and social recreation. Those who did not fit in or committed breaches of etiquette had a less enjoyable time; three or four of them, having dined with the commandant's cook, were set upon by Repington and his friends and were nearly drowned in the lake. J.F.C. Fuller, who entered the college in 1897, regarded the whole atmosphere as basically 'Crimean', with antiquated courses and some eccentric tutors.[21]

When a Select Committee, chaired by A. Akers-Douglas, examined the two academies during the Second Boer War, it generally approved of the instruction at Woolwich but heavily criticised Sandhurst. It found that the cadets at the latter lacked any incentive to work, as they were likely to be commissioned even if they failed to attain the low qualifying standard in the final examinations. It deprecated the lack of practical emphasis in the course – the failure to test musketry or revolver shooting, the limited amount of riding instruction (thirty-nine hours per annum), the failure to instruct cadets in how to drill a squad or a company, and the minimal emphasis on tactics, which were allotted only half the marks given to military engineering and little more than half those given to topography in the final examination. Above all, it criticised the prevailing ethos, commenting

that the majority of young officers will not work unless compelled; that 'keenness is out of fashion'; that 'it is not the correct form'; the spirit and fashion is 'rather not to show keenness'; and that the idea is . . . to do as little as they possibly can.[22]

Despite these shortcomings, Sandhurst at least provided its cadets with a reasonably extensive military training. As neither the Militia nor the regular regiments could emulate this instruction (because many of the latter were quartered in urban barracks, bereft of training facilities, or were located in inadequate colonial stations), the Akers-Douglas Committee favoured the retention of the college and an expansion of its course from eighteen months to two years. It calculated that Sandhurst and Woolwich, on their existing establishments, could not produce more than 410 officers per annum (with the 150 from Woolwich providing the thirty to forty officers normally required by the Royal Engineers and some 100 required by the three branches of the Royal Artillery). It learnt from the War Office that it would require seventy officers for the cavalry (Household and line), 460 for the Foot Guards and infantry, twelve for the West India Regiment and 120 for the Indian Staff Corps. The committee accepted that the army would have to continue finding the bulk of its line officers from the Militia (as Sandhurst met most of the demands of the Indian Staff Corps, the Guards and the cavalry), but hoped that it could increase its commissions from the universities, which had rarely numbered fifty per annum in the pre-war period. In effect, the committee conceded that the army would remain dependent upon the Militia for a substantial body of officers, many of whom had failed the entrance examinations for Sandhurst, and all of whom had missed both the military training and the sense of cohesiveness instilled by a college education.[23]

Another small source of officer supply came from the promotion of noncommissioned officers (NCOs). The army had regularly appointed NCOs as quartermasters and riding masters, but rarely as second lieutenants: in the period from 1885 to 1899, the annual number of NCOs promoted as second lieutenants in the cavalry, infantry, artillery, engineers and the Army Service Corps ranged from a low of nine in 1897 to a maximum of forty-one in 1888. Even during the Second Boer War, the largest annual intake was only forty-eight in 1900. The lack of numbers did not reflect any lack of aptitude; well acquainted with the habits and trickery of the private soldier, the NCOs were unlikely to be deceived by any malingering, and those who were former colour-sergeants understood the intricacies of regimental accounting. Yet their prospects were blighted by a deeply rooted prejudice against promotion from the ranks. The former NCO, argued General Charles Philip de Ainslie, could perform the duties of an officer, but he would always lack the necessary instincts: 'although it is certain that the mere fact of being an officer does, in a sense, make a man a gentleman, it is the individual born, educated, and possessing the innate feelings of one that is required . . .'.[24] In short, the officer gentleman tradition remained pervasive.

An officer had to act in accordance with the norms of gentlemanly behaviour, including an emphasis on honour, integrity and courage, a capacity for generosity and unselfishness, and a conformity with the etiquette, dress and deportment of persons in polite society. An officer had to uphold these standards of behaviour to maintain the harmony and concord of the officers' mess and to earn the respect and obedience of the rank and file. Indeed, the ranks were thought to dislike being officered by promoted NCOs, purportedly because they preferred the leadership of their social superiors and resented those with ambitions above their station. If impossible to prove, these assumptions may have had some plausibility, especially if the promoted rankers proved to be stricter disciplinarians than the officers from Sandhurst. Whether true or not, these assertions were often repeated: 'the British soldier', wrote Wolseley, 'has always evinced an aversion to the men of his own class who had become officers . . . .'[25]

Accordingly, promotion from the ranks was never really encouraged. The financial impediments were neither removed nor substantially alleviated. When William Robertson sought a commission in the late 1880s, he reckoned that a cavalry officer could not live in his regiment without a private income of £300 a year (but the actual sum may have been much larger – in 1902, a Select Committee estimated that the annual expenses of dining in the mess, sport, social recreation and the constant moving of army life presumed a private income of £100 to £150 for an infantry officer and of £600 to £700 for a cavalry officer).[26] As a promoted ranker, Robertson received an outfit allowance of £150 and immediately transferred to the Indian service, where the allowances were more generous and the costs were less. More intangible but just as serious were the social discomforts which attended promotion. Although some of those promoted were gentlemen rankers (individuals who had often enlisted in the hope of obtaining a commission, having failed to secure one by the normal methods), many like Robertson were not. Even if they encountered a cordial reception and correct behaviour when they entered the officers' mess, they could not easily bridge the social gulf which divided them from their fellow subalterns. As Robertson's biographer notes, 'A true ranker could never disguise his origin. He was continually being given away by his accent, tastes, habits, jokes, relations, friends (or the lack of them), enforced parsimony, or whatever.'[27]

The army had effectively preserved its social homogeneity, partly by the increasing dependence upon the commissioning of ex-public schoolboys and partly by the monetary qualifications for military service. Parental support and a private income were essential for anyone who aspired to enter a home-based regiment. Although these requirements pertained in other nineteenth-century professions, the scale and duration of the necessary support were exceptional in the army. Parents had to pay some £175 per annum to cover the full fees and uniform at Sandhurst (part of which was returned to the cadet as pay to meet his daily expenses). On joining his regiment, each subaltern had to provide his own uniform, cases, furniture, mufti, servant's outfit and incoming mess contribution. Whereas these items cost about £200 for an infantry officer, the more expensive uniform, saddlery, mufti and the purchase of two chargers required an expenditure of £600 or even of £1,000 for a cavalry officer, depending on the customs of his regiment. Thereafter the annual expenses of dining and entertaining in the mess, sport, social entertainment, the upkeep of the regimental band, the purchasing of silver for the mess (upon occasions such as promotion, marriage and the departure of officers from the battalion) and the constant moving of army life presumed a substantial private income.[28]

Officers could not possibly meet these expenses from their pay, which was based upon rates established in 1806. These rates ranged from 5s 3d a day for an ensign or later for a second lieutenant to 17s a day for a lieutenant-colonel (with an extra 3s a day if the latter commanded a regiment). The Guards received more generous rates of pay, especially from the rank of captain upwards (a lieutenant-colonel in the Foot Guards received £1 6s 9d per day). Cavalry rates of pay were also slightly higher than those of the infantry, but the differential narrowed considerably when cavalry rates were reduced following the abolition of the forage stoppage in 1881 (ranging thereafter from 6s 8d a day for second lieutenants to £1 1s 6d a day for a lieutenant-colonel). Some officers received extra allowances – another 1s a day for lieutenants after seven years' service, an allowance for adjutants, a contingent allowance for the captains of companies, 'working pay' for the task of superintending working parties, a 'non-effective' allowance of about £20 per annum for the senior lieutenant-colonel and major of a regiment, and distinguished service pay. There were additional allowances for messing, for soldier servants, and for living out (a 'fuel and light and lodging allowance'), awards for linguistic proficiency, opportunities for extra remuneration on some campaigns (such as the 3s a day 'Khedival allowance' earned in the Sudan), and the more generous pay and allowances to be gained by service in India and the colonies. Officers from less wealthy or only marginally wealthy backgrounds normally sought service in India, where they could enjoy the sport, social life and the experience of practical soldiering at much less cost. India acted as a syphon, removing a large pool of potential discontent from the regimental messes in Britain. As Wolseley snobbishly observed,

The great bulk of the young men who then usually went to India were socially not of a high order. Of course, though very poor, many were sons of old officers of good families, whose poverty compelled their sons to serve in India, if serve they would in the Army. But the great bulk of those I met at Chatham, and afterwards in India and Burmah, at that time [the 1850s], struck me, I remember, as wanting in good breeding and all seemed badly educated.[29]

All officers were expected to comply with the standards and customs of their regiment and its mess. Whereas some like Robertson constantly economised to bear their share of the regimental expenses (in his case, 'drinking water . . . when others were drinking champagne'), others like Lord Gleichen happily went into debt: 'it never worried me for a subaltern's views on the subject of cash are always pleasantly buoyant'.[30] Those who failed to match the spending of their brother officers, or offended against the etiquette of the mess, risked the possibility of social ostracism and flagrant bullying: some were driven from the regiment. 'Officers,' wrote Captain W.E. Cairnes, 'have lived in the 10th [Hussars] with an allowance of only £500 a year in addition to their pay, but they have rarely lasted long . . .'.[31] Occasionally the ragging was so vicious, notably in the cases of Second Lieutenants Bruce and Hodge, that complaints were made in Parliament. These officers had been gazetted into the 4th Hussars in the 1890s, with private incomes of £500 and £300 respectively, but were informed that these incomes were quite inadequate. They were then bullied for over two months, subjected to a remorseless boycott, and forced to leave the regiment, with Hodge requiring medical treatment for a period of three months thereafter. Of more significance than the occurrence of hazing, which was a fairly prevalent pastime in Victorian public schools, was the implicit connivance of some senior officers. Wolseley even condoned such behaviour in his memoirs. He recalled how he had participated, as a subaltern, in the bullying of four ensigns who had joined his regiment from the Militia in the 1850s. These ensigns, he noted, 'had practically no pretensions to the rank of gentlemen'; they would have been 'absolutely useless as officers, and we soon got rid of them'.[32]

Once commissioned, subalterns entered the cavalry and infantry as an ensign or cornet until 1871, as a sub-lieutenant until 1877, and as a second lieutenant thereafter. On account of their longer courses at Woolwich, the young gunner or sapper officer joined his corps with the rank of lieutenant antedated by six months (hence in the defence of Rorke's Drift Lieutenant Chard, RE, assumed command over Lieutenant Bromhead of the 2nd Battalion, 24th Foot, despite Bromhead's extra one year's service). After the reduction in the length of course at Woolwich (1878) the antedation was removed, and, in 1887, the rank of second lieutenant was restored to graduates of the academy.[33]

Second lieutenants underwent a period of training on joining their regiment or corps (and in the cavalry this involved six months' arduous instruction as a 'recruit officer', being drilled in the saddle and afoot on the same basis as the troopers). Henceforth, unless compelled by the shortage of officers to assume the command of a company prematurely (as sometimes happened), they learnt about the life and organisation of their units until promoted to the rank of lieutenant, becoming the second-in-command in one of the eight companies commanded by captains. The commanding officer chose one lieutenant to serve as the adjutant and so undertake some of the busiest and most responsible duties in the battery or battalion. The adjutant had to superintend the pre-breakfast drilling of recruits and guard mounting, present delinquents to the commanding officer, prepare regimental orders as directed by the commanding officer, arrange the details of duty for the following day, attend courts-martial, check the accuracy of the monthly returns, attend the evening parade, and write any letters required by the commanding officer.

The other captains and lieutenants had less demanding duties (except in the artillery, where the battery organisation gave each subaltern specific responsibilities). Captains had a nominal responsibility for the guards, drills and inspections of their companies. They often supervised the management of canteens, shops and libraries, participated in boards of examination, courts of inquiry and courts-martial, and, above all, had to oversee the company accounts (replacing any losses caused by deserters or by the faulty accounting of their pay-sergeants). Though numerous, these tasks hardly consumed all the time and energies of captains and their seconds-in-command. Lord Gleichen, who joined the Grenadier Guards in 1881, recalled that 'we thought ourselves badly used if (except on guard days) we did not find ourselves free by luncheon time'. His fellow officers expected six months' leave and sometimes got eight, and the battalion only drilled seriously from the middle of March to the middle of July.[34] J.F.C. Fuller had similar memories: 'it was a delightful life, mostly duck shooting and hunting in the winter, and tennis and cricket in the summer'.[35]

Several factors accounted for the perfunctory nature of an officer's regimental training and for his nominal duties as a subaltern. First, some officers served in bases like Gibraltar, Bermuda, Malta or Aden where the lack of ground and/or the climatic conditions militated against practical training. Many others began their duties in urban barracks in the United Kingdom, where the training facilities were unduly cramped or lacked basic requirements. Secondly, captains tended to become preoccupied with or diverted by various administrative tasks and rarely concentrated upon the training of their junior officers. The frequent interruptions of peacetime service undermined any continuity of instruction within the battalions. Thirdly, military training within the home-based battalions was all too often artificial, as the companies were depleted by the annual provision of drafts and by the employment of men in fatigues, working parties, and non-military duties such as those of clerks, orderlies, grooms, groundsmen, and waiters in canteens and regimental institutes. In effect, officers rarely saw the men for whom they were responsible, and, as a consequence, specialists undertook most of the training. The adjutant, assisted by the sergeant-major, taught drill; the musketry instructor taught rifle-shooting or at least ensured that the regulation number of rounds were fired; and the riding master taught riding in the mounted corps. Finally, the young officers were largely unprepared for the financial responsibilities of company command. Uninstructed in the tasks of keeping battery or company accounts or in the monitoring of clothing accounts or in the preparation of pay lists, they all too often depended upon the skills of their colour-sergeants and pay-sergeants. In these circumstances, argued Sir Evelyn Wood, military training was 'absolutely impossible'. The Akers-Douglas Committee agreed with the Adjutant-General; the system, it affirmed, had prevented young officers from developing the 'habit of promptly assuming the initiative' and had stifled their 'readiness to accept responsibility'.[36]

Second lieutenants still had to pass formal examinations before they could be considered for promotion to the rank of lieutenant, and later to captain. The first examination, known as A and B, on drill and interior economy, was none too demanding. The district commanding officer appointed a board of three officers from the candidate's garrison to prepare the questions, which normally covered the rudiments of drill and regimental duties. Few officers experienced any difficulty with this examination, but several years later many returned to their crammers to prepare for examinations C, D and G on military law, tactics, military topography, field fortification and military administration. These examinations, which officers had to pass before they could be promoted to the rank of captain, were held twice yearly at the principal military stations. They were conducted by a board of officers, presided over by a field officer, with two or more field officers or captains chosen from regiments other than those of the candidates. The written papers were prepared and marked by the department of the Director-General of Military Education, but parts of the examination were conducted *viva voce* and with practical work in the field. Even so, the Akers-Douglas Committee felt that the examination concentrated excessively upon testing the candidate's knowledge of formulae, of the precise number of stores required to carry out certain works, and of various data which could be memorised from textbooks rather than examining how these principles could be applied in practice.[37]

More significantly, the examinations hardly furnished any incentive for the officer to study his profession on a serious and sustained basis. Passing the examinations merely established an eligibility for promotion, but, in the post-purchase army, promotion was normally on the basis of seniority, tempered by the rejection of the unfit. The Duke of Cambridge would not countenance promotion on the basis of merit, arguing that he could not adjudicate between the 6,000 confidential reports annually submitted by commanding officers. He did not believe that comparisons could be made between the service of officers in the field in India or elsewhere and those who undertook garrison duties at home or in the West Indies. He feared, too, that he would undermine regimental *esprit de corps* if he used the confidential reports to 'pass over' certain officers, as distinct from identifying those who were utterly inefficient in the hope of persuading them to retire. He disparaged any notion that promotion should be based upon the results of competitive examination, and doubted that the best officers – even for staff duties – were necessarily obtained from the graduates of the Staff College (indeed, these officers were not guaranteed junior staff appointments). The Duke maintained that 'a man who will stick to his regiment will learn his profession in that regiment much better than in any college. I would prefer selecting a man even for the staff from the best regimental officers in the whole army.'[38]

The Duke's attitude to promotion, and his hostility to the concept of a General Staff, provided scant encouragement for the Staff College, which had been founded at Camberley in 1858. By 1870 the college was languishing, without much appeal for the more able and ambitious junior officer. Those who aspired to undertake the two-year course generally received little encouragement from their regiments: indeed, those aspirants were widely regarded as 'slackers' who wished to evade their regimental duties, with a view to spending an idle two years at college, followed by choice staff appointments.[39]

Nevertheless, the reputation of the college improved, partly on account of some outstanding appointments to the Camberley staff. Sir Edward Hamley, who was Commandant from 1870 to 1877, infused a new spirit into the College. As the author of the widely acclaimed *The Operations of War*, he gave the college some prestige and credibility within the army. He used an increased training grant, secured by Cardwell, to extend the scope of the outdoor exercises, especially in reconnaissance and sketching. He reduced the emphasis on mathematics and on personal competition in the final examinations, and lessened the parochial atmosphere by enabling six officers from the Indian Army to attend the course. Another considerable influence was Colonel J.F. Maurice, who was the Professor of Military Art and History at the college in the later 1880s. A conscientious and innovative teacher, if notoriously absentminded, he continued Hamley's battlefield tours of western Europe and enabled his students to meet foreign officers.[40]

The number of officers who attended the college significantly increased, too. In 1870 the establishment numbered only forty, with twenty admitted each year, purely on the basis of their examination results, with only one student coming from a regiment in any one year. The establishment rose to forty-eight in 1884 and to sixty-four in 1886. By increasing the numbers and by altering the rules on admission (to include Indian Army officers, more than one entrant from a regiment, and four entrants nominated by the Commander-in-Chief), the army widened its search for the best staff material. Yet anomalies persisted in the selection process and in the final examinations. The selection system severely restricted the intake from the scientific corps, reserving a mere six places for their officers compared with eighteen places for the cavalry and infantry. Although some restriction was probably necessary to prevent a monopoly of the college by the gunners and sappers, the chosen ratio regularly ensured that some of their officers were rejected despite excellent examination results, while less able officers gained admission from the infantry and cavalry, including some who had actually failed the examination. Having gained entry, however, officers did not have to attend the course to pass the terminal examination and gain a 'p.s.c.' (passed Staff College). They missed thereby all the benefits of the college experience, which Robertson described as 'a feeling of self-reliance', 'a smartening friction with other brains', rubbing shoulders with officers of 'their own standing' from other arms and from overseas, and learning the same principles of strategy and tactics and the same methods of military administration.[41] Notwithstanding the anomalies of selection and examination, the reputation of the Staff College improved, not least because Wolseley favoured p.s.c.s in his staff appointments. Several prominent members of the 'Ashanti ring', including Colley, Wood, Buller and Maurice, were recent graduates of Camberley, and, in the Egyptian campaign of 1882, thirty-four Camberley men held staff appointments. If these officers, as members of Wolseley's 'ring', earned a degree of resentment within the army, their appointments exemplified the career opportunities which could be pursued by Staff College graduates. Admittedly Wolseley, as a field commander, had a distinctly limited view of staff duties. He relied largely upon his own judgement and initiative, especially in the planning of campaigns and in the preparation of operations. He looked to his staff to provide administrative support in his headquarters, to furnish information on local intelligence and reconnaissance, and to supervise the vital matters of communications and supply. He consulted close subordinates, like Wood, Buller and Sir Herbert Stewart, but never really encouraged initiative in a 'chief of staff'. Nevertheless, he promoted Camberley by his appointments and by encouraging young officers to compete for the college; he also urged the appointment of first class Commandants and staff.[42]

Two of Wolseley's protégés had a profound influence upon the Staff College in the 1890s, namely his former staff officer, Colonel H.J.T. Hildyard (Commandant, 1893–98) and Colonel G.F.R. Henderson, the author of *Campaign of Fredericksburg*, who succeeded Maurice as Professor of Military Art and History. Hildyard sought to make the course more practical and to undermine the penchant for cramming by abolishing the final examination. He preferred to classify students by their work during the course and by the assessments of their instructors. Henderson was particularly influential as a teacher, partly on account of his zeal and thoroughness, and partly on account of an approach which was both analytical and fundamentally practical. His students, wrote Jay Luvaas,

found themselves expected to replace the actors, to work out the operations step by step with map and compass, to investigate the reasons behind each decision, to ascertain the relative importance of moral and physical factors, and to deduce the principles on which the generals had acted.[43]

As the reputation of the college improved in the 1890s, it attracted some of the more talented and ambitious officers, many of whom would obtain field commands in South Africa and later the command of armies, corps and divisions in the First World War. The illustrious roll of graduates included Spencer Ewart, Henry Wilson, Henry Rawlinson, John Cowans, Edmund Allenby, Douglas Haig, James Edmonds, William Robertson and Hubert Gough. Their college experience had shortcomings. The absence of officers from the Royal Navy and the dominions hardly enhanced the study of combined operations and the problems of imperial defence. The small staff (one Commandant, six instructors and two civilians) was barely sufficient to supervise the work of sixty-four students, especially if some members were less industrious than others. Some instructors, too, lacked any staff experience, and the recruitment of suitably qualified instructors remained a difficulty. The course itself was limited in scope (apart from the tours of Continental battlefields and many outside tasks, such as making sketch maps, digging trenches, erecting wires, and small-scale tactical activities, there were few staff tours or war games and no preparation for undertaking large-scale operations). Finally, the Staff College produced only thirty-two graduates per annum, so ensuring that a large proportion of the staff appointments in peace, and even more in war, would be filled by regimental officers, lacking both the training and the experience of a college education.[44]

This approach to staff duties aroused less controversy in the 1890s than it would do subsequently, because the army never anticipated that it would be sent to fight in a large-scale, Continental conflict or even in a protracted war in South Africa. Wolseley recognised that officers had to study the history of recent wars and to train for wars under modern conditions. He believed, nonetheless, that they would only develop the necessary self-reliance if they possessed the appropriate character and learnt their profession in the field. Their qualities of command, he argued, derived from their noble and manly qualities as gentlemen, from their innate love of sport and adventure, and their 'varied experience and frequent practice in war'. The 'British officer', he contended, 'is by birth and education the natural leader of the British private . . .'.[45]

The attitudes of officers towards their men varied considerably. On the one hand, Sergeant Wyndham complained that certain officers knew nothing of their men, rarely came in contact with them, and were indifferent towards their wants.[46] Officer neglect was quite plausible, since officers enjoyed lengthy periods of leave and did not mix with their men other than on special or festive occasions. On the other hand, regimental officers had pioneered the establishment of libraries and savings banks for the other ranks, and many regiments had charities to provide clothing for the children of private soldiers or to support their widows. Officers' wives, taking their cue from the colonel's lady, played a vital role in sustaining these benevolent traditions. They were expected to visit the married quarters, collect money for, and show a general interest in, the welfare of the rankers' wives. Officers helped to launch the National Association for the Employment of Reserve and Discharged Soldiers (1885) and the Army Temperance Association (1893). Wolseley, Buller and Roberts among others consistently advocated improvements in the conditions of service at home and abroad. They expressed concern about the pay, food, clothing and living conditions of the ranks before a succession of Select Committees and Royal Commissions.

Pragmatism and paternalism underpinned this concern. More and more officers adopted an enlightened approach towards man-management, partly because they had to do so after the abolition of flogging, partly because they wished to do so. Wolseley was frankly pragmatic; he doubted that the army could attract the necessary recruits without an increase in pay and improved conditions of service. Roberts agreed that a voluntary army could not compete for recruits in the labour market unless the men were dealt with fairly and honestly, with due attention to their wants and grievances.[47] Paternalism, though, was increasingly in vogue. The concept of a gentleman had changed during the nineteenth century, with the suppression of the duel and the greater emphasis upon Christian virtues – the unselfishness, thoughtfulness and sense of *noblesse oblige* which were intrinsic aspects of Matthew Arnold's ideal of a Christian gentleman. By accepting the values which were implicit in *noblesse oblige*, many officers recognised, perhaps more conspicuously than in former years, their paternalistic responsibilities towards the other ranks. There were also extremely devout officers, such as Sir Hope Grant and Charles 'Chinese' Gordon, who never concealed their deeply held religious convictions. If outward displays of religious zeal were still considered eccentric, that eccentricity was generally tolerated. In the 1870s, for example, Sir Hope Grant used to convene meetings of soldiers with the aim of inculcating notions of temperance, thrift and a few biblical precepts.[48]

Paternalism of course had not been unknown in the early nineteenth century, when officers like the Duke of York (Commander-in-Chief, 1789–1809 and 1811–27) and Sir Charles Napier had cared deeply about their men. If there was a change in this respect latterly, it was largely a matter of degree; indeed, among the officers generally, the elements of continuity were probably more apparent than the signs of radical change. Despite the abolition of purchase, officers came predominantly from the same groups in society, with their social homogeneity increasingly reflecting a public school education and the possession of private means. They cleaved to their honorific and gentlemanly code of values, indulged their passion for sports, especially field sports, and preserved the customs, traditions and social life within the mess. There were some changes in their educational opportunities, at least for the small minority who entered Camberley in the 1890s, and some reflection of the changes in attitudes within society, including more evidence of paternalism. By promoting a greater awareness and concern about the conditions of service endured by the rank and file, officers drew attention to the many difficulties which bedevilled the recruitment of a volunteer army.

Notes

1   *Report of the Royal Commission on Army Promotion and Retirement; together with minutes of evidence, appendix, and index,* hereafter referred to as the *Penzance Report,* C. 1569 (1876), XV, pp.viii, 227–34.

2   *Ibid.,* pp.xi, xxviii, xxxi.

3   *Ibid.,* pp.xvii–xxii, xxv–xxviii, xli.

4   *Parl. Deb.,* Third Ser., Vol.262 (24 June 1881), col.1232.

5   *Revised Memorandum showing the Principal Changes in Army Organisation, etc., intended to take Effect from 1st July 1881,* C. 2922 (1881), LVIII, pp.8–10.

6   Lt.-Col. C. à Court Repington, *Vestigia* (Constable; London, 1919), p.37; Gen. Sir J. Adye, *Recollections of a Military Life* (Smith Elder; London, 1895), pp.324–8; Anglesey, *A History of the British Cavalry 1816–1919,* Vol.3, p.92; Keegan, 'Regimental Ideology', p.10.

7   Field-Marshal Viscount Wolseley, *The Story of a Soldier's Life,* 2 Vols. (Constable; London, 1903), Vol.1, p.5; General Sir H. Gough, *Soldiering on* (Morrison & Gibb; Edinburgh, 1954), p.27; Sir H. Smith-Dorrien, *Memories of Forty-eight Years' Service* (John Murray; London, 1925), p.2; I. Hamilton, *Happy Warrior: A Life of General Sir Ian Hamilton* (Cassell; London, 1966), p.11.

8   Field-Marshal Earl Roberts, *Letters written during the Indian Mutiny* (Macmillan; London, 1924), p.xvii; R. Holmes, *The Little Field-Marshal: Sir John French* (Jonathan Cape; London, 1981), p.17.

9   Earl of Dundonald, *My Army Life* (E. Arnold; London, 1926), p.4.

10   J. Connell, *Wavell: Scholar and Soldier* (Collins; London, 1964), p.34.

11   Susan Countess of Malmesbury, *The Life of Major-General Sir John Ardagh* (John Murray; London, 1909), pp.1 and 4–5; W. Hillcourt, *Baden-Powell: The Two Lives of a Hero* (Heinemann; London, 1964), pp.32–4; Gen. Sir A. Wavell, *Allenby: A Study in Greatness* (Harrap; London, 1940), p.35; W.S. Churchill, *My Early Life* (Thornton Butterworth; London, 1930), p.19.

12   G. Harries-Jenkins, *The Army in Victorian Society* (Routledge & Kegan Paul; London, 1977), pp.24–5.

13   Wavell, *Allenby: A Study in Greatness*, p.35.

14   Lt. E. Longueville, diary, Longueville Mss., NAM, 7711–113, appendix.

15   A.H.H. MacLean, *Public Schools and the War in South Africa* (Stanford; London, 1902), p.12; see also C.B. Otley, 'The Educational Background of British Army Officers', *Sociology*, Vol.7, no.2 (1973), pp.191–209.

16   G. Best, 'Militarism and the Victorian Public School', in B. Simon and I. Bradley (eds.), *The Victorian Public School* (Gill & Macmillan; London, 1975), p.143; see also Harries-Jenkins, *The Army in Victorian Society*, p.148.

17   *First Report of the Royal Commission appointed to inquire into the Present State of Military Education and into the Training of Candidates for Commissions in the Army*, C. 4221 (1868–69), XXII, pp.14–17; *Minutes of Evidence taken before the Royal Commission appointed to inquire into the Present State of Military Education and into the Training of Candidates for Commissions in the Army; with appendix*, C. 25 (1870), XXIV, pp.19, 101, 124, 178, 186, 230.

18   Brigadier Sir J. Smyth, *Sandhurst: The History of the Royal Military Academy, Woolwich, the Royal Military College, Sandhurst, and the Royal Military Academy Sandhurst 1741–1961* (Weidenfeld & Nicolson; London, 1961), pp.95–101, 115–18; H. Thomas, *Sandhurst* (Hutchinson; London, 1961), pp.124–7; *Report of the Committee appointed to consider the Education and Training of Officers of the Army*, hereafter referred to as the *Akers-Douglas Report*, Cd. 982 (1902), X, p.23.

19   Goodenough and Dalton, *The Army Book for the British Empire*, pp.225, 240, 316, 425.

20   C.B. Otley 'The Social Origins of British Army Officers', *Sociological Review*, Vol.18 (July 1970), pp.213–39; Spiers, *The Army and Society*, pp.6–7; *Akers-Douglas Report*, pp.86, 112.

21   Repington, *Vestigia*, pp.38–9; Churchill, *My Early Life*, pp.43–5; Maj.-Gen. J.F.C. Fuller, *Memoirs of an Unconventional Soldier* (Nicholson & Watson; London, 1936), pp.5–6.

22   *Akers-Douglas Report*, pp.15, 20–3, 29.

23 *Ibid.*, pp.9–12, appendices XX, XXV, and XXXVII, pp.84, 105 and 124–5; Harries-Jenkins, *The Army in Victorian Society*, pp.153–4.
24 Gen. C.P. de Ainslie, *Life as I have found it* (Blackwood; Edinburgh, 1883), pp.488–9; *Return as to the Number of Commissions granted during each of the Years 1885 to 1913 inclusive (in continuation of No.525 of 1912)*, No.224 (1914), LI; H. Wyndham, *The Queen's Service* (Heinemann; London, 1899), pp.252–3.
25 Viscount Wolseley, 'The Army', in T.H. Ward (ed.), *The Reign of Queen Victoria*, 2 Vols. (Smith, Elder & Co.; London, 1887), Vol.1, p.167.
26 Field-Marshal Sir W. Robertson, *From Private to Field-Marshal* (Constable; London, 1921), p.30; *Report of the Committee appointed by the Secretary of State to enquire into the Nature of the Expenses incurred by Officers of the Army*, hereafter referred to as the *Stanley Report*, Cd. 1,421 (1903), X, pp.7–8.
27 V. Bonham Carter, *Soldier True: The Life and Times of Field-Marshal Sir William Robertson, 1860–1933* (Muller; London, 1963), p.30.
28 *Stanley Report*, pp.7–8, 25; A British Officer, *Social Life in the British Army* (John Long; London, 1900), pp.9–10.
29 Wolseley, *The Story of a Soldier's Life*, Vol.1, p.10; for data on the costs of an officer's life-style, see D.M. Henderson, *Highland Soldier: A Social Study of the Highland Regiments, 1820–1920* (John Donald; Edinburgh, 1989), pp.143–51; Anglesey, *A History of the British Cavalry 1816 to 1919*, Vol.3, pp.90–1; P. Mason, *A Matter of Honour: An Account of the Indian Army its Officers and Men* (Jonathan Cape; London, 1974), pp.372–3; *Royal Warrant 1878 Parts 1 and 2 Pay and Non-effective Pay*, pp.69–71, 89–99.
30 Robertson, *From Private to Field-Marshal*, p.42; Lord E. Gleichen, *A Guardsman's memories* (Blackwood; London, 1932), p.47.
31 A British Officer, *Social Life in the British Army*, p.36.
32 Wolseley, *The Story of a Soldier's Life*, Vol.1, p.226; *Parl. Deb.*, Fourth Ser., Vol.41 (19 June 1896), cols.1481–4.
33 Callwell and Headlam, *The History of the Royal Artillery*, Vol.1, pp.69–70, 98–9.
34 Gleichen, *A Guardsman's Memories*, p.17; Churchill, *My Early Life*, p.63; Henderson, *Highland Soldier*, pp.84–5; Sir C. Fortescue-Brickdale (ed.), *Major-General Sir Henry Hallam Parr: Recollections and Correspondence* (Fisher Unwin; London, 1917), p.66; Gen. Sir H.E. Wood, qs.50 and 54, Maj.-Gen. Sir C. Grove, q.635, Col. G.R. Challenor, q.2003 and Lt.-Col. G.R. Henderson, q.6415 evidence before the *Akers-Douglas Committee*, Cd. 983 (1902), X, pp.4, 27, 78 and 239.
35 Maj.-Gen. J.F.C. Fuller, *The Army in my Time* (Rich & Cowan; London, 1935), p.62.
36 *Akers-Douglas Report*, p.30; Wood, qs.51–61, Grove, qs.635 and 641, Challenor, q.2003, Col. H. Mends, qs.2180–7, Henderson, qs.6412–15 evidence before the *Akers-Douglas Committee*, pp.4, 27, 78, 84, 239.
37 *Akers-Douglas Report*, pp.30–1; Anglesey, *A History of the British Cavalry 1816 to 1919*, Vol.3, pp.96–7.

38 Cambridge, qs.6–7, 21–2, 33–7, 54–60, 69–70, 92, 106, 110, 209, 214 evidence appended to the *Penzance Report*, pp.21–7, 33.

39 Gleichen, *A Guardsman's Memories*, p.110; Gen. Sir I. Hamilton, *Listening for the Drums* (Faber & Faber; London, 1944), pp.119–20; B. Gardner, *Allenby* (Cassell; London, 1965), p.14.

40 B. Bond, *The Victorian Army and the Staff College 1854–1914* (Eyre Methuen; London, 1972), pp.132–3, 136–7.

41 Robertson, *From Private to Field-Marshal*, pp.88–9; Bond, *The Victorian Army and the Staff College*, pp. 133, 138–9.

42 *Ibid.*, pp.128–31; Maj.-Gen. Sir J. Adye, *Soldiers and Others I have known* (H.Jenkins; London, 1925), p.136; Sir G. Aston, *Memories of a Marine* (John Murray; London, 1919), p.208.

43 Luvaas, *The Education of an Army*, p.242; Brev. Major A.R. Godwin-Austen, *The Staff and the Staff College* (Constable; London, 1927), p.231; Bond, *The Victorian Army and the Staff College*, pp.154–8.

44 Bond, *The Victorian Army and the Staff College*, pp.167–9, 176–7.

45 General Viscount Wolseley, 'The Standing Army of Great Britain', *Harper's New Monthly Magazine* (European edition), Vol.LXXX (February 1890), pp.331–47 and 'The Army', pp.167 and 186.

46 Wyndham, *The Queen's Service*, p.152.

47 Wolseley, qs.4469 and 4480 evidence appended to the *Wantage Report*, pp.158–9; Lt.-Gen. Sir F.S. Roberts, 'Free Trade in the Army', *Nineteenth Century*, Vol.15, (1884), pp.1054–74.

48 H. Knollys (ed.), *Life of General Sir Hope Grant*, 2 Vols. (Blackwood; London, 1884), Vol.2, p.317; W.L. Burn, *The Age of Equipoise* (Allen & Unwin; London, 1964), pp.259–60.

5

The rank and file

Recruiting sufficient men by voluntary enlistment to offset the annual wastage caused by deaths, discharges, desertion and other causes was a perennial problem for the late Victorian army. It was exacerbated by the periodic expansions of Britain's overseas commitments and by the urgency with which troops were required for colonial campaigns. It had ramifications throughout the service, impinging directly upon the strength and effectiveness of the home-based battalions and upon their ability to supply sufficient drafts for linked battalions overseas. Sustaining the flow of recruits, and hopefully improving their quality, became the aim of many reformers and several Secretaries of State. Reformers described improvements in pay and changes in the terms and conditions of service as not only intrinsically worthwhile but also as inducements which might enhance the appeal of service life. Although the authorities proved unwilling to concede a substantial increase in the basic rates of pay, they implemented many reforms in the terms and conditions of service. Nevertheless, shortfalls in recruiting constantly recurred, indicating the intractability of the problem and the inherent difficulty of persuading men to join the army.

Long service enlistment, even though the initial term was reduced to twelve years after 1847, had rarely produced sufficient recruits. The prospect of spending a protracted period of service overseas had only a limited appeal, and, by the 1860s, the effective strength of the army was steadily falling (see Table 4). Moreover, long service precluded the creation of a Reserve of trained ex-regulars, a requirement underlined by the reorganisation of Continental armies, particularly Prussia's. When Cardwell addressed these problems in 1870, shortening the terms of enlistment for the infantry of the line

Table 4 *Manpower requirements for the rank and file, 1868–98*

Year	Effective strength on 1 Jan.	Establishments on 1 Jan.	Increase				Decrease			
			Recruits	From desertion	Other sources	Total increase	Dead	Discharge including reserves	Desertion and other causes	Total decrease
1868	172,014	172,633	17,060	1,221	–	18,281	2,685	16,419	3,431	22,535
1872	166,985	170,029	17,791	1,855	20	19,666	2,546	11,570	6,602	20,718
1876	159,640	160,537	29,370	2,063	21	31,454	1,998	16,921	6,516	25,435
1880	167,909	164,115	25,622	1,557	3	27,182	3,186	20,802	5,903	25,435
1884	158,029	165,386	35,653	1,568	1,415*	38,636	1,521	24,874	4,762	31,157
1888	186,839	186,180	25,153	1,737	29	26,919	1,852	20,882	4,484	27,218
1892	186,447	191,348	41,659	1,944	61	43,664	1,859	30,261	5,424	37,544
1896	195,980	192,054	28,532	1,533	57	30,122	1,769	26,021	3,637	31,427
1898	194,705	195,304	40,729	1,789	4,578*	47,096	2,578	29,892	4,646	37,116

* From Army Reserve.

Sources: *General Annual Returns of the British Army . . .*, C. 3083 (1881), LVIII, p.10 and C. 9426 (1899), LIII, p.10.

to six years with the Colours, followed by six years in the Reserve, he accelerated the turnover of men and set new targets for the recruiting process. He optimistically reckoned that an annual intake of 32,000 recruits would replace each year's wastage and produce a Reserve of 178,000 men by 1883.[1]

Although there was a substantial increase in the numbers enlisted over the next thirty years, recruiting seldom met its annual targets. From the sample examined in Table 4, the effective strength of the army at the end of each year only reached the establishment voted by Parliament on three out of nine years. Even in these years, the intake of recruits often failed to replace the annual wastage from deaths, discharges, desertion and other causes. It had to be bolstered by returning deserters and by extraordinary intakes from the Army and Militia Reserve. Wastage remained substantial throughout this period – a problem compounded, after 1876, by the effects of short service enlistments. Admittedly, the short service men who left the Colours hardly constituted a net loss to the service; they formed an Army Reserve which numbered nearly 80,000 men by 1899, and they proved their worth in the Second South African War and later in the First World War. In the short term, however, the annual transfer of trained soldiers placed an additional strain on the home-based battalions, many of which were largely composed of raw recruits. Recruitment never fully alleviated this strain, and the authorities had to adopt various expedients to bolster the annual intake.

There were three main expedients. In the first place, the War Office sometimes offered bounties to tempt soldiers into extending their service with the Colours. The War Office deprecated any recourse to bounties (it had abolished enlistment bounties in 1870), and, in trying to induce re-engagements, disliked nullifying the principle of short service. Yet it periodically did so; in 1883 it offered bounties of £2 to soldiers due to return home from India to extend their service to twelve years with the Colours, and later permitted all men in the line to extend their service to twelve years, whereupon they could re-engage and complete twenty-one years' service with a pension, provided that they had good characters.[2] Such temporary palliatives had little effect (Table 5) as most men who had enlisted for short service proved reluctant to serve for more than the minimum term.

A less expensive expedient was the lowering of the minimum physical standards required of new recruits. Altering the physical standards was a traditional ploy; whenever the authorities needed

Table 5   *The number of men re-engaging for a second period of service with the Colours, 1875–98*

Year	After 6 years' service	After 7–10 years' service	After 11 years' service	After discharge	Total	Percentage of re-engagements to number of men serving
1875	109	2,762	202	55	3,128	1·7
1879*	14	1,065	792	8	1,879	1·0
1883	–	207	1,381	–	1,588	0·8
1885	–	207	1,357	–	1,564	0·8
1887	–	397	1,294	–	1,691	0·8
1891	–	498	1,347	–	1,845	0·9
1895	–	894	2,053	–	2,947	1·3
1898	–	931	2,050	–	2,981	1·4

* Re-engagements after discharge were discontinued
Sources: *General Annual Returns of the British Army* . . ., C. 6196 (1890), XLIII, pp.10, 31; C. 9426 (1899), LIII, pp.8, 33.

fewer recruits or anticipated a buoyant recruiting season they raised standards, when they desperately needed more recruits they lowered standards. In May 1869, after the relatively buoyant recruiting of the previous two years, the minimum height was set at five feet six inches, but, as short service failed to produce the extra recruits, the standard was promptly reduced to five feet four inches in August 1870. Short service had a limited appeal; it enabled the War Office to raise the minimum age from seventeen to eighteen years in 1871 and to raise the standard of height by another inch. The War Office periodically altered these standards thereafter. It experimented with a recruiting age band of nineteen to twenty-five years from 1881 to 1883 before restoring eighteen to twenty-five years. It frequently changed the standards of height, sometimes raising them to five feet six inches for infantry recruits but more often lowering them (from 1883 to 1889 the standard was only five feet three inches, from 1889 to 1897 it was five feet four inches, and from 1897 it fell again, plummeting to five feet three inches in 1900). In 1884 the authorities stipulated that the minimum weight should be 115 lb and that the minimum chest measurement for recruits under five feet six inches in height should be thirty-three inches. In other words, at a time when the health and stature of the people were steadily improving (the Anthropometric Committee of 1883 reckoned that the average stature of a boy of eighteen years was about sixty-seven inches in height and 137 lb in weight, with a chest measurement of thirty-four inches),[3] the army was forced to lower its standards and accept smaller and younger men.

Even so, the army had to resort to a third expedient, namely 'special enlistments' or recruits who failed to meet one of the minimum requirements. In effect the army was willing to accept recruits who were slightly below the minimum standards but who, in the view of their medical officers, promised to become efficient soldiers. These 'specials', largely under-age or underdeveloped adolescents, were expected to become fit for their duties in about four months, even if they could not carry their complete accoutrements. Although the Select Committee, chaired by Lord Wantage, which examined the terms and conditions of service in the army accepted this rationale, it contended that 'the enlistment of any large number of men below the present low standard of 5 feet 4 inches in height, 33 inches round the chest, and 115 lb. in weight, is to be deprecated'.[4] The Inspector-Generals of Recruiting had little option, however. They could not meet, or even approach, their recruiting targets without a substantial dependence upon 'special enlistments' (that is, from 18 per cent to 36 per cent of their annual intakes during the 1890s).[5]

Finally, the official statistics undoubtedly concealed some element of fraudulent enlistment. The medical officers who inspected the prospective recruits had no means of checking their ages. They suspected that some of those presented as just over eighteen or just under twenty-five were trying to enter the army because they were either lads earning boys' wages or mature men, sometimes in their thirties or even older, who were out of work. They realised, too, that the recruiting officers might have connived in this deception, as they were largely paid by results. Under the 'bringing in' system of the late 1870s, each recruit was worth 25s, shared between the officer who examined him and signed his attestation papers, the recruiting sergeant, and the soldier, civilian or pensioner who brought the recruit in. As the system tainted recruiting with fraud and dissolution (since the 'bringers' habitually frequented public houses, where they plied prospective recruits with drink), it was abolished in 1888 and paid recruiters were established (at 2s a day and lodging money if away from headquarters or 1s a day if based at the recruiting headquarters). These recruiters still received 5s for every recruit passed and finally approved for the Guards, the Royal Artillery (gunners only) and the Royal Engineers (sappers only), and 2s 6d for all other recruits, and some of them still conducted their activities in public houses.[6] Medical officers could not be too fastidious in their inspections as they were already rejecting some 20–30 per cent of the prospective recruits (see Table 6). In 1879, Lieutenant-Colonel J. Logan, the superintending officer of recruiting for the London district, testified that

If I were to try to find out too much, the recruiting would fall off very materially. It would not at all do for me to make any close enquiries as to the antecedents of recruits who come to enlist, especially in London. Most of them would refer me to a common lodging-house if I were to ask them where they lived.[7]

Recruiting difficulties were much more apparent in some arms than in others. The recruiters found little difficulty in securing men for the Royal Engineers, the Army Service Corps and the Medical Staff Corps, where recruits could follow their trades and benefit from extra duty payments. Conversely, they frequently struggled to find sufficient gunners for the Royal Artillery and to replace the excessive wastage in the Foot Guards. Both corps required men of superior physique – to handle the heavy ordnance of the field and garrison artillery and to act as the sovereign's body-guard – and so competed in the labour market for full-grown and able-bodied men (in 1894, seeking men of five feet six and a half inches for field gunners, men of five feet seven inches for garrison gunners, and men of five feet nine inches for the Foot Guards). The Foot Guards had to replace the losses from abnormally high wastage rates (their tally of sick and invalided being attributed to the severity of the sentry duties in London). The cavalry also demanded high physical standards (from five feet six inches to five feet eleven inches in 1894), but attracted a large number of recruits. In 1891 Colonel John Russell, commanding the cavalry depot at Canterbury, exuded confidence about continuing to meet his recruiting targets. 'Many men,' he claimed, 'are attracted by the uniform and the swagger, and this accounts in a great measure for the better class of recruits who join the Cavalry.'[8]

In the hope of attracting more recruits, particular classes of recruits, and an improved quality of recruit, extensive efforts were made to reform the recruiting system. In 1867 the office of Inspector-General of Recruiting was established to curb the irregularities and impose some uniformity on the methods employed. Sweeping

Table 6 Wastage rate in recruiting, 1870–98

Year	Number of men enlisted	Rejected by the authorities	Absconded	Paid smart	Deserted	Losses from other causes	Number who joined units
1870	34,547	8,278 (24·0%)	501	2,370	248	133	23,017 (66·7%)*
1874	30,356	6,208 (20·5%)	667	2,588	323	248	20,312 (73·9%)
1878	42,734	9,556 (22·4%)	903	3,248	525	393	28,109 (65·8%)
	Number of men served with notice papers		Failed to come up for attestation				
1882	45,385	12,487 (27·5%)	8,841		279	234	23,555 (51·9%)*
1886	71,786	22,593 (31·5%)	9,725		370	127	38,953 (54·3%)*
1890	61,434	20,518 (33·4%)	9,628		245	107	30,918 (50·3%)*
1894	70,999	28,349 (39·9%)	8,618		424	167	33,441 (47·1%)
1898	84,626	32,330 (38·2%)	12,732		593	81	38,890 (46·0%)

* There are slight irregularities in the data for these years, underlining the difficulties of monitoring the men in the enlistment process.
Sources: *General Annual Returns of the British Army . . .*, C. 1323 (1875), XLIII, p.22; C. 6196 (1890), XLIII, p.28; C. 9426 (1899), LIII, p.30.

changes were soon introduced. The expensive employment of pensioners, which had produced many disreputable recruits, was greatly curtailed. Recruiting parties were instructed to remove their activities from public houses (an instruction more easily stated than enforced). Advertisements were required to be clear and honest in their statements. Enlistment bounties were prohibited and measures taken to make medical examinations more rigorous and searching. Free discharges were instituted for any recruit who could prove that he had been deceived during the process of enlistment, and the recruiters responsible were required to bear the expenses incurred. The display of posters, distribution of pamphlets, and the use of advertisements in the local and national press became more extensive. Traditional recruiting marches were supplemented by public displays, like the Royal Naval and Military Tournament, which was held annually after 1893.

Cardwell had also hoped that the linking of battalions and the assignment of territorial recruiting areas would strengthen local ties and feelings and so 'bring into the army a better class of men and a greater number of men than now present themselves'.[9] The localisation of 1872 divided the military districts of the United Kingdom into sixty-six sub-districts for infantry, twelve for artillery and two for cavalry. Each infantry sub-district was to support the recruiting of the two line and affiliated Militia battalions which shared a brigade depot within the sub-district. The linking proved less than popular. Many depots took several years to form (only thirty-three had all their barracks and other facilities by 1875). Some battalions had few associations with their linked battalion and disliked the depot base assigned to them. Many prospective recruits did not wish to enlist in their local regiments and expressed preferences to join specific regiments (and these were usually met if there were vacancies in the regiments concerned).[10]

In 1881 Childers replaced this scheme by abolishing the old regimental numbers, relinking and renaming the battalions to form the first and second battalions of one regiment, with specific geographical recruiting areas, to be known as regimental districts. Local Militia and Volunteer units were integrated with the parent regiment and the regular depot became the Militia headquarters. The Militia battalions became the third, and, where appropriate, the fourth battalions of the parent regiment. The twelve artillery districts were retained, and the cities of London, Dublin and Liverpool were worked as recruiting districts outside the territorial system. Recruiting was also undertaken at the headquarters of the regiments of cavalry, battalions of infantry and batteries of Royal Artillery. The Guards took recruits from all regimental districts and sent fifteen special recruiters from their regiments to recruit in different parts of the country.

Undoubtedly this scheme had some beneficial effects, even if it caused considerable resentment when it was first introduced. Some regiments rapidly established, or quickly developed, their local roots and became identified with the counties in which they were based. By 1883 forty-three of the sixty-six districts were supplying their regiments with over 50 per cent of their recruits, and fifteen of these were supplying over 80 per cent. Militiamen supplied 12,450 of the army's 33,096 recruits in 1883, and 51 per cent of those volunteered for their linked units. Inevitably there were some regiments, especially in the Highlands, which struggled to find recruits in large and predominantly rural districts. Lieutenant-Colonel A.Y. Leslie, the commanding officer of the 1st Battalion, the Queen's Own Cameron Highlanders, regarded his recruiting district of Inverness-shire as 'miserable in its unproductiveness', with very few recruits coming from the Inverness Militia, commanded by Lord Lovat. He had to find men from other parts of Scotland and England, and, when the 2nd Battalion, the Queen's Own Cameron Highlanders, was raised in 1897, it was given the whole of Scotland as its recruiting area.[11]

However desperate the search for recruits, recruiters had to operate within certain limitations. They could not exceed the numbers voted by Parliament and so, in prosperous recruiting years, if the intake threatened to exceed the targets (usually when the home establishments were full just before the embarkation of reliefs in September), they had to curtail recruiting. As the home-based units lost numbers later, usually reaching their nadir in May when the last of the invalids and time-expired men were struck off, recruiting often had to be resumed to replace these losses. The Wantage Committee criticised these constraints, but the War Office only permitted the recruitment of an additional 1,000 men each year, if necessary, above the establishments of the infantry battalions.[12]

Recruiting, finally, was never so dire that the army was willing to accept grossly undernourished, malformed or disease-ridden men. Of those who accepted the Queen's shilling and received notice papers to appear for medical inspection, barely half ever joined the ranks. Although the medical inspections varied in their thoroughness from district to district, they were never a simple formality. As the army became increasingly dependent upon urban areas for recruits, it rejected between a quarter and a third of those who presented themselves (inspecting them before attestation and later when they appeared at regimental headquarters, see Table 6). Men seeking confirmation as eligible soldiers had to present themselves before a magistrate between twenty-four and ninety-six hours after they had accepted the shilling. Thereupon, the particulars of their background were recorded (they were rarely checked) and, if satisfactory, the magistrate would administer the oath of allegiance. Theoretically, men could be rejected as ineligible if they admitted being married, or being an apprentice, or if they were in certain trades (for example, a sailor), but, as they could fill in any details without fear of scrutiny, few were rejected. If men had second thoughts about entering the army at this stage, they either absconded before seeing the magistrate or paid £1 'smart money' before the process of attestation or deserted thereafter (see Table 6).

If intrinsically worthwhile, reforming the process of recruiting could not in itself enhance the appeal of military service. Indeed it was widely believed that this appeal was so limited that men frequently turned to the army in desperation, prompted in the vast majority of cases by unemployment. Although the army never tabulated its dependence on the unemployed (recording the previous trades of recruits but not whether they were employed in them), it was a commonplace assumption, voiced before numerous Select Committees and Royal Commissions, that recruiting flourished whenever unemployment was high, and that it slumped as the terms of trade improved. In 1890 the War Office tried to substantiate this correlation by publishing a graph which compared the trends of imports and exports, pauperism, and recruitment for the army and Militia over the period from 1859 to 1888. The apparent correlation, as Alan Skelley has argued, rests on tenuous foundations. The graph only compared national statistics and could not account for the regional variations in pauperism and recruiting. Nor could the graph allow for other factors which might affect recruitment, like alterations in the terms and conditions of service and the excitement generated by war or the threat of war. The simplified correlation was also less than conclusive (when pauperism fell to its lowest total of nearly three-quarters of a million in 1877–78, recruiting, instead of falling too, remained relatively high, at 28,280). Market forces, in short, never operated in conditions of perfect freedom. The War Office regulated the intake by altering the age and physical standards, and Parliament limited the numbers by imposing rigid establishments on an annual basis. Even so, the vast majority of the unemployed preferred the condition of unemployment to military service. Whereas the army never recruited more than 39,552 men in any of the years from 1859 to 1888, the number of paupers never fell below 745,453 in the same period. Many of the latter would have been too old or too unfit for military service, but there was still a vast reservoir of eligible unemployed men which the army, though recurrently short of recruits, failed to attract.[13]

A large proportion of the recruits undoubtedly came from the ranks of the unemployed. Robert Blatchford was only one of many who met a recruiting sergeant when he was penniless and hungry.[14] Whether the numbers constitued 70–80 per cent of the intake in the 1890s, as Sergeant Robert Edmondson supposed, cannot be proved, but his estimate compares with an Army Medical assessment in 1909 that 'well over 90 per cent' of those inspected were out of work.[15] Yet hunger and poverty were not the sole motives for enlistment. Some enlisted to escape from their domestic circumstances, especially from their amatory mistakes. Some enlisted on impulse, following a mere whim or fancy either to travel abroad or to join family and friends in the ranks or to escape from a tedious menial occupation. A small but conspicuous number of gentlemen entered the ranks, often seeking promotion to an officer's commission (they were mainly students or professional men who had encountered setbacks in their former careers). Some recruits appear to have been fascinated by the glamour or excitement of a soldier's life, and a substantial proportion (nearly 40 per cent in the 1890s) had already served in the Militia before they enlisted. Finally, the sons, brothers or orphans of soldiers constituted another source, particularly the boy soldiers under seventeen years of age. They either joined the regiments direct or came from the schools set up to educate soldiers' children: the Royal Military Asylum, Chelsea, and the Royal Hibernian Military School, Dublin.[16]

Regardless of motive, those who enlisted came primarily from the least skilled sections of the working class. Casual labourers comprised the bulk of the recruits from the urban and rural areas

(Table 7). Admittedly the returns from the Army Medical Department have to be treated with caution, as the occupations recorded were either notional in some cases or were classified in categories too all-embracing to be meaningful, but the dependence upon unskilled labour was abundantly clear.

Although the recruiting returns did not record the diminishing intake from the rural areas (at least until the Edwardian years, when agricultural labourers constituted a mere eleven per cent of the national recruitment),[17] the diminution had been apparent for many years and had been a source of great regret. Agricultural labourers were widely regarded as stronger, healthier and more obedient than their slum-bred counterparts. Indeed, recruiting officials complained not only about the diminishing pool of potential recruits from the rural communities, but also about the increasing opportunities for muscular men to find alternative work in the cities, particularly in the police force and the railways. Unable to compete financially for these men or for most men in regular employment, the army had to seek recruits from the less able or the less motivated and from the less physically fit. Cardwell had tried to halt this trend by introducing his

Table 7 *Previous civilian occupations of recruits, 1870–1900, expressed in percentage terms*

Year	Labourers	Manufacturing artisans	Mechanics	Shopmen/ clerks	Professions	Boys
1870	64·7	7·5	19·5	6·5	0·7	1·2
1873	58·9	10·1	21·4	7·4	0·6	1·6
1876	61·0	12·0	17·5	6·8	0·8	1·9
1879	59·4	10·1	19·5	8·1	0·9	2·0
1882	59·5	13·8	15·9	6·7	1·3	2·8
1885	64·1	14·5	13·4	5·4	0·8	1·8
1888	61·6	15·7	12·0	6·6	1·2	2·9
1891	64·0	15·8	10·8	5·7	1·0	2·7
1894	65·1	14·7	9·9	6·4	1·2	2·7
1897	64·0	14·8	10·2	7·3	1·0	2·7
1900	61·6	14·2	13·3	7·0	1·0	2·9

Note: The classifications of the Medical Department, cited above, were as follows:
1. Labourers includes servants and husbandmen;
2. Artisans includes cloth-makers, lace-makers and weavers;
3. Mechanics includes trades favourable to physical development like smiths, carpenters and masons;
4. Boys were under seventeen years of age.

localisation scheme, with the aim of recruiting as effectively as possible in every part of the country, but the rural-based regiments, particularly in the Highlands, could never find sufficient recruits from their designated areas.[18]

Reflected in the urbanisation of the late Victorian army was the continuing transformation of its national composition. Whereas Ireland and Scotland had provided over half the noncommissioned officers and men in the 1830s, their contributions had slumped with rural depopulation and the massive emigration from Ireland. By 1870 the Irish proportion of the army had fallen to 27·9 per cent, and by 1898 to 13·2 per cent (but this recruitment at least kept pace with Ireland's share of the United Kingdom population). The Scottish proportion had dwindled too, falling to 9·6 per cent of the army in 1870 and to 8·0 per cent in 1898, so failing to keep pace with her growth of population Table 8.

Table 8 *Nationalities of men serving with the Colours, 1870–99, expressed in percentage terms*

Year	England and Wales	Scotland	Ireland	Others and those not reported
1870	60·3	9·6	27·9	2·2
1873	67·0	8·5	23·6	0·9
1876	68·3	7·9	22·7	1·1
1879	66·8	7·7	20·3	5·2
1882	69·3	7·6	20·6	2·5
1885	71·6	7·7	17·4	3·3
1888	74·3	8·5	15·6	1·6
1891	76·2	8·3	13·9	1·6
1894	77·5	8·1	12·6	1·8
1897	77·0	7·8	12·4	2·8
1899	76·6	8·0	13·2	2·2

Sources: *General Annual Returns of the British Army* . . . C. 3803 (1881), LVIII, p.65 and C. 9426 (1899), LIII, p.94.

If recruiting from English cities largely compensated for the declining numbers of Scots and Irish soldiers, only some Englishmen were attracted to the Colours. The army remained 'un-English', as H. J. Hanham observed, because it grossly under-represented the Nonconformist religions. Until the 1860s the army had only recognised the Church of England, the Roman Catholic Church and the

Presbyterians, and had classified the religions of new recruits in a brusque and summary manner. Those who could not profess any religious adherence were arbitrarily allocated, usually as 'C of E', and those who affirmed belief in a Dissenting creed were required to join any of the three religions. Once 'Other Protestants' and later Wesleyans were permitted to register separately, their numbers gradually expanded until they constituted about 5–6 per cent in the 1890s. So small a proportion emphasised the class basis of both the army and the Nonconformist creeds.[19] As the rank and file were recruited overwhelmingly from the working class, and usually from the least respectable sections of the working class, it held little attraction for religious groups which, apart from the Methodists, were preponderantly middle-class in composition.

The army, in short, had failed to broaden the base of its social composition. Despite reforming the methods of recruitment and altering the physical standards, all attempts to improve the quality of the recruiting intake had foundered upon the profound contempt with which a military career was viewed. The army never eroded the stigma which was attached to enlistment, aptly described by John Fraser when he recalled the reaction of his father to his own enlistment in 1876:

Never have I seen a man so infuriated. To him my step was a blow from which he thought he would never recover, for it meant disgrace of the worst type. His son a soldier! . . . Rather would he have had me out of work for the rest of my life than earning my living in such a manner. More than that, he would rather see me in my grave, and he would certainly never have me in his house again in any circumstances.[20]

Table 9   *Religious denominations of noncommissioned officers and men,*
1868–98, expressed in percentage terms

Year	Church of England	Presby-terians	Roman Catholics	Wesley-ans	Other Protestants	Not reported
1868	58·2	9·6	28·4	n.a.	3·1	0·7
1873	64·5	8·8	22·8	n.a.	3·3	0·6
1878	64·5	7·8	23·0	n.a.	3·9	0·8
1883	64·3	7·6	22·9	3·7	0·6	0·9
1888	66·7	7·8	19·7	5·0	0·6	0·2
1893	68·2	7·3	17·9	5·2	0·7	0·7
1898	68·0	7·3	17·5	5·2	0·9	1·1

Sources: *General Annual Returns of the British Army . . .*, C. 3083 (1881), LVIII, p.66 and C. 9426 (1899), LIII, p.94.

Should a man enlist with the support of his family, it was usually where there was already a service connection. The profound and widely held reservations about the character and life-style of the serving soldier, and of his prospects once he returned to civilian life, persisted throughout this period. As Lord Wavell recollected, 'There was in the minds of the ordinary God-fearing citizen no such thing as a good soldier; to have a member who had gone for a soldier was for many families a crowning disgrace.'[21]

Many of those who enlisted in the late Victorian army did so in the confident expectation of receiving the regular payment of 1s a day. When Cardwell entered office, the basic rate of pay in the infantry had just been raised to 1s 2d per day, supplemented by an allowance of 1d per day for beer (in the other corps the wages were slightly higher). These rates hardly compared with the weekly wages of unskilled urban labourers (which rose in London from 22s 3d in 1867 to 29s 2d in 1899), or even with those of agricultural labourers in England and Scotland, if not Ireland,[22] but the prospect of regular payment was probably the main attraction, at least for those who were unemployed or who were dependent upon seasonal or irregular work. Yet the rates of pay were unlikely to attract a better class of recruit, especially as the soldier never received 1s a day because of the stoppages deducted for messing expenses, clothing and equipment replacement, washing, hair-cutting and barrack damages.

Cardwell recognised that more attractive financial inducements could enhance recruiting, but he had limited resources at his disposal and had to offset any additional spending, if possible, by savings elsewhere (for example, by terminating bounties on enlistment). He abolished the stoppage of 4½d a day by making the basic bread, meat and potato ration free; reduced the amount stopped for medical care from 9d to 7d daily; and established that good conduct badges, for which soldiers received extra payments, could be earned after two, six, twelve, eighteen, twenty-three and twenty-eight years' service. He made some savings by abolishing the beer allowance and by removing the extra 2d per day which had been granted in 1867.

Faced with the need to attract more recruits annually under the short service system, a War Office committee proposed in 1875 that deferred pay should be introduced to make the army more attractive. Gathorne Hardy acted upon this recommendation; in 1876, he introduced the requirement that 2d per day should be credited as deferred pay for up to twelve years, and that this money should be paid as a lump sum when the soldier left the Colours. He also modified the terms for good conduct badges, allowing them to be earned after two, five, twelve, sixteen, eighteen, twenty-one and twenty-six years.

Stoppages, though, remained a persistent and deeply resented feature of army life, especially among new recruits. Men had enlisted expecting to receive a free kit which would become their own property. The initial issue of clothing and equipment was free, and some items such as tunics, boots, trousers and helmets were reissued without charge, but the uniform remained the property of the State (in the vain hope that veterans or beggars would not beg in uniform). Soldiers had to pay for all alterations and personal markings, maintain their own underclothing, socks and cleaning materials, and replace all items lost, damaged or worn out before the date of re-issue. Soldiers received no credit for making their kit last longer than expected and suffered financially whenever their kit deteriorated from heavy wear on manoeuvres or on military exercises. Moreover, if recruits were issued with items of their kit missing, they incurred stoppages to replace the losses. The burden of these deductions proved so severe that the army had to issue a regulation, specifying that a minimum of 1d per day should be left to the soldier after stoppages.[23] In 1890, 694 privates kept a record of the stoppages from their average pay of £18 5s per annum (see Table 10).

Fortunately many soldiers did not depend entirely upon their regimental pay. In all units some men could augment their pay as cooks, mess waiters and as the 'soldier servants' of officers (paid by regulation at 2s 6d per week in the cavalry and 1s 6d in the infantry). Artillerymen and engineers could earn 'working pay' of up to 2s a day for extra duty work in road and bridge building, surveying and telegraphy. Carpenters, shoemakers, tailors and men with similar skills could also supplement their wages. Wives could earn as much as 4–5s a week by washing for the regiment. Cavalrymen could draw additional pay as grooms for sergeant-majors, quartermaster-sergeants, sergeants and farriers. Some men earned gratuities for distinguished service or special awards for success in musketry or in swordsmanship competitions. Finally, rankers received an extra penny a day whenever they were awarded a good conduct badge (and over 40 per cent of privates possessed one or more badges in this

Table 10 *Stoppages from pay at Aldershot, 1890; average pay £18 5s*

Stoppage item	Total amount for 694 men			Average amount per man		
Tailor's bill	£213	17s	4d		6s	2d
Shoemaker	£176	12s	11½d		5s	1d
Regimental necessaries	£487	6s	8½d		14s	0d
Barrack damages	£156	18s	7½d		4s	5d
Deficiencies in old clothing	£92	10s	2½d		2s	7d
Washing	£414	9s	5½d		11s	10d
Hair cutting	£31	4s	11d			9d
Library	£59	1s	0d		1s	7d
Fines	£14	12s	6d			4d
Repair of arms & accoutrements	£7	2s	2½d			2d
Other stoppages, including groceries and extra rations	£3,366	19s	5¾d	£4	17s	0d
Total	£5,020	15s	4¾d	£7	3s	11d

Source: *Return of the Average Number, during the Year 1890, of Private Soldiers in each of the No. 1 Companies of the Line Battalions now stationed at Aldershot: of the Total Stoppages from the Pay of the Private Soldiers, thus classified . . .*, C. 209 (1890–91), L, p.1.

period, see Table 11).

Men could further enhance their prospects by seeking promotion, but many short service soldiers, though suitably qualified, had little desire to accept the added responsibility and pursue a military career. Some commentators ascribed this reluctance to the frequent altering of War Office regulations, which left soldiers uncertain about their entitlement to re-engage for twenty-one years and receive a pension, even if they had been permitted to extend their first engagement to twelve years. Others suspected that the rates of pay were not sufficiently attractive (in 1876 an infantry corporal earned 1s 4d a day and a sergeant 2s 1d a day), especially as the ranks above lance corporal were not given good conduct pay. Promotion could actually involve financial losses, at least initially, because of the additional expenses incurred by NCOs, who not only paid the regulation stoppages but often paid men to clean their equipment and undertake various tasks for them (and all sergeants, including lance sergeants, were expected to join the sergeants' mess and meet their share of mess expenses). Finally, the rapid turnover of men in the short service army, particularly in the home-based battalions, had imposed a considerable extra burden upon NCOs, so prompting 'an

Table 11 *Number and proportion of privates in possession of good conduct badges, 1870–99 (as at 1 January)*

Year		One	Two	Three	Four	Five	Six	Total (one or more)
*1870	No.	34,801	29,607	10,822	3,154	712	165	79,261
	%	22·2	18·9	6·9	2·0	0·5	0·1	50·5
†1878	No.	34,697	25,707	9,849	9,738	308	11	80,310
	%	20·9	15·5	5·7	5·9	0·2	0·007	48·3
1886	No.	47,465	15,764	5,271	3,405	345	95	72,345
	%	26·8	8·9	3·0	1·9	0·2	0·05	40·9
1894	No.	64,826	24,610	2,686	971	289	117	93,499
	%	33·4	12·7	1·4	0·5	0·1	0·06	48·2
1898	No.	74,215	24,480	2,951	1,264	158	125	103,193
	%	38·1	12·6	1·5	0·6	0·8	0·06	53·0

* After 1870 badges could be earned in two, six, twelve, twenty-three and twenty-eight years.

† After 1876 badges could be earned in two, five, twelve, sixteen, eighteen, twenty-one and twenty-six years.

Sources: *General Annual Returns of the British Army* . . ., C. 1323 (1875), XLIII, p.49; C. 6196 (1890), XLIII, p.67: C. 9426 (1899), LIII, p.69.

undesirably large proportion' of lance corporals to request permission to resign their stripes. As concern about the predicament of NCOs was voiced in Parliament, the press, and in evidence before various Select Committees,[24] it could hardly be ignored.

The military authorities had always recognised the importance of maintaining a strong cadre of NCOs (in a ratio of about one NCO, including corporals, to every six enlisted men). The noncommissioned officer fulfilled a vital role in the training, discipline and internal functioning of every military unit, and served as an indispensable link between the officer and the rank and file. Moreover, the War Office could improve the pay and privileges of the noncommissioned officer without incurring a vast financial burden. Accordingly, it permitted the secondment of NCOs to special duties in several military departments, so enabling about a thousand men to earn salaries which ranged from 1s 8d to 7s 6d a day. It created the rank of warrant officer for senior NCOs in 1881 and augmented their salaries (by 1896, regimental sergeant-majors were earning 5s a day in the infantry and 6s a day in the Royal Engineers and Royal Horse Artillery). After repeated protests, notably by the Wantage Committee in 1892, the War Office also removed the anomaly whereby lance corporals and lance sergeants drew the same pay as the ranks below them. By 1896 the daily rates for lance corporals and corporals ranged from 1s 3d to 1s 8d per day in the infantry to 1s 8d to 2s 8d per day for acting bombardiers and bombardiers in the Royal Horse Artillery. These enhanced rates of pay complemented the privileges which noncommissioned officers already enjoyed. They occupied positions of prestige and responsibility within their own regiments. The sergeants had their own mess and enjoyed more liberal marriage provisions (whereas only 4–7 per cent of the ranks could marry officially, all warrant officers and staff sergeants could marry and 50 per cent of all other sergeants). They were also eligible for promotion to commissioned rank, although the numbers promoted in peacetime were never substantial.[25] In short, the authorities enhanced the attractions of promotion within the lower ranks and significantly compensated the NCO for his additional burdens under the short service system.

Nevertheless, the vast majority of soldiers remained in the ranks, dependent upon a meagre wage, supplemented in many cases by a good conduct badge. As the offer of a notional 1s a day became increasingly less competitive in the labour market, many campaigned for a substantial increase in army pay. Their protests reached a crescendo in the evidence before the Wantage Committee. Wolseley insisted that a voluntary army had to be a highly paid army: 'unless we can give a very high rate of pay, we shall always be obliged to take in "the waifs and strays" '.[26] Many of the witnesses agreed with Wolseley, but some, including the Duke of Cambridge and Sir Redvers Buller, then Adjutant-General, demurred. The Duke doubted whether increasing the basic rate of pay was as important as modifying deferred pay, which discouraged men from re-engaging for a further period of service. Buller endorsed these views and recommended that soldiers should be given free groceries rather than increased pay.[27] The committee embraced many of these proposals. It advocated the abolition of all stoppages; the provision of a messing allowance of 3*d* a day in addition to the free ration of bread and meat; the provision of a more ample supply of clothing, which should last the prescribed period of time and ultimately become the property of the soldier; a further reduction of the periods of service required to earn good conduct badges; and the substitution of gratuities of £1 for each year of service in place of deferred pay. It contended that the effect of these measures would be to raise the pay of the soldier to approximately 'the ordinary market rate given for unskilled labour'.[28]

Arthur Haliburton, then Under-Secretary of State and later Permanent Under-Secretary of State at the War Office (1895–97), issued a lengthy minority report, firmly opposing these recommendations. He doubted whether an increase in pay, other than an extremely large one, would have any effect on recruitment.[29] Stanhope and Campbell-Bannerman agreed: indeed, Campbell-Bannerman later claimed that the inducement to enlist was not pay but 'the military life, the adventurous life and the change'.[30] Nevertheless, some marginal increments in army pay were conceded. In 1898 deferred pay was replaced by a messing allowance and a gratuity of £1 for each year of service, which brought the basic rate of pay for an infantry private to 1*s* 3*d* a day. The deduction of stoppages, though, still ensured that soldiers were not receiving a clear 1*s* a day as their basic pay.

Soldiers were not only miserably paid but were also indifferently housed. By the late nineteenth century they were quartered in barracks which varied enormously in size and amenities. Some were in ancient forts and castles, such as the Tower of London and the castles in Edinburgh, Stirling and Dover; some were in forts and barracks erected to overawe the Highlanders or to garrison Ireland in the eighteenth and early nineteenth centuries; some were in forts hastily built in response to the French and Napoleonic Wars; some were in barracks located in the centre of manufacturing towns in the Midlands and the north of England, where the military had aided the civil power in the early nineteenth century; and some were in the large camps at Aldershot and the Curragh. Many barracks, in effect, had outlived their original purpose, and some temporary buildings, notably the wooden huts at Aldershot, had become permanent accommodation. A few barracks such as those at Weedon and Woolwich were reasonably spacious and well appointed, but many were extremely small, needed repairs, and lacked sufficient ancillary buildings (adequate laundries, drying rooms, cookhouses, married quarters, drained latrines, etc.). Men were often crowded into cramped, insanitary and poorly ventilated rooms.

Sharing these spartan quarters were the wives and children of the soldiers who had married with the permission of their regimental colonels. Although the army accepted the need for some wives to wash and sew for the men, to help with nursing and midwifery, and to act as a morally steadying influence, it also regarded women and children as a liability, adversely affecting the 'mobility, discipline and efficiency' of the service.[31] It permitted only 4–7 per cent of private soldiers to marry 'on the strength', allowing their wives to live inside the barracks, feed free on half rations, and enrol their children in the regimental schools. But the lack of separate married quarters meant that marriages often had to be consummated and babies born in the corners of communal barrack rooms, screened by flimsy curtains.

The importance of improving these conditions had been recognised ever since the revelation of the Army Sanitary Commission that only twenty out of the 251 stations in the United Kingdom in 1857 had separate married quarters. Separate quarters were constructed in newly built barracks, but the renovation of existing accommodation was costly and proceeded slowly. Separation allowances were instituted in 1871 and increased in 1882 (so that an NCO's wife received 8*d* a day and 8*d* from her husband's pay, a private's wife 8*d* a day and 4*d* from her husband's pay, with small additional payments for each child). Medical care for wives and children was approved in 1878 and a maternity and child care service begun in

1880, although the accommodation for women and children in garrison hospitals was scarcely adequate in the 1880s. In 1881 a gratuity of one year's pay was awarded to the widows of non-commissioned officers and men who were killed in action, or who died as a result of wounds in action. These provisions only accentuated the division between marriages 'on' and 'off the strength'. The wives of the latter were not allowed in the barracks nor granted separation allowances nor entitled to accompany their husbands abroad. Undoubtedly these women suffered considerably from the regulations imposed by the army. They were forced to eke out a living as seamstresses or servants: some perforce had to live off the parish or off the streets.[32]

Living conditions had improved since the criticisms voiced during and immediately after the Crimean War, but the achievements were fairly limited. The sheer magnitude of the task, which involved over 250 barracks accommodating 97,832 men in 1860, limited the rate of progress. The costs of repairing, renovating and enlarging barracks were not only formidable but they were also constantly expanding, as the army endeavoured to meet new minimum requirements in public health, hygiene and sanitation. Even if the additional expenditure had been authorised, many barracks could not have been modernised completely because of their age and structural limitations, while others suffered from appalling locations, far from exercise and training areas. Renovation, in short, had to be accompanied by considerable reconstruction, but governments were reluctant to sustain the necessary expenditure once the initial furore over barrack reform had subsided. Only the occasional scandal, like the revelation of the insanitary and fever-ridden conditions within the Royal Barracks, Dublin, in the 1880s, shamed the authorities into facing their responsibilities. Under immense parliamentary pressure, compounded by the critical reports of several committees of inquiry, the government prepared a new plan of barrack building and renovation in February 1890 to be funded by loans outside the Army Estimates. Successive governments sustained this programme over the next sixteen years, spending over £12,000,000 in the last eleven years.[33]

An important aspect of these reforms was the installation of kitchens and various cooking facilities in many barracks. These constituted a step towards an improvement of the soldiers' dietary provisions. The basic ration of 1 lb of bread and ¾ lb of meat remained unchanged, but it was usually supplemented by the vegetables, spices, tea and butter which regiments could contract for and supply. After the establishment of a School of Cooking at Aldershot in 1870, the regiments began to benefit from the services of trained cooks. Real improvements in catering, though, proved fitful, and the diet varied considerably from one unit to another. By the late 1880s the 1st Royal Irish Rifles was one of several regiments which provided a remarkably varied and imaginative range of meals, within the limits of the existing messing allowance. Sir Stafford Northcote's committee of inquiry was impressed and wished that many more regiments would follow its example. The committee recommended that special classes should be held to instruct medical and young regimental officers in the task of inspecting meat; that more supervision should be exercised over the supplies received and over the preparation of army meals; that more instruction should be given in how the variety and appeal of the food could be enhanced; and that bread should be baked in 2 lb instead of 4 lb loaves to improve the quality and reduce the waste.[34] Yet the standards were hardly transformed. Sergeant Horace Wyndham, who enlisted in 1890, recollected that the quality of the food which was served in Dublin was reasonable, but that there was simply not enough of it, especially after an hour's pre-breakfast drill. A.F. Corbett, who also served in the 1890s, vividly recalled the pangs of hunger which he felt at night: 'Fortunately the heavy drinkers were light eaters, and many times I have felt along the barrack shelves and found a dry crust for my supper.'[35]

The army, nonetheless, was still providing regular meals which were more substantial, at least in the daily quantities of meat, than those regularly consumed by many manual labourers in London. Moreover this diet, coupled with more sanitary living conditions, the regular exercise and physical training of army life, had a beneficial effect upon the health of the other ranks. Admittedly any improvements occurred at a time, after 1880, when the standards of public health and medical knowledge were improving. These standards had led to the control, and in some cases the extinction, of infectious diseases like smallpox and cholera, but the army was still finding the bulk of its recruits from the lower urban working class, the most vulnerable group in society. It was also increasingly dependent upon 'special enlistments', many of whom came from appalling urban environments. The army expected that these recruits would make rapid gains in weight and in muscular development. These gains not only occurred in many cases, but the army also sustained the diminution of its mortality rates and the proportion of men hospitalised in the home army (Table 12).[36]

Table 12 *The health of the rank and file, 1861–99*

Year	Mortality rate per 1,000 men: NCOs and other ranks in the home army	Number of hospital admissions per 100 men in the home army
1861	9·2	102·5
1867	9·4	87·0
1873	7·9	75·9
1879	7·6	82·2
1885	6·7	87·7
1891	4·9	77·2
1897	5·4	64·1
1899	4·3	67·1

Sources: *Reports of the Army Medical Department . . .*, C. 3233 (1863), XX1, C. 4185 (1868–69), XXXVII, C. 1374 (1875), XLIV, C. 2960 (1881), LIX, C. 5128(1887), LI, C. 7047 (1893), LII, C. 8936 (1898), LIV, Cd. 521 (1901), XLI.

Despite the benefits of more wholesome rations and more sanitary surroundings, the daily routine of the ordinary soldier changed remarkably little. After reveille at 6.00 or 6.15 a.m., the ranks paraded and breakfasted at about 8.00 a.m. Thereafter recruits were drilled for an hour, orderly-room business was completed, including the disposal of prisoners, and fatigue duties undertaken (like polishing kit, peeling potatoes, cleaning barrack rooms and latrines). After another parade, dinner was served at about 1.00 p.m. Recruits were drilled from 2.00 to 3.00 p.m. and, after tea at 4.00 p.m., the ranks enjoyed a period of free time until 9.30 p.m., when a roll call was taken of each company, followed either by guard duty or 'lights out' at 10.15 p.m. Cavalrymen had a much more arduous schedule, caring for their horses on a daily basis, and maintaining their saddlery and stables. The routine was not 'static', inasmuch as men were constantly going or returning from furlough, prison, hospital or detachment duties; recruits were joining or passing into the ranks; and some men were being specially employed. It was monotonous, nonetheless, and was rarely interrupted by military training. There were route marches in the winter months, and drills and rehearsals for the half-yearly inspections and the periodic field days, but large-scale exercises and combined arms training were comparatively rare (large-scale manoeuvres were only held in 1871, 1872, 1873 and 1898). Overall, fatigue duties probably loomed larger in the consciousness of the peacetime soldier than military training; the underemployment was enervating, the routine dull and tedious. 'Idleness,' recalled Sergeant Menzies, 'is the bane of the soldier, and the hardest foes to overcome are not always to be found on the field of battle.'[37]

Underemployed, soldiers sought solace and comfort in drink, and so drunkenness persisted as a military problem (as it did for the class of society from which the army drew the bulk of its recruits). Drunkenness was not only a military crime but it also contributed to other crimes, like desertion and the spread of venereal disease. The weekly pay days frequently occasioned bouts of heavy drinking, followed by rowdy barrack room scenes and a rash of crimes — insubordination, absence without leave (AWOL), violence towards a superior officer, and drunkenness itself. The Inspector-General of Military Prisons reported that soldiers often deserted to avoid the consequences of becoming absent without leave after a drinking spree.[38] The heavy drinking also correlated with the high incidence of venereal disease, as soldiers all too often shunned the dreary surroundings and high prices of the barrack canteens for more congenial drinking haunts.

Venereal disease was so extensive, accounting for 33 per cent of the home-based forces in 1862, that the authorities sought to protect the soldier and sailor against their 'natural inclinations' by regulating prostitution. The Contagious Diseases Acts of 1864, 1866 and 1869 provided for the compulsory hospitalisation of any woman accused by a policeman before a magistrate of being a prostitute within certain districts, for the detention of diseased women for three months (and later, under the 1869 Act, nine months), for the registration and regular examination of suspected women, and for an extension of the radius of protected areas to fifteen miles around the major garrison and seaport towns. The Acts aroused passionate opposition, largely on moral grounds (that the vice of prostitution should be removed and not regularised) but also on pragmatic and libertarian grounds (that the Acts were ineffective and denied their victims the rights of habeas corpus). Parliamentary opponents agitated throughout the 1870s and early 1880s for the repeal of this

legislation. Supported by a substantial extra-parliamentary movement, including radicals, middle-class feminists, Nonconformist
bodies, and many working-class men, they eventually gained the
endorsement of the National Liberal Federation, which ultimately
persuaded Gladstone not to oppose repeal in 1886.

Whether the Acts had as much effect as their supporters claimed
upon the declining incidence of venereal disease is doubtful. They
probably had some effect, but the statistics supplied by the Army
Medical Department are not wholly reliable, and the army may
have benefited from a long-term decline in the virulence of the
disease during the latter half of the nineteenth century. Higher public
standards of sanitation and cleanliness may have contributed, too;
the army's hospital admissions for venereal disease continued to
decline after the repeal of the CD Acts (accounting for only 11·2 per
cent of the home-based forces in 1899).[39] Another contributory
factor may have been the far greater provision for recreational
pursuits to occupy the soldier's time. By the late nineteenth century,
regimental sports were firmly established; they institutionalised the
enthusiasm for football and boxing and added the competitive spice
of inter-regimental rivalry. Music was also encouraged; the training
of military musicians had improved since the founding of the Military School of Music in 1856, and regimental bands had formal and
informal duties (at parades, funerals, on the line of march, in battle,
in entertaining officers and men, and in public entertainments and
recruiting marches). Barrack facilities were greatly improved; the
provision of soldiers' day rooms had been under way since the
1860s, and, by 1900, many regimental and garrison institutes had
been built, comprising games rooms, grocery shops, canteens, luncheon rooms and, in a few cases, theatres and halls.

Complementing the proliferation of these amusements was the
extension of army education. Even in the pre-Crimean army, regimental libraries had been perceived as an alternative haven to the
barrack canteen. By 1876 there were 150 libraries in the United
Kingdom and the colonies, containing nearly 230,000 volumes, but
their appeal perforce was limited to those who were literate and who
were prepared to eschew the dissipated habits of many of their
barrack-room comrades. Literate soldiers comprised a relatively
small fraction of the rank and file, despite the startling improvements
in army literacy recorded in the annual returns. By 1889, 1·9 per cent
of the other ranks were described as illiterate and 85·4 per cent were

rated as possessing a 'superior education'. However, these findings contrasted sharply with those of the Director-General of Military Education. In 1888, he recorded that over 60 per cent of the ranks had failed to attain even the lowest army education certificate (the fourth class, involving simple reading and a few sums at a level that might be attained by an eight-year-old child). The annual returns were reclassified in the 1890s to confirm that throughout the decade over 60 per cent of the ranks failed to obtain any certificate. In other words, thirty years after the passage of Forster's Education Act (1870) and the 1872 Scottish Education Act, and after nearly two decades in which school attendance was compulsory for new recruits (1871–88), the ranks still contained 60 per cent who were either illiterate or barely literate. Even the standards attained by the remainder were 'elementary at best', in spite of the inducement from 1889 onwards that the possession of a first and second-class certificate of education was among the requirements for promotion to sergeant and corporal respectively.[40]

The establishment of 'Soldiers' Homes' or mission centres near many of the large garrisons represented another attempt to wean soldiers from the demon drink. They were founded by concerned citizens (after the first had been founded by the Wesleyan Charles Henry Kelly at Chatham in 1861, Mrs Louisa Daniell opened the second at Aldershot in 1862, and, after several branches had been opened near other English garrisons, Elsie Sandes opened the first soldiers' home in Ireland in 1877). They provided meeting halls, smoking and games rooms, tea and coffee bars, baths and sleeping quarters. As Mrs Daniell and her lady helpers were primarily engaged in the saving of souls, they distributed religious tracts within the homes, prohibited the consumption of liquor, and held Bible classes nightly. Notwithstanding this proselytising, the homes provided a range of facilities in comfortable surroundings which had generally been lacking for the common soldier. Undoubtedly, they contributed to raising the standards of behaviour in the army, even if the extent of their impact was never entirely clear.[41] The Churches and various religious societies were active, too, particularly in the crusade against drunkenness. In 1893 they joined forces to form a non-denominational Army Temperance Association. By 1895, it claimed 8,641 members and within a few years, 20,000. The Association almost certainly had some influence beyond its nominal membership, although this may have been relatively small in view of the well known suspicion of religion within the ranks, reflecting the dislike of Sunday parades and the resentment of religion being forced upon them.[42]

Even so, drunkenness and other crimes markedly diminished within the late Victorian army (see Chapter 3). When coupled with the termination of corporal punishment, the decline of recidivism might have been expected to enhance the status and appeal of military life. This did not occur or at least not sufficiently to broaden the social composition of the rank and file. The deeply rooted prejudice against military service, so keenly felt within respectable working-class families, could not be allayed by mere statistics or recruiting publicity. That prejudice was understandable, whether directed at the rates of pay, which became increasingly less competitive with civilian wages, or at the plight of the ex-ranker. As the short service army provided few opportunities for a soldier to learn a trade, soldiers often left the Colours unskilled and handicapped in their search for work by their age and their Reserve obligations. All too many of them appear to have squandered their deferred pay in 'drink and dissipation', and to have lapsed thereafter into itinerant vagrancy.[43]

Secretaries of State from Cardwell onwards had urged government departments to employ more ex-servicemen, but only the Post Office had responded on a significant scale. Even after the recommendations of the Wantage Committee, when it was agreed that some positions as prison and customs officials, park keepers, messengers and clerks should be set aside, the numbers were modest (only 4,687 places in government departments were found for the 40,393 ex-soldiers who officially registered from 1894 to 1898).[44] Benevolent societies and employment agencies were formed, often by former officers, to compensate for the government's provisions. The Army and Navy Pensioners' and Time-Expired Men's Society and the Corps of Commissionaires already existed but the National Association for the Employment of Reserve and Discharged Soldiers was established in 1885 and the Soldiers' and Sailors' Help Society in 1899. These and other private agencies provided considerable assistance (in 1900 the Pensioners' Society and the National Association had placed over 4,000 men in work, and, by 1904–05, the Commissionaires had found employment for 3,046 men). Some civilian employers, notably the police and the railway companies, began to hire larger numbers of ex-servicemen, but the prospect of unemployment persisted. It afflicted not only a proportion of those with good characters on the official registers (by the Edwardian period, about one in four of these men failed to find work), but also the itinerants who lost touch with the official registers and those who had left the Colours with 'less than good characters' (about one in four of the total in 1896).[45]

Army pensioners were sometimes reduced to an even more parlous predicament. Only in the wake of the Wantage report was the maximum pension for an NCO raised to 5s a day, but privates had to wait until after the South African War before their minimum rate of 8d a day was raised to 1s a day. Admittedly, many civilian firms did not pay any pension at all, but the police pensions were much more generous, and, after twenty-one years of service, the employment prospects of an army pensioner, especially a private, were fairly bleak. Moreover, unless invalids incurred their disability in action, they were discharged without any pension. By December 1897 there were 1,905 army pensioners, 320 reservists, and another 6,662 ex-servicemen in receipt of poor relief.[46]

If the sight of old soldiers begging in the streets hardly enhanced the appeal of service life, the depth of popular contempt for a military career almost certainly reflected more profound emotional feelings. As the army maintained its cohesiveness by enforced discipline, communal living, and a sacrifice of individual liberty, it was bound to have a fairly limited appeal. Some may have deplored the purpose of military training; others probably feared that a boy once enlisted would become lost to his family and friends, if not necessarily corrupted, at least changed beyond all recognition by the experience of service life. For families with genteel aspirations, these fears had a semblance of truth. As Horace Wyndham, a gentleman ranker in the 1890s, recalled, 'Those who have not actively experienced what a barrack-room, crowded with noisy, foulmouthed, and more or less drunken men, means at night cannot conceive what a man who is in the slightest degree sensitive feels at such times.'[47] Service in the ranks remained a career of lowly status and of little esteem.

Notes

1   *Parl. Deb.*, Third Ser., Vol.205 (16 March 1871), col.129. For the effects of long service, see *Report of the Commissioners appointed to inquire into Recruiting for the Army*, C. 3752 (1867), XV, pp.v, vii–xvi; B.J. Bond,

'Recruiting the Victorian Army 1870–92', *Victorian Studies*, Vol.V (September 1961), pp.332, 334.

2   *Parl. Deb.*, Third Ser., Vol.279 (1 June 1883), cols.1555–9; (4 June 1883), cols.1641–3; *Annual Report of the Inspector General of Recruiting*, C. 3911 (1884), XVII, p.2.

3   *Memorandum by the Inspector General of Recruiting*, C. 57 (1870), XLII, p.1; *Report upon Recruiting for the Regular Army for the Year 1871*, C. 495 (1872), XIV, p.4; Maj.-Gen. J.H. Rocke, q.836 and 'Return showing the Standards of Age and the Physical Qualifications, etc.' evidence appended to the *Wantage Report*, pp.29, 520; *Elgin Report*, p.65; Skelley, *The Victorian Army at Home*, pp.237–8.

4   *Wantage Report*, p.10; Col. G. Barton, q.4767 evidence appended to the *Wantage Report*, p.170.

5   Rocke, q.439 evidence appended to the *Wantage Report*, p.17; *Annual Reports of the Inspector General of Recruiting . . .*, C. 7659 (1895), XVIII, p.6; C. 9185 (1899), XI, p.9.

6   Surgeon-Major D.A. Campbell Fraser, qs.130–2, Lt.-Col. J. Logan, qs.170, 211, and J. Donald, q.3761 evidence appended to the *Airey Report*, pp.135, 137, 139, 336; Capt. E. Turner, qs.7716–32, 7753 evidence appended to the *Wantage Report*, pp.251–2; Robertson, *From Private to Field-Marshal*, p.1; Wyndham, *The Queen's Service*, p.1.

7   Lt.-Col. J. Logan, q.205 evidence appended to the *Airey Report*, p.139.

8   Col. J. Russell, q.12582 evidence appended to the *Wantage Report*, p.429; see also *Wantage Report*, p.22; Rocke, qs.513, 532, 751–5 and Maj.-Gen. E. Markham, q.12776 evidence appended to the *Wantage Report*, pp.20, 27 and 438; *Annual Reports of the Inspector General of Recruiting . . .*, C. 1149 (1875), XV, p.3 and C.7659 (1895), XVIII, p.5.

9   *Parl. Deb.*, Third Ser., Vol.209 (22 February 1872), col.901. On the recruiting reforms, see Skelley, *The Victorian Army at Home*, pp.242–3.

10   *Report upon Recruiting for the Regular Army for the Year 1874, to the Adjutant-General of Her Majesty's Forces, by the Inspector-General of Recruiting, C. 1149 (1875), XV, p.2*; Henderson, *Highland Soldier*, pp.39–40; Anglesey, *A History of the British Cavalry 1816 to 1919*, Vol.3, p.50.

11   Lt.-Col. A.Y. Leslie, qs.12256, 12271, 12290 and Rocke, qs.463, 532 evidence appended to the *Wantage Report*, pp.416–17, 418, 420; *Annual Report of the Inspector General of Recruiting*, C. 3911 (1884), XVII, pp.1, 3; Henderson, *Highland Soldier*, p.27.

12   *Wantage Report*, p.7; *Annual Report of the Inspector General of Recruiting for 1894*, C. 7659 (1895), XVIII, p.3; 'Revised Summary of Recommendations of Lord Wantage's Committee, and of Decisions Thereon', July 1895, PRO, WO 33/55.

13   *Report of the Committee on Questions (Recruiting, etc.) with respect to Militia; with evidence and appendices*, C. 5992 (1890), XIX, Appendix 2; Skelley, *The Victorian Army at Home*, p.248.; Spiers, *The Army and Society*, pp.44–5.

14   R. Blatchford, *My Life in the Army* (The Clarion Press; London,

n.d.), p.5.

15   R. Edmondson, *Is a Soldier's Life Worth Living?* (Twentieth Century Press; London, 1902), p.5; *Report of the Health of the Army for the Year 1909*, Cd. 5477 (1911), XLVII, p.2.

16   Skelley, *The Victorian Army at Home*, p.249; Rocke, qs.485–6 evidence appended to the *Wantage Report*, p.19; *Annual Reports of the Inspector General of Recruiting* C. 7659 (1895), XVIII, p.6 and C. 9185 (1899), XI, p.10.

17   Spiers, *The Army and Society*, p.48.

18   *Ibid.*; J. Donald, q.3755 evidence appended to the *Airey Report*, p.335; Col. R. Upcher, qs.4285–91, the Duke of Connaught, q.9472, and Col. H. Trotter, qs.11136–8 evidence appended to the *Wantage Report*, pp.151, 311 and 355; Henderson, *Highland Soldier*, p.43; E. and A. Linklater, *The Black Watch: The History of the Royal Highland Regiment* (Barrie & Jenkins; London, 1977), p.227.

19   H.J. Hanham, 'Religion and Nationality in the mid-Victorian Army', in M.R.D. Foot (ed.), *War and Society* (P. Elek; London, 1973), pp.163–4.

20   J. Fraser, *Sixty Years in Uniform* (Stanley Paul; London, 1939), p.42.

21   Field-Marshal Sir A. Wavell, *Soldiers and Soldiering* (J. Cape; London, 1953), p.125.

22   Royal Commission on Labour, *The Agricultural Labourer*. Vol.III, *Scotland*, Part I, C. 6894–XXXVI (1893–94), XV, pp.19–20; A.L. Bowley, *Wages and Incomes in the United Kingdom since 1860* (Cambridge University Press; Cambridge, 1937), p.10.

23   'The Pay Allowances and Stoppages of Privates of Infantry from 1660–1891', 27 June 1891, PRO, WO 33/51; Skelley, *The Victorian Army at Home*, pp.182–4, 188–9; E.C. Grenville Murray, *Six Months in the Ranks* (Smith, Elder & Co.; London, 1881), pp.69–71; *Wantage Report*, p.13; Robertson, *From Private to Field-Marshal*, p.5.

24   *Parl. Deb.*, Third Ser., Vol.222 (8 March 1875), col.1450; Vol.227 (2 March 1876), cols.1260–1; *The Times*, 18 March 1881, p.9; Lt.-Col. G.H. Adams, qs.1783–9, Maj.-Gen. G.H.S. Willis, q.2766 and Lt.-Col. Hon. R.H. de Montmorency, q.4260 evidence appended to the *Airey Report*, pp.211, 266 and 373; *Airey Report*, pp.27–31; *Short Service Report*, pp.15–17; *Wantage Report*, p.20.

25   Skelley, *The Victorian Army at Home*, pp.196–201; *Report of the Principal Changes in Army Organisation Effective 1 July 1881*, C. 2922 (1881), LVIII, p.5; 'The Advantages of the Army', 1 November 1896, *Pamphlets showing the Conditions of Service in the Army and Militia respectively*, No.81 (1898), LIV, pp.6–9.

26   Wolseley, q.4480 evidence appended to the *Wantage Report*, p.159.

27   Buller, qs.129, 155, 162, 324 and Cambridge, qs.2046, 2121, 2148–56 evidence appended to the *Wantage Report*, pp.6, 8, 13, 74, 78–9.

28   *Wantage Report*, pp.14–17, 27.

29   A.L. Haliburton, 'Dissent', 20 February 1892, appended to the *Wantage Report*, pp.35 and 40.

30   *Parl. Deb.*, Fourth Ser., Vol.93 (13 May 1901), col.1501 and Vol.10 (17 March 1893), col.409.

31 M. Trustram, *Women of the Regiment: Marriage and the Victorian Army* (Cambridge University Press; Cambridge, 1984), pp.29–30.
32 *Ibid.*, pp.84–5, 90–3; Maj. D.D. Maitland, 'The Care of the Soldier's Family', *Royal Army Medical Corps Journal* (1950), pp.107–25; *Report of the Commissioners appointed to inquire into the Regulations affecting the Sanitary Condition of the Army, the Organisation of Military Hospitals, and the Treatment of the Sick and Wounded*, C. 2318 (1857–8), XVIII, p.xviii.
33 E.M. Spiers, 'The Reform of the Front-line Forces of the Regular Army in the United Kingdom, 1895–1914', unpublished Ph.D. thesis (University of Edinburgh, 1974), Appendix X; Skelley, *The Victorian Army at Home*, pp.38–40; Henderson, *Highland Soldier*, pp.167–76.
34 *Report of the Committee appointed to enquire into the Question of Soldiers' Dietary, with appendices*, hereafter referred to as the *Stafford Northcote Report*, C. 5742 (1889), XVII, pp.8–10, 15–20.
35 Wyndham, *The Queen's Service*, pp.31–4; A.F. Corbett, *Service through Six Reigns* (Norwich, 1953), p.10.
36 *Stafford Northcote Report*, p.7; Skelley, *The Victorian Army at Home*, pp.24–7.
37 Sergeant J. Menzies, *Reminiscences of an old Soldier* (Crawford & McCabe; Edinburgh, 1883), p.3; Robertson, *From Private to Field-Marshal*, pp.6, 14–17; Wyndham, *The Queen's Service*, pp.43–4; Henderson, *Highland Soldier*, pp.210–15.
38 *Report on the Discipline and Management of Military Prisons*, C. 4209 (1868–69), XXX, p.4.
39 Trustram, *Women of the Regiment*, pp.118–26; F.B. Smith, 'Ethics and Disease in the later Nineteenth Century: the Contagious Diseases Acts', *Historical Studies*, Vol.15, No.57 (October 1971), pp.118–35; P. McHugh, *Prostitution and Victorian Social Reform* (Croom Helm; London, 1980), p.260; E.M. Sigsworth and T.J. Wyke, 'A Study of Victorian Prostitution and Venereal Disease', in M. Vicinus (ed.), *Suffer and be Still* (Indiana University Press; Bloomington, 1973), pp.77–99; R.L. Blanco, 'The Attempted Control of Venereal Disease in the Army of mid-Victorian England', *J.S.A.H.R.*, Vol.45 (1967), pp.234–41.
40 Spiers, *The Army and Society*, pp.63–4; Skelley, *The Victorian Army at Home*, pp.89–98, 163; *Reports of the Director of Military Education*, C. 1885 (1877), XXX, p.xxiv and C. 5805 (1889), XVII, p.21; *General Annual Returns of the British Army . . .*, C. 6196 (1890), XLIII, p.85 and C. 9426 (1899), LIII, p.96.
41 Hanham, 'Religion and Nationality in the mid-Victorian Army', pp.169–71; Anderson, 'The Growth of Christian Militarism', pp.59–60.
42 Hanham, 'Religion and Nationality in the mid-Victorian Army', pp.170–1; Robertson, *From Private to Field-Marshal*, p.8; Wyndham, *The Queen's Service*, p.68.
43 Upcher, q.4234, Leslie, q.12385, and Fraser, q.12967 evidence appended to the *Wantage Report*, pp.150, 420–1, and 449.
44 Skelley, *The Victorian Army at Home*, pp.213–14; 'Summary of the Recommendations of the Wantage Committee and of Action taken'; *Annual Report of the Inspector-General of Recruiting for 1898*, C. 9185 (1899), XI,

p.23.
45 *Report of the Committee on the Civil Employment of ex-Soldiers and Sailors*, C. 2991 (1906), XIV, p.5; *Annual Reports of the Inspector-General of Recruiting* . . ., C. 8370 (1897), XVI, p.17, C. 110 (1900), X, pp.21–2, and C. 519 (1901), IX, pp.23–4; J.M. Brereton, *The British Soldier: A Social History from 1661 to the present Day* (The Bodley Head; London, 1986), pp.93–4, 102; Spiers, 'The Reform of the Front-line Forces of the Regular Army in the United Kingdom, 1895–1914', appendix XI.
46 'The Advantages of the Army', p.10; *Wantage Report*, pp.17–18; Brereton, *The British Soldier*, pp.101–2; Skelley, *The Victorian Army at Home*, pp.208–10; *Return of the Discharged Soldiers chargeable on the Poor Rates of England, Scotland and Ireland in the Month of December 1897, as Inmates of Workhouses and in receipt of Out-door Relief*, No.332 (1898), LXXVIII, p.8; Brodrick, q.21807 evidence appended to the *Elgin Report*, Cd. 1791 (1904), XLI, p.556.
47 H. Wyndham, *The Queen's Service*, p.84.

6
Civil–military relations

In view of the reforms implemented in the late Victorian period, and the controversies which attended them, civil–military relations were often fraught with difficulties. Tensions were all too apparent in the relationships between various Secretaries of State and their military advisers; they found reflection in the correspondence and published pronouncements of some senior officers, in the reports of several Select Committees and Royal Commissions, and in the debates conducted in Parliament and the press. The debates focused upon issues of considerable importance, including the sanctity of long established parliamentary principles, the implications of imperial expansion, the viability of home defence, and the ethos, efficiency and role of the army itself. The outcome would depend partly upon the manner in which the army, despite its factious high command, presented its case and cultivated support, partly upon the response of successive governments in an increasingly partisan political climate (after the secession of the Liberal Unionists), and partly upon the salience or perceived significance of the issues themselves.

By the late nineteenth century, military participation in politics had a long established pedigree. Although officers took an oath of loyalty to the Crown and often depicted themselves as above party politics, they could still write and speak openly. They could promote or castigate army reforms, and they could serve in local or national politics. Wolseley was particularly prominent as an advocate of reform. In speeches and articles he championed the virtues of short service, the Army Reserve, and the localisation and linking of battalions, despite frequent rebukes from the Queen and the Duke of Cambridge. In his public advocacy, Wolseley recognised that political initiatives could provide a vital spur to reform. He regarded the army as a naturally conservative institution, inhibited by its discipline, deference to authority, and respect for tradition from reforming itself. Even the 'young school with advanced ideas', he argued, was held in check by habits of discipline and respect for authority. He feared that the service was likely to oppose any reforms emanating from the War Office or a Liberal government, especially if the Horse Guards let it be known that the proposals threatened cherished traditions. 'Great reforms', he concluded, would only be accepted after great reverses: 'discipline', he observed, 'is apt to make parrots of us all; we have much less individuality than the members of civil professions'.[1]

Having perceived the crucial role of politicians in instigating reform within the peacetime army, and having openly and vigorously supported their endeavours, Wolseley was deeply disappointed by their failure to sustain the process. After some seven years as Adjutant-General, he unfolded an extensive critique of the policies pursued by successive governments in *Harper's New Monthly Magazine* (February 1890). He ascribed the persistence of military shortcomings to a level of funding which neither buttressed the Cardwell reforms nor met the burgeoning commitments of Empire. Additional battalions, he insisted, had to be raised to restore the balance between those at home and those abroad, and so relieve the debilitating strain upon the home-based forces. More attractive rates of pay had to be offered if the voluntary army was to compete in the labour market for a better quality of recruit. More resources had to be invested if the Army Reserve was ever to be drilled, the armament of the horse and field artillery standardised, and the soldiers' barracks made more habitable and comfortable. False economies, argued Wolseley, had impaired the efficiency of the service, effectively preventing it from fulfilling its duties at home and abroad. Although the Commander-in-Chief had drawn attention to these deficiencies, he could neither correct them nor even apprise the public – the only factor which, in Wolseley's view, could have any effect upon party government. 'Our system of military administration has been growing more and more civilian in character since the days of Wellington. . . . Soldiers don't think the arrangement a good one.'[2]

Privately he deplored the baleful effects of party considerations upon contemporary politics. He was convinced that Ministers would never act on a 'great measure' unless forced to do so by public opinion and the risk of electoral losses. Indeed, he asserted that 'party government' involved 'the controlling of public opinion, diverting it into side issues so as to avoid expenditure which would be inconvenient from a party standpoint'.[3] He periodically despaired of the consequences of the democratic process – 'pandering to the whims of a mob in order to gain and retain power'.[4] He even yearned for a time when

the licence of democracy & socialism will be conquered by the sword, and succeeded by cruel military despotism. Then it will be that the man of talk will give way to the man of action, and the Gladstones, Harcourts, Morleys & all that most contemptible of God's creatures will black the boots of some successful Cavalry Colonel. A new Cromwell will clear the country of these frothing talkers, & the soldiers will rule. Would that my lot could have been cast in such an era.[5]

Wolseley never acted on these Caesarist sentiments. Although his determined quest in the mid to late 1870s for the command of a localised Indian Army independent of Horse Guards control might have been, as Adrian Preston asserts, 'the closest thing to a drift towards Caesarism that the Victorian Age experienced',[6] he only aspired to influence and control the military policy of the State, not the State itself. However much he might laud the achievements of Cromwell or Bonaparte in private, he still saw himself, as did most officers, as a servant of the Crown, and hence of Her Majesty's government. If he often criticised the policies of various governments, and the partisan divisions of contemporary politics, he neither questioned the legitimacy of the civilian administrations nor the principle of civilian supremacy. On the contrary, he favoured a more prominent role for the military within the policy-making and decision-taking process, and so advocated that the Commander-in-Chief should be able to report direct to Parliament upon the state of the nation's defences. Although successive governments blocked this proposal, which the Stephen Commission had endorsed, and circumscribed the role of the Commander-in-Chief still further, Wolseley never contested the paramountcy of civilian authority.[7]

Nevertheless, he realised that the conduct of brisk, successful and economical campaigns, and the staunch advocacy of military reforms, could make him both 'politically indispensable and nationally popular'. As a consequence, he expected accelerated promotions or field commands and a larger share in the making of military policy. He sought, thereby, to circumvent the traditional sources of patronage and to become relatively autonomous as a commander, possessing his own sources of patronage.[8] Many officers, taking their cue from the Duke of Cambridge, deprecated such political involvement. In serving the Queen, they saw their role as above and beyond the vagaries of party politics and as one which carried a superior social status. Wolseley endorsed their views on status. Ever contemptuous of his political masters, he delighted in comparing their profession with his own: 'The foolish public,' he informed the Queen, 'prefer believing the tradesman who has become a politician to the gentleman who wears Your Majesty's uniform.'[9] Yet he still believed that soldiers had to be involved politically, if only to mitigate the impact of ill-informed civilian Ministers. He believed, too, that well-advised Ministers, like Cardwell and Childers, could instigate reforms which would enhance the functioning of the service. In this respect, he was probably in a small minority; many shared the fears of the Duke of Cambridge that army reform would undermine

the old regimental system of our glorious Army. It has stood many shocks, and has done its duty nobly by the Crown and by the Country. It is worth saving.[10]

Officers who held such views might seem – in the terminology of Alfred Vagts – to be representatives of a militarist rather than a military army: an army more concerned with the maintenance of its customs, status and prestige than with its military efficiency.[11] The contrast, though, is too stark and has to be placed in context. Many of these officers probably shared the concern of the Duke of Cambridge about the rapid changes in society and the emergence of values which seemed inimical to the traditional ethos of the army. If they subsequently developed a citadel mentality and feared lest reform would weaken their status and prestige, this was largely a defensive reaction to the political and social changes around them. Moreover, they did not see any contradiction between the traditions and interests which they upheld, especially the importance of regimental *esprit de corps*, and the maintenance of military efficiency. As the heirs of the Wellingtonian army, they regarded these traditions and interests as vital to the army's effectiveness in the field, and, since war was an uncertain business, they assumed that success in the future could only be based on the tried and tested methods of the past. Where they erred was not so much in emphasising the importance of *esprit de corps*, but in asserting its supposed fragility. Regimental spirit proved remarkably pliable and resilient; it survived the introduction of short service, linked battalions, and the loss of historic numbers and facings. Although some friction erupted initially over the linking of regiments, it proved much less persistent and the changes much less deleterious than many had feared. Finally, some traditions from which regiments derived their *esprit de corps* were closely related to their proficiency as military units. Several regiments, notably the Rifle regiments, the 27th and the 58th Foot, took a positive pride in their musketry talents. They regarded their skill with a rifle as much a part of their *esprit de corps* as any other aspect of their history and traditions. After a disappointing performance in the First Boer War (1881), the 58th Foot (the 2nd Battalion, the Northamptonshire Regiment) resolved to improve its standard of musketry and entered the next South African War, in 1899, with a musketry standard averaging 'marksmen'.[12]

Nevertheless, the fears for the status, traditions and prestige of the army ensured that officers who championed reform, like Wolseley and his 'ring', remained a small and isolated group. Those officers, who deplored the Liberal reforms, placed a premium not only on loyalty and obedience to the Duke but also on conformity, on a solid wall against the enemy. Disparaging the activities of the Wolseley 'ring', they exaggerated its significance, so exacerbating a division which Secretaries of State could readily exploit. The further rivalry and competition for staff appointments between the 'rings' supporting Roberts and Wolseley merely emphasised that the army was not a monolithic body. The movement in favour of reform was split, with Roberts advocating proposals which differed radically from those of Wolseley inasmuch as they reflected his own military experience and strategic priorities shaped by service on the Indian subcontinent.[13] Even the 'rings' were not always cohesive: Wolseley's 'ring' was sometimes known as 'the young school with advanced ideas' and it suffered from the features which distinguished its members as a group, namely their youth, their ambition, and their extensive wartime service. Serving in small colonial wars earned them public acclaim, opportunities for faster promotion, and the wartime experience upon which they based many of their proposals, but it also meant that they spent considerable time either preparing for wars or fighting in wars. This impaired the momentum of reform at home and, during the Gordon Relief Expedition, the unison of the group. Several members of the 'ring' eagerly sought promotion, especially those, like Brackenbury, who came from less wealthy or only marginally wealthy backgrounds, but they sometimes suppressed their reforming zeal for fear of offending the Duke and of jeopardising their careers.[14]

Compounding these rivalries were the structural divisions within the army between the various arms and between the separate regiments. The Royal Engineers had several able, influential and well-connected senior officers, notably Lord Napier of Magdala, who kept 'one courtly step ahead of Wolseley in his wars and chief commands', and Sir John Lintorn Simmons, who advised Disraeli on the Eastern Question, accompanied the Prime Minister to the Congress of Berlin, and was Wolseley's main rival for the Egyptian command in 1882.[15] More fundamentally, the regimental system thwarted the emergence of a cohesive officer corps, with a common sense of identity, interests and grievances. As Michael Howard observed, the regimental system effectively tamed the officers, inhibiting any disposition to intervene politically by 'fixing their eyes on minutiae, limiting their ambitions, teaching them a gentle, parochial loyalty difficult to pervert to more dangerous ends'.[16] The late Victorian army, in short, was riven with internal divisions; it lacked the cohesion, the motives and the inclination to challenge the principle of civilian supremacy.

Nor did it have much opportunity to intervene. Although officers deeply resented the Liberal government which refused to avenge the defeat of Majuba Hill (1881) and failed to authorise a prompt relief of Gordon in Khartoum, many were serving in further campaigns, or were stationed overseas, or were scattered across the British Isles in isolated barracks. Some, too, had had first-hand experience of the difficulties and choices involved in political and civil administration. Seconded by various governments, officers acted as civil servants in numerous appointments throughout the Empire. While senior officers frequently assumed administrative responsibility for various colonies (Wolseley as Lieutenant-Governor of Natal in 1875 and the High Commissioner in Cyprus in 1878, Kitchener as Governor-General of Eastern Sudan in 1886–88 and Butler as the High Commissioner in South Africa in 1898–99) or commanded local armies (Evelyn Wood as Sirdar in the Egyptian Army), many others filled a variety of positions ranging from proconsular appointments and comptrollers to minor administrative posts (Brackenbury organised a force of military police and remodelled the prison service in Cyprus before serving as private secretary to the Viceroy in India). In readily changing from military to civil posts and back again, officers became imbued with a sense of imperial service and duty. They gained experience in the exercise of civil authority and some understanding of the constraints and difficulties of colonial administration. Above all, in accepting these appointments, they strengthened the links with their civilian counterparts and ensured that they did not feel isolated from the civil power.[17]

Complementing these overseas appointments was the extensive employment of officers and former officers in local politics and in administration within the United Kingdom. This was particularly apparent within the counties, where officers, who were scions of the local gentry, could undertake or were expected to undertake numerous duties in the making or implementation of administrative policies and in the maintenance of law and order. As W.L. Guttsman observed, the representatives of large landed interests were 'not only patrons of livings and Justices of the Peace but on them rested generally the major share of responsibility for the running of village schools, infirmaries, and other local welfare institutions'.[18] As many officers came from these families and assumed responsibilities as members of the rural elite, this helped to prevent the military from becoming self-contained and isolated from the rest of society.

Officers or more commonly former officers served at the apex of county society. In 1881, thirty-seven of the 122 Lords-Lieutenant in the United Kingdom had served in the army. Some like Lord Lurgan and the Duke of Richmond and Gordon had only served briefly, but the eighth Duke of Beaufort, the Lord-Lieutenant of Monmouthshire, had spent twenty years in the army, and Sir Charles Yorke, the Lord-Lieutenant of Tower Hamlets, was a Peninsular War veteran, who gained the rank of field-marshal in 1877 after seventy years of military service. There were also Lords-Lieutenant chosen from the major landowners outside the peerage such as Sir Robert Anstruther, the Lord-Lieutenant of Fifeshire. A former lieutenant-colonel in the Grenadier Guards, he owned 38,718 acres in Fife and Caithness. Traditionally, in the appointment of Lords-Lieutenant, the possession of military experience had had some relevance. Throughout most of the century they undertook specific military responsibilities within their counties. They appointed officers to commissions in the local Militia, accepted administrative responsibility for the local Volunteer forces, and, in the event of an emergency, would have taken command of all local forces. Even after the War Office assumed administrative responsibility for the Volunteer forces in 1871, many Lords-Lieutenant continued to serve as colonels of the newly formed regiments.

Another aspect of their 'guardian' role was the maintenance of law and order, primarily through the appointment of local magistrates. Until the creation of county councils in 1888, these magistrates were not merely responsible for dispensing justice but also had to exercise financial control of the police through quarter sessions, and implement parliamentary legislation by serving on local boards, like the boards of guardians, boards of health, and the highway boards. Many officers, whether retired or on half pay, met the criteria for serving as magistrates. They were socially respectable, law-abiding, had the leisure time to attend the petty and quarter sessions, and had the inclination to uphold the traditions and customs of rural society. The military magistrates included the sons of aristocratic families (such as the Marquess of Abergavenny, formerly of the 2nd Life Guards, who was a JP and DL for the county of Sussex, and the Earl of Lindsey, a former captain in the Grenadier Guards, who became JP and DL for the county of Lincoln), the owners of large landed estates (including Henry Arthur Herbert, JP and DL, formerly of the Coldstream Guards, who owned 47,238 acres in county Kerry, and Ewen Macpherson, JP and DL, who was a captain in the 42nd Highlanders and owned 42,000 acres in Inverness-shire), and several lords of the manor, like Lieutenant-Colonel John Marcon and Major William Lyon. Some officers followed their fathers in serving on the bench, including Major-General George Sandham, Warden Sergison, formerly a captain in the 4th Hussars, and Henry T. Boultbee, formerly a captain in the Royal Artillery. A few lacked any connection with the landed interest but merely undertook a magistracy as part of their post-service career. As Harries-Jenkins perceptively noted,

In a period when few other institutions could rival the position of the military as a complex bureaucratic organisation, military administrative experience was a positive asset to the potential magistrate.[19]

This experience seemed particularly appropriate for the task of administering the police forces under the County and Borough Police Act of 1856. Magisterial responsibilities reflected the quasi-military ideals which underpinned much of mid-nineteenth-century policing, especially the image of the police as 'servants', assisting their masters in the defence of property and social order in the countryside, and as possessing an ability to confront insurrection (and hopefully overcome it) in the towns. In the boroughs, magistrates often served on the watch committees of the town councils which had the power to select, direct and dismiss the borough policemen. As the latter had to operate within the framework of borough bye law, the watch committees enjoyed considerable latitude and financial autonomy (the central government originally provided only 25 per cent of the funds for the police forces, doubling this proportion in 1874). In the counties, where the Chief Constable enjoyed a statutory autonomy in the appointment, regulation and dismissal of his policemen, the magistrates, acting individually or corporately in quarter sessions, were still critically important. In the majority of English counties, individual magistrates served at the apex of the local police forces, which were deployed and organised on the basis of the petty sessional divisions. The magistrates levied the county rate from which they extracted the police fund, and their powers derived from the disposal of the police fund, including the payment of the county police, and from the selection of the Chief Constable for the county.[20]

In choosing their Chief Constables, magistrates tended to prefer men from a similar social background and with some military experience. Twenty-two of the twenty-four Chief Constables appointed between 1856 and 1880 had served in the army or navy, and eleven came from the ranks of the landed gentry. Several former officers also served in the police inspectorate; in 1869, Colonel Cobbe succeeded Major-General William Cartwright as the Inspector of Constabulary for the Midland region, and in the same year Lieutenant-Colonel Sir Edmund Henderson, RE, became the Chief Commissioner of Police. Major-General Sir Charles Warren proved a highly controversial appointment as the Chief Commissioner of the Metropolitan Police (1886–88). He was criticised for his purported 'militarisation' of police organisation and procedures, for the appointment of ex-army men to the new positions of Chief Constable and Assistant Chief Constable, for his impatience with 'civilian' interference from the Home Office and Scotland Yard, and for his handling of the Trafalgar Square disorders in 1887. Nevertheless, another officer, Colonel Sir Edward Bradford, was appointed as the Commissioner of the Metropolitan Police in 1890 and held the post until 1903. Appointing former officers reflected a desire to ensure that the police forces were organised, disciplined, and able to exert a degree of social control. In the counties it met the need, as expressed by the Home Office and felt by the justices themselves, that the autonomous Chief Constables should have an equal social standing with the county magistracy. These links were occasionally cemented by family ties; of John Barker's thirteen children, 'two sons became Deputy Lieutenants and J.P.s in Staffordshire, one became a Shropshire J.P., one became rector of Henstead in Suffolk, one served in the army, and one crowned an army career by becoming Chief Constable of Birkenhead'.[21]

The passage of the County Electors Act (1888) undoubtedly affected the ease with which officers and former officers participated in local administration through their membership of the magistracy. Although some stood for election under the restricted franchise and proved successful (the Rt. Hon. Sir Richard Paget, formerly of the 56th Foot and chairman of the Somerset quarter sessions, became the first chairman of the county council), others chose not to do so. In Cheshire, for example, the large land-owning families largely remained aloof from the county council elections of 1889; only thirty-four county magistrates offered themselves for election in the fifty-seven divisions, and a mere five of the fourteen chairmen of the petty sessions stood for election. The old patterns of social dominance within the counties, if not swept away, had certainly been diminished, and with them the assumption of some Victorian officers that they had an automatic right to exercise administrative responsibilities within their counties.[22]

Even so, the military still participated in national politics through their substantial presence in the House of Lords and the House of Commons. Throughout the nineteenth century, army officers formed a conspicuous group within the House of Lords, and their presence was all too apparent in the late Victorian period. In 1870, 1885 and 1898, there were 111, 132 and 182 officers in the Lords, comprising about 23, 27 and 35 per cent respectively of the total membership.[23] Their number included some distinguished officers who were ennobled during this period, including Napier (1868), Roberts (1880), Wolseley (1882) and Kitchener (1898), officers who had served with distinction in earlier campaigns (Lords Seaton and Strathnairn), and peers who had spent a lifetime of service in the army (including the second Viscount Templetown, the third Earl of Lucan and the fourth Earl de la Warr, headed by the Duke of Cambridge). For many others military service, often in a fashionable regiment, only lasted for a few years before they began to manage their country estates and assume the national and local responsibilities expected of them.

The military peers varied considerably in their contribution to the debates of the House of Lords and to the affairs of government. Some, such as the sixteenth Earl of Derby, the third Earl of Longford and Lord Wantage, VC, either served in government or participated in Select Committees or Royal Commissions; many others made only a notional contribution, rarely appearing in the House. Occasionally, as in the debates over the abolition of purchase or other military reforms, the military peers and their supporters could cause difficulties, and sometimes governments would try to counter their influence. Conflicts, though, were not particularly frequent; more generally the military peers exercised a degree of political influence collectively by their membership of the House of Lords, and individually, in many cases, by their family connections, territorial status, and their extensive powers of patronage.[24]

Another traditional form of military participation in politics was through membership of the House of Commons. Following a pattern established in the unreformed House, and sustained in the wake of the Reform Act of 1832, some officers regularly sought entry into the House of Commons. In February 1870 there were 102 Members of Parliament who had served in the army (see Table 13). Comprising some 16 per cent of the total membership of the House, the military Members constituted a significant proportion of both parties (fifty-eight were Conservative and forty-four Liberal). They reflected the continuing appeal and acceptability of their dual role, especially for the heirs or the younger sons of the peerage.

These Members of Parliament brought a wide range and diversity of military experience into the House. Although the vast majority had spent only a few years in a fashionable regiment (and some like Sir Henry Bruce and Sir Watkins Wynn barely more than a year in the 1st Life Guards), several had distinguished records of military service. Robert Lloyd-Lindsay, Henry Wilmot and the Hon. Augustus Anson held the Victoria Cross for acts of personal bravery during the Crimean War or the Indian Mutiny; some had spent a lifetime of service in the army (thirty years by Major-General Sir

Table 13 *The background and rank of the military interest in the House of Commons in February 1870*

Military rank	Kin of peer	Son of baronet	Gentry	Other	Total
Colonels and all generals	5	1	1		7
Lt-Colonels	1	1	8		10
Majors	3	3	2	1	9
Captains and subalterns	40	10	23	3	76
Total	49	15	34	4	102

Sources: M. Stenton (ed.), *Who's Who of British Members of Parliament* (Harvester; Hassocks, 1976), Vols. 1 and 2; *McCalmont's Parliamentary Poll Book British Election Results 1832–1918* (Harvester; Hassocks, 1971), E. Walford, *The County Families of the United Kingdom*, J.H. Burke, *Peerage and Baronetage*, *The Dictionary of National Biography*.

Percy Egerton Herbert, over forty years by Sir Henry Ferguson Davie and the Rt. Hon. George C. Forester, who retired as general in 1877). If few officers had served in the Royal Artillery or the Royal Engineers (two and one respectively), some had or would command their regiments (including Edward H. Clive, who became the lieutenant-colonel commanding the Grenadier Guards from 1880 to 1885).

Officers probably embarked upon a political career for a variety of reasons. Some held strong political convictions; Guildford Onslow, for example, favoured shortened parliaments, an extension of the franchise, the introduction of the ballot and the abolition of Church rates. In this period, though, there were few officers who sought to emulate those mid-century Radicals, Lieutenant-General Sir George De Lacy Evans and Lieutenant-Colonel Thomas Perronet Thompson, in promoting various reforms and in challenging the civil power. The majority of officers probably entered politics either in the quest for individual preferment or to advance their family interests. As a military career held little prospect of either tangible rewards, material advantages or rapid promotion, some officers understandably chose to pursue their political ambitions. Lord George Hamilton, the third son of the first Duke of Abercorn, who entered Parliament in 1868, chose to concentrate on politics after a successful maiden speech on the Irish Church Bill. He retired from the army in 1869, after a mere five years of service, and pursued a political career which brought him appointments as Under-Secretary of State for India (1874–78), First Lord of the Admiralty (1885–86 and 1886–92), and Secretary of State for India (1895–1903).[25] Preserving family interests probably motivated many political aspirants. Some, who came from families which wielded considerable territorial influence, represented the proprietory boroughs over which their families had long held sway. Captain Mervyn Archdale, formerly of the 6th Inniskilling Dragoons, represented the county of Fermanagh from 1834 to 1874, in which he owned 27,410 acres. Similarly, Lord Claud Hamilton represented County Tyrone from 1839 to 1874, a county in which his brother, the Duke of Abercorn, owned 60,000 acres. The territorial influence wielded by various peers, such as the Earl of Lichfield and the Marquess of Anglesey, enabled them to promote the political careers of members of their respective families, irrespective of whether or not they had served in the army. This equally applied to some large land-owning families, such as Munro-Ferguson of Raith House, Kirkcaldy, and Acland-Hood of St Audries, Bridgwater. They both sustained successive generations of military Members of Parliament; indeed, the Hood family provided three Members of Parliament for West Somerset (1847–51, 1859–68 and 1892–1911).

Peers sometimes expected their heirs to enter politics in the hope of preparing them for their future responsibilites. As Harries-Jenkins indicates, there was virtually a 'socialisation process', beginning with education at a public school, followed by a further course at university or Sandhurst, a brief period of service in a fashionable regiment, and a short spell as a member of the House of Commons. In many families only the younger sons joined the military establishment, but there were several examples of heirs passing through this process, including Viscount Seaham, who spent three years in the Life Guards and seven years in the House of Commons before succeeding as the fifth Marquess of Londonderry, and the Hon. Edward Douglas-Pennant, who spent six years in the Scots Fusilier Guards and five years in the Commons before succeeding as the third Baron Penrhyn.[26]

In some boroughs local political parties wished to return a military or naval officer to the House of Commons. This was fairly rare; in many instances the wealth and influence of the prospective candidate and of his family were of much more importance than his service background. Captain Henry Jervis-White-Jervis, for example, appealed to the notoriously venal electors of Harwich because of his personal wealth, the influence of his father-in-law, J.C. Cobbold, who was a large local landowner, and his subsequent appointment to the board of the Great Eastern Railway, which had invested heavily in the borough. Nevertheless, in boroughs based upon garrison towns and dockyards, with small electorates and a history of closely contested elections, both parties recognised that a member of the armed services might attract some crucial votes. In 1868 the Liberals retained Chatham with Arthur J. Otway, formerly of the 51st Foot, defeating Rear-Admiral G. Elliot in a re-run of their contest in 1865. Six years later Elliot gained his revenge, defeating Otway. Nominating service candidates, with strong local connections, may have helped the Liberals to capture one of the Canterbury seats (in 1868) and Winchester (in 1880) – two cathedral towns with a strong military presence and small electorates. The Conservatives, however, quickly recaptured both boroughs, and, by the mid-1880s, could apparently rely on the support of the vast majority of their military electors (estimated to number 200 out of 2,048 voters in Winchester, and about 130 out of 3,508 in Canterbury). In larger constituencies, with a larger military presence (such as Hampshire North, containing the Aldershot garrison and training area, and Woolwich, with its barracks, academy, and arsenal employing several thousand people), the Conservative strength was overwhelming. The Conservatives did not need to nominate service candidates for either constituency, and the Liberals either struggled to find suitable candidates (sometimes failing to do so in Hampshire North) or hoped that service candidates could erode the Conservative majority in Woolwich, which they never did.[27]

The parties were also willing to sponsor officers to fill specific appointments at junior ministerial level. Cardwell sought the appointment of Major-General Sir Henry Storks as Surveyor-General of the Ordnance in 1870, and his nomination for the borough of Ripon in the following year, largely to compensate for his own lack of knowledge about military subjects and to share his parliamentary burdens in the Commons. Although Gladstone endorsed this request, he deplored Cardwell's subsequent suggestion that Sir William Mansfield, the former Commander-in-Chief in India, should replace him as Secretary of State for War. The Premier maintained that 'the qualities of a good administrator and statesman went further to make a good War Minister than those of a good soldier'.[28] Military experience, in short, had a fairly limited appeal, at least for political purposes.

The political contributions of the military Members of Parliament were as varied as those of any other group in the Commons. Radical suspicions that many of them abused their parliamentary privileges for their own professional purposes (either defending their role in disputed military incidents or championing the privileges of their regimental comrades or trying to influence Ministers on matters of military procedure)[29] were almost certainly exaggerated. While some may have done so, others were certainly not preoccupied with service issues and many were relatively inconspicuous on the floor of the House. A few, nonetheless, pursued distinguished political careers. William Cowper-Temple spent forty-five years in the Commons, holding numerous appointments, including President of the Board of Health (1855–57, 1857–58), Paymaster-General (1859–60) and Commissioner of Works and Buildings (1860–66). Lord Eustace Cecil was Surveyor-General of the Ordnance (1874–80) and the chairman of several companies. Colonel the Hon. F.A. Stanley, later the sixteenth Earl of Derby, became Secretary of State for War (1878–80), for the Colonies (1885–86), President of the Board of Trade (1886–88) and Governor-General of Canada (1888–93).

Collectively the service Members, known as 'the Colonels' during Cardwell's term in office, had a fairly limited impact. Split between the two main parties (so posing only a limited threat to the Liberal majority), they lacked any formal leadership, organisation or group cohesion, and rarely mustered their full support. Indeed, they never formed a separate bloc, and many, having served so briefly in their regiments, did not identify with 'the Colonels' and their concerns. These divisions were sharply exposed during the committee stages of the Army Regulation Bill. In the critical vote on 25 May 1871, when the Liberal majority slumped to a bare sixteen votes, only thirty-eight service Members voted in the opposition lobby while another sixteen and Sir Henry Storks voted for the government. On the third reading of the Bill, the Liberal whips ensured a government majority of fifty-eight votes (see Chapter 1).

The political convulsions of the 1870s and 1880s transformed the political composition of the service membership, if not its influence. The upheavals were particularly dramatic in southern Ireland, where the Home Rule movement of the early 1870s introduced a purely

Irish party into Irish politics, and where the Ballot Act of 1872 reduced, albeit partially, the political influence of the landowners. Several officers still contested elections as Home Rule candidates, and five were Members of Parliament in 1885, but their numbers steadily dwindled. By February 1896, Ireland had five service Members (compared with twenty-two in February 1870) and only one was a Nationalist (Major James Jameson). Similarly the proportion of officers on the Liberal benches fell sharply after 1885 (when there were seventeen Liberals in addition to the thirty-seven Conservative and five Home Rule officers). Of the Liberals, eight retired in 1885 or 1886, five were defeated in the elections of 1885 and 1886, three became Liberal Unionists (and another of the retired Members, the Hon. F.W. Lambton, eventually re-entered the Commons as a Liberal Unionist in 1900). Only one remained in politics as a Gladstonian Liberal – General Sir George Balfour, representing Kincardineshire until 1892. Admittedly a few more officers entered politics as Liberals (there were four in addition to the fifty-five Conservative and Liberal Unionist Members in February 1896), but the Liberal schism of 1886, with the loss of so many Whigs from the Liberal ranks, had gravely weakened the party, particularly in the English counties. Henceforth the service Members would be overwhelmingly Conservative in their political allegiance.[30]

The service Members participated prominently in the army reform debates of the 1890s.The basis for a political controversy over army reform had been laid in the late 1880s by the reports of various Royal Commissions, the well publicised criticisms of Wolseley, and the findings of the Select Committees appointed at the request of Lord Randolph Churchill after his resignation as Chancellor of the Exchequer over the scale of army expenditure. The committee of 1887 issued five reports of testimony by military and civilian authorities, which found that the costs of the army had risen not on account of general extravagance but because of decisions by successive governments. Instead of discovering waste and mismanagement, the committee accepted the need for large appropriations to facilitate the mobilisation of two army corps. Reconstituted in 1888, the committee found that the politicians, and not the military, were responsible for the large expenditure upon the Army without securing an adequate return for it. The committee realised, too, that the requirements of national security had been compromised by political considerations.[31] As successive governments embarked

upon further campaigns in the 1890s – the Ashanti War, the Second
Sudan War, and several on the North West Frontier – without
adding a battalion (until 1897), they exacerbated the strain upon the
home-based battalions.

The consequences were examined by three distinct groups – a
small clique of civilian reformers, Lord Roberts and his advisers in
India, and a large proportion of the service Members of Parliament.
The civilian reformers included Henry Spenser Wilkinson, a jour-
nalist and military historian, Sir Charles Dilke, a Radical Member of
Parliament who specialised in matters pertaining to imperial
defence, and Hugh Arnold-Forster, a Liberal Unionist Member of
Parliament who possessed a considerable knowledge of the technical
details of naval and military organisation. These writers kept abreast
of military developments in Britain and Europe; attended
manoeuvres, military exercises and gunnery displays; and provided
the literary and intellectual leadership of the campaign. They gained
military endorsement from those officers in India who supported
Lord Roberts in his rivalry with Viscount Wolseley, and military
advice from Roberts himself. They relied upon the service Members
to proffer assistance in Parliament and in their campaigns to
influence the cabinet.

Initially it proved quite difficult to forge sufficient cohesion among
these groups. In the autumn of 1893 Wilkinson suggested that the
civilian reformers should seek some agreement among themselves,
and, at a subsequent dinner with Dilke and General Sir George
Chesney, a Conservative MP and writer of books on home defence
and the Indian Army, they agreed to draft a letter of common
principles on imperial defence and send it to Gladstone, then Prime
Minister, and the leaders of the opposition – Lord Salisbury, the
Duke of Devonshire, Arthur Balfour and Joseph Chamberlain. It
took until 4 February 1894 before they could compose their
differences. In their letter, dated 12 February 1894, they emphasised
that imperial defence was an issue which transcended party political
differences, and that it was too complicated to be left to the separate
departments of the War Office and the Admiralty. They asserted that
the cabinet would only be able to consider war as a whole if one
Minister held the offices of Secretary of State for War and First Lord
of the Admiralty (or if these offices were amalgamated), and if the
cabinet had the advice of professional officers from each service.
They conceded, however, that if a difference of opinion occurred

between the cabinet and its naval or military adviser on an important issue of policy, the latter would have to resign. None of the political leaders supported this idea, but Balfour believed that a defence committee of the cabinet could achieve some co-ordination between the two services. Dilke doubted that this compromise would guarantee an examination of the requirements for war, but he accepted it as a step forward and welcomed the creation of a committee by the incoming Conservative government in August 1895.[32]

Fundamentally, the reformers believed that imperial defence was a topic which embraced both the army and navy, even if the Senior Service had the primary role. Wilkinson had converted Dilke to this point of view during their joint compilation of *Imperial Defence* in 1891. They agreed that the supplementary duties of the army included the maintenance of the overseas garrisons; home defence (against a *coup-de-main* and not the massed invasion of 150,000 men which the War Office feared and which the reformers dismissed as incredible on account of Britain's naval power); the policing of the Empire in colonial warfare; counter-attack in a major war once command of the sea had been secured; and resistance *en masse* in the extreme case of naval disaster. They feared that the army, as fashioned by Cardwell and Childers, could never meet these requirements. In numerous works, they argued that the imbalance of battalions at home and abroad had impaired the efficiency of the home battalions, reduced their officers to little more than training instructors, and forced the enlistment of 'specials' to sustain the levels of recruiting. They condemned the unprecedented peacetime despatch of battalions from the Brigade of Guards to Gibraltar, a station devoid of training facilities, and deprecated the shortage of horses for the cavalry, the lack of batteries for the artillery, and the disorganised, under-manned, and ill-equipped condition of the auxiliary forces.[33]

The reformers asserted that the Cardwell system had caused the breakdown. They denounced the effects of the short service system and deferred pay, arguing that the current terms of service were an unsatisfactory compromise between a genuine short service enlistment and a full military career with pension rights. They condemned the linking of battalions, claiming that it was illogical to expect a battalion to serve as both a depot and a fighting unit. They questioned the achievements of territorial localisation, noting that some battalions could never rely on their depopulated districts for sufficient recruits, and stressing that the constant movement of battalions meant that some were only infrequently quartered in their own districts. Finally, they castigated the main achievement of the Cardwell system – the Army Reserve. They deprecated the absence of any prescribed period of training for reservists, which meant that the Reserve would always be an unknown quantity in its military skills, physical fitness and discipline. They complained, too, that the wartime role of the Reserve differed from that of foreign reserves, that is, it was not intended as a supplement to the peacetime army but as a substitute for the ineffectives and shortages in the home-based battalions. Consequently, the army was liable to exhaust the Reserve quickly in a major war, while finding it impossible to mobilise without the Reserve in a minor war.[34]

To remedy these deficiencies, the critics advocated the complete removal of the Cardwell system.They adopted the proposal, previously advanced by Lord Roberts, of replacing the present terms of enlistment with two separate terms of enlistment for the home and overseas armies. Wilkinson had originally favoured the creation of two separate armies, but Roberts persuaded him that the home army could be manned by men recruited for three years in the Colours, followed by nine years in the Reserve, and the overseas army by men who had enlisted for twelve years, with the option either of serving for three years in the Reserve or of an additional nine years' service with pension rights. The reformers argued that concomitant long and short terms of service, if buttressed by other reforms – the abolition of deferred pay and grocery stoppages, improvements in barrack and canteen facilities, more government employment of discharged soldiers, and the introduction of differential rates of pay for boys and efficient soldiers – would prove attractive to potential recruits and provide seasoned soldiers for Indian service. They also advocated the unlinking of battalions, the restoration of the old regimental numbers, and the feeding of overseas battalions from large depots. They insisted that the artillery and cavalry had to be supplied with sufficient guns and horses to permit realistic training in peacetime and to facilitate mobilisation planning. Finally, they demanded a devolution of administrative responsibility to an intermediate level between the War Office and the 141 battalions, and the replacement of the territorial localisation by a quartering of the home army in which divisions and corps could be trained as units and their commanders and staffs gain experience in the handling of large formations.[35]

In presenting these proposals, the reformers sought to exert pressure on the government by three methods – parliamentary debates, direct appeals to cabinet Ministers, and campaigns in the press. The debates and appeals, which relied upon the support of the service Members, proved the least successful. After the service Members, supported by other backbench Conservatives, had precipitated the fall of the Liberal government over the cordite vote (21 June 1895), they returned to the subsequent Parliament with an inflated view of their own importance. Their opinion, argued Sir Henry Havelock-Allan, VC, 'was of such weight and importance that it could not be disregarded by any government however strong'.[36]

This influence proved more apparent than real. On the one hand, the service Members enjoyed the caustic criticisms which Dilke and Arnold-Forster hurled at both front benches, and used the literary talents of these civilians to express their own fulminations over the crisis in the home army. In a letter addressed to Lord Lansdowne, the committee of service Members supported Dilke and Arnold-Forster in claiming that the military crisis had been caused by the malfunctioning of the Cardwell system, the erosion of regimental spirit, and the malevolent influence of War Office clerks. On the other hand, these Members had little to offer in support of specific reforms. While some simply endorsed the views of Dilke and Arnold-Forster, others thought that the Cardwell system could be made to work, but the overwhelming majority had neither studied the finer points of army organisation nor had any interest in problems outside those of their own particular regiment or military arm. Campbell-Bannerman shrewdly observed that 'it is the barrack-yard alone that is represented among the militaries in the House of Commons', and Wilkinson recognised 'the difficulty of getting the service members to appreciate a sound system'.[37]

In sum, the civilian reformers found little support for a positive and coherent campaign within Parliament. Even when they simply criticised the malaise within the home army, the service Members provided vocal rather than voting support. They were reluctant to vote against the government and recoiled at the prospect of sharing a lobby with Radicals and Irish Members, who readily supported any division against the Army Estimates. On 8 February 1897, when Dilke divided the House over short service enlistment, the service Members, including three naval officers, voted 33 to 10 against the motion, which was defeated by 197 to 63 votes.[38] The service Members were only an irritant for the Conservative government, one which it occasionally felt compelled to appease, but one which it rarely, if ever, had cause to fear.

The reformers achieved more from the press campaign initiated by Arnold-Forster. The well timed campaign from November 1897 to January 1898 coincided with the discussion of the Army Estimates within the cabinet, and followed the public admission of Wolseley, in receiving the freedom of the city of Glasgow, that 'our army machinery is overstrained and is out of gear . . . no longer able to meet effectively the demands now made upon it'.[39] Brodrick, the Under-Secretary of State for War, publicly agreed that the calls upon the army had become incessant, with 50,000 men now engaged on the North West Frontier, and that the Cardwell balance had been deranged, with 56,000 men at home and 78,000 abroad.[40] In seven letters to *The Times*, Arnold-Forster did not add to his previous criticisms of the Cardwell system, but, after the admissions of Wolseley and Brodrick, his comments aroused much greater interest. Sir Arthur Haliburton, the former Permanent Under-Secretary of State, wrote several letters of reply *to The Times*, vehemently defending the Cardwell system as the source of all improvements in the army since 1870. Any failings, he asserted, only reflected a failure to develop fully the original proposals, and so only marginal reforms were necessary – a limited liability upon reservists to serve abroad in small wars and an increase in the number of batteries and battalions to realise a parity between the battalions at home and abroad and to augment the proportion of guns to sabres. He insisted that the War Office was the true custodian of army reform, and that the advocates of change in 1897 were little different from the opponents of change in 1870.[41]

After the presentation of these uncompromising positions, Lord Lansdowne entered the fray with a far less rigid defence of the Cardwell system. As a newcomer to the War Office, he had not manned the barricades for the past generation in the defence of the Cardwell principles. A former Governor-General of India (1888–93), he had established far better relations with Roberts, an enthusiastic reformer, than he would do with Wolseley, and he praised Roberts and Dilke as 'high military authorities'. Yet he had to answer the questions raised by Arnold-Forster, both publicly and in cabinet, and had to reassure his cabinet colleagues, even offering to resign over the issue.[42]

In cabinet memoranda, and in an address to the Primrose League in Edinburgh on 9 December 1897, Lansdowne argued that the principles of the Cardwell system were inherently sound. He claimed that the army of 1897 was substantially stronger than the army of 1870, and that the proposed reforms would prove costly (possibly increasing the pension bill by £2,000,000 per annum), would not supply the same quality of drafts from depots as the home battalions had done, and that a short service army would be even more dependent upon the Reserve than the present force. He admitted, though, that the Cardwell system had lacked elasticity and had been far too easily disorganised. He endorsed demands for increases in the size and number of the home battalions, in the proportion of guns to sabres, and for the introduction of a limited liability upon some Reservists to serve abroad in small wars. Lansdowne also agreed to experiment with three-year enlistments and to improve the conditions of service for efficient soldiers, promising to abolish grocery charges and deferred pay, introduce differential payments, improve opportunities to learn a trade in the Colours, and give more preference to discharged soldiers in government employment. By pressing for substantial increases in men and *matériel*, and by offering concessions in detail and in minor structural changes, he hoped to preserve the Cardwell system.[43]

Lansdowne had effectively used and controlled the reform debate. By appearing as a conciliatory figure, untrammelled by departmental dogma and yet unwilling to cast aside a functioning system for an untried alternative, he used the reform agitation as a bargaining lever within the cabinet. In support of his artillery proposals, he claimed that 'public opinion is apparently unanimous in demanding a large augmentation of the Force'.[44] As a result he secured the army's largest establishment and its greatest increase in peacetime (fifteen new batteries, thirty-two extra horses for each of the eight cavalry regiments on a higher establishment, another eighty men for each home battalion, a Special Reserve of 5,000 men with a limited liability to serve abroad in their first year of reserve service, and another six battalions to be linked with existing battalions in fours, so enabling three to be sent abroad at one time).[45] This achievement mellowed the service Members and prompted Dilke to withdraw his ritual amendment to the Army Estimates. Lansdowne's success underlined the inherent strength of the department when assumptions were shared by the War Office and its critics. On this occasion, there was a consensus that a crisis existed, and that it had adversely affected the home battalions. Lansdowne, therefore, was able to limit the scope of the debate; by concentrating upon increased numbers and improved conditions of service, he deflected criticism from the purposes and priorities of the Cardwell system.

The civilian authorities, in short, had never been seriously challenged during the late Victorian period. They had faced criticism and protests from their military advisers, and a more expansive critique from the army reformers, but never any challenge to their political supremacy. Although the Duke of Cambridge and Wolseley struggled unsuccessfully for a more influential role in policy formation, army officers sustained their involvement in politics and public administration. They served in the magistracy, in colonial administration, and in local and national politics. Admittedly, relatively few officers appeared to have any political aspirations, and the collective achievement of those who entered politics, and acted as service Members of Parliament, was hardly considerable. The army reform movement only achieved a measure of success in the late 1890s because of the articulate and skilful leadership of some well informed civilians, the widespread perception of a military crisis, and the willingness of the War Office to press demands for more men and *matériel*. Even so, the military were never isolated; their officers participated in the debates within the War Office, Parliament and the press, and made a generally positive contribution to civil–military relations.

Notes

1   Maj.-Gen. (later Lt.-Gen.) Sir G. Wolseley, 'England as a Military Power in 1854 and in 1878', and 'Long and Short Service', *Nineteenth Century*, Vol.111 (March 1878), pp.433–56 and Vol.IX (March 1881), pp.558–72.

2   General Viscount Wolseley, 'The Standing Army of Great Britain', pp.336–45.

3   Wolseley to Brodrick, 3 October 1890, Midleton Mss, PRO, 30/67/1, f.34.

4   Wolseley to Lady Wolseley, 1 October 1884, Wolseley Mss., W/P 13/22.

5   Wolseley to Lady Wolseley, 1 November 1890, Wolseley Mss., W/P 19/51.

6   A. Preston, 'Introduction', in P. Dennis and A. Preston (eds.), *Soldiers as Statesmen* (Croom Helm; London, 1976), p.31.

7   Wolseley, 'England as a Military Power in 1854 and in 1878', p.452; Hamer, *The British Army*, pp.122–3; S.E. Finer, *The Man on Horseback: The Role of the Military in Politics* (Pall Mall Press; London, 1962), p.30.

8   A. Preston, 'Introduction', p.29 and 'Frustrated Great Gamesmanship: Sir Garnet Wolseley's Plans for War against Russia, 1873–1880', *International History Review*, Vol.11 (January 1980), pp. 239–65.

9   Wolseley to Queen Victoria, 22 March 1885; in Buckle (ed.), *The Letters of Queen Victoria*, Second Ser., Vol.3, p.632.

10 Cambridge to Queen Victoria, 27 December 1880, in Verner, *The Military Life of H.R.H. Duke of Cambridge*, Vol.2, p.217.

11 A. Vagts, *A History of Militarism* (Norton; New York, 1937), p.13.

12 Col. J.K. Dunlop, *The Development of the British Army 1899–1914* (Methuen; London, 1938), p.37; Regimental Historical Records Committee, *The Royal Inniskilling Fusiliers*, pp.339–40.

13 Lt.-Gen. Sir F.S. Roberts, 'Free Trade in the Army', *Nineteenth Century*, Vol.15 (1884), pp.1055–74.

14 Brackenbury to Blackwood, 27 November 1874 and 11 October 1880, Blackwood Mss., National Library of Scotland, MS 4,315 and 4,403.

15 A. Preston, 'Wolseley, the Khartoum Relief Expedition and the Defence of India, 1885–1900', *Journal of Imperial and Commonwealth History*, Vol.6 (1978), pp.260, 270–1.

16 M. Howard, 'Soldiers in Politics', *Encounter*, Vol.XIX (September 1962), pp.77–81; Keegan, 'Regimental Ideology', pp.14–15.

17 Harries-Jenkins, *The Army in Victorian Society*, pp.217–18.

18 W.L. Guttsman, *The British Political Elite* (Macgibbon & Kee; London, 1965), p.142.

19 Harries-Jenkins, *The Army in Victorian Society*, p.255; the data on the Lords-Lieutenant and the magistracy for 1881 was culled from E. Walford, *The County Families of the United Kingdom*, J. Bateman, *The Great Landowners of Great Britain and Ireland*, J. Burke, *Peerage and Baronetage, The Dictionary of National Biography* and F. Boase, *Modern English Biography*.

20 C. Steedman, *Policing the Victorian Community: the Formation of English Provincial Police Forces, 1856–80* (Routledge; London, 1984), pp.3, 37, 43–50, 54.

21 F.M.L. Thompson, *English Landed Society in the Nineteenth Century* (Routledge & Kegan Paul; London, 1963), p.128; V. Bailey, 'The Metropolitan Police, the Home Office and the Threat of outcast London' in V. Bailey (ed.), *Policing and Punishment in Nineteenth Century Britain* (Croom Helm; London, 1981), pp.106–7; Steedman, *Policing the Victorian Community*, pp.47–9.

22 J.M. Lee, *Social Leaders and Public Persons* (Clarendon Press; Oxford, 1963), pp.56–7; Harries-Jenkins, *The Army in Victorian Society*, pp.256–7.

23 *Ibid.*, p.218; data on the Lords for 1870 were culled from the sources which are mentioned in n.19 above and from the Hon. Vicary Gibbs *et al.*, *The Complete Peerage*, 13 Vols. (St. Catherine's Press; London, 1910–38)

and L. G. Pine, *New Extinct Peerage* (Heraldry Today; London, 1972).
24 Harries-Jenkins, *The Army in Victorian Society*, p.219; Guttsman, *British Political Elite*, p.111; for attempts to counteract the influence of the Duke of Cambridge and his supporters in the House of Lords, see Preston, 'Wolseley, the Khartoum Relief Expedition and the Defence of India, 1885–1900', p.269.
25 Hamilton, *Parliamentary Reminiscences and Reflections 1868–1906*, Vol.1, p.15.
26 Harries-Jenkins, *The Army in Victorian Society*, pp.230–42.
27 H. Pelling, *Social Geography of British Elections 1885–1910* (Macmillan; London, 1967), pp.11–12, 37, 40, 81, 131 and 138; *The Constitutional Yearbook 1885*, pp.145 and 159; H.J. Hanham, *Elections and Party Management* (Harvester Press; Hassocks, 1978), pp.60–2.
28 Gladstone to Cardwell, 5 January 1871; see also Cardwell to Gladstone, 17 November 1870 and 3 January 1871, Gladstone Mss., B.L. Add. Mss.44,539, f.124; 44,119, ff.173–4 and 191–2.
29 G. Hooper, 'The Army', *Questions for a Reformed Parliament* (Macmillan; London, 1867), p.227.
30 On the Irish political developments, see Hanham, *Elections and Party Management*, pp.183–6 and F.S.L. Lyons, *Ireland since the Famine* (Fontana; London 1973), pp.153 and 169; on the effects of the Liberal schism, see R. Blake, *The Conservative Party from Peel to Churchill* (Eyre & Spottiswoode; London, 1970), pp.153, 159–60 and R. Douglas, *The History of the Liberal Party 1895–1970* (Sidgwick & Jackson; London, 1971), pp.4–5.
31 Hamer, *The British Army: Civil–Military Relations 1885–1905*, pp.96–113; the reports from the Select Committee on Army and Navy Estimates were C. 216, 223, 232, 239 and 259 (1887), VIII and from the Select Committee on Army Estimates were C. 120, 212 and 225 (1888), VIII and C. 269 and 285 (1888), IX.
32 S. Gwynn and G.M. Tuckwell, *The Life of Sir Charles W. Dilke*, 2 Vols. (John Murray; London, 1917), Vol.2, pp.417–23; Chesney to Wilkinson, 4 February 1894, Wilkinson Mss., Army Museums Ogilby Trust, 13/9.
33 Dilke and Wilkinson, *Imperial Defence*, pp.138, 140–3; H.O. Arnold-Forster, *Army Letters 1897–8* (E. Arnold; London, 1898), pp.18–60; Sir C.W. Dilke, *Army Reform* (Service & Paton; London, 1898), p.27.
34 H.O. Arnold-Forster, 'Memorandum with regard to the condition of the Army and the existing military system', 16 June 1897, Balfour Mss., B.L. Add. Mss.49,722, ff.20, 22–3, 31–3 and *Army Letters 1897–8*, pp.72–8, 86–9, 98–9 and 100; Dilke and Wilkinson, *Imperial Defence*, pp.143 and 149; and Dilke, *Army Reform*, p.67.
35 Roberts, 'Free Trade in the Army', pp.1062–5; Wilkinson to Roberts, 20 May 1892, Roberts Mss., NAM, 7101–23–87–3, Arnold-Forster, 'Memorandum . . .', ff.35–6 and 40; Dilke and Wilkinson, *Imperial Defence*, pp.155–60; Dilke, *Army Reform*, pp.61–4; *Parl. Deb.*, Fourth Ser., Vol.41 (19 June 1896), col.1477 and Vol.54 (25 February 1898),

cols.75–6.

36 *Parl. Deb.*, Fourth Ser., Vol.51 (23 July 1897), cols.942–3. For an account of the tactics used over the cordite vote, see Sir A.S.T. Griffith Boscawen, *Fourteen Years in Parliament* (John Murray; London, 1907), pp.72–3.

37 Campbell-Bannerman to Haliburton, 6 January 1898, in J.B. Atlay, *Lord Haliburton: a memoir of his public service* (Smith, Elder & Co.; London, 1909), p.212; Wilkinson to Dilke, 20 March 1900, Dilke Mss., B.L. Add. Mss.43,916, f.198; Services Committee to Lord Lansdowne, 20 January 1898, in H.O. Arnold-Forster, *Army Letters, 1897–8*, pp.187–91; *Parl. Deb.*, Fourth Ser., Vol.51 (23 July 1897), cols.943–4 and Vol.54 (25 February 1898), cols.91–2; Tearem, MP, 'The Military Amateurs', *Contemporary Review*, Vol.LXXIII (March 1898), pp.335–45.

38 *Parl. Deb.*, Fourth Ser., Vol.45 (8 February 1897), cols.1625–8.

39 *The Times*, 24 September 1897, p.4.

40 *The Times*, 14 October 1897, p.4.

41 Arnold-Forster's letters were published in *The Times* on 11, 16, 18, 20, 23, 30 November 1897 and 3 December 1898 and were re-published in his *Army Letters 1897–8*; Haliburton's letters were published in *The Times* on 3, 6, 9 December 1897 and 11 January 1898 and were re-published in Sir A. Haliburton, *A Short Reply to Long Service* (E. Stanford; London, 1898).

42 Lansdowne, 'Outlines of Army Proposals', 2 December 1897, p.17; 'Mr Arnold-Forster's Letters to the *Times*, December 1897 and January 1898', 13 January 1898 and 'Linked Battalions versus Depots', 25 January 1898; Lord Salisbury to Queen Victoria, 18 December 1897, PRO, CAB 37/45/42, CAB 37/46/4, CAB 37/46/11 and CAB 41/24/24; Lansdowne to Salisbury and Salisbury to Lansdowne, 2 February 1898, Lord Newton, *Lord Lansdowne: A Biography* (Macmillan; London, 1929), pp.149–51.

43 Lansdowne, 'Outlines of Army Proposals', pp.1–2, 13–17; *The Times*, 10 December 1897, p.10.

44 Lansdowne, 'Note on Proposals made by the Chancellor of the Exchequer', 26 January 1898, PRO, CAB 37/46/13.

45 *Memorandum of the Secretary of State relating to the Army Estimates, 1898–99*, C. 8742 (1898), LIII, pp.3–4.

7

The army in an age of imperialism

The army enjoyed unprecedented popular appeal and esteem during the last three decades of the nineteenth century. Through numerous expeditions and small colonial wars, it earned more popular adulation than ever before over a comparable period of time. Although the army neither faced a European foe nor encountered a crisis as grave as the Indian Mutiny, generals such as Wolseley, Buller and Roberts became popular heroes, Gordon gained veneration as a martyr, and 'Tommy Atkins' earned lasting acclaim. The popular esteem reflected the pervasive influence of imperial propaganda, the recurrence of conflicts in exotic surroundings, the periodic fears of invasion, and the development of a peculiar form of militarism embodied in the liberal political culture and in much of Anglican and Nonconformist Christianity.[1] Underpinning this upsurge of interest was the convergence of various political, religious and cultural ideas, the propagation of pro-military images and beliefs in a variety of media, and the extensive coverage of the army in its colonial activities.

Political attitudes shifted decisively in the 1870s. The radical patriotism of the Chartist era, already fragmented and weakened, encountered a formidable challenge from Benjamin Disraeli as he sought to wean his party from its cautious non-interventionist foreign policy and to identify it with the 'national interest'. As Freda Harcourt argues, he probably perceived the potential of imperialism as a response to external pressures in the late 1860s (when the Abyssinian campaign of 1867–68 could be mounted without risk of conflict with France or Russia), and as a means of unifying the nation and diverting attention from domestic troubles.[2] During his premiership, the Conservative government purchased the Suez

Canal shares, consolidated imperial ties with the East by making Victoria Empress of India, and sought to unify the country by adopting a resolute attitude towards Russia in 1878. Elsewhere the government generally adopted the imperial policies of its predecessor until situations arose in which forceful 'men on the spot' – Sir Bartle Frere and Lord Lytton – were able to precipitate the 'forward policies' in South Africa and Afghanistan in 1878. Disraeli endeavoured to identify the Conservatives with patriotism, royalism and imperialism – feelings which reached a popular crescendo with the jingoistic outbursts of 1878, combining fervent Russophobia (as the Russians advanced on Constantinople) with antagonism towards the Liberals who advocated peace.[3]

Although jingoism proved an ephemeral force, and did not prevent the return of a Liberal government in 1880, defensive imperial sentiment became widespread in Britain, affecting Conservatives, Liberal Unionists and Liberal Imperialists alike. It found reflection in much of Fleet Street and in some Ministries of State, where concern was expressed about Britain's isolation, her industrial weaknesses, and the perceived challenge of foreign rivals. By the early 1890s, its broader political significance had become evident when Gladstone's fourth Ministry acquiesced in the retention of Egypt and Uganda rather than risk losing the support of Lord Rosebery and the other Liberal Imperialists. Indeed, Sir Edward Grey was able to make his notable declaration that any French advance into the Bahr-el-Ghazal would be construed as an unfriendly act – the first public claim that the ownership of the Sudanese desert might be worth a war. Even if the Liberal Imperialists had reservations about imperial expansion, they accepted the need for policies which would ensure the possession and retention of the existing Empire. They also appreciated the electoral dangers which could befall the Liberals if they appeared as 'unpatriotic' in promoting anti-imperial policies. In short, a popular sense of imperial mission had developed, often coloured with assertions of Anglo-Saxon superiority. If neither a constant nor a dominant factor in British politics (and only one factor among several in determining the outcome of the 'khaki election' of 1900), it periodically erupted whenever challenges from within and without the Empire recurred.[4]

Several religious groups embraced the ideas of imperialism and militarism. Many Wesleyan Methodists differed from the preferences of the more radical Nonconformist sects and favoured the imperial cause. As a propertied community, occupying a middle ground between Establishment and Dissent, the Wesleyan Methodists enjoyed a large middle-class support in particular regions of the country and a vast following overseas. Their lay and ministerial leaders, with some notable exceptions, saw little virtue in Little Englandism, and, in the 'khaki election' of 1900, those Wesleyans who staunchly supported the Boer War commanded considerable support among the Wesleyan electorate. As Stephen Koss observed, 'Weslyan Methodists were relieved to see class antagonisms and sectarian divisions submerged in a tidal wave of race patriotism.'[5]

Even by the late 1860s, Christian militarism had firmly established itself. The Crimean War had fostered the image of the private soldier as an object of evangelical compassion, and precipitated an unprecedented volume of voluntary work among the troops, aimed at ameliorating living conditions, promoting temperance, and saving 'souls'. The image of a Christian army had gained credibility during the Indian Mutiny, both from the task of stemming a heathen rebellion and from the example of Major-General Sir Henry Havelock, who became revered as a Christian hero for the sacrifice of his life in defence of the Empire. At a time when educated people were reading about and evincing enthusiasm for Cromwell and the Ironsides, the notion of 'Christian Soldiers' became increasingly commonplace. The War Office encouraged this view, making the army 'less exclusively Anglican, but more obtrusively Christian, than it had ever been since the Restoration'.[6] Having flouted ecclesiastical law and certain statutory privileges of the Church of England, the army had made comprehensive provision for the religious care of the troops, and, in 1881, had placed the Wesleyans on an equal footing with Anglican, Presbyterian and Roman Catholic chaplains. Many Christians, though, did not merely laud the achievements of the army in colonial conflict, but also imitated the uniforms, discipline, titles and rhetoric of the military in their own activities (notably in the foundation of the Salvation Army, the Church Army and the Boys' Brigade between 1878 and 1883). If the military motivation often came from external factors, such as Garibaldi's example in the unification of Italy – a struggle as much against Papal as against Austrian domination – or the themes expressed in the literature, propaganda and battle hymns of the North in the American Civil War, the paramilitarism still reflected a growing militarism within

British society as a whole.

Christian militarism found its ultimate apotheosis in Major-General Charles 'Chinese' Gordon, who was slain in Khartoum on 26 January 1885. He was already a popular legend before he was sent to Khartoum, partly for his exploits in quelling the Taiping rebellion in China and in suppressing the slave trade in the Sudan, and partly on account of his unconventional piety, which was thought to have an almost mystical hold over the 'native mind'. In the wake of the Mahdi's revolt, and the annihilation of General Hicks's army at El Obeid (5 November 1883), the Gladstone government had resolved to withdraw the Egyptian garrisons from the Sudan. Gordon, who had just returned from Palestine, gave an interview to W.T. Stead, the editor of *The Pall Mall Gazette*, and denounced the idea of evacuation as dishonourable and impracticable. Stead printed the interview and, in a front page editorial, advocated the despatch of Gordon, claiming that he had 'on more than one occasion . . . proved himself more valuable than an entire army' to the Sudan.[7] Other newspapers echoed these sentiments, prompting the government to send for Gordon and to charge him with implementing its policy in the Sudan. Once in Khartoum, however, Gordon renounced the proposed evacuation and resolved to challenge the Mahdi. The press mounted another campaign to relieve Gordon, now beleaguered in Khartoum. It gathered political support through the spring and summer of 1884 until the Gladstone government, faced with the threat of Lord Hartington's resignation, capitulated. On 5 August Gladstone moved a vote of credit to facilitate the relief expedition, which arrived two days too late to save Gordon.

The circumstances of Gordon's death – often portrayed as God's chosen servant standing alone against the powers of darkness – aroused the belief that he was 'an uncalendared saint, a Christian hero and martyr'.[8] A day of national mourning was declared and memorial services were held at Westminster Abbey, St Paul's Cathedral and other churches throughout the country. A ferocious outcry erupted in Parliament and the press, denouncing the dilatory despatch of the relief expedition. In the music halls, Gladstone's initials, G.O.M. ('Grand Old Man'), were changed to M.O.G. ('Murderer Of Gordon'). Gordon was eulogised by the press, by soldiers, including Wolseley and Butler, by imperial societies like the Primrose League, by schoolbooks, pamphlets and popular hagiographies such as *Gordon, the Christian Hero, A Book for the Young* by Abraham Kingdom. Commemorated in statues, busts, jugs, and bookmarks, he was revered by Queen and commoner alike. His Khartoum journals, published in 1885, were extensively read and his fate re-enacted on the stage. A Gordon cult swept Britain and continued for over twenty years, finding more lasting reflection in a memorial school, later to become a University College in Khartoum, and in homes for boys who would later enter the army.

Gordon's death clearly embarrassed Gladstone's government and may have contributed, at least partially, to its fall from office. Admittedly the Conservative leadership, having denounced the muddle and indecision of the Liberals, did not press for the reconquest of the Sudan; indeed, once in office, it continued the policy of evacuation inherited from the Liberals. Moreover, when Lord Salisbury eventually approved an invasion of the Sudan in 1896, he did so for the strategic reason of excluding the French from the Valley of the Nile and justified the move with the pretext of supporting the Italians in Kassala after their defeat by the Abyssinians at Adowa. Nevertheless Gordon, as Douglas Johnson argues, had become 'a symbol of the rightness and righteousness of imperialism', and his death had placed the national honour at stake. He was more than the hero 'of an hour', and Kitchener's subsequent campaign, which involved the crushing of the Khalifa's forces at Omdurman (2 September 1898), carried overtones of 'restitution and reparation',[9] at least in popular perception. George Warrington Steevens, who covered the war for *The Daily Mail*, described the memorial service for Gordon in the ruins of his palace:

We came with a sigh of shame: we went away with a sigh of relief. The long-delayed duty was done. The bones of our countrymen were shattered and scattered abroad, and no man knows their place; none the less Gordon had his due burial at last . . . . We left Gordon alone again – but alone in majesty under the conquering ensign of his own people.[10]

Imperialism gained further support and justification from the popularised notions of Social Darwinism towards the end of the nineteenth century. Writers such as Benjamin Kidd and Karl Pearson applied the ideas of organic evolution and natural selection to international affairs, emphasising the frequency of struggle between nations, the tendency of the strong to prevail over the weak, and the superiority of particular races. The phrases 'struggle for existence' and 'survival of the fittest' became increasingly prominent in, or served as implicit assumptions for, the writings of many imperialists and politicians. These concerns seemed particularly appropriate at a time of growing challenges to imperial frontiers, periodic naval and invasion 'scares', and debates about the nation's industrial difficulties.[11]

Social Darwinism, moreover, provided an ideological rationale for colonial war and conquest. By depicting enemies as 'inferior peoples', the destruction of their armies could be justified as part of a constructive and civilising mission, a precursor to bringing them the unquestioned benefits of trade, technology, Christianity and British rule. The war correspondents who accompanied Kitchener to Khartoum regarded the squalor, cruelty and degradation of the Mahdist regime as ample justification for the campaign. They emphasised the lust and filth of Khartoum: as Steevens observed, 'the whole city was a huge harem . . . a montrosity of African lust . . . . And foul. They dropped their dung where they listed . . . . The reek of its abominations steamed up to heaven to justify us of our vengeance.' He claimed, too, that the regime was 'the worst tyranny in the world', and argued that 'the Sudan's gain is immunity from rape and torture and every extreme of misery'.[12] Ernest N. Bennett agreed that Mahdism had 'proved the most shameful and terrible instrument of bloodshed and oppression which the modern world has ever witnessed': by crushing it, Britain had advanced 'the cause of civilisation'.[13]

Social Darwinism, finally, aroused a new interest in war as the ultimate test of national power. War was regarded as a natural occurrence, either a form of inevitable struggle between States or an endemic phenomenon which afflicted States at certain stages in their development (both in competition between rising States and in conflict between these States and their declining counterparts). In the battle for survival, nations were thought likely to prevail only if they possessed the best human material and the most modern weapons, and if they prepared efficiently for future conflicts. Although new technology was thought likely to reduce the duration of modern warfare, it was never perceived as a substitute for the decisive human qualities – patriotism, duty, honour, courage, endurance, and a willingness to meet a noble death. War was still depicted as a struggle of national wills; it was, argued Wolseley,

a manly, elevating aspiration [which] exercises a healthy influence on all classes of society . . . . War, though it may mean a hard struggle for national existence, is the greatest purifier to the race or nation that has reached the verge of over-refinement, or of excessive civilization.[14]

Many Britons did not subscribe to these views. Most were not outright pacifists, but they still regarded war as an expensive, risky and destructive course of action, if sometimes a regrettable necessity. They deprecated any glorification of war, and, during the Second Boer War, Campbell-Bannerman spoke for many Liberals when he claimed that Britain's 'position in the world has been made and is held by commerce and peace and amity; it must be maintained in the same manner, and not by the stirring up of the military spirit'.[15] They criticised the wastage of human and financial resources involved in war, and in the preparation for war, insisting that this level of investment should be kept to a minimum and should avoid conscription. Above all, they deplored the tendency of war or the threat of war to stimulate unruly passions at home. Nothing more alarmed the Liberals in 1900 than the recrudescence of jingoism. Sir William Harcourt did not distinguish between the jingo mobs and the Mafeking celebrations; he simply hoped that peace would 'inspire a soberer sentiment in the people of this country, and that a time will come when the melodies of the music halls and the Mafeking mobs will not be regarded as the exponents of English statesmanship'.[16] Even the Liberal Imperialist, Sir Edward Grey, who admitted being stirred by the onset of war, insisted that it had

no business to be popular, and the cry for Revenge for Majuba dishonours us and destroys our reputation for good faith. I should like to break the heads of all the Music halls first and then go out and teach the Boers gravely and sternly the things which they do not know.[17]

Yet Liberals and other sceptics struggled against the floodtide of imperial propaganda and the adulation of the army in its colonial exploits. Various societies and pressure groups sought to generate support for imperial unity. The Tory-based Primrose League, claiming a membership of one million by 1890, was one of the more active bodies. By its lectures, pamphlets, exhibitions, magic lantern displays, and children's fiction, it generated an emotional enthusiasm for the Empire. More broadly based groups, like the British Empire League and the Imperial Federation Defence Committee (both offshoots of the short-lived Imperial Federation League) sought to educate the public about the Empire or to promote a common interest in the maritime defence of the Empire. Both the

Victoria League and the Imperial South Africa Association were formed during the Second Boer War and actively supported the war effort by the mass distribution of pamphlets and leaflets and by the organisation of public meetings. These bodies enabled the committed elite to establish links between themselves, to act as a channel for the flow of funds from companies and private individuals, and to promote contacts with politicians, journalists and other opinion-formers. Their educational endeavours, though, were only one of many forms of imperial propaganda.

The popular songs of the period were no longer vehicles of dissent, but often focused on topical events, delivering judgements in a chauvinistic and xenophobic manner. They glorified military triumphs and revelled in the defeat of 'inferior peoples'. 'By Jingo', written by G.W. Hunt in 1877, and performed by G.H. Macdermott throughout the crisis of 1877–78, was only one of several songs which reflected the defensive nationalism and Russophobia of the 1870s. A more assertive nationalism appeared in the songs and spectacles of the 1880s (*Britannia*, shown at Oxford in 1885, *Our Army and Navy* at the Alhambra in 1889, and *The Girl I Left Behind Me*, depicting soldiers and sailors on imperial service at the Empire, Leicester Square, in 1894). These patriotic extravaganzas emphasised the loyalty of the colonies and the unity of the Anglo-Saxons, as did the highly popular song of Charles Godfrey, 'It's the English Speaking Race against the World'. These jingo songs and elaborate spectacles were apparently favoured by the proprietors of large music halls catering for a socially mixed clientele.[18]

In the smaller halls, 'penny gaffs', and popular theatres, the patriotic theme, often expressed in melodrama, differed in tone and content. Melodrama depended upon a polarisation of good and evil, so facilitating the presentation of British heroes confronting and overcoming the barbarous 'fuzzy-wuzzy'. If they stereotyped contemporary racial attitudes, these melodramas celebrated the achievements of individual soldiers and sailors, and emphasised that justice and freedom flowed from British rule. The liberating emphasis appeared to diminish after the 1870s, possibly as the ideal seemed at odds with the prolonged resistance to British rule in the Sudan and South Africa. The depiction of the ordinary soldier changed, too. The themes of heroism and self-sacrifice in the songs of the 1870s ('The Dying Soldier', 'Think of me, Darling', 'Let me like a Soldier Fall') were significantly amplified in Leslie Stuart's 'Soldiers of the

Queen' (1881) and Rudyard Kipling's, 'The Absent-minded Beggar' (1899), which emphasised the role of the ordinary soldier in defending the Empire. Both became immensely popular during the Boer War, with 'The Absent-minded Beggar' raising a quarter of a million pounds for soldiers' families.[19]

Many plays were also strikingly topical, rapidly transferring contemporary news to the stage. Various Zulu titles appeared after 1879, with two plays, *The Zulu Chief* and *Cetewayo at Last*, commemorating Cetewayo's visit to Britain in 1882. The British role in Egypt became the theme of several plays after 1882 and in South Africa during the Second Boer War. Gordon's martyrdom was re-enacted in a four-act drama, *Khartoum*, and the ill-fated attempt to rescue him in the five-act drama, *The Fall of Khartoum* (although in the latter the British army, having arrived too late, defeated the Mahdi and recaptured Khartoum, anticipating events by thirteen years). If far less numerous than the plays on romantic and domestic themes, these colonial plays still constituted a significant proportion of all those performed during the period. Some contained elements of satire, but most evinced profound respect for the flag, royalty and authority, and they treated moments of crisis, like the fall of Khartoum and the Boer War, with immense seriousness. The plays had respectable runs in London and the provinces, and, in combination with the music halls, they reflected the widespread enthusiasm for performances based on military exploits and patriotic sentiment. Indeed, this enthusiasm appears to have crossed class barriers and to have been an enduring phenomenon.[20]

Large-scale exhibitions further exploited the imperial fascination. The Colonial and Indian Exhibition (1886) attracted 5,500,000 visitors, and, in 1895, the Hungarian-born entrepreneur, Imre Kiralfy, began a series of exhibitions on imperial themes in Olympia and Earl's Court. His Greater Britain Exhibition of 1899 was particularly extravagant, featuring the 'Kaffir Kraal' containing 174 Africans, and the 'Savage South Africa' display, with re-enactments of the Matabele War of 1893 and the Rhodesian rebellion of 1896–97. This was, as Ben Shephard noted, 'an explicit piece of economic and physical exploitation, using Africans to project to British audiences a series of stereotypes of savagery, darkness and cruelty'.[21]

The army also exploited its own appeal, especially the popularity of military music and of public displays. It held open-air band performances and organised the Royal Naval and Military Tournament as anannual event from 1893 onwards. Sir Evelyn Wood, when Adjutant-General, made facilities available for R.W. Paul to make a series of about twenty films, illustrating, as Paul claimed, 'the life and career of a soldier, and the work of each branch of the Service'. The first of these films was shown at the Alhambra on 18 September 1900, and, in the same year, the two films, *The British Army* and *The British Navy*, were made by Cecil Hepworth. The filming of the army blossomed during the Boer War, stimulating the development of the newsreel industry. Some scenes, filmed at home, covered the departure and return of troops; others, taken in Africa, recorded events well behind the firing line. There were some short drama films, like *The Call to Arms*, exploiting sentimental and heroic themes, and some action sequences, notably Joe Rosenthal's *A Skirmish with the Boers near Kimberley by a Troop of Cavalry Scouts Attached to General French's Column*. In response to the demand for more excitement, film-makers produced several films using faked sequences taken at home.[22]

Arguably, imperialistic propaganda may have had more effect when it was more precisely targeted, particularly at impressionable minds in public schools. These schools, which provided a classical education and made a cult of team games, were enthusiastic exponents of the new militarism. They promoted the values of duty, loyalty, discipline and self-abnegation, and perceived that the qualities required for success in games could serve as a preparation for success in battle. Some schools had army classes for boys seeking entry to Sandhurst or Woolwich, and many formed cadet corps. Several headmasters – J.E.C. Welldon of Harrow, H.W. Moss of Shrewsbury, C. Norwood of Marlborough (and Harrow), M.J. Rendall of Winchester, H.H. Almond of Loretto and E. Warre of Eton – were unabashed imperialists. They proselytised the virtues of patriotism and imperial service in chapel sermons, prize day speeches, magazine editorials, classroom lectures and informal conversation. Their influence was bolstered by iconography on school walls, illustrating the achievements of nautical and military heroes, by history texts, particularly *The Expansion of England* (1883) by John R. Seeley, extolling the moral and uplifting aims of the Empire, and by geography texts, steeped in Social Darwinism, describing the economic benefits of imperial expansion. Undoubtedly this schooling had some effect: the emphasis upon character training and the lauding of patriotism, imperial service and martial self-sacrifice probably influenced some public schoolboys, either predisposing or confirming them in a desire to serve in the army and in the colonies.[23]

Although State schools took the public schools as their model, their prime concerns were the creation of a system of organised instruction and the imparting of basic skills in reading, writing and arithmetic. The Board schools, nonetheless, firmly believed in the virtues of classroom discipline and many accepted that marching drill helped to inculcate obedience among working-class youth. Whether it did or not, drill blatantly copied and helped to popularise military practices. Paramilitarism flourished, too, outside the school system. Cadet corps, which Charterhouse and Dulwich had founded in the 1870s, proliferated in late 1880s and 1890s. In London they were usually based on working-boys' clubs, associated with public school missions or university settlements. The corps normally obtained their officers from the middle-class residents of these missions and settlements, and sought uniforms from local bankers, employers and city manufacturers. The cadet corps attracted a mixed group of boys: some probably believed that membership of the corps might enable them to gain employment in trades, which placed a premium upon discipline and respectability, and some unskilled boys joined prior to entering the army.[24]

Paramilitarism was also a conspicuous feature of the larger youth movements which developed in the 1880s and 1890s. When William Alexander Smith founded the Boys' Brigade in 1883, he combined elements from the Volunteers and the Christian youth clubs (namely a weekly drill parade, using dummy rifles, a uniform comprising belt, haversack and pillbox cap, and rules on Sunday school and Bible class attendance). By 1896 the Boys' Brigade had 264 companies in Scotland and 435 in England and Wales and a national membership of over 30,000, which rose to nearly 45,000 by the turn of the century. In 1891 Walter Mallock Gee formed the Anglican Church Lads' Brigade, a more miltaristic and middle-class body which gained strong support from the army (in 1893, Lord Chelmsford became the first in a long line of high-ranking army officers to serve as Governor of the Brigade). By 1897 the Church Lads' Brigade had companies in every diocese in England and Wales. Other religious denominations followed suit, with the foundation of a Jewish Lads' Brigade in Whitechapel (1895) and the Catholic Boys' Brigade in Bermondsey (1896). The twelfth Earl of Meath formed a non-denominational body, the Lads' Drill Association, in 1899. More militaristic than the religious brigades, it was dedicated to the systematic physical and military training of British lads and their instruction in the use of the rifle. Although the appeal of the larger religious organisations may have proved less comprehensive than their founders had hoped, particularly among the unskilled working-class, they established a presence within districts occupied by skilled manual workers and other working class residents. The organisations varied considerably in their military emphasis: whereas Smith merely regarded it as a framework for the good-citizenship and evangelical purposes of the Boys' Brigade, Gee, a member of the Volunteers, regarded it as more central to the purposes of the Church Lads' Brigade.[25]

The juvenile interest in war and militarism found a further stimulus in the boys' literature of the period, which expanded in scope and volume after the passage of the 1870 Education Act. Of the new journals, the *Boy's Own Paper* (1879–1967) proved the most popular; by the mid-1880s it claimed a circulation in excess of one million. Unlike the 'penny dreadfuls', its heroes were figures of authority, willing to defend or expand the Empire and able to triumph over formidable odds. Many of the stories contained grisly descriptions, but the violence and bloodshed were generally directed towards the spread of civilisation, Christianity, and Just Rule. Juvenile writers such as W.H.G. Kingston, R.M. Ballantyne, Rider Haggard and, above all, George Alfred Henty specialised in adventure tales, set in exotic locations, with schoolboy heroes facing imaginary challenges, full of narrow escapes and exciting fights. Often the heroes were placed in the midst of contemporary events, particularly colonial wars, which enabled Henty, an ex-war correspondent, to transfer his style of reporting and some of his campaign experiences into his fiction. His heroes were usually 'typical public schoolboys', who revelled in adversity and overcame their difficulties. In this literary context, war served as 'a purifying experience . . . making huge demands upon bravery, physical endurance, group loyalty, and ultimately patriotic self-sacrifice'.[26]

Visual imagery complemented and reinforced these perceptions. Printed or painted pictures of colonial forces, military heroes and frontier warfare were conveyed through advertisements, postcards, cigarette cards and toy soldiers. They were reproduced in almanacs and encyclopaedias, and were exploited along with royalty and the flag in the commemorative market by tea, biscuit and tobacco companies. During the jubilees of 1887 and 1897, and in the Second Boer War, there was a profusion of mugs, cups, plates and tins embellished with royal and military images. Much of the popular art appropriated images already created by the battle painters and war artists of the period. There were about a dozen artists who worked either partially or primarily as battle painters. Some of these had served as special war artists, notably Charles Edwin Fripp, Godfrey Douglas Giles and Frederick Villiers, but their work hardly differed in approach from the paintings of those who had never been to war, like Lady Butler, Richard Caton Woodville and Robert Gibb (apart from a greater awareness of terrain and the confusion of battle). All painters emphasised the colour, drama and heroism of war, deliberately selecting the nobler themes and heroic scenes, and excluding the more horrific aspects (the agony, suffering and mutilations of war). Their war portrayal was partly descriptive, partly a matter of historical record (and hence the great emphasis placed on accuracy of detail), and partly inspirational.[27]

Elizabeth Thompson, later Lady Butler, was the most famous of the battle painters. 'The Roll Call', which she exhibited in 1874, proved an outstanding success. It became 'the hit of the season' with the members of the public and London society who saw it, earned the approval of many Crimean War veterans, and enhanced the status of battle painting in Britain. The Queen purchased it and Miss Thompson sold the copyright for £1,200. Thereafter she was acclaimed and lionised by royalty, the aristocracy and the military establishment. The army facilitated many of her subsequent works, mounting displays and exercises for her benefit, lending her soldiers in period uniform as models, and volunteering expert advice. She worked prodigiously, producing seventeen major battle paintings between 1874 and 1899 (portraying contemporary events as well as incidents from the Napoleonic, Crimean and, in one case, the Franco–Prussian conflicts). She depicted war as a spectacle, focusing upon scenes such as 'the march past', 'reveille', 'the square', 'the charge', 'after the battle', and 'the highlander' (as an embodiment of the warlike spirit). She preferred not to portray conflict, and had to be pressed to paint 'The Defence of Rorke's Drift, January 22nd, 1879' for the Queen. She avoided the squalor, dirt and suffering of warfare but paid close attention to the detail of uniform. She largely reinforced the romanticised warrior ethos which underpinned the popular militarism of the period. She sold paintings for over £1,000 each, which were hung in clubs, mess rooms, homes and institutes, and received even larger sums from the Fine Art Society for the right to publish prints and engravings from her work.[28]

Other artists did not share her reticence about painting scenes of conflict. Robert Caton Woodville, another highly successful painter, began his career as a London-based illustrator for *The Illustrated London News*, portraying incidents from colonial wars in a wholly imaginative way, without any assistance from the sketches of the special artists. Having begun to exhibit at the Royal Academy in 1879, he was commissioned by the Queen to paint the Duke of Connaught at the battle of Tel-el-Kebir. Once he had received royal approval for this painting, he was soon able to command prices of £1,000 for his canvases. Like Lady Butler, he continued battle painting into the First World War, employing throughout a highly distinctive style: with figures grouped and posed, their eyes staring and rifles ready, all drama and movement but no agony. Carnage was more prominent in one of the more powerful paintings of the period, Charles E. Fripp's 'The last Stand of the 24th Regiment at Isandhlwana'. Impressively set on the African veldt, the scarlet clad British forces were depicted in their last stand, with corpses of British and Zulu soldiers scattered over the foreground and Zulus shown in the act of killing. By focusing upon a back-to-back stand, with a resolute sergeant in the centre and a drummer boy at his side, Fripp manipulated the poignancy of the juxtaposition. He conveyed the image of disciplined soldiers, standing together against overwhelming odds and dying bravely.

Nevertheless, battle painting appears to have been a minority taste among the art-loving public. The receptions accorded to 'The Roll Call' and Robert Gibb's 'The Thin Red Line' were unusual, and few painters earned a living from battle painting alone, even if they sustained a regular supply of battle paintings, commemorating highlights and episodes from the recurring colonial conflicts. As their paintings were frequently displayed in the summer exhibitions of the Royal Academy, with reproductions in mess rooms, clubs, schools and institutes, and with prints on classroom walls and in school history textbooks, they probably compounded support for the imperial wars and increased the popularity of the army. They reinforced the popular perception of war, and provided a second-hand sense of the adventure and romance which underpinned the thinking and assumptions of late Victorian imperialism.[29]

Battle painting, though, only built upon the imagery already evoked by the reports and sketches of contemporary journalism. The work of the war correspondents and special artists had the initial advantage of topicality, and a longer-term influence as it met the public expectations of thrilling, dramatic and heroic warfare. This was the golden age of war correspondence, occasioned by the varied and frequent wars, minimal official restrictions on the correspondents, the rapid transmission of reports by telegraph and ocean cable, and an insatiable demand for war news. The reporting and the sketches undoubtedly boosted newspaper sales at a time of great expansion and rivalry in the industry, fuelled by the growing population, increased standards of living, the expansion of primary education, and the technological changes which increased the scope for advertising and lowered production costs. As the number of newspapers doubled between 1880 and 1900, and the popular press mushroomed, editors invested heavily in journalists who could produce rapid and vivid descriptions of the courage and carnage of battle.[30]

War illustrators and reporters quickly became the well paid elite of the journalistic profession. An essentially, though not exclusively, London-based group, they travelled together and messed together on campaign, often helping each other but sometimes keeping an eye on each other's movements. They included many different personalities. Some gloried in the discomforts of war, scorning luxuries and never washing; others, like Melton Prior of *The Illustrated London News*, ensured that they travelled as comfortably as possible, sparing no expense upon servants, transport, and copious supplies of whisky. Some like Prior or Bennet Burleigh of *The Daily Telegraph* covered numerous campaigns, becoming the *doyens* of their profession; others like Ernest Bennett were non-journalistic amateurs, who paid their own expenses and had to secure a permit to act as a newspaper correspondent. They all shared the hardships and rigours of the campaigns, sometimes participating in the fighting and helping with the wounded. Several died in battle or during a campaign (there were seven deaths during the Sudan wars of 1883–85), and some died of disease, notably G.W. Steevens of *The Daily Mail* during the siege of Ladysmith.[31]

Their writing and sketching flourished amid the peculiar circumstances of colonial campaigning – the picturesque locations, the small scale of the operations, and the lengthy delays in reaching the battle zones. Indeed, their preliminary reports and sketches not only built up interest in the campaigns but also focused upon their own adventures, establishing their legendary or heroic credentials. The 'specials' enjoyed a further advantage, inasmuch as photography, which antedated pictorial journalism, could not compete as a visual medium. On account of technological difficulties, cameramen could only photograph static scenes and so never captured the colour, movement, action and emotion of war. Above all, the correspondents understood the twin imperatives of their trade: they had to press as close as possible to the front line in battle, and they had to send their despatches and sketches as quickly as possible (usually employing native runners to carry their reports and tracing sketches across hostile territory). 'A war correspondent,' wrote Winwoode Reade, who reported on the Ashanti War for *The Times*, 'can witness nothing unless he goes very near the enemy. In thick bush there are no bird's eye views to be had.'[32] Archibald Forbes of *The Daily News* agreed. He had cleverly used the telegraph and knowledge of Saxon plans to 'scoop' William Howard Russell during the Franco–Prussian War, and gained lasting fame for his 'ride of death' over 100 miles to file the first reports of the battle of Ulundi. 'In modern war correspondence,' he wrote, 'the race is emphatically to the swift, the battle to the strong.'[33]

The journalists largely shared the attitudes and values of the officers whom they accompanied. They depended upon the army for assistance with their supplies, transport, and sometimes their communications. They relied upon the field commanders and their staff for information and generally worked more effectively with the goodwill of these officers. Although they sometimes criticised senior officers (Forbes denounced Lord Chelmsford's handling of the Zulu War and, like Russell, criticised the Gordon Relief Expedition), they generally lavished praise upon field commanders and never mocked them (Prior refused to sketch Wolseley when the latter fell off his camel). War correspondents saw themselves neither as dispassionate observers nor as commentators upon the moral or political aspects of war. Their role, as Forbes observed, was to record 'how our countrymen, our dear ones, toil and thole, vindicate Britain's manhood, and joyously expend their lives for Queen and fatherland'.[34]

Even so, the relationship between the army and the press was rarely close. Reconciliation was never likely between correspondents and those officers, headed by the Duke of Cambridge, who had deplored Russell's reporting from the Crimea. Some officers, nonetheless, realised that the press could boost their careers and reputations: Wolseley conciliated and manipulated correspondents to his own advantage, despite disparaging them as 'curses to armies' and as 'drones' who leaked information and ate the rations of fighting men. Yet neither he nor any other officer readily accepted criticism from reporters, many of whom had either aborted military careers at an early age or had never served in the army. When Russell dared to criticise Wolseley's choice of staff in South Africa, Wolseley disparaged him as 'no gentleman', a fellow 'who has behaved like the scoundrel and low snob he always was'.[35] More seriously, the military felt concerned about their inability to control the flow of news from the field of battle. Official despatches, bearing the imprint of the commanding officer, had lost their impact, and the journalistic reports and sketches always carried the risk of revealing secrets or intentions which could be of use to the enemy. Hence commanders periodically censored the reports or restricted the movements of correspondents and special artists, occasionally expelling those who tried to circumvent the restrictions (including Hector Macpherson of *The Standard* during the Afghan War and Edward Kyran Moylan of *The Times* in the Burma War). These occurrences were exceptional, and the correspondents, though irked by the restrictions, were still effusive in their praise, even of the noncommittal Kitchener. Steevens could not imagine Kitchener other 'than as seeing the right thing to do and doing it. His precision is so inhumanly unerring, he is more like a machine than a man'.[36]

In their reports, correspondents provided much more than praise and adulation. They proffered remarkable accounts of military campaigning in the 1880s and 1890s, particularly the rigours and difficulties of moving men, arms and supplies through mountains, over vast tracts of desert, and of hauling boats up the Nile through the series of cataracts, or rock-strewn rapids. They described the minutiae of field life, including the care of the wounded in ambulance boats and in camel-borne ambulance chairs. They recognised the value of careful logistic preparations: Steevens described the Sudan Military Railway as 'the deadliest weapon Britain has ever used against Mahdism'.[37] They criticised failings of military equipment; Burleigh's condemnation of the swords and bayonets which bent in the battle of Abu Klea (17 January 1885) aroused a storm of con-

troversy about the standard of British weaponry, and thirteen years
later Steevens caused a similar outcry over the standard of British
boots.[38]
Nevertheless, the reports and sketches of battle provided the
customary climax of campaign reporting. Steevens was particularly
evocative in his writing from the Sudan. At the battle of Atbara
(1898), he described the calm and phlegmatic officers who 'despised'
danger, with 'their locked faces turned unswervingly towards the
bullets . . .'. The 'unkempt, unshaven Tommies' were transformed in
battle; they moved forward, stirred by the bagpipes, and 'whether
they aimed or advanced they did it orderly, gravely, without
speaking. The bullets had whispered to raw youngsters in one breath
the secret of all the glories of the British army'. He magnified his
accounts of sterling British fortitude, coupled with passing
references to the admirable fighting of the native auxiliaries, by
reference to the courage and fanatical zeal of the Dervishes. At
Omdurman, he wrote, 'no white troops would have faced that
torrent of death for five minutes', but eventually that 'dusky line . . .
bent, broke up, fell apart, and disappeared'. Unlike some commentators, he described the costly, if courageous, charge of the 21st
Lancers at Omdurman as 'a gross blunder' and commented upon the
'most appalling slaughter' of the Dervish army. However, he
regarded this massacre, including the killing of many wounded, as
'absolutely unavoidable', and attributed the British successes to
superior leadership, planning, morale, and disciplined firepower. All
this, he claimed, vindicated the nation's 'self-respect'.[39]
   Whether this writing in Britain's largest-circulation newspaper
'co-opted the masses' to imperialism, as H. John Field implies, is
arguable, but so is claim of Richard Price that popular journalism
had relatively little impact upon working-class attitudes. On the one
hand, it would seem unwise to impute too much influence to the
writing when the socio–economic composition of *The Daily Mail*'s
readership is not accurately known: on the other hand, it would seem
unreasonable to discount the influence of the press entirely. The
campaign coverage almost certainly had *some* effect upon readers
and their families, friends, and associates – anyone with whom the
news was discussed. By minimising the agony and suffering of war
and by emphasising the heroism, adventure, drama and glory, the
press probably reinforced popular preconceptions. It undoubtedly
sustained a widespread interest in the army, and in its imperial role,

sustaining popular support for the 'little wars' of the late Victorian period.[40] Newspaper coverage, if more topical than any other medium, complemented the values and ideas expressed elsewhere, not least in fictional and non-fictional literature. Writing on military or quasi-military themes was extremely popular; Wolseley, Hamley, Brackenbury and Maurice were among the many officers who wrote military histories, biographies and campaign accounts. Sir William Butler was one of the more prolific military writers, producing works on his travels in North America, a regimental history, a boys' adventure story, an anonymous prophetic novel, *The Invasion of England* (1882), lively accounts of the Ashanti War and the Gordon Relief Expedition, and biographies of Gordon, Napier and Colley. War correspondents like Forbes, Winwoode Reade and Henty also turned from journalism to writing about military history, famous regiments, distinguished generals, or pure fiction based on a military theme.

Invasion fantasies proved a highly popular form of fiction. Captain (later General Sir) George Chesney pioneered the genre with his vigorous narrative, 'The Battle of Dorking', published in *Blackwood's Edinburgh Magazine* in 1871. At a time when the Prussian victories in France had caused considerable anxiety in Britain, his account of a successful German invasion of England, exploiting Britain's defensive weaknesses, caused considerable commotion. So popular was the work that it was promptly reproduced in book form, and even Gladstone felt compelled to speak out against the dangers of alarmist literature. Although the immediate controversy would quickly abate, and it failed to arrest the falling enrolments in the Volunteers, Chesney made his fame, fortune and reputation from the book. He prompted many scholars, servicemen and sensationalists to try to emulate his achievement over the next thirty years. Usually they followed his formula of employing a survivor to relate the disaster and to identify its causes – short-sighted politicians, unprepared defences, ill-trained troops, technological advances exploited by the enemy, and strategic blunders (the possible construction of the Channel Tunnel becoming an acute source of concern). By the 1890s many of these stories originally appeared as serials in the large-circulation newspapers and magazines, and ran for several weeks or months. Often they were reprinted as lavish books, which ran through several editions. Popular journalists such as Louis Tracy, George Griffith and William Le Queux wrote their racy narratives around the major anxieties of the moment, finding an enthusiastic mass readership, attracted by the themes of war, jingoism and xenophobia.[41]

Of the various writers in the 1880s and 1890s, none was more influential than Rudyard Kipling. Although he spent seven formative years in India from 1882 to 1889, he never saw a shot fired in anger until 1900. Nor did he have much knowledge of Egypt and Burma, other than a passage through the Suez Canal in 1882 and a brief visit to Rangoon and Moulmein as a steamship passenger in 1889. As a consequence, his Burmese works, like 'The Ballad of Boh da Thone' (August 1888) and 'A Conference of the Powers' (May 1890), though vividly descriptive of wartime incidents, lack the local colour and insights of his Indian stories. In writing about army life in India he relied heavily upon secondary sources, culling yarns and anecdotes from the files and reference works of *The Civil and Military Gazette*, his father's library, and from his father's immense knowledge of India. 'The Drums of the Fore and Aft' was a story recorded by Robert Orme in his history of British military activities in India; 'Snarleyow' was an episode in Sergeant Bancroft's history of the Bengal horse artillery; and 'The Taking of Lungtungpen' was a fictionalised version of an achievement of the 2nd Queen's Regiment, which Kipling wrote only a few weeks after the event had been reported in *The Civil and Military Gazette*. He also formed many military contacts while based in Lahore, the capital of the Punjab. In this outpost of the Empire, still policed by the army, the military ethos was more pronounced than in the rest of British India. Various regiments were stationed in the cantonment of Mian Mir, just outside Lahore, where Kipling often dined in the mess. He met the officers and men, from whom he derived his fascination with army life and his awe of the 'military virtues'.[42]

In his earliest writing about the army Kipling focused upon the life-style and attitudes of the young subalterns. Several of the stories reproduced in *Plain Tales from the Hills* (1887) described the horseplay and practical jokes of life in the officers' mess, notably 'The Arrest of Lieutenant Golightly' and 'His Wedded Wife'. In 'Only a Subaltern', Kipling's hero, 'Bobby Wicks', encapsulates the virtues of honesty, loyalty, propriety, and unflinching moral and physical courage, so exalted in the code of an officer gentleman. In 'Arithmetic on the Frontier' Kipling described the rigours, hardships and the possibilities of an unheroic death:

> A scrimmage in a Border Station –
>   A canter down some dark defile –
> Two thousand pounds of education
>   Drops to a ten-rupee jezail –
> The Crammer's boast, the Squadron's pride,
>   Shot like a rabbit in a ride.[43]

Kipling was much more original in his writing about the private soldier. *Soldiers Three* (1890) and *Barrack-Room Ballads* (1892) were utterly new in their style and subject matter to the Victorian reading public. No one had chosen to write so extensively about the serving soldier (as distinct from the retired soldier, who figured fairly prominently in English literature). No one had fully understood the importance of dialect and used it other than for comic effect. He made his Irishman, 'Mulvaney', his cockney, 'Ortheris', and his West Riding dalesman, 'Learoyd' – the characters of 'The Three Musketeers' (March 1887) and *Soldiers Three* – use local words, grammatical forms, and speak in a language both convincing and appropriate. He used the vernacular of the London working class for the majority of his speakers in the *Barrack-Room Ballads*. In the period of Yeats, Conrad and Wilde, he was the first author to compose his work 'in the language of the people and with the rhythm of the music-hall'.[44]

Equally impressive was the stark realism of his depiction of army life in India. His 'Tommy Atkins' led a boring and tedious life, with few pleasures, little glamour, and lowly status. Serving in India, as Kipling described it, was a life of grinding inactivity, dominated by the climate, and bedevilled by recurrent epidemics of cholera. To escape from the heat and the fever, his soldiers sought solace in drink, whoring, and barrack-room brawling. His characters, though, were never standardised. Speaking in soliloquies, or occasionally in dialogues, the characters revealed themselves as decent and deceitful, as honest and wayward, as heroes and cowards. Some were idiosyncratic, like the 'gentlemen rankers'; a few were female – women of the camp, 'ruined' and deserted by their roguish amours; all were different. Keenly aware of detail, Kipling recorded a profoundly realistic picture of the British Tommy:

> Wot makes the soldier's 'eart to penk, wot makes 'im to perspire?
> It isn't standin' up to charge nor lyin' down to fire;

But it's everlastin' waitin' on a everlastin' road
For the commissariat camel an' 'is commissariat load.[45]

Kipling's work earned criticism as well as plaudits. His writing failed to impress Oscar Wilde and aroused the everlasting antipathy of Max Beerbohm. His characterisation of Tommy Atkins neither convinced nor pleased some retired soldiers. Robert Blatchford, a former NCO, doubted that the tales of the *Soldiers Three* were particularly realistic. He questioned whether any noncommissioned officer would have permitted the excesses and latitude enjoyed by Kipling's heroes. He also maintained that the dialect of the *Barrack-Room Ballads* was little more than 'comic caricature'. Although he accepted that barrack-room slang was prevalent, and that many soldiers came from the 'illiterate classes' in London, he still believed that

soldiers speak more correctly than civilians of their own rank in life, the tendency of barrack life being to assimilate all dialects and slightly to amend the level of merit in grammar and pronunciation – the amendment being partly due to travel and experience and partly to the example of educated officers.[46]

If plausible in some respects, this criticism should be juxtaposed with the subsequent reflection of Sir George Younghusband. He agreed that in his youth neither he nor any of his brother officers had ever heard the words and expressions used by Kipling's soldiers, but, several years later, 'the soldiers thought, and talked, and expressed themselves exactly like Rudyard Kipling had taught them in his stories! . . . Rudyard Kipling made the modern soldier.'[47] If possibly exaggerated, this assertion still indicated the immense popularity of Kipling's works within the ranks, a point corroborated by the hearty receptions, he received wherever he met the troops in the South African War. He had empathised and sympathised with them. He had stripped away the pretence, and, within the realms of poetic licence, had described their lives with 'bitter honesty'.[48]

Kipling's works, and the war literature in general, proved immensely popular. They testified to the pervasive appeal of militarism and popular imperialism, and to a profound sense of national superiority. They complemented the commercial successes of patriotic plays, songs and spectacles; the veneration of Gordon; the demand for prints and reproductions of battle paintings; the voluminous sales of militaristic juvenile fiction; the growth of paramilitary youth movements; and the insatiable appetite for war news. Despite this widespread interest, which almost certainly transcended class barriers, there was never any rush to the Colours. The vast majority of the populace shunned enlistment, and many discriminated against soldiers in uniform. Whereas soldiers left for wars amidst cheering throngs of people and were enthusiastically greeted on their return, they were often rejected in peacetime. Soldiers were frequently prevented by steamship companies from using second-class saloons, they were barred by some theatres and music halls from occupying particular places in their auditoriums, and, occasionally, they were even banned from riding on omnibuses. The paradox baffled Theodore von Sosnosky, a foreign observer of the army. 'How this blind glorification and worship of the Army,' he wrote, 'continues to coexist with the contemptuous dislike felt towards the members of it, must remain a problem in the national psychology.'[49]

In seeking to unravel this paradox, the evidence of popular imperialism, racialism and militarism has to be placed in perspective. Undoubtedly these attitudes were prevalent amidst the intellectual and social currents which intertwined nationalism and imperialism in the last decades of the century. They also straddled class and party lines, periodically erupting as outbursts of indignation which policy-makers could hardly ignore in moments of crisis, even if they were often transitory in form and were usually bracketed by longer periods of quiescence. Moreover, imperialistic feelings, as Michael Howard observes, generally existed 'in very mild solution': they were expressed 'without rancour or fanaticism; still underpinned by a strong Christian ethic and leavened by the values of Victorian liberalism'. He adds, too, that imperial defence was perceived as fundamentally a naval and not a military responsibility. If Britain lost 'command of the sea', she risked losing not only her Empire but also her immunity from invasion.[50] Whenever governments responded to invasion scares and alarmist literature, it was primarily the Royal Navy and not the army that benefited.

Quite apart from the primacy accorded to the Senior Service, the adulation of the army may have proved counterproductive. The reporting and descriptions of military successes, or the recovery from periodic disasters, simply buttressed confidence in the commanders and in the abilities of the small, voluntary army. They hardly con-firmed the claims that the army could not fulfil its responsibilities or that it required drastic reorganisation. Neither those who advocated a vast increase in military expenditure nor those who favoured wholesale reform had much influence until the disasters of 'Black Week' (10–15 December 1899) and Spion Kop (24 January 1900) in the early months of the Second Boer War.

Distance, finally, may have lent enchantment. The reporting, painting and glorifying of wars in distant, and often exotic, locations may have served as a vicarious outlet for those living drab or monotonous lives. People may have distinguished between the army as an institution, undertaking an honoured role in garrisoning, defending and expanding the Empire, and the army as a possible career for themselves or for their children. Indeed, the writing of Kipling probably reinforced traditional attitudes towards military life – that it was poorly paid, lacked status, and was bereft of prospects; that it attracted recruits from the least respectable sections of the population; and that its soldiers periodically indulged in drunken and licentious behaviour. Similarly, those who popularised the army by romanticising warfare, extolling the warrior ethos, and glorifying the imperial mission, may have confirmed instinctive feelings that this was a life-style and value system utterly remote from civilian professions and trades, and that its primary remit, unlike that of the Volunteers, was geographically remote too.

Notes

1 A. Summers, 'Militarism in Britain before the Great War', *History Workshop*, Issue 2 (autumn 1976), pp.104–23; J.M. MacKenzie, *Propaganda and Empire: The manipulation of British public opinion 1880–1960* (Manchester University Press; Manchester, 1984), p.5.

2 F. Harcourt, 'Disraeli's Imperialism, 1866–1868: A Question of Timing', *Historical Journal*, Vol.23 (1980), pp.87–109.

3 P.J. Durrans, 'A Two-edged Sword: The Liberal Attack on Disraelian Imperialism', *J.I.C.H.*, Vol.X (May 1982), pp.262–84; H. Cunningham, 'The Language of Patriotism, 1750–1914', *History Workshop*, Issue 12 (autumn 1981), pp.8–33 and 'Jingoism in 1877–78', *Victorian Studies*, Vol.14 (June 1971), pp.429–53; C. de B. Webb, 'The Origins of the War: problems of interpretation' in A. Duminy and C. Ballard (eds.), *The Anglo–Zulu War New Perspectives* (University of Natal Press; Pietermaritzburg, 1981), pp.1–12; T.A. Heathcote, *The Afghan Wars* (Osprey; London, 1980), pp.94–102.

4 P. Kennedy, *The Rise of the Anglo–German Antagonism 1860–1914* (Allen & Unwin; London, 1980), pp.308–9 and *The Realities Behind Diplomacy* (Fontana; London, 1981), pp.26–7, 30–1, 42–3, 59, 67; J.M.

MacKenzie (ed.), *Imperialism and Popular Culture* (Manchester University Press, Manchester, 1986), pp.4–5; R. Robinson and J. Gallagher with A. Denny, *Africa and the Victorians: The Official Mind of Imperialism* (Macmillan; London, 1961), pp.318–22, 335–6; *Parl. Deb.*, Fourth Ser., Vol.32 (28 March 1895), cols.405–6; H.C.G. Matthew, *The Liberal Imperialists* (Oxford University Press; London, 1973), p.151.

5 S. Koss, 'Weslyanism and Empire', *Historical Journal*, Vol.18 (1975), p.110; Cunningham, 'The Language of Patriotism, 1750–1914', p.22.

6 Anderson, 'The Growth of Christian Militarism in mid-Victorian Britain', p.64.

7 *Pall Mall Gazette*, 9 January 1884, p.1; C. Chenevix Trench, *Charley Gordon: An Eminent Victorian Reassessed* (Allen Lane; London, 1978), pp.194–206.

8 R. Hill, 'The Gordon Literature', *Durham University Journal*, Vol.XLVII (June 1955), pp.97–103; see also A. Nutting, *Gordon: martyr and misfit* (Constable; London, 1966), pp.11, 276–80; MacKenzie, *Propaganda and Empire*, pp.28, 51, 150–1, 181 and 213; D.H. Johnson, 'The Death of Gordon: A Victorian Myth', *J.I.C.H.*, Vol.10 (May 1982), pp.285–310.

9 Johnson, 'The Death of Gordon: A Victorian Myth', pp.301–4; Robinson and Gallagher with Denny, *Africa and the Victorians*, pp.24, 151–5, 346–54.

10 G.W. Steevens, *With Kitchener to Khartum* (Blackwood; Edinburgh 1898), pp.315–16.

11 W.L. Langer, *The Diplomacy of Imperialism 1890–1912* (Alfred Knopf; New York, 1951), pp.85–9; Kennedy, *The Rise of the Anglo–German Antagonism 1860–1914*, pp.308–9; H.W. Koch, 'Social Darwinism as a Factor in the New Imperialism' in H.W. Koch (ed.), *The Origins of the First World War: Great Power Rivalry and German War Aims* (Macmillan; London, 1972), pp.329–54.

12 Steevens, *With Kitchener to Khartum*, pp.301, 309, 324.

13 E.N. Bennett, *The Downfall of the Dervishes* (Methuen; London, 1898), pp.201–2.

14 Wolseley, *The Story of a Soldier's Life*, Vol.1, p.20; see also MacKenzie, *Propaganda and Empire*, p.6; Z.S. Steiner, *Britain and the Origins of the First World War* (Macmillan; London, 1977), pp.155–7; J. Gooch, *The Prospect of War: Studies in British Defence Policy 1847–1942* (Frank Cass; London, 1981), pp.41–3.

15 *Parl. Deb.*, Fourth Ser., Vol.90 (14 March 1901), col.1612.

16 *Parl. Deb.*, Fourth Ser., Vol.90 (14 March 1901), col.1640; for the debate over the composition of the mobs, see R. Price, *An Imperial War and the British Working Class* (Routledge & Kegan Paul; London, 1972), ch.IV; M.D. Blanch, 'British Society and the War' in P. Warwick (ed.), *The South African War: The Anglo–Boer War 1899–1902* (Longman; London, 1980), pp.216–30; P. Summerfield, 'Patriotism and Empire: Music-Hall Entertainment 1870–1914' in MacKenzie (ed.), *Imperialism and Popular Culture*, pp.17–19.

17 Sir E. Grey to K. Lyttelton, 17 October 1899 and to N. Lyttelton, 23

October 1899, Lady K. Lyttelton Mss., Queen Mary and Westfield College, University of London.

18 Summerfield, 'Patriotism and Empire: Music-Hall Entertainment 1870–1914', pp.25–30.

19 *Ibid.*, pp.31–7; MacKenzie, *Propaganda and Empire*, p.45.

20 MacKenzie, *Propaganda and Empire*, pp.49–51, 62–3.

21 B. Shephard, 'Showbiz Imperialism: The Case of Peter Lobengula' in MacKenzie (ed.), *Imperialism and Popular Culture*, p.107; MacKenzie, *Propaganda and Empire*, pp.101–4.

22 R. Low and R. Manvell, *The History of the British Film* (Allen & Unwin; London, 1948), pp.55–6, 66–9, 95–7.

23 J.A. Mangan, 'The Grit of our Forefathers' in MacKenzie (ed.), *Imperialism and Popular Culture*, pp.113–39 and 'Images of Empire in the late Victorian Public School', *Journal of Educational Administration and History*, Vol.XII (January 1980), pp.31–9; G. Best, 'Militarism and the Victorian Public School', pp.129–46; P. Burroughs, 'John Robert Seeley and British Imperial History', *J.I.C.H.*, Vol.1 (1972–73), pp.191–211; Steiner, *Britain and the Origins of the First World War*, p.157; MacKenzie, *Propaganda and Empire*, pp.5–6, 179–85, 193–4; V.E. Chancellor, *History for their Masters: Opinion in the English History Textbook, 1800–1914* (Adams & Dart; London, 1970), pp.122–38.

24 Mangan, 'The Grit of our Forefathers', p.116; Blanch, 'British Society and the War', pp.211–13; J.O. Springhall, *Youth, Empire and Society: British Youth Movements, 1883–1930* (Croom Helm; London, 1977), pp.71–7.

25 P. Wilkinson, 'English Youth Movements 1908 30', *Journal of Contemporary History*, Vol.4 (April 1969), pp.5–6; J.O. Springhall, 'Lord Meath, Youth, and Empire', *Journal of Contemporary History*, Vol.5 (1970), p.100; Mangan, 'The Grit of our Forefathers', p.128; MacKenzie, *Propaganda and Empire*, pp.242, 245–7; J.O. Springhall, *Youth, Empire and Society*, pp.24–8, 37–9, 41–3.

26 MacKenzie, *Propaganda and Empire*, p.207; J. Springhall, 'Rise and Fall of Henty's Empire', *Times Literary Supplement* (3 October 1968), pp.1105–6; P.A. Dunae, 'Boys' Literature and the Idea of Empire, 1870–1914', *Victorian Studies*, Vol.24 (1980), pp.105–21.

27 R.T. Stearn, 'War Images and Image makers in the Victorian Era: Aspects of the British Visual and Written Portrayal of War *c.* 1886–1906', unpublished Ph.D. thesis (King's College, University of London, 1987), pp.116–19; J.O. Springhall, 'Up Guards and at them! British Imperialism and Popular Art, 1880–1914' in MacKenzie (ed.), *Imperialism and Popular Culture*, p.52.

28 P. Usherwood and J. Spencer-Smith, *Lady Butler: Battle Artist 1846–1933* (Alan Sutton; Gloucester, 1987), pp.59, 79; R.T. Stearn, 'War and the Media in the Nineteenth Century: Victorian Military Artists and the Image of War, 1870–1914', *Journal of the RUSI*, Vol.131 (September 1986), pp.58–9; Springhall, 'Up Guards and at them!', pp.65–7; J.W.M. Hichberger, *Images of the Army: The Military in British Art, 1815–1914* (Manchester University Press; Manchester, 1988), p.77.

29 Springhall, 'Up Guards and at them!', p.69; Usherwood and Spencer-Smith, *Lady Butler: Battle Artist 1846–1933*, pp.168–9; Hichberger, *Images of the Army*, pp.101–2; I. Knight, *Brave Men's Blood: The Epic of the Zulu War, 1879* (Guild Publishing; London, 1990), p.10.

30 Stearn, 'War and the Media in the Nineteenth Century', pp.55–6; Kennedy, *The Rise of the Anglo–German Antagonism 1860–1914*, pp.361–2; P. Knightley, *The First Casualty: The War Correspondent as Hero, Propagandist, and Myth Maker from the Crimea to Vietnam* (André Deutsch; London, 1975), p.42; L. Brown, *Victorian News and Newspapers* (Clarendon Press; Oxford, 1985), pp.7–25.

31 P. Hodgson, *The War Illustrators* (Osprey; London, 1977), pp.20–1; P. Johnson, *Front Line Artists* (Cassell; London, 1978), pp.80, 82, 114–15; R. Wilkinson-Latham, *From Our Special Correspondent: Victorian War Correspondents and their Campaigns* (Hodder & Stoughton; London, 1979), pp.170, 190–1; Bennett, *The Downfall of the Dervishes*, pp.71–7.

32 *The Times*, 17 March 1874, p.11. See also Johnson, *Front Line Artists*, pp.29, 135.

33 A. Forbes, *Memories and Studies of War and Peace* (Cassell; London, 1895), p.225; Johnson, *Front Line Artists*, pp.99, 153–4; R.T. Stearn, 'Archibald Forbes and the British Army', *Soldiers of the Queen*, Issue 61 (June 1990), pp.6–9; P. Knightley, *The First Casualty*, pp.47–8.

34 A. Forbes, 'War Correspondents and the Authorities', *Nineteenth Century*, Vol.7 (1880), pp.190–1; Bennett, *The Downfall of the Dervishes*, p.70; Stearn, 'War Images and Image Makers in the Victorian Era', pp.158–61 and 'Archibald Forbes and the British Army', p.8; Johnson, *Front Line Artists*, p.136.

35 Wolseley to LadyWolseley, 2 January 1880, Wolseley Mss., W/P, P/1; G.J. Wolseley, *The Soldier's Pocket Book*, 3rd edition (Macmillan; London, 1874), pp.93, 97.

36 Steevens, *With Kitchener to Khartum*, p.46; Wilkinson-Latham, *From Our Special Correspondent*, pp.141–2, 199.

37 Steevens, *With Kitchener to Khartum*, p.22; Johnson, *Front Line Artists*, pp.115–16, 132.

38 Wilkinson-Latham, *From Our Special Correspondent*, pp.196, 227; Steevens, *With Kitchener to Khartum*, pp.69–71.

39 *Ibid.*, pp.146–7, 150–2, 264, 282, 285, 292–3, 318; see also R.T. Stearn, 'G.W. Steevens and the Message of Empire', *J.I.C.H.*, Vol.XVII (January 1989), pp.210–31.

40 H.John Field, *Toward a Programme of Imperial Life: The British Empire at the Turn of the Century* (Clio Press; Oxford, 1982), chs.4, 5; Price, *An Imperial War and the British Working Class*, pp.2, 140; Shephard, 'Showbiz Imperialism', pp.94–5; Springhall, 'Up Guards and at them!', p.69; Stearn, 'G.W. Steevens and the Message of Empire', p.231, n.151.

41 I.F. Clarke, *Voices Prophesying War 1763–1984* (Oxford University Press; London, 1966), pp.33–9, 59, 65; H.R. Moon, 'The Invasion of the United Kingdom: Public Controversy and Official Planning 1888–1918', Ph.D. thesis, 2 Vols. (University of London, 1968), Vol.1, p.117; I.F.W.

Beckett, *Riflemen Form: A Study of the Rifle Volunteer Movement 1859–1908* (The Ogilby Trust; Aldershot, 1982), p.105.
42 C. Carrington, *Rudyard Kipling: His Life and Work* (Penguin; London, 1970), pp.141–4.
43 *Rudyard Kipling's Verse: Definitive Edition* (Hodder & Stoughton; London, 1946), p.45.
44 P. Mason, *Kipling: The Glass, the Shadow and the Fire* (Jonathan Cape; London, 1975), p.73; P. Keating, *The Working Classes in Victorian Fiction* (Routledge & Kegan Paul; London, 1971), pp.139–66.
45 'Oonts', *Rudyard Kipling's Verse*, p.408.
46 R. Blatchford, *My Life in the Army* (Daily Mail novels; London, 1910), p.160.
47 Sir G.T. Younghusband, *Soldier's Memories in War and Peace* (H. Jenkins; London, 1917), p.187.
48 M. Edwardes, 'Oh to meet an army man' in J. Gross (ed.), *Rudyard Kipling: the man, his work and his world* (Weidenfeld & Nicolson; London, 1972), p.41; M. Seymour-Smith, *Rudyard Kipling* (Queen Anne Press; London, 1989), p.93.
49 T. von Sosnosky, *England's Danger: The Future of British Army Reform* (Chapman & Hall; London 1901), p.80. On the pervasiveness of the popular imperialism, MacKenzie, *Propaganda and Imperialism*, pp.253–5; Summerfield, 'Patriotism and Empire', p.42; H.M. Hyndman, *Further Reminiscences* (Macmillan; London, 1912), pp.165, 168; on popular military departures, Sergeant C. Spraggs, diary, 30 July 1882, Spraggs Mss., NAM, 7706–14–9; Corporal W. Roe, diary, 25 February 1879, Roe Mss., NAM, 7504–18; and returns, Brig. B.W. Webb-Carter, 'A Subaltern in Abyssinia', *J.S.A.H.R.*, Vol.38 (1960), pp.144–9.
50 M. Howard, 'Empire, Race and War', *History Today*, Vol.31 (December 1981), pp.4–11.

8

Military duties in the United Kingdom

The army had a wide array of home-based duties. As the Stanhope memorandum indicated, its prime task was to provide 'effective support of the civil power in all parts of the United Kingdom', and, after the provision of reliefs for India and the garrisoning of fortresses at home and abroad, it had 'to be able to mobilise rapidly for home defence two Army Corps of Regular troops, and one partly composed of Regulars and partly of Militia . . .' (Appendix 3). Although this ordering of priorities has been criticised as 'more suited to the conditions of 1818 than those of 1888', and as the reason for the failure to prepare plans 'for the defence of the Empire as a whole',[1] they reflected a range of contemporary concerns. Threats to public order, if not as serious as those in the early nineteenth century, recurred in the late Victorian period. During the 1880s there were notable disturbances in Lancashire, the Western Isles, north Wales and, above all, Trafalgar Square (13 November 1887). The 'condition of Ireland' remained an acute concern, and panics about the possibility of invasion periodically aroused protests in the press and Parliament. In these circumstances military deployments, or plans for military deployments, were one of several methods by which successive governments sought to preserve order and restore confidence.

Violent disturbances and riots, occasioned by elections, religious processions, industrial disputes, and other large public gatherings, were common phenomena. The vast majority of these events were either controlled by the police or subsided of their own accord. During the years from 1869 to 1908 the military were only called out to restore public order on twenty-four separate occasions in England and Wales, although troops were either alerted or requested during many other disputes, notably the London dock strike of 1889 and the police, postal and gas strikes of 1890.[2] Soldiers opened fire in one incident, killing two people at the Featherstone riot (1893), and charged a mob (Leigh, 1881), using the flats of their swords to disperse it. Called out during ten of the twenty-five Murphy riots (June 1866 to April 1871), where Irish Catholics clashed with supporters of Murphy, an anti-Catholic demagogue, the mere presence of the army was often sufficient to check the riots. Soldiers were deployed during election campaigns, agricultural protests, industrial disputes, and religious conflicts, including some disturbances which followed the mass meetings and processions of the Salvation Army.[3] Proffering assistance in the maintenance of public order remained a prime and demanding duty.

In discharging this duty, soldiers acted as citizens and had to conduct themselves within the remit of the law. They were bound by two main principles:

That every citizen is bound to assist the Civil Authority in repressing disorder when called upon to do so, an obligation which admits of no distinction as between civil and military status.

That for such purposes of repression or suppression no more force than is necessary can be lawfully used.[4]

However simple, these principles did not allow for the fact that soldiers, unlike civilians, formed part of a disciplined organisation and, if they had to act, could employ deadly weapons. Although soldiers normally acted at the behest of a civilian magistrate, the absence of a magistrate did not absolve a soldier from acting against rioters. If a magistrate called for assistance, any refusal to render assistance would be liable to punishment as a misdemeanour in the civil courts. If the soldier failed to use sufficient force to quell disorder, he could be court-martialled for negligence. If the soldier used excessive force, he could be tried for manslaughter or murder, and a magistrate's order to fire had no legal effect in law. The order would not justify the firing if the magistrate was later found to be wrong by a court, and the absence of an order would not excuse the soldier for declining to fire when the necessity arose. The reading of the Riot Act did not interfere with these principles. Its only effect was to make it a felony if a crowd failed to disperse one hour after a reading of the proclamation. Should an outrage take place after the reading but before an hour had elapsed, the common law duty of soldiers as citizens remained in force. Only after the hour had elapsed was it lawful to shoot people, if the felony could not be stopped in any other way.[5]

The civil authorities were not expected to call upon the military except as a last resort. Technically the military were not entitled to act unless summoned by the magistracy or 'in cases of great and sudden emergency'. Thereupon the officer in command had to act with great discretion in deploying his men. Under Queen's Regulations he had to march his troops in regular order and had to ensure that they were 'not scattered, detached, or posted in a situation where they may not be able to act in their own defence'. Once they had arrived at the point designated by the magistrate, the officer had to decide what action should be taken. He alone could command his soldiers to fire but had to exercise a 'humane discretion' regarding the line of fire. Although he could authorise firing if his forces were attacked, or if they could not hold their positions without doing so, he would normally give the command only if required to do so by the magistrate in attendance. As Sir Redvers Buller acknowledged, Queen's Regulations expected that soldiers would open fire 'under the greatest restrictions and the strictest discipline possible'.[6]

The magistrates exercised a vital role in the summoning of troops. In extreme emergencies this was the only practical arrangement, as sending an application through the Home Office could incur disastrous delays. Nevertheless, Home Secretaries and their Permanent Under-Secretaries were frequently concerned lest magistrates should panic and call out troops unnecessarily. They feared not only the possibility of bloodshed but also the misuse of troops, which could aggravate the situation and ultimately discredit the government. They knew, too, that magistrates could summon the military without worrying about the expense. Whereas the local authority bore the cost of summoning police from other boroughs or counties, the War Office met the bulk of the costs of any military deployments. Consequently, the Home Office sometimes censured local authorities for requesting troops unnecessarily, and periodically insisted that the soldiers should be withdrawn in spite of local opposition.[7]

The army performed various duties in aid of the civil authorities. Occasionally their mere arrival in the midst of a community served as a deterrent to further disorder. Often they were used to relieve the police of certain duties, such as the guarding of public buildings and homes, so that the police could concentrate their resources against the mob. Sometimes they were employed in accompanying magistrates as they served writs or in separating rival mobs or in acting as a rearguard for the police when they tried to disperse demonstrators. Their length of employment varied with the nature of the disturbance; the 5th Dragoon Guards were only briefly deployed during an election at Northampton (March 1882), but served for several weeks during protracted industrial disputes (such as the cotton weavers' strike in Lancashire in 1878, when B, D and G Troops spent several weeks in Accrington, Burnley and Blackburn, or in the Liverpool dock strike of February 1879, when G Troop was quartered in the Artillery drill shed for nineteen days).[8]

Employing the military had many advantages. As these interventions were relatively rare, they appeared as drastic steps, bringing the power and prestige of the State to bear upon local incidents or disputes. In certain areas, which were not effectively policed, military intervention often proved decisive. During the Scottish 'Crofters' Land War', in which crofters in the Western Isles had seized land and refused to pay rent, Arthur Balfour advised his cabinet colleagues that the local police were held in 'uttermost contempt' and were 'regarded as emissaries of the landlords' and not 'as vindicators of the law'. He was convinced that

the people will never for an instant attempt to resist the forces of the Crown, partly through fear of the results, and partly because they recognize in them what they decline to recognize in the police, i.e., that they are emissaries of the central authority.[9]

Underpinning this respect for central government in some communities was a basic patriotism, coupled with a belief that if only the Queen and government knew what was happening an inquiry and justice would follow. Accordingly, the military were sometimes well received; when the 9th Lancers appeared in Denbigh (May 1888), during the Welsh 'Tithe War', they were cheered repeatedly and money was collected to give them drinks.[10] On the other hand, fraternisation could prove counterproductive. As Balfour reflected upon an earlier use of the marines in the Western Isles, when troops were scattered in small groups under no official supervision and had nothing to do other than forge friendly relations with the crofters, the deployments simply fostered the belief that in the event of an emergency 'the marines would side with them against their officers'.

In 1886, he advocated sending parties of fifty to 100 marines to land by sea and act in concert with the police, serving writs for rent and rates and arresting deforcers 'on the spot'.[11]

Balfour was reflecting a widespread view that the military, if called out as a last resort, should act in a prompt, concerted and systematic manner, employing the minimum of force. These precepts were underlined in the handling of the 'Bloody Sunday' riots in Trafalgar Square (13 November 1887). These riots were the culmination of many years of agitation for the right to hold mass meetings in Hyde Park and Trafalgar Square. Only one year previously, on 8 February 1886, a mob had debouched from the Square and rampaged through Piccadilly and Pall Mall, smashing windows and destroying property. The revelation that the nation's capital had been inadequately policed (and that the District Superintendent in charge had had his pockets picked) caused widespread alarm. Indignation mounted in the wake of the riot as the police advised shopkeepers to close their premises, thereby admitting inability to maintain order. The Home Secretary, who was responsible for the capital's safety, resolved that similar events should not recur and appointed Sir Charles Warren as the new Chief Commissioner of the Metropolitan Police to placate his critics. When the latter protested over outbreaks of disorder following mass meetings of the unemployed in Hyde Park in the autumn of 1887, the Home Secretary prohibited further mass meetings in the vicinity of Trafalgar Square. On 13 November a large mob tried to contest the order but Warren had taken elaborate precautions. He not only deployed his constables in strength but also called upon four squadrons of Life Guards and 400 Foot Guards to act in support. He deployed two squadrons of Life Guards in the Square, another in Waterloo Place, and held more mounted troops in reserve in Horse Guards. He required the 400 Foot Guards to line the north side of the Square, so enabling the police to concentrate on dispersing the mob. These tactics proved so effective that *Reynolds's Newspaper* was reduced to complete fabrication when it claimed that the military had been ordered 'to shoot down the unarmed bread earners of London in cold blood'. In fact, the military never opened fire, as the police managed to disperse the mob.[12]

Where effective precautions were not taken, though, military intervention could prove costly. The disturbance caused by a large and apparently hostile crowd at Ackton Hall Colliery, Featherstone, on 7 September 1893 occurred when the bulk of the local constabulary were policing the Doncaster races. The Chief Constable found that he could not provide the police protection requested by Mr Holiday, the colliery manager, and by Lord St Oswald, a county magistrate, who faced another hostile crowd at Nostell Colliery. He duly requested military assistance from Bradford, but then chose to split the small force, sending Captain Digby Barker and twenty-eight men from the 1st Battalion, South Staffordshire Regiment, to Ackton Hall while a lieutenant and another twenty-five men travelled on to Nostell. On arriving at Featherstone, Captain Barker found that there was not a magistrate available to accompany him, and that his force was greatly outnumbered by a crowd of some 500 to 600 people, armed with sticks and cudgels. He led his detachment into an engine shed to await the arrival of a magistrate, but, as dusk fell, the crowd began to bombard the shed with stones and lumps of iron, breaking windows and beating down the doors. While some surged in, demanding the removal of the troops, others tried to start a fire to burn them out. Barker undertook to remove his men, if the mob dispersed immediately. He struck a bargain to this effect, and withdrew to the nearby station at about seven o'clock, whereupon the rioters began to burn down the colliery buildings. When a magistrate belatedly arrived, he and Captain Barker repeatedly urged the mob, now estimated to number 2,000, to disperse. They were attacked with showers of stones and bricks, and the reading of the Riot Act by lantern light at 8.40 p.m. merely provoked further stone throwing. When the troops fixed bayonets and advanced, they came under further attack and eventually, at 9.15 p.m., the magistrate decided that the troops had to open fire. It took two volleys to subdue the mob, leaving about a dozen people injured and two men, both spectators, dead, one of whom was a local Sunday school teacher.

As the two coroner's juries which held inquests on the dead men differed about whether there had been sufficient reason for the soldiers to open fire, Herbert Asquith, the Home Secretary, faced critical questioning in the House of Commons. He responded by constituting a committee, composed of Lord Bowen, Richard Haldane and Sir Arthur Rollit, to investigate the issue. It criticised the concentration of police at the Doncaster races, the division of the soldiers, and the initial absence of a magistrate. It also concluded that after the failure of conciliation, the onset of darkness, and the eruption of a riot, with colliery buildings blazing and a defiant mob, the troops 'had no alternative but to fire'. It took evidence from Sir

Redvers Buller, the Adjutant-General, about the adequacy of the existing legal arrangements and the lethality of modern armaments. He deprecated any modification of the current legal provisions and opposed the retention of two different types of cartridges, with a less powerful form reserved for riot control. He feared that it would not only be difficult to ensure that the appropriate ammunition was always available, but also that arming the military with a less lethal weapon might increase the frequency with which it was requisitioned. In short, preserving the current arrangements would underline the gravity of summoning the military and ensure that it only happened as a last resort.[13]

At a separate conference in the Home Office, Buller pressed for a change in the summoning procedure. He suggested that all requests for military assistance from a particular county should be channelled through the Chief Constable, and that the latter should be able to exercise his discretion in passing on the request. The conference approved this proposal, and a similar measure whereby all requests from boroughs were to be channelled through the mayor and not individual magistrates. The Home Office hoped that this would reduce unnecessary demands, as the Chief Constables were usually reluctant to make requests which reflected upon their policing arrangements. The Home Office also agreed that a magistrate should always accompany troops whenever they were acting in aid of the civil power, but that he should no longer give an order to open fire, only an order for the military to 'take action'. The responsibility for the particular form of action would rest with the officer in command.[14]

Nevertheless, acting in aid of the civil power remained a disliked and disagreeable duty. Senior officers, including the Duke of Cambridge, Wolseley and Buller, evinced little enthusiasm for the task, especially as it was not one for which the army was specially trained. 'We have no practice of firing at a mob,' admitted Buller.[15] In effect, the army depended upon its discipline, its cohesion and the deterrent posed by its weaponry whenever it had to assist in the maintenance of public order. Fortunately it received relatively few requests. Successive governments sought to establish the 'legitimacy' of their authority, minimising their use of force, tolerating freedom of expression, and relying upon an unarmed police. In post-Chartist Britain the authorities tended to fear sudden outbreaks of mass disorder rather than any organised movement of rebellion, and their

confidence reflected the readiness of Radical and trade union movements to seek reform through constitutional means and not through
recourse to violence.

Ireland posed more acute problems. Successive governments had
demonstrated their determination to uphold the Act of Union of
1800 and the integrity of the Empire. The bungled Fenian rising of
1867 had ensured that future governments would be determined to
maintain public order, even if they were also prepared, as some were,
to countenance limited measures of reform. In fact, the main threats
to public order came not from armed insurrection but from agrarian
'outrages', sectarian disturbances, and the tensions aroused by
various murders, including the Phoenix Park murders of 6 May
1882. The agrarian vendettas, often prompted by the eviction of
tenants for the non-payment of rents, were particularly prominent
during the late 1870s and 1880s. They took the form of intimidating
other tenants, maiming cattle, burning haystacks and farm buildings, and making attempts on the lives of landlords and their agents.
At the height of the agitation in 1880, when over 2,000 families were
driven from their homes, the outrages numbered 2,590.[16]

To assist local authorities throughout Ireland, the army normally
deployed some 25,000 to 30,000 troops in two divisions, with a
cavalry brigade, under the Irish Commander-in-Chief, based in
Dublin. One division, known as the northern command, had its
headquarters at the Curragh, where the cavalry brigade was
stationed. This command supplied forces for the Dublin and Belfast
areas, and stationed units in garrisons such as Dublin, Belfast,
Newry, Londonderry, Enniskillen, Mullingar, Birr, Athlone,
Dundalk, Belturbet, Dundalk and Castlebar. The other division,
known as the southern command, was based at Cork, and provided
troops for southern and western outposts, including Limerick,
Tipperary, Clonmel, Fermoy, Nenagh, Kinsale, Waterford,
Templemore, Kilkenny and Buttevant. This dispersal of troops
reflected the primacy of the public order role and the number of
relatively small Irish barracks, the majority of which had been built
between 1786 (Enniskillen) and 1813 (Kilkenny). The distribution,
as the Duke of Connaught recognised, had a debilitating effect upon
military training:

It is horrible for efficiency & discipline the way they are scattered in small
Detach[ment]s : *all* over the country. Concentration in Large Barracks &

Stations is what is most urgently required, but this means building & money.[17]

Nevertheless, the army was able to respond promptly to calls for assistance and to proffer support for magistrates and the Royal Irish Constabulary. As police resources were stretched to respond to the many and various disturbances in the 1870s and 1880s, the military received numerous requests from the civil authorities. Repington, who served with the 3rd Rifle Brigade in western Ireland in 1880, when tensions had risen after the murder of Lord Mountmorres (25 March 1880), recalled that companies had to be scattered across Galway, Headford, Tuam, Oughterard, Ballinakill and other places to be able to support the summons from the police. He spent the winter at Oughterard, often mounting night patrols two or three times a week, which involved marches of 'sixteen or twenty miles to search for men drilling and to impress the people'.[18]

The work was arduous and involved considerable privations. Night patrols in midwinter were often bitterly cold, and the peat fires in the elderly Irish barracks emitted little heat. Although units sometimes moved by train to their various districts, some incidents occurred in fairly inaccessible areas. In moving from Belfast to Letterkenny, the 5th Dragoon Guards had to undertake four one-day marches, each of thirty miles, with all their equipment and provisions on their saddles, as wheeled transport could not accompany them. The deployments were sometimes lengthy, particularly during the season of the Orange and Roman Catholic marches and demonstrations. Just as the 5th Dragoon Guards served in Belfast during July and August 1873, the 27th Foot spent the same months in Belfast in 1876, occupying strategic positions in the city and moving when necessary to prevent collisions between the rival factions. During the major riots in Belfast in 1886, various regiments supplied pickets of about 100 men each to support the police in various parts of the town and to guard key buildings. Throughout this period the civil authorities repeatedly sought the assistance of cavalry units, either to disperse street mobs or to overawe them. Although Sir Thomas Steele, the Commander-in-Chief in Ireland (1880–85), accepted that cavalry could render useful service in towns, he still feared lest they should 'come to grief' in confined areas. He admitted, though, that he could not refuse the magistrates, who 'always ask for Cavalry'.[19]

Relations between the military and the agitators varied greatly. In the north, relations between the Protestant mobs and the military were often good. The 27th Foot (the Royal Inniskilling Fusiliers) earned widespread plaudits for their patience, good temper and discipline when they were deployed in Belfast from April to October 1873. Indeed, the mobs frequently turned their wrath upon the police or the opposite faction, and, in stoning these targets, raised the cry, 'don't touch the soldiers, but aim over them.' Regimental recruiting flourished during this period, with 292 recruits joining at the regiment's headquarters – a large proportion from Belfast. During the Belfast riots of 1886 the appearance of the military often curbed the stoning of the police, and cavalry units regularly dispersed the mobs, without incurring deep resentment. Only in Catholic areas, like the Falls Road, were the troops stoned. In the rural areas of south and west Ireland, the receptions were more variable. If the locals were reluctant to confront the military openly (and Repington recalled that the tension of many evictions was defused by a combination of perfect military and police discipline and Irish humour), relations could be extremely strained. When some 7,000 troops guarded fifty volunteer Orangemen as they harvested the crops of Captain Boycott in Lough Mask, County Mayo, one of the officers, a veteran of Isandhlwana, claimed that he had never experienced as much 'personal discomfort' as he did then.[20] Yet attacks on the soldiers were fairly rare; only one assault occurred, nearly killing two riflemen, during Repington's tour of duty in Galway. The company promptly retaliated by ambushing the assailants, attacking them with shillelaghs, and hospitalising twenty-four of them. 'After that night,' he noted, 'our men were let alone. We had spoken in the Galway dialect.'[21]

Even so, the duties in aid of the civil power in Ireland were intermittent, and, in the intervening periods, officers had considerable amounts of free time to enjoy the attractions of Ireland. In Galway, at the height of the outrages, Repington found plenty of rough shooting at Oughterard, both duck shooting on the lake and woodcock shooting in the woods of Lord Ardilaun's estate at Cong. He also enjoyed the trout fishing on Lough Corrib, and, on returing to the Curragh, revelled in the hunting, racing, polo, racquets and cricket. Colonel Charles Head recalled excellent hunting with the Tipperary Hounds when he was based at Clonmel, and Colonel Sir Percival Marling had similar experiences at Cahir, Tipperary, where

'Nobody seemed to have an idea in the world beyond whisky and horses, and hunting and shooting; they didn't care a bit about hounds, which they said got in the way'.[22] Sir Edward May recalled how the gunners relished their opportunities to ride over the 'broad pastures of Meath', where they encountered little or no wire, hunting with the Meath and Kildare Foxhounds and with the Ward Union Staghounds. In his memoirs, May poignantly reflected upon his Irish service in the early 1880s, especially the regimental races, the hunting and cricket: 'such sport I have never had before or since . . . .'[23]

The social opportunitites were abundant, too, particularly in Dublin. The mess at the Portobello Barracks was unusually large, accommodating three batteries of Horse Artillery, and so facilitated lively nights for the junior officers. Indeed, the officers not only entertained guests in the mess but were also in demand socially, especially during the Dublin season, when the nobility and county families of Ireland flocked to Dublin for the balls, dances and dinners. The Commander-in-Chief had to sustain a tradition of hospitality at the Royal Hospital, hosting numerous balls, dinners and parties for the Punchestown Races and the annual Horse Show. In return the military were royally entertained and military manpower was much in demand by the Dublin hostesses. As May remembered, 'we officers dined out a great deal at pleasant parties, such as have gone out of fashion now. There was very good claret in Dublin, and witty conversation over it after dinner . . .'.[24]

Underpinning these links was the welcome extended by the Anglo–Irish community. Although some middle-class Roman Catholic families, other than those fiercely anti-British, were not slow to greet the military, especially their array of eligible young officers, the Anglo–Irish were particularly keen to foster links with the army. They welcomed the military presence, as it embodied the British connection, offered the prospect of additional protection for their persons and property, and bolstered their claims to political and social supremacy in Ireland. Their Loyalism, as described by Nora Robertson, combined loyalty to Crown, country and Protestant religion, in return for which they expected protection of their family and property and, above all, their class superiority (which was felt as keenly by 'Protestant charwomen' as by daughters of the Anglo–Irish gentry). In this respect, she observed, 'the close association of the officer class with civilians of like mind created and encouraged a

Loyalist standpoint which no other influence could have created'.[25]

As the army also contributed to the trade and social life of small communities, it was warmly received. During his childhood, Colonel Head recalled, it was almost venerated by some Anglo–Irish families:

Nothing I enjoyed more, when driving into Birr, than seeing the red-coated soldiers walking along the road in or out of the town. They looked such gentlemen compared with the local inhabitants. And the officers that I came in contact with always appeared to me to be veritable gods from Olympus.[26]

The Anglo–Irish country gentleman, argued Nora Robertson, who was the daughter of an Anglo–Irish colonel, 'took their colour absolutely from the garrison', not merely the latter's patriotic attitudes but also their social and cultural values: 'it had become obligatory to look and speak like an English public school man'. The women, she thought, were probably even more impressed; they rarely inhibited their daughters from consorting with 'these fascinating creatures, so kind and well turned out, and so ready to enjoy themselves'.[27] Indeed, this was hardly surprising in view of the long-established military connections of many Anglo–Irish families. Not only had many of them lengthy military pedigrees, but their sons had fewer professional options than their contemporaries in England and Scotland. Unable to live off the returns from coal or railways or industrial sites on their land, and with diminishing rentals and few opportunities for appointments at Dublin Castle, many from the more wealthy families pursued a military career (Table 3).

The warmth of this welcome almost certainly conveyed a distorted impression of Ireland, isolating the army from the depth of nationalist resentment and the changes in the nature of Irish society and politics. Nora Robertson loved living in the barracks at Fermoy in the 1890s but admitted that any suggestion

that it introduced me to anything Irish but the scenery is absurd. The barracks dominated my outlook except for visits . . . to large and bitterly cold country houses. Even there a British military milieu was only exchanged for a rigidly Anglo–Irish country atmosphere.[28]

Admittedly, these memories may not reflect impressions formed in earlier years, when soldiers found their barracks regularly stoned in Dublin and they acted more often in aid of the civil power. By the 1890s, the agitation and violence had largely subsided, partially on account of the policies of coercion and conciliation applied by

Arthur Balfour as Chief Secretary, and partially on account of the divisions within the Parnellite party and the death of Charles Stuart Parnell in 1891. Yet the army had never been used provocatively in Ireland; it had remained in a reserve or supportive role, with units sometimes kept in barracks during peaceful processions and demonstrations. The police had usually taken the initiative in implementing the policies of coercion (even killing three and wounding two when they fired on a large crowd in the Mitchelstown 'massacre' of September 1887). Accordingly, the Royal Irish Constabulary had born the brunt of the nationalist wrath.

Military life in Ireland, nonetheless, had depressing aspects. Many of the small and elderly barracks were ill-constructed and unsuitably arranged by contemporary standards. Officers complained of the overcrowding, the lack of amenities, especially in the smaller rural outposts, inadequate stables, and the appalling standards of hygiene in the Royal Barracks, Dublin. Located beside the river Liffy, which exuded foul odours in the summer months, the Royal Barracks were periodically swept with fever in the 1870s and 1880s. Enteric fever hospitalised a higher proportion of soldiers in Dublin than in any other military district in the United Kingdom, and caused a higher mortality rate among the troops than among the civil population in Dublin. After numerous reports from committees of inquiry, and parliamentary protests, the government eventually launched a barrack renovation programme in 1890. Although the programme produced desirable improvements, including the provision of cubicles in the Royal Barracks, the sheer scale of the Irish problem, particularly the continuing need for scattered deployments, limited the impact of the reforms.[29]

Military training also required an overhaul. It had always proved extremely difficult for forces scattered across the country in small outposts, bereft of training facilities. Even the gunnery range at Glenbeigh on the Kerry coast was hardly adequate, and at times dangerous, as the locals concealed themselves over the range in the hope of gathering bits of brass and copper from the exploded shells before the range-parties could do so. Admittedly, the forces quartered near Phoenix Park, and even more so at the Curragh, had access to more spacious training areas, but the field days at the Curragh were not always as useful as they might have been (Lord Sandhurst, as Commander-in-Chief 1870–75, once put his troops through a representation of the battle of Aliwal, in which he had participated in 1846). Under Wolseley's command (1890–95), the field days appear to have become more realistic exercises, including night operations, lengthy marches, and deliberate battlefield manoeuvres. Lord Roberts, who succeeded him as Commander-in-Chief, was used to military training in India, and he condemned the facilities at the Curragh, since they meant that 'manoeuvres on an extended scale are out of the question'.[30]

However concerned about improvements in training and conditions in Ireland, Wolseley shared the anxieties so often expressed by other civil and military authorities about the reliability of Irish Catholic soldiers. If Wolseley's fears reflected his own fierce brand of Anglo–Irish loyalty, they coincided with the forebodings revived by the Fenian infiltration of the army in the 1860s. If by no means as serious a threat as the sepoy revolt of 1857, it indicated a possible or potential threat from Irish soldiers, whether serving in Irish or non-Irish regiments or in the Reserve. Arguably reservists, once freed from military discipline, might have proved the greatest potential problem, especially if they found themselves destitute on leaving the Colours. Consequently W.H. Smith, as Secretary of State, asked the Chief Secretary in Ireland

if we could in some way or other obtain civil employment for Army reserve men in Ireland. They are probably disposed to be loyal when they are discharged into the Reserve from the Army and it is just as well to make it worth their while to remain so. On the other hand they would add strength to any movement against the Govt. if they joined the rebel forces.[31]

Concern about the loyalty of the Irish Catholic soldiers reflected racial stereotypes rather than any substantive evidence of disaffection. The 'native Irish' were perceived as alien in race and inferior in culture to the Anglo-Saxons, and Irish soldiers were often depicted as simple, genial, prone to drink, and likely to relish a good fight. The Connaught Rangers, as characterised by General George de S. Barrow, had 'something of a child in their dispositions; they were careless, untidy, negligent and happy-go-lucky, while reacting readily to discipline; loving a scrap without malice'.[32] Whether regarded as charmingly idiosyncratic, with virtues which outshone their faults, or as utterly frustrating characters, of whom too much could not be expected,[33] Irish soldiers were perceived as essentially malleable. They were thought to be susceptible to discipline but also as likely to be led astray, especially if under the influence of drink. Wolseley was particularly worried about their reliability; during his command, he reported upon an Irish private in the Scots Guards who had headed an 'amnesty procession', and some sixty, apparently drunken, Munster Fusiliers who ran amok in a railway train. He even advised the Duke of Cambridge

to get *all* the Irish Regts. out of Ireland as soon as possible & not to send any more until Mr Gladstone dies or is turned out of office. I would not trust them in a riot here, & any bad behaviour on the part of Her Majesty's soldiers in the North of Ireland just at present, might be most disastrous.[34]

Wolseley's request was not acted upon, and Lord Roberts, his successor, found little cause for complaint about the soldiers under his command. He recognised that few soldiers, Irish or non-Irish, relished service in the small towns of Ireland, but he attributed these feelings to living in cramped and ill-designed barracks, with scant amusement for their off-duty hours. Irish soldiers, in fact, proved neither disloyal nor collectively unreliable; indeed, they served with distinction in the Second Boer War, prompting Queen Victoria to mark her appreciation of their services by visiting Dublin in 1900 and awarding them the privilege of wearing a shamrock on St Patrick's Day.[35]

The Irish military establishment remained relatively static throughout this period, limiting the ability of the home-based army to prepare for other eventualities. Apart from aiding the civil power, the other major role was home defence – a task which, in Stanhope's memorandum, assumed priority over the preparation of an expeditionary force (Appendix 3). Traditionally, the defence of the British Isles had always been the primary responsibility of the Royal Navy, and doubts about the ability of the navy to undertake this mission had only arisen during the invasion panics of the mid and late nineteenth century. These panics, which occurred in 1846, 1851 and 1859, had usually reflected anxiety engendered by an upsurge of hostility from France and concern lest the French exploit new technological innovations (such as the first steam-powered ironclad battleship, built in 1859) to lure away or disperse the fleet and deploy an invading army. In 1871, Chesney had adapted this theme in his alarmist work, 'The Battle of Dorking', to incorporate the fanciful prospect of a Prussian invasion while the Channel Fleet was destroyed by a secret device. Although the controversy aroused by this work quickly abated, without any tangible benefit for Volunteer recruiting, the concern would recur.

In 1882 there were further alarms over invasion aroused by the proposal of the Channel Tunnel Company to construct a tunnel under the English Channel. The proposed linking of England and France provoked a furious reaction, with denunciations by leading generals, admirals, newspaper editors and a multitude of novelists. James Knowles, the editor of the prestigious periodical *The Nineteenth Century*, organised a mass petition against the the 'military dangers and liabilities' of the proposal. He gained the support of prominent intellectuals, churchmen, peers, politicians, the editors of four newspapers, the Governor of the Bank of England, seventeen admirals, fifty-nine generals and about 600 eminent persons. A Military and Scientific Committee, under the chairmanship of Major-General Sir Archibald Alison, issued a critical report on 12 May 1882, concluding that the prearranged measures for rendering the tunnel impassable could not meet every conceivable contingency. Wolseley and the Duke of Cambridge both prepared lengthy critical memoranda for parliamentary committees of inquiry. Wolseley argued that the seizure of the tunnel by a *coup de main* would be 'a very simple operation, providing it be done without any previous warning or intimation whatever by those who wish to invade the country'. During a period of 'profound peace', he argued, England could be surprised and the Dover entrance taken by 'a few thousand men . . . sent at night through the tunnel itself', so leaving the country at the mercy of an invader. At the very least, he concluded, the tunnel would represent 'a danger to the national existence of England'. The Duke of Cambridge, though less willing to speculate upon theories of a *coup de main*, still accepted that the tunnel represented a danger of considerable magnitude. Only a few years ago, he reflected, the Fenians had tried to sieze Chester Castle and no-one could guarantee that Dover Castle could not be taken once the tunnel was built. The French, he noted, had failed to destroy the Vosges tunnels in 1870, enabling the Prussian armies to use them. He contended that it was quite possible that an enemy could at some time secure possession of both ends of the tunnel and so be able to 'pour an army through it unopposed'. He also agreed with General Sir J.L.A. Simmons that if Britain became a Continental power, she would have to accept Continental risks and take out the same insurance which was required of Continental powers, namely a large standing army, based upon compulsory service.[36]

A Joint Parliamentary Select Committee, chaired by Lord Lansdowne, met to review the tunnel proposal on 20 April 1883. It reviewed the various reports and memoranda, and interviewed leading naval and military authorities. In its draft report of 10 July 1883 it cast doubt upon most of the theories of the means by which the tunnel could be seized in peace or war, particularly the notion of a *coup de main* during a period of peace. It also noted the numerous ways in which the tunnel could be obstructed or flooded in an emergency. Nevertheless, the committee agreed with the Alison Committee that Britain could not rely upon even the most 'comprehensive and complete arrangements' to deny the tunnel to an enemy 'in every imaginable contingency'. It recognised, too, that immense costs would be involved in building and manning a first-class fortress to defend the exit and land-based portion of the tunnel and in the reorganisation and re-equipment of the forces available for home defence. Finally, it accepted that only a large standing army, based upon compulsory service, could guarantee the nation's safety if the tunnel existed. Unwilling to endorse this 'gigantic evil', a majority of the committee advised that Parliament should not approve the proposal – a conclusion which sounded 'the death blow of the Channel Tunnel scheme'.[37]

The controversy had confirmed the degree to which Britain depended upon the Royal Navy for its protection. It had also brought to light the inadequacy of the military provisions for home defence, namely an inability to place more than 70,000 men in the field, backed by reserve forces which were bereft of artillery, organisation, and field equipment. It had revealed anxiety in some quarters about the prospect of a surprise attack. In his memorandum Wolseley had alluded to the recurrence of surprise attacks since 1700, implicitly referring to the findings of research undertaken by Colonel John Frederick Maurice in the Intelligence Branch, which were subsequently published in 1883 as *Hostilities without Declaration of War*. Having reviewed the period from 1700 to 1871, Maurice concluded that there were 107 instances in which armed conflicts had begun without any declaration of hostilities. Although the Lansdowne Committee shrewdly distinguished between the formality of declaring war and the attainment of complete surprise, arguing that most wars began after a period of warning, the notion of a 'Bolt from the Blue' had gained a degree of quasi-official backing. It became the basis of speculation about the possibility of a future invasion.[38]

This concern was further heightened by the shattering of public confidence in the invincibility of the navy. On 15 September 1884, W.T. Stead, the editor of *The Pall Mall Gazette*, began a series of articles entitled 'What is the Truth about the Navy?' He revealed that France, on account of her large shipbuilding programme, had nearly attained parity with Britain in numbers of first-class battleships, and that Britain's former supremacy at sea had diminished significantly. His articles aroused a widespread clamour, which prompted the Gladstone government to spend an extra £3,100,000 upon warships and £2,400,000 upon naval ordnance and coaling stations. The forebodings proved difficult to allay completely, partly on account of the fears evoked by the belligerence of France's War Minister, General Georges Boulanger, and the possibility that he might seize power, and partly on account of the recrudescence of Anglo–Russian enmity over Afghanistan in 1885. Should Russia, which was building up its fleet, consider a naval alliance with France, these powers had the potential to impose a pincer upon the under-strength Mediterranean Fleet.[39] Facing the prospect of a serious naval challenge, or the possible diversion of part of the Home Fleet, alarm about home defence quickly resurfaced.

Major-General Henry Brackenbury provided the stimulus for a thorough review of the military provision for home defence. Appointed Deputy Quartermaster-General and head of the Intelligence Branch in 1886, he sought to remedy the lack of any up-to-date mobilisation plan within the War Office. In his review of the existing provisions, he recognised that Britain could not 'place two complete Army Corps in the field, either for foreign service or for home defence', and, in seeking to establish criteria for mobilisation planning, he catalogued the deficiencies of the United Kingdom's defences. He noted the lack of any comprehensive plan of defence and hence the absence of organisational provision for the assembly, supply or transport of the scattered forces. He emphasised that the Commissariat staff could only support one army corps, and that there were completely undefended points on the coast, within an easy four days' march of London, which were suitable for the landing of a large force. 'London,' he concluded, 'the richest town in the world, lies undefended at the mercy of the invader.'[40]

Brackenbury regarded mobilisation planning as an immense additional burden upon his tiny staff, which already had to collect, analyse and produce military intelligence on a worldwide basis. He was heavily involved in seeking extra funds and additional appointments for intelligence collection (including another seven staff captains, so doubling the number of officers serving long tours at the branch), and in enhancing its status by gaining the transfer of the branch to the more prestigious Adjutant-General's department (June 1887), with direct access between himself and the Commander-in-Chief. The reputation of the branch received a further boost when it was redesignated as a directorate in mid 1887, and later as a division (January 1888). To cope with the minutiae of mobilisation planning, Brackenbury sought and secured Treasury approval for the creation of a new Mobilisation and Home Defence Section to be headed by Colonel John Ardagh (October 1887). In informing Ardagh of his appointment, Brackenbury urged the latter to hasten his return from Egypt, as Stanhope was 'very anxious' to have some plan devised for training the auxiliary troops in the places which they would have to occupy in the event of war. He added, too, that 'the whole scheme for mobilisation of our field army for home defence has yet to be worked out'.[41]

Although Ardagh quickly produced a proposal for an exercise of the metropolitan Volunteers, Stanhope found that he could not raise the 'extra money' to implement it.[42] Ardagh persevered, nonetheless, preparing elaborate schemes for the 'Defence of England' and the 'Defence of London'. He assumed that the warning might be little more than a week 'at the outside', and that a landing could hardly be contested, if supported by a coastal bombardment. Indeed, he feared that the 'enormous wealth' of London could tempt an invader, and that a landing of 30,000 men in the Thames estuary could come as a 'complete surprise', causing panic and dismay. As he clearly doubted whether the cabinet would approve the expenditure of £3,000,000 upon thirty permanent forts, with barracks, magazines and heavy guns, to protect the approaches to London, he proposed that London should be defended by mobile forces. He recommended that these should be deployed in two rings – an outer ring of two regular army corps and one partially composed of regulars and the Militia, and an inner ring of three Volunteer corps.

His calculations were highly theoretical. He assumed that regular battalions and cavalry regiments could be removed from Ireland and replaced by Militia and Yeomanry units. He deducted some units to guard Ireland and the Channel Islands and to man fortresses at home and abroad, but did not deduct the untrained, the unfit, or those Militiamen who were absent, with or without leave, from his calculations. He also assumed that the eighteen Volunteer brigades could be supported by 331 pieces of assorted artillery, the majority of which were guns of position (twenty and forty-pounders), heavy ordnance, and pieces in the siege trains. Although these weapons were movable, and possessed much more power than any guns which might accompany an invading army, they were neither modern nor particularly mobile. Hence Ardagh requested the purchase of '150 pieces of the most modern type . . . and 120 machine guns firing small-arm ammunition'. Finally, he optimistically claimed that the Volunteer corps did not need the same level of logistic support that an army would need in a country ill-provided with railways or roads. Ammunition, medical support and the commissariat train could be moved by the abundance of horses and vehicles: all that was needed, he claimed, was an 'organised method' of using them.[43]

Complementing these official proposals were the debates in Parliament and the press over the Volunteers and home defence. In the House of Commons, Sir Edward Hamley had championed the cause of the Volunteers over a period of three years. He had advocated additional expenditure to improve their uniforms, their arms, and their opportunities for more practical training. He had also favoured the construction of defensive works around London so that the Volunteers could co-operate effectively with the regulars. Wolseley proved more influential when he intervened in a debate in the House of Lords on 14 May 1888. He declared that on account of the country's naval weakness, and the dispersal of the army all over the world,

our defences at home and abroad are at this moment in an unsatisfactory condition, and that our military forces are not organised or equipped as they should be to guarantee even the safety of the capital . . . .[44]

Even Lord Salisbury, the Prime Minister, had to concede that this was a 'very grave statement', although he was clearly sceptical about Wolseley's assumptions and questioned the propriety of debating this issue in public. He knew that Wolseley had the support of the Duke of Cambridge on home defence (and the latter would reiterate this support publicly), and so responded by trying to defuse the debate with the appointment of a Royal Commission. To the dismay of Wolseley and the Duke, this commission, chaired by Lord Hartington, was only to inquire into the relationship between the army and navy departments and between these departments and the Treasury; it was neither an inquiry into the provisions for home defence nor into the broader missions of the services and their inability, without further expenditure, to fulfil them.[45] Meanwhile naval propagandists mounted a powerful counterattack. Vice-Admiral Philip Colomb, the naval historian, and his brother, Captain Sir John C.R. Colomb, MP, an eminent naval strategist, asserted that the navy had absolute primacy in home defence. Instead of accepting a divided naval and military responsibility, which the fortification experts of the War Office had advocated since 1860, the Colombs stressed a purely naval concept. Only four days after Wolseley's speech in the Lords, Admiral Colomb launched his broadside in a lecture before the Royal United Service Institution. He argued that if the navy was augmented, and so enabled either to blockade enemy ports or to keep an intact fleet in reserve, then there was no need for expensive fortifications. Although his paper proved highly controversial, not least among some senior admirals, it had launched a navalist case, known as the 'Blue Water' campaign, which quickly found more supporters. While Sir John Colomb argued in similar vein in the House of Commons, others challenged Wolseley's 'Bolt from the Blue' thesis in newspapers, journals, books and pamphlets. They had several advantages over Hamley and the Volunteer lobby; they could appeal to different audiences in different ways, promoting the navy as an economic alternative to militarism, fortresses and large standing armies, as the only viable means of defending the United Kingdom and the Empire, as the prerequisite for the delivery of any counterstroke strategy by the army, and as the embodiment of national tradition and scientific progress. Moreover, the naval manoeuvres of 1888 underscored the need for substantial improvements to the fleet, as it became patently clear that the navy could not blockade even a single enemy and simultaneously discharge its other wartime duties. Faced with the embarrassing divisions between the services and the evidence of chronic naval incapacity, the government resolved to maintain a two-power naval standard. In introducing the National Defence Bill before Parliament in 1889, the government sought approval for the expenditure of £21,500,000 on the construction of eight battleships, thirty-eight cruisers and twenty-two gunboats. It proffered a mere £600,000 to the army to improve the defences against invasion.[46]

The army would not admit defeat. Maintaining even a minimal role in home defence preserved a prized responsibility and cushioned the service against possible reductions. On 11 March 1889 Stanhope announced plans to purchase thirteen sites for the construction of entrenched camps around London. These were to constitute the second line of defence along the main roads and railway routes, with each serving as a mobilisation centre for the Volunteers and their guns of position. The sites included Epping (North Weald), Farningham, Halstead, Betson's Hill (Westerham), Woldingham, Foster Down (Caterham), East Merstham, West Merstham, Reigate, Betchworth, Dorking (Box Hill), Dorking (Denbies), Guildford (Pewley Hill) and Guildford (Henley Grove). The War Office planned to build storage accommodation on the sites to facilitate rapid mobilisation and to entrench the sites, if the necessity arose, so that they could serve as defensive positions to be held by the Volunteers. The preoccupation with home defence remained pervasive: Coleridge Grove, Stanhope's military secretary, was characterised as 'recasting the various schemes from the point of view of the probability of our finding the French army on our breakfast tables with *The Times* to-morrow morning', and when Colonel Gerald Ellison joined the mobilisation section in 1890 he found it absorbed with the problems of fortifying London.[47]

Admittedly there were divergent currents of thought within the War Office. Major-General Edward Chapman, who succeeded Brackenbury as Director of Military Intelligence in 1891, had considerable Indian experience and close ties with Lord Roberts. He believed that Britain's strategic planning should move beyond the defence of the British Isles and the protection of the capital, particularly after the signing of the Franco–Russian alliance in 1894. Concerned primarily about a possible threat to the North West Frontier, he soon came to the conclusion that a full-scale invasion of Britain was unlikely, and that a small coastal raid was the most that the French might attempt. Chapman, though, had much less influence within the War Office than either his predecessor or his successor, Ardagh. He suffered on account of his Indian background and his lack of good connections with the Foreign and Colonial Offices. Ardagh, who served as Director of Military Intelligence from 1896 to 1901, was much more closely identified with traditional thinking on home defence. Although he was willing to concede the primacy of command of the sea in home defence, he maintained that 'there is a considerable element of chance in naval supremacy, and that mere superiority of numbers is precarious until battles have been fought and won'. Ardagh accepted, nonetheless, that the government would not authorise the £3,000,000 required to fortify the sites purchased around London, even if there was 'much to be said in favour of this means of defence': that option, he conceded, 'was not now under discussion'.[48]

During the 1890s, military planning had moved away from the focus upon home defence in two critical respects. First, the Salisbury government had been so appalled by the lack of agreement, or even basic co-operation, between the two services that it had imposed inter-service committees, like the Landing Places Committee, from above. If these tended to perpetuate disagreements (the Landing Places Committee met on eleven occasions between 1891 and 1894, without being able to compose the differences between the services), at least naval and military representatives met more regularly to exchange their points of view. Secondly, and more significantly, the Mobilisation Department began to amend the mobilisation plan, devised for the defence of London, to accommodate the despatch of troops overseas. Backed by Wolseley as Commander-in-Chief, the department and the Army Ordnance Department prepared a plan which would permit the mobilisation of units at the same place, whether mobilised for home or overseas service. This place was normally to be the peacetime station of the unit, and for formations, like supply columns, which did not normally exist in peacetime, the London mobilisation centres such as Croydon or Caterham would be used. At least these arrangements, which eventually facilitated the despatch of the field force to South Africa in 1899, indicated some flexibility in planning, even if not any strategic reappraisal.

When fears of an invasion resurfaced during the Boer War, disagreements recurred within the War Office. Sir William Nicholson, appointed Director-General of Mobilisation and Military Intelligence in 1901, required Lieutenant-Colonel E.A. Altham to conduct a survey of Britain's strategic requirements against the most threatening of opponents, France and Russia. Altham argued that if Britain lost command of the sea, then 'however large a home army we maintain, we shall be starved into surrender without the landing of a single French soldier on our shores'. He claimed, too, that the insular preoccupation had led to 'a flagrant neglect of vital factors, such as the defence of India, Egypt, and the power of striking effective blows at the enemy'. Accordingly, he advocated increasing the size of the Indian Army and the Egyptian garrison, diminishing and reorganising the forces earmarked for home defence, and preparing an expeditionary army of about 200,000 men.[49] Nicholson and Lord Roberts, then the Commander-in-Chief, broadly endorsed these findings, but Roberts also approved of another paper, by Lieutenant-Colonel W.R. Robertson of the Intelligence Department, which recounted all the traditional arguments about the 'attractive and feasible' option of a French invasion. Roberts realised that this paper could justify the creation and retention of a large home-based army. Considering it 'imprudent to rely absolutely and exclusively on the navy for home defence', he suggested that an army corps of regulars should be maintained in England, bolstered by Militia and Volunteers (with the training and organisation of the Militia enhanced by compulsory service). Brodrick, the Secretary of State, queried whether the French would be able to collect and protect their transports while preparing for an invasion. Roberts referred him to the calculations of the military members of the Landing Places Committee and drew his attention to the provisions which had been made to defend the country in 1798, when 180,000 regulars and Militia were ready to defend the country, backed by 400,000 volunteers. He questioned whether 'our military strength and organization' had since been developed in proportion to the 'military development of our continental neighbours, or to our own increase in population and wealth'. Brodrick duly agreed to pass on the paper to the defence committee of the cabinet.[50]

Throughout this period, in short, the War Office repeatedly sought to fashion and promote a role for the home army. Assisting in the maintenance of public order in Ireland and in the rest of the British Isles was a necessary but hardly sufficient task; it neither provided a clear focus (since the difficulties arose on an episodic basis) nor facilitated the organisation of the forces retained at home. The defence of London and the United Kingdom offered much more scope, but, without cabinet backing, the various proposals remained essentially theoretical. Nevertheless, the War Office was reluctant to accept the full implications of 'Blue Water' thinking, as they seemed likely to deny the army a role and leave it ripe for further reductions.

Notes

1   Gooch, *The Plans of War*, p.12; Robertson, *From Private to Field-Marshal*, p.92.

2   E. Stanhope to Cambridge, 26 August 1889, Wolseley to Cambridge, 23 September 1890, and Cambridge to Stanhope, 24 September 1890, Cambridge Mss., RA, E/1/12476, E/1/12656 and E/1/12658; Stanhope to H. Matthews, 7 July 1890 and G. Hamilton to Stanhope, 30 September 1890, Stanhope Mss., Kent Archives Office, 0298/2 and 0319; I.F.W. Beckett, 'The Stanhope Memorandum of 1888: a Reinterpretation', *Bulletin of the Institute of Historical Research*, Vol.LVII (November 1984), pp.240–7.

3   C.E. Troup, qs.26–7 evidence appended to the *Report of the Select Committee on the Employment of the Military in Cases of Disturbances*, hereafter referred to as the *Paulton Report*, Cd. 236 (1908), VII, pp.5–6; J.P.D. Dunbabin, *Rural Discontent in Nineteenth Century Britain* (Faber & Faber; London, 1974), p.91; see also D. Richter, 'The Role of Mob Riot in Victorian Elections, 1865–1885', *Victorian Studies*, Vol.XV (September 1971), pp.19–28; T.A. Critchley, *The Conquest of Violence* (Constable; London, 1970), pp.160, 178.

4   *Paulton Report*, p.iii.

5   *Manual of Military Law*, p.107; Critchley, *The Conquest of Violence*, pp.74–5; *Report of the Committee appointed to inquire into the Circumstances connected with the Disturbances at Featherstone on the 7th of September 1893*, hereafter referred to as the *Featherstone Report*, C. 7234 (1893–94), XVII, pp.10–11; R.B. Haldane, q.134 evidence appended to the *Paulton Report*, p.15.

6   Buller, qs.5307–13 evidence appended to the *Featherstone Report*, pp.121–2; Troup, q.17, Sir A.P. MacDonnell, q.516 and Appendix 1 evidence appended to the *Paulton Report*, pp.4, 38, 45; *Queen's Regulations and Orders for the Army 1873* (HMSO; London, 1873), sect.8, IV, pp.221–3.

7   Troup, qs.8, 25–6, 30–1, and Capt. Tomasson, qs.382–5 evidence appended to the *Paulton Report*, pp.3, 5–6, 31; see also P.T. Smith, *Policing Victorian London: Political Policing, Public Order, and the London Metropolitan Police* (Greenwood Press; Westport, Connecticut, 1985), p.119.

8   Maj. the Hon. R.L. Pomeroy, *The Story of a Regiment of Horse: being the Regimental History from 1685 to 1922 of the 5th Princess Charlotte of Wales' Dragoon Guards*, 2 Vols. (Blackwood; Edinburgh, 1924), Vol.1 pp.199–200; Steedman, *Policing the Victorian Community*, p.37.

9   A.J. Balfour, memorandum, 15 September 1886, PRO, CAB 37/18, No.44.

10   *Denbighshire Free Press*, 26 May 1888, p.6.

11   A.J. Balfour, memorandum, 15 September 1886, PRO, CAB 37/18, No.44.

12   *Reynolds's Newspaper*, 20 November 1887, p.1; Critchley, *The Conquest of Violence*, pp.145, 148–57; V. Bailey, 'The Metropolitan Police, the Home Office and the Threat of Outcast London', in V. Bailey (ed.), *Policing and Punishment in Nineteenth Century Britain* (Croom Helm;

London, 1981), pp.96–105; A. Babington, *Military Intervention in Britain* (Routledge; London, 1990), pp.121–2.

13   *Featherstone Report*, pp.1–11; Babington, *Military Intervention in Britain*, pp.123–30; Buller, qs.5313, 5316–18, evidence appended to the *Featherstone Report*, p.122.

14   Tomasson, q.256 and Troup, qs.7, 8 and 33, evidence appended to the *Paulton Report*, pp.26, 3 and 6.

15   Buller, qs.5327 and 5357, evidence appended to the *Featherstone Report*, pp.122–3; Cambridge to Stanhope, 24 September 1890, Cambridge Mss., RA, E/1/12658.

16   Lyons, *Ireland since the Famine*, pp.137, 165, 168; see also A.J. Semple, 'The Fenian Infiltration of the British Army', *J.S.A.H.R.*, Vol.52 (autumn 1974), pp.133–60.

17   Duke of Connaught to Wolseley, 2 December 1890, Wolseley Mss.; Henderson, *Highland Soldier*, pp.172–3; E.A. Muenger, 'The British Army in Ireland, 1886–1914', unpublished Ph.D. thesis (University of Michigan, 1981), p.73.

18   Repington, *Vestigia*, pp.64–5.

19   Sir T. Steele to Cambridge, 4 November 1883, Cambridge Mss., E/1/10534; Repington, *Vestigia*, p.65; Pomeroy, *The Story of a Regiment of Horse*, Vol.1, pp.197–8; Regimental Historical Records Committee, *The Royal Inniskilling Fusiliers*, p.340; *Report of the Belfast Riots Commissioners*, C. 4925 (1887), XVIII, p.20 and Capt. Evans Loome, qs.5890–93, 5906 evidence appended to this report, pp.186–79; R. Hawkins, 'An Army on Police Work, 1881–2', *The Irish Sword*, Vol. XI (Winter 1973), pp. 75–117.

20   Maj.-Gen. Sir E. May, *Changes and Chances of a Soldier's Life* (Philip Allan; London, 1925), p.82; R.Kee, *The Green Flag*, 3 Vols. (Quartet Books; London, 1976), Vol.2, p.81; Pomeroy, *The Story of a Regiment of Horse*, Vol.1, p.198; Repington, *Vestigia*, p.64; Moore, qs.5570, 5572, 5581, 5707–8 and Evans Loome, qs.5893, 5906, evidence appended to the *Report of the Belfast Riots Commissioners*, pp.175–7, 181, 186–7; Regimental Historical Records Committee, *The Royal Inniskilling Fusiliers*, p.340.

21   Repington, *Vestigia*, p.65.

22   Repington, *Vestigia*, pp.66, 69; Lt.-Col. C.O. Head, *No Great Shakes: An Autobiography* (R. Hale; London, 1943), pp.78–9; Col. Sir P. Marling, *Rifleman and Hussar* (John Murray; London, 1931), p.168.

23   May, *Changes and Chances of a Soldier's Life*, pp.72, 84.

24   *Ibid.*, pp.70, 73, 84; Gen. Sir N. Lyttelton, *Eighty Years Soldiering, Politics, Games* (Hodder & Stoughton, London, 1927), p.284; J. Lehmann, *All Sir Garnet: A Life of Field-Marshal Lord Wolseley* (Jonathan Cape; London, 1964), p.23.

25   N. Robertson, *Crowned Harp* (Allen Figgis & Co.; Dublin, 1960), pp.24, 36–7.

26   Head, *No Great Shakes*, pp.24–5; T. De Vere White, *The Anglo–Irish* (Victor Gollancz; London, 1972), pp.252–3; Robertson, *Crowned Harp*, pp.23, 99; May, *Changes and Chances of a Soldier's Life*, p.288.

27 Robertson, *Crowned Harp*, pp.24, 101; Maud Gonne Macbride, *A Servant of the Queen* (Victor Gollancz; London, 1974), p.40.
28 Robertson, *Crowned Harp*, p.38; Muenger, 'The British Army in Ireland, 1886–1914', p.82.
29 *Report on the Prevalence of Enteric Fever in the Royal Barracks, Dublin*, C. 5292 (1888), XXV, pp.13–17; *Interim Report on the Sanitary Condition of the Royal Barracks, Dublin*, C. 5653 (1889), XVII, pp.4–8; *Parl. Deb.*, Third Ser., Vol.333 (11 March 1889), col.1434; Maj.-Gen. May, *Changes and Chances of a Soldier's Life*, p.88; Pomeroy, *The Story of a Regiment of Horse*, Vol.1, p.194; Henderson, *Highland Soldier*, p.172; Steele to Cambridge, 20 November 1883, Cambridge Mss., E/1/10548.
30 Roberts to Secretary of State for War, 8 January 1897, Roberts Mss., NAM, 7101–23–107, f.85; Wolseley to Cambridge, 29 October 1890 and 27 August 1892, Cambridge Mss., E/1/12666 and 12842; Lyttelton, *Eighty Years*, pp.72–3; Marling, *Rifleman and Hussar*, p.171.
31 W.H. Smith to Sir M. Hicks Beach, 15 November 1886, PRO, Smith Mss., WO 110/5, f.849; Wolseley to Cambridge, 23 April 1893, Cambridge Mss., E/1/12945.
32 Gen. Sir G. de S. Barrow, *The Fire of Life* (Hutchinson; London, 1941), p.7; L.P. Curtis, *Anglo–Saxons and Celts: A Study of anti-Irish Prejudice in Victorian England* (New York University Press; New York, 1968), p.5.
33 Brig.-Gen. Sir J. Willcocks, *From Kabul to Kumassi: Twenty-four Years of Soldiering and Sport* (John Murray; London, 1904), pp.7–8, 101–2; Col. Sir T. Montgomery-Cuninghame, *Dusty Measure: A Record of Troubled Times* (John Murray; London, 1939), p.29.
34 Wolseley to Cambridge, 23 April 1893 and letters of 2 February 1893 and 17 November 1893, Cambridge Mss., E/I/12945, 12818 and 12996.
35 Roberts to the Rev. W.J. Mathins, 23 May 1899 and Roberts secretary to C. Welby Eyre, 17 April 1898, Roberts Mss., NAM, 7101-23-110-1 and 7101-23-107; B. Farwell, *For Queen and Country* (Allen Lane; London, 1981), pp.34–5; Robertson, *Crowned Harp*, pp.54–5.
36 Sir G. Wolseley, 'Memorandum', 16 June 1882 and 'Observations by His Royal Highness the Field-Marshal Commanding in Chief', 23 June 1882, *Correspondence with reference to the Proposed Construction of a Channel Tunnel*, C. 3358 (1882), LIII, pp.271–98, 299–305; Sir J.L.A. Simmons, 'The Channel Tunnel', *Nineteenth Century*, Vol.XI (May 1882), pp.663–7; Clarke, *Voices Prophesying War 1763–1984*, pp.110–11.
37 'Précis of the Channel Tunnel Negotiations', PRO, WO 32/5299; *Report from the Joint Select Committee of the House of Lords and the House of Commons on the Channel Tunnel; together with the Proceedings of the Committee, Minutes of Evidence, and Appendix*, hereafter referred to as the *Lansdowne Report*, C. 243 (1883), XII, pp.xx–xxvi, xxxv–xxxviii, xliv–xlv.
38 *Lansdowne Report*, p.xx; Gooch, *The Prospect of War*, p.6; Luvaas, *The Education of an Army*, p.184.
39 P.M. Kennedy, *The Rise and Fall of British Naval Mastery*

(Macmillan; London, 1983), p.178; 'What is the Truth about the Navy?'
Pall Mall Gazette (15 September 1884), p.1.
   40 Brackenbury to the Quartermaster-General, 14 April 1886, and
'General Sketch of the Situation Abroad and at Home from a Military
Standpoint', 3 August 1888, PRO, WO 33/46; T.G. Fergusson, *British
Military Intelligence, 1870–1914 The Development of a Modern Intelligence Organisation* (University Publications of America; Frederick,
Maryland, 1984), p.84.
   41 Brackenbury to Ardagh, 13 October 1887, Ardagh Mss., PRO
30/40/2; Fergusson, *British Military Intelligence, 1870–1914*, pp.84–5.
   42 Stanhope to Ardagh, 31 January 1888, Ardagh Mss., PRO 30/40/2.
   43 Col. J.C. Ardagh, 'Defence of England', 17 April 1888 and 'Defence
of London', 16 July 1888, Ardagh Mss., PRO 30/40/13. Compare Ardagh's
calculations on the Militia with those of Simmons, q.2047 evidence
appended to the *Lansdowne Report*, pp.199–200.
   44 *House of Lords*, Third Ser., Vol.326 (14 May 1888), cols.100–1;
Hamley, 'The Defencelessness of London', pp.633–40; Luvaas, *The Education of An Army*, pp.159–61.
   45 *House of Lords*, Third Ser., Vol.326 (14 May 1888), cols.105–8 and
Vol.327 (29 June 1888), cols.1695–8; *Parl. Deb.*, Third Ser., Vol.326 (15
May 1888), col.374.
   46 Salisbury to Queen Victoria, 3 and 7 December 1888, PRO, CAB
41/21; Moon, 'The Invasion of the United Kingdom: Public Controversy
and Official Planning 1888–1918', Vol.1, pp.44–6, 60–5, 76–9; D.M.
Schurman, *The Education of a Navy: The Development of British naval
strategic Thought, 1867–1914* (Cassell; London, 1965), pp.46–51; *Parl.
Deb.*, Third Ser., Vol.326 (4 June 1888), cols.1099–102; A.J. Marder, *The
Anatomy of British Sea Power* (Hamden, Connecticut, 1964), pp.107–9;
Gooch, *The Prospect of War*, p.7.
   47 G.D.A. Fleetwood Wilson to Ardagh, 15 August 1889, Ardagh Mss.,
PRO, 30/40/13; G. Ellison, 'From here and there: reminiscences',
Lancashire Lad, No.50 (October, 1934), pp.6–7.
   48 Maj.-Gen. E. Chapman to Roberts, 19 October 1892 and to
Brackenbury, 29 October 1892, PRO, WO 106/16; Beckett, 'The Stanhope
Memorandum of 1888: a Reinterpretation', p.246; Maj.-Gen. J.C. Ardagh,
'The Defence of London', 19 January 1897, Ardagh Mss., PRO, 30/40/14;
Fergusson, *British Military Intelligence*, 1870–1914, pp.106–7.
   49 'Military Needs of the Empire in a War with France and Russia', 10
August 1901, pp.17, 49, PRO, CAB 3/1/1A; Moon, 'The Invasion of the
United Kingdom: Public Controversy and Official Planning 1888–1918',
Vol.1, p.187; J. Gooch, *The Prospect of War*, p.9.
   50 'The Military Resources of France, and probable Method of their
Employment in a War between France and England', 27 December 1901,
PRO CAB 3/1/4A and Lord Roberts, minutes on Paper 4A, 29 January 1902,
CAB 3/1/5A; Moon, 'The Invasion of the United Kingdom: Public Con-
troversy and Official Planning 1888–1918', Vol.1, pp.190–2.

9

Arms, tactics and training

During the late nineteenth century, profound changes occurred in military technology which greatly enhanced the potential effectiveness of firepower and stimulated a wide-ranging debate about the possible modification of tactics for the infantry, cavalry and artillery. These changes included the introduction of breech-loading rifles and guns, the adoption of smaller-calibre ammunition, the refinement of the machine gun, the subsequent incorporation of smokeless powder and magazine rifles, and the prospect of quick-firing artillery. Some of these innovations had been tested in battle, others not, but their combined effects portended a massive increase in firepower. Officers examined the effects of those weapons which had already been used in Continental wars or had been developed by European armies; they also debated their potential significance for British military tactics and sought to incorporate tactical changes into peacetime training.

The Prussians had been the first to introduce breech-loaders and had demonstrated the marked superiority of their needle gun over the Austrian muzzle-loader in the war of 1866. Essentially breech-loaders were much easier to load, obviating any need to place a cap on the nipple, or to bite the cartridge to free the powder, or to drive the ramrod down the barrel. They doubled the rate of fire to some six or seven rounds per minute. The loading process was not only much quicker but could also be undertaken in any position, thereby enabling the soldier to fire from a prone position and present a smaller target. Like the French, who introduced the Chassepot – an even better weapon than the needle gun – in 1866, the British followed the Prussian example. By fitting a Snider breech mechanism to their Enfield rifles, they converted their muzzle-loaders into breech-loaders. They also replaced the paper cartridge, which had fouled the breech-loaders and emitted hot gases from the breech, with the first brass cartridge, invented by Colonel Boxer of the Royal Laboratory, Woolwich. Robust and waterproof, the brass cartridge simplified the process of loading and extraction and sealed the breech during the explosion, allowing a more accurate aim. By March 1868, the British had converted 350,000 arms.

The Snider rifle never fully exploited the advantages of loading from the breech. As the Chassepot confirmed, it was now possible to fire bullets of a smaller calibre (0·43 inches) from a breech-loader. A smaller-calibre bullet encountered less resistance in the air, travelled over a flatter trajectory, and struck targets at a longer range. Moreover, if the bullet was composed of a harder metal, it would retain its penetrative and man-killing properties at a longer range when the velocity was diminishing. Whereas the Enfield barrel required a projectile composed of soft lead to take its three deep grooves and reduce the degree of windage (the gap between the projectile and the sides of the barrel which had impaired accurate firing), a rifled barrel with more numerous, if shallower surfaces, could permit the use of a harder bullet. When the War Office Small Arms Committee examined these aspects, it found that the seven-groove barrel invented by Alexander Henry would fire a bullet of 0·450 inches instead of the 0·577 fired by the Enfield. In addition, it found that von Martini, an Austrian, had developed a simpler and more efficient breech mechanism, which consisted of a block, hinged at its rear end, and contained a coiled spring in place of a hammer. The breech was opened whenever a lever under the trigger was pulled down, lowering the front end of the block, ejecting the previous empty cartridge and cocking the striker. A loaded cartridge could then be inserted by hand and the breech closed by raising the lever. A rifle comprising the Martini breech and the Henry barrel was approved in 1871, and, after experimental trials, was issued to soldiers in 1874.

Weighing 8 lb 12 oz and sighted up to 1,400 yards, the Martini-Henry was a popular and highly regarded weapon. Simple and easily operated, it was accurate at long range and contained a safety device so that it could be carried without any danger of accidental firing. But it was only a single-shot weapon, possessed a vicious recoil, and was prone to jamming and barrel-fouling. After complaints about jamming during the Egyptian campaign of 1885, a committee recommended that the calibre should be further reduced to increase the range and flatten the trajectory. It also seemed timely to incorporate a magazine system for rapid firing, as the Turks had demonstrated the potential of the Winchester magazine rifle in their war with Russia in 1877–78. Although this rifle proved apt to jam and could not be loaded singly, James Paris Lee had patented a more reliable bolt mechanism and magazine. Adding a magazine, though, required further changes. As soldiers were bound to use more ammunition, they had to carry additional bullets in their two pouches (ninety instead of seventy per person). They could only carry the extra number if the calibre (and therefore the weight) of each bullet was reduced, and the latter was only possible, without diminishing the man-stopping properties of the bullet, if the muzzle velocity could be increased. By using a compressed charge of black powder, and a hardened bullet which could withstand being propelled at a faster rate down the barrel (achieved by encasing the lead bullet in a covering of hardened metal), the calibre of the British bullet was reduced to 0·303 inches. Introduced in 1888, the new bullet was designed for a weapon which combined the Lee bolt mechanism with the shallower grooves of the rifling perfected by William Ellis Metford. Known as the Lee-Metford rifle, it had a magazine which originally held eight cartridges (later increased to ten) and could be closed by a cut-off, converting it to a single-shot weapon and so conserving ammunition, while retaining the magazine rounds for an emergency.[1]

In 1892 a smokeless propellent, cordite, was added. Based upon the discoveries of the Swiss engineer, Alfred Nobel, cordite (a compound of nitroglycerine and nitro-cellulose made in the form of sticks or cords) had several advantages over gunpowder. As a chemical compound, it had an exact relationship between its constituent parts and proved uniform in action. It was easier to store, less susceptible to damp, and safe to handle. It was virtually smokeless, as it emitted gaseous products when used, and, weight for weight, proved more powerful than gunpowder, increasing the muzzle velocity from 1,800 to 2,000 feet per second. Cordite, however, had a higher flame temperature than gunpowder and so tended to corrode the shallow grooves of the Metford barrel. A new barrel was duly constructed at Enfield in 1895 with five deeper grooves and was combined with the Lee bolt mechanism. The Lee-Enfield rifle became standard issue for the infantry, but single-shot weapons were retained for other arms to conserve ammunition (a large number of Martini rifles and carbines were converted to Martini-Metfords and

Martini-Enfields). A Lee-Metford magazine carbine was produced for the cavalry in 1894, and a Lee-Enfield magazine carbine in 1896. All artillery carbines remained single-shot weapons, and the colonial troops at the start of the Boer War were armed with the Martini-Enfield.[2] Smokeless powder realised the full potential of the magazine rifle. It permitted a rifleman to sustain rapid, aimed fire without smoke, obscuring his field of vision. This had an immense potential on the field of battle, as it increased the tactical power of the rifleman on the defensive. Henceforth he could retain the advantages of cover and shoot without fear of betraying his own position. Conversely, offensive forces lost the covering screen of smoke and had to cross or outflank much longer fields of fire from flat-trajectory bullets. As these changes had revolutionary implications for each of the three arms, their possible effects upon tactics were extensively debated in the 1890s.

The revolution in small arms represented only part of the changes in firepower generally. By 1868 the Royal Artillery had already adopted rifled breech-loading (RBL) guns in wrought iron jackets, but like the Royal Navy had become dissatisfied with the Armstrong breech mechanism. The removable breech-piece proved unable to withstand the shock of quick-burning powders, especially from the charges which propelled shot with sufficient velocity to penetrate the armour of the new French ironclads. As Joseph Whitworth, another British manufacturer, had challenged Lord Armstrong's monopoly of producing guns for the armed services in 1863, the Royal Arsenal, Woolwich, conducted numerous trials between breech and muzzle-loaders throughout the 1860s. Various committees reported that the breech-loader failed to show any significant advantages in range, accuracy or rapidity of fire over the simpler and less costly muzzle-loader. They favoured conversion to rifled muzzle-loaders (RML) which began with the seven-pounder mountain gun, used in Abyssinia in 1868, followed by the adoption of the nine-pounder and sixteen-pounder RML guns in 1871 for the horse and field artillery respectively. The manufacture of new guns of position also began in 1871 with the forty-pounder RML guns, followed by the twenty-five-pounder RML gun in 1874. Coastal batteries retained a mixture of ordnance, including some of the discarded RBL guns of position, converted smooth-bore muzzle-loaders (sixty-four and eighty-pounders), the 10 inch RML gun from 1870 onwards, and some 38 ton RML guns of 12·5 inch calibre. A new siege gun gained approval in 1872, namely the 8 inch RML howitzer, followed by the lighter 6·3 and 6·6 inch howitzers later in the decade. Finally, a new mountain gun appeared in 1879, the jointed 2·5 inch RML gun of 400 lb, known as the 'screw gun', which was much more powerful than the seven-pounder of 200 lb.[3]

In 1878 the British authorities, still unconvinced about the virtues of breech-loading, approved experiments with a thirteen-pounder RML design which proved a more accurate and a longer-range gun than either the nine-pounder or the sixteen-pounder. In 1880 the army began to issue the thirteen-pounder to both horse and field artillery and employed it in Egypt in 1882. The thirteen-pounder, however, possessed a violent recoil and never matched the potential attributes of the improved breech-loaders which the French and Germans had adopted. As the breech-loader had both ends open, it was easier to manufacture, rifle and load. Operationally, it left the gun crew less exposed, reduced the degree of windage, and lessened the likelihood of accidents from smouldering remnants of cartridge. Incorporating a breech mechanism now posed fewer difficulties, as the strain on the gun had been reduced by the introduction of slower-burning propellants and by the 'chambering' of the barrel (giving the bore a slightly larger diameter at the breech than along the remainder of its length to allow the pressure to rise more gradually). Having examined the interrupted screw mechanism, developed by the French designer de Bange, the British found that 6 inch RBL guns possessed more accuracy and a longer range than the 38 ton gun and had a higher muzzle velocity than either the 81 ton or the 100 ton gun. Somewhat belatedly, in 1885, the Royal Artillery began a reversion to breech-loaders, establishing the twelve-pounder RBL, sighted to 5,000 yards, as their standard piece for the horse and field artillery.[4]

Nevertheless, artillery armament remained a source of continuing controversy. In the first place, as the old muzzle-loaders remained in service, the regulars and Volunteers possesssed a heterogeneous collection of weapons. The horse and field artillery retained four different calibres of guns, some loading from the breech, some from the muzzle, which complicated the supply of ammunition in the field. There were complaints, too, from Lord Roberts, an experienced gunner and Commander-in-Chief in India, that the the twelve-pounder, once equipped with the Mark II carriage (to absorb its violent recoil), was too heavy for horse artillery, and that its shell was too light for field batteries. In 1892, after cordite had been adopted as a propellant, a Committee under the chairmanship of Sir Robert Biddulph examined the suitability of the twelve-pounder. It recommended that the existing guns should be converted into fifteen-pounders for the field artillery, and that a lighter twelve-pounder, weighing 6 cwt instead of 7 cwt, should be introduced for the horse artillery. Sighted to 5,500 yards, these weapons became the standard field guns of the Boer War, firing shrapnel shell primarily but also some case shot. As neither the trajectory of these guns nor the weight of the shell was particularly effective in the bombardment of buildings and trenches, high-angled howitzers were reintroduced in 1896. Separate howitzer batteries were formed, each armed with six 5 inch breech-loading howitzers, firing a 50 lb projectile with a new high explosive, lyddite. While the 5 inch was employed successfully in the bombardment of Omdurman, a range of howitzers was designed exclusively for use in India – the 5·4 inch, the 6 inch and a portable 4 inch, jointed RML howitzer.[5]

The government produced much of this equipment itself, maintaining major factories to make guns (the Royal Gun Factory), carriages (the Royal Carriage Department) and ammunition (the Royal Laboratory) – all in the Woolwich Arsenal. It also produced explosives at Waltham Abbey and small arms at Enfield and Sparkbrook, Birmingham, but still depended upon the additional capacity of the private sector, especially the major munition contractors (Armstrong, Vickers and Whitworth who produced artillery, the Birmingham Small Arms Co. and the London Small Arms Co., which manufactured service rifles, and Webley, who made the service revolvers). These firms found themselves in the position of selling government-approved designs to a government buyer in competition with government factories. In spite of a notional commitment to free competition, the government acted as a monopoly buyer with a strategic and not an economic imperative. As R.C. Trebilcock has argued, governments developed a 'special relationship' with the leading armament manufacturers, in the hope of creating and sustaining extra capacity among the private firms which could be quickly used in war. It forged close relations with particular firms (Vickers and Armstrong had representatives on the Ordnance Council) and engaged in a selective tendering policy, sometimes described as 'creating a trade by orders'. Although this policy enabled the government to exert control, including price control, over the markets, it inhibited private innovation or, as alleged in the 'cordite scandal' of 1893, resulted in private information being copied without recognition. Admittedly, the 'special relationship' failed to emulate the French in producing a quick-firing gun before the outbreak of the Boer War, but it was, as Trebilcock claimed, a quite sophisticated process:

The government factory led prices and pioneered techniques, the Contracts branch controlled the markets by fixing tenders and prices, brought along new firms, and calculated the amount of expansion necessary to meet a given military situation.[6]

The machine gun, employed in the American Civil War (1861–65) and the Franco–Prussian War, was the other major innovation in firepower. Despite its poor performance in the battles of 1870–71, it had a potential for a sustained, rapid rate of fire which attracted widespread interest. Having tested the Gatling machine gun in 1869, the army adopted it as an auxiliary weapon two years later, but the artillery mounted it on fixed artillery carriages, so precluding any traversing of the gun and thereby reducing its effectiveness. Even so, the Gatling was employed in several colonial campaigns, enhancing the volume of fire at the battles of Gingindhlovo (2 April 1879) and Ulundi (4 July 1879). The army and navy experimented with various machine guns, including the Gardner and the Nordenfelt in the Egyptian and Sudanese campaigns of 1882 and 1884–85. Senior officers seemed generally impressed with them, despite the jamming of the Gardners at critical moments in the battles of Tamai (13 March 1884) and Abu Klea (17 January 1885). Lord Chelmsford extolled the contribution of the machine guns in the Zulu War, arguing that they should 'not be attached to artillery, but should be considered as essentially an infantry weapon . . . . So utilized, they might, I feel sure, be used most effectively not only in defence, but in covering the last stage of an infantry attack . . .'. Wolseley was equally enthusiastic: 'the fire of this small arm, firing from a fixed carriage at ascertained ranges of 2000 up to 3000 yards and beyond, will be most effective'.[7]

As the Gatling, Gardner and Nordenfelt were all crank-operated weapons, their rate of fire depended upon someone continuously turning their handles. It was not until the mid-1880s that a genuinely automatic firing system became available when Hiram Maxim produced a weapon which used the force of the recoil to operate the rejection, loading and firing mechanism, with the initial trigger pull making the firing automatic until the trigger was released. As the Maxim gun required only one barrel and not several, it was much lighter than other machine guns. Weighing only 40 lb, it was a genuinely mobile weapon which could be used in support of the cavalry. It was capable of firing ten rounds per second, over a range of 2,500 yards. Wrested from the control of the artillery, machine guns were deployed in two gun sections with every brigade of infantry, although some battalions had additional guns. They were still perceived as primarily auxiliary weapons more effective in defensive than in offensive operations for the infantry, and as capable of proffering support for the cavalry, either relieving them of the necessity to dismount or of augmenting their firepower in pursuit or of covering a retreat.[8]

The tactical implications of these weapons aroused considerable interest within the late Victorian army. They were examined by the authors of campaign studies, particularly of the Austro–Prussian and Franco–Prussian Wars, and by those who wrote tactical textbooks. They were also debated in the lectures of the Royal United Service Institution (RUSI) and the Aldershot Military Society, and by contributors to the *Journal of the RUSI* and the *United Service Magazine* (particularly after its purchase by John Frederick Maurice in 1890). Admittedly these commentators were probably exceptional; those who belaboured the short service system, localisation, and the various reforms of officer education and training in the *Army and Navy Magazine* and in the *United Service Magazine* in the 1870s and 1880s probably represented a broader swathe of opinion. Nevertheless, there was a significant number of officers who deliberated upon the lessons of recent Continental wars or their own colonial experience, and who had the interest and encouragement of senior officers, such as Wolseley, Henry Brackenbury, Redvers Buller and Evelyn Wood.[9]

Several officers were particularly impressed with the Prussian performance in 1866 and 1870–71. Captain Charles Brackenbury had seen the conflicts at first hand and chose thereafter to extol the innovations and achievements of the Prussian military. He stressed the virtues of the swarm formation (an open order and vastly extended firing line, fed by supports, and finally strengthened by reserves at the critical time and thrown *en masse* towards the decisive point) and the primacy of the offensive. 'It is a very ugly thing,' he wrote, 'to attack against breech-loaders, but it has to be done . . . it is moral force which will most prevail.'[10] Commentators quoted liberally from the English translations of Continental works, elevating the swarm formation into a basic principle of modern tactics. Colonel Lonsdale Hale and Captain F.N. Maude advocated either the detailed study of the battles of 1870–71 or the emulation of the Prussian standards of organisation, training and commitment to the offensive. Several authors of tactical textbooks, C.B. Mayne, Francis Clery and Colonel W.H. James, consistently stressed that lessons should be learned from studying Continental tactics. Mayne feared that the British army, like the French, could become too preoccupied with its own colonial experience, and that its thinking could suffer as a consequence. Finally, Sir Edward Hamley extensively revised his Staff College text, *The Operations of War*, to take account of the Austro–Prussian and Franco–Prussian conflicts. Even if he did not regard the Prussian tactics in 1870 as the best possible in the circumstances, he paid a conspicuous tribute to 'the discipline and training and spirit' of their units.[11]

These writers, though, had a fairly limited influence upon the thinking of the late Victorian army. Hamley reached the apogee of his career during his period as Commandant of the Staff College (1870–77), but, after gaining his first field command in Egypt in 1882, lost the confidence of Wolseley and much of his former influence within the army. In 1894, one year after his death, *The Operations of War* was discontinued as the sole text for the Staff College entrance examination. Many of the other Continentalists – Charles Brackenbury, Mayne, Lonsdale Hale and Maude – became quite rigid in their views, fixated in Hale's case upon the events of 1870–71, and extreme in the commitment of the others to the offensive. They seemed to have little influence within the War Office and had less and less to contribute to the thinking about the logistical and tactical requirements of an imperial army. Indeed, some deprecated the value of British military experience: as Hale observed,

An officer who has seen service must sweep from his mind all recollections of that service, for between Afghan, Egyptian, or Zulu warfare and that of Europe, there is no similarity whatever. To the latter the former is merely the play of children.[12]

Several officers had questioned whether the Prussian performance should be emulated without reservation. Major-General Patrick

MacDougall was one of the few British officers who had taken a keen interest in the American Civil War. He had predicted that improved firearms and rifled artillery would enhance the scope of the defensive, compelling attacking infantry to advance in extended order and diminishing the scope for shock tactics by the cavalry. In his opinion the Franco–Prussian War had largely confirmed these predictions. In *Modern Infantry Tactics* (1873), and in subsequent writing, MacDougall accepted that the attacker still had moral advantages, but that the defender had gained significantly from the acquisition of the breech-loader. He contended that the swarm formation had become too disorderly with the delegation of critical decisions to company commanders, and saw little reason to alter the traditional British line formation, screened by skirmishers.[13]

Lieutenant (later Major-General Sir) John Frederick Maurice took a somewhat similar view of the Prussian achievements. As a Staff College officer, he won the essay prize offered by the second Duke of Wellington in 1872 with an analysis of 'The System of Field Manoeuvres Best Adapted for Enabling our Troops to Meet a Continental Army'. Unlike many British officers, Maurice was neither surprised by the French defeat nor terribly impressed with the improvised Prussian tactics. He accepted that assaulting troops, faced with breech-loaders, had to adopt more flexible formations and make better use of the ground. Officers and noncommissioned officers would have to be better trained, preferably in larger companies, and ought to undertake regular combined manoeuvres to maximise co-operation between units. He favoured the adoption of an offensive strategy and defensive tactics to overcome the firepower of the modern breech-loader (that is, by entrenchments at the front and then by attacking the extended forces of an adversary at their weakest point and, if necessary, by using shelter trenches in the attack). British infantry tactics, he reckoned, needed only minor modifications; skirmishing should no longer merely protect the following columns but should require those columns to feed successive supports and reserves into the skirmishing line. Maurice remained more conventional in his thinking on cavalry tactics; he doubted that a hybrid was possible, whereby troops could be trained to fight equally well on horse or dismounted. Cavalry, he claimed, even confronted by modern firearms, could make local attacks and exploit victory by a vigorous pursuit.[14]

If these individual commentaries barely dented the Continentalist predominance in the early 1870s, they at least indicated some ideas, reflecting a more distinctively British tradition, which would appear in the subsequent revisionism. Howard Bailes argues that this revisionism developed as a cumulative process over the next twenty years, incorporating elements of chauvinism and reasoned analysis. A distinctively British response seemed increasingly necessary after the studies of of the Russo–Turkish War of 1877–78, the diverse experience gained in colonial campaigning, the sceptical reports of the tactics displayed in foreign manoeuvres, and the challenges of the so-called 'second tactical revolution' of the 1890s, wrought by smokeless powder, magazine rifles and quick-firing artillery.[15]

The Russo–Turkish War was the first test of a mass conscript army, equipped with breech-loaders, since 1871. The three costly and abortive Russian assaults on the Turkish entrenchments at Plevna, followed by the lengthy siege, contrasted sharply with the Prussian performance in France. As the classical account of the war, written by the American military attaché at St Petersburg, Lieutenant Francis Vinton Greene, concentrated upon the Russian ineptitude (tactical blunders, divisions within the high command and the chronic lack of intelligence and reconnaissance), the conflict hardly seemed like a model for the future. Several British commentators produced similar interpretations, including Captain George S. Clarke, who published an account under the auspices of the Royal Engineers' Institute. He asserted that much could be learned from the Russian mistakes, particularly the reliance upon frontal assaults, the lack of sustained artillery support for the infantry, and the failure to equip the soldiers with sufficient supplies of entrenching tools. Although these were pertinent observations, the preoccupation with Russian failings enabled commentators like C.B. Mayne to argue that they merely confirmed 'the experiences and deductions of the Franco–Prussian War'. Such complacency obscured the more fundamental lessons which could have been drawn from the war of 1877–78, namely the failure of massive artillery bombardments to breach well constructed entrenchments, the lack of opportunity for shock tactics by the cavalry, and the defensive power of the breech-loading rifle.[16]

Britain's colonial experience complicated the debate still further. It emphasised the problems of logistical support, tactical flexibility, and the maintenance of a strategic offensive, but the sheer diversity of the campaigns, coupled with the range of tactics employed (see

Chapter 10), raised questions about the value of the lessons learned and their applicability to a European context. Some officers perceived lessons of lasting value. Henry Brackenbury, commenting upon Wolseley's directions for bush fighting in the Ashanti War, was adamant that they breathed 'spirit' into the teaching from the Franco–Prussian War:

It recognises, amongst other points, the vital importance of giving independence of action to small units, and proposes to carry out on this system exactly what had been done by our fathers, in the days when the Light Division in the Peninsula could beat all other troops in the world in skirmishing . . . .[17]

Even Colonel Charles Callwell, who claimed in his authoritative work, *Small Wars* (1896), that this form of war constituted an 'art by itself', insisted that it did not diverge 'so widely' from regular warfare that comparisons with the latter could not be made.[18] Several commentators had anticipated Callwell in their writings upon particular campaigns; others saw less and less need to indulge in 'slavish imitations from the Prussian',[19] and some rather belatedly came to the conclusion that the American Civil War had bequeathed tactical lessons of more significance than recent Continental experience. Wolseley, Maurice and, above all, G.F.R. Henderson, the doyen of the British school of military training, asserted that the American conflict had been the first of the great modern wars, and that important lessons could be learnt from it.

In *The Campaign of Fredericksburg* (1886), which largely created a new interest in the American Civil War, Henderson asserted that the modern battle had enhanced the importance of leadership and discipline. Junior officers, he argued, whether commanding soldiers in entrenched defensive positions and directing fire by volleys, or leading forces in marches around the enemy flanks, had to assume greater responsibilities. In this context, he extolled the light infantry training advocated by Sir John Moore during the Peninsular War, based upon the physical training of the soldier, practice over difficult ground, careful instruction in skirmishing, and the inculcation of the correct habits of command into regimental officers. Like MacDougall, he deprecated the Prussian tactics of allowing company commanders latitude to manoeuvre and to seek cover at the expense of abandoning the direct line of attack. He maintained that the company commander had to persevere, 'regardless of losses', and that frontal attacks in close order at the decisive moment would prove more decisive than the extended order which had proved so popular after 1870. In effect, he asserted that the lessons of the American Civil War had merely reinforced the traditional British notion of skirmishing. By the early 1890s, he still maintained that the role of skirmishers was to cover the advance of successive lines of infantry, which, 'moving shoulder to shoulder, was to pass through the firing line and carry the position with the bayonet'. He had modified this view by the eve of the Boer War, arguing that the bayonet had become subordinate to the bullet, and that the infantry had to make more use of cover and employ light infantry tactics. Nevertheless, he retained his faith in frontal attacks and in a distinctive British response to the challenges posed by smokeless powder and magazine rifles. Britain, he affirmed, had 'no need to ask another nation to teach us to fight'.[20]

Underpinning this resurgence of self-confidence in the 1890s was a widespread belief that the army had profited immensely from its protracted experience in colonial warfare. By 1890, argued Wolseley, the British army had practised the arts of war far more frequently than any other nation, particularly the Germans, who had not fired 'a shot in anger' for twenty years.[21] The Germans had partially offset this lack of campaign experience by undertaking regular and large-scale military manoeuvres. British observers generally applauded this mode of training; they praised the value of practising the deployment of large bodies of troops, the standards of rapidity and precision attained by the attacking forces, and the minimal reliance upon commands by senior officers. Admittedly, some observers criticised the tactics demonstrated by the Germans, and even more by the French, who took the cult of the offensive to greater extremes. They argued that some offensive formations seemed unrealistic and risked colossal losses if they were adopted on battlefields swept by flat-trajectory bullets. Even Henderson, who extolled the offensive spirit which seemed all-pervasive at the French manoeuvres of 1891, criticised the neglect of cover during the advance. Although he lauded the French army for not relying exclusively upon shock tactics, he thought it odd that the opposing sides should stand 'in the open, blazing away at each other at 200 or 300 yards range, with the lines beautifully dressed, and the second line lying down a short distance in the rear'.[22]

Official infantry tactics mirrored the ebb and flow of tactical thought. Whereas the infantry manual of 1870 still advocated close order advances in line formation, screened by skirmishers, by 1877 a section on 'extended order' had replaced the regulations on skirmishing but without allowing company commanders the same latitude as in the Prussian army. In trying to combine British and Continental ideas, the first line became divided into a firing line, supports and reserves, but without the admixture of units implicit in the swarm formation. The army, argued Maurice, had in essence 'taken up a skirmishing form of fighting in place of masses and line'.[23] During his term as Adjutant-General, Wolseley sought to reorder the priorities of *Field Exercise and Evolutions of Infantry*. He contended that more time should be devoted to practical training, that drill movements should be reduced in number, and that annual inspections should focus upon fighting proficiency and not parade ground precision. He believed, too, that the army should learn from its practical experience and should not simply follow, even in a modified form, the Prussian model. Accordingly the first edition of *Infantry Drill* (1889), prepared while he was in office, preserved the traditional British line and recognised the battalion as the main tactical unit.[24]

Successive editions built on this approach. Although they did not prescribe formations, the manuals stated that troops should 'usually reach the field of battle in column of route or in battalion quarter columns' and should open 'for the attack only when the necessity arises'. Thereafter all movements in contact with the enemy should be covered by a screen of troops in extended order, supported normally by three lines – a firing line, generally moving in extended order, to engage the enemy and launch the assault, a second line of supporting soldiers to aid the assault, and a third line of reserves either to complete the success or cover a retreat. Close formations, though still useful in colonial warfare, were deemed impractical against troops equipped with modern arms. Excessive extensions were also deprecated, particularly in the final attack (where soldiers had to withstand any counter-attacks, deliver sufficient firepower to prepare the assault, and absorb the losses from enemy fire). Although smokeless powder had enhanced the scope for independent firing, collective fire by volleys remained the general method of developing an attack. As *Musketry Regulations* argued, volleys controlled the direction and concentration of fire, regulated the expenditure of ammunition, and served as 'an aid to discipline'. In complementing the drill book, it asserted that volley firing should be sustained in the attack for 'as long as possible'.[25]

The drill book recognised some of the constraints imposed by breech-loading magazine rifles. It advocated practice in night operations, in the construction of shelter trenches, and in the use of cover in 'the direct line of advance'. It asserted that training should aim to imbue all ranks with a knowledge of the principles of how movements should proceed under fire and should encourage individual self-reliance:

The conditions of modern warfare render it imperative that all ranks shall be taught to think, and, subject to their general instructions and to accepted principles, to act for themselves.

Finally, the drill book emphasised that the moral advantage still lay with the 'bold attack', and described a final assault in which 'the men will cheer, drums be beaten, bugles sounded, and pipes played'.[26]

The Franco–Prussian War had a less immediate impact upon artillery tactics. Several commentators, notably Henry and Charles Brackenbury and Lieutenant-Colonel C.H. Owen, the Professor of Artillery at Woolwich, praised the performance of the Prussian gunners. The latter, after their disappointing display at Sadowa (1866), when they held back too long on the line of march and entered the battle too late, had pushed forward boldly in 1870. Accompanying the infantry into the attack, they had operated in masses and prepared positions for assault by suppressing the French artillery and bombarding their infantry, so diminishing the firepower of the Chassepot. By their audacity and skill the Prussian gunners had demonstrated that the arm had a potential for independent action in battle. The Duke of Cambridge tacitly acknowledged this in his directive of 1871, stating that the artillery no longer had to conform to the movements of the infantry but could select its own positions from which to cover an attack or retreat. By this new freedom of manoeuvre, field artillery commanders could avoid deployments within the traditional case shot range of 350 to 400 paces of the enemy, but still contended that their batteries could smartly advance in open order, take up fire positions with a clear line of sight to the enemy, and proffer direct support from relatively short range. Major A.W. White recognised that modern rifles could fire up to ranges of 1,500 yards, but doubted, on account of ranging difficulties, whether 'infantry fire at distances over 600 yards will ever prove worth the great expenditure of ammunition and waste of energy involved'.[27]

The arm did not even prepare a manual on tactics until 1892 (the first publication of the regiment, the *Manual of Field Artillery Exercises*, issued in 1875, was largely an attempt to standardise parade ground movements). Nor did it have much opportunity to practise its tactics in massed formations at a time when batteries were scattered around a myriad of small stations at home and abroad, rarely saw active service in large numbers other than in Egypt in 1882 (see Chapter 10), and lacked a sizeable training facility until the acquisition of Okehampton in 1877. During this period the gunners also had to cope with many changes of equipment, not merely new patterns of guns and the switch from breech to muzzle-loading and from muzzle-loading to breech, but also the adoption of Scott's telescopic sights, mechanical range-finders, new gun carriages in 1890, and clinometers (devices for measuring slopes and elevations).

Interest in tactical doctrine revived with the translation of the *Letters on Artillery* by Prince Kraft zu Hohenlohe-Ingelfingen in 1887. Written in a simple, forthright and attractive style, Hohenlohe's work had an immediate and lasting appeal. He dismissed the 'scientific' approach to gunnery and the practice of indirect firing from hidden positions behind cover. Guns, he argued, should move in 'as close as possible to the enemy', with the aim of winning the decisive artillery duel at ranges between 2,700 and 2,200 yards, and then of pushing forward, disdaining any search for cover, to support the infantry fire from positions up to 1,000 yards from the enemy's ranks. He emphasised that the guns had 'staying power', and that gunners, if they learned to hit by constant drill, could make a vital contribution by precise and accurate gunnery. 'A line of artillery,' he argued, by 'resolutely' advancing at a 'rapid pace straight at the enemy' could seek a 'decisive engagement' within 1,000 to 2,000 paces.[28] Although written with reference to the Franco–Prussian War, his precepts seemed to vindicate the Royal Artillery's preference for a bold, highly mobile and direct contribution to the battle. By emphasising precise and accurate gunnery, he set new standards for gunnery which could be measured by competitive tests at Okehampton, and introduced the concept of fire discipline which enhanced the control of battery firing. Hohenlohe's writings were widely regarded as authoritative and were reflected in the priorities and ranges adumbrated in the the first edition of the

Field Artillery Drill. Major (later Major-General Sir) Edward S.
May, who advised Wood on artillery matters at Aldershot, lauded
Hohenlohe's work, as it was based on a 'unique experience of
modern war'.[29]

Ironically the Royal Artillery had embraced the views of
Hohenlohe at a time when the German artillery were substantially
modifying them. Concerned about the defensive advantages of
breech-loaders, firing from field entrenchments, especially after the
failure of the Russian guns to breach the defences at Plevna, the
Germans had sought to support their infantry with high-angled
shellfire from heavy field howitzers. Once the Krupp works at Essen
had produced the mobile 150 mm howitzer in 1886, the Germans
acquired an ideal weapon for indirect firing. Having experimented
with siege artillery, the Germans found that field artillery could also
be employed effectively in indirect firing, especially with smokeless
powder and their pivot-based *richt fläche* line-of-fire sight. As
reports from the German manoeuvres described how their artillery
unlimbered in the rear, ran up their guns by hand (unless horses
could move under cover) and employed gun pits, British gunners
began to debate the issue of indirect fire. In 1896 a young infantry
officer, Captain Thomas D. Pilcher, threw down the challenge and
gained support from the maverick gunner Major (later Lieutenant-
General Sir) John L. Keir. They argued that indirect firing, with
modern clinometers, could exploit the potential of smokeless powder, avoid exposing gunners unnecessarily to rifle fire, and sustain an effective concentration of fire. Captain (later Major-General
Sir) John Headlam deplored this heresy; he stressed that there were
important differences between the German guns and sights and their
British equivalents, but, more important, feared that 'if you train
Field Artillery to consider firing from behind cover as "practically
the rule" . . . you will destroy the whole spirit of the arm'.[30]

Headlam found overwhelming support for his sentiments; senior
gunners, including Brigadier-General Charles H. Spragge, Commanding Royal Artillery, Bombay Army, Colonel (later Major-
General Sir) George H. Marshall and May vehemently contested the
claims of Keir, even although the latter was only suggesting indirect
fire as an auxiliary and not as a replacement for direct fire. The
debate raged for over two years in the regimental journal before Keir
abandoned the challenge. He admitted that he had failed to persuade
three different groups of officers – those who relied on military

history, implicitly the Franco–Prussian War, to teach the tactical lessons of the future; those who regarded Continental methods as unnecessary because they doubted that they would ever have to fight on the Continent; and the largest group, more or less trained in the 'Asiatic school of tactics', who saw no need to adopt German artillery tactics. He prophetically concluded that 'so long as neither side can claim practical experience, the verdict of time alone can decide'.[31] Throughout the debate the *Field Artillery Drill*, as updated in 1896, had offered little guidance. On the critical issue of choosing ground, it listed the priorities as obtaining a clear view of the target, a good platform for the guns, ensuring no obstacle to movement, maximising the difficulties of the enemy approaching or ranging on the guns, and 'lastly – cover'. If this was somewhat ambiguous, the manual never explicitly sanctioned the use of indirect fire and so effectively thwarted this option. It set set distant to medium artillery ranges at 3,500 to 2,500 yards, discounted infantry fire at ranges over 1,000 yards, and stressed that the guns had to be concentrated in support of the infantry. Above all, it urged gunners to place the defeat of the enemy above any thought of personal protection; indeed, Marshall, when commanding the Royal Artillery at Aldershot, in 1899, argued 'that the best protection from the enemy's fire is to overwhelm him with your own'. Similarly, he doubted whether the introduction of new weaponry, particularly the quick-firing guns which the French had displayed at their manoeuvres in 1897, would alter any of the 'main principles' of artillery tactics. 'More than ever,' he contended, 'we shall have to pay attention to fire discipline and accuracy of shooting.'[32]

The cavalry also clung to certain fundamentals in tactics but did so despite a much more contentious debate about their role on the field of battle. By confirming the massive increase in the effectiveness of firepower, the American Civil War and the Continental wars of the 1860s and 1870s had raised questions about the efficacy of shock tactics by massed cavalry formations, relying upon the *arme blanche*. In view of the expansion in the size of armies and the extension of battle fronts, a mobile arm was still essential to undertake the tasks of scouting and reconnaissance, the protection of marching columns, and the mounting of raids deep into an enemy's rear to disrupt his communications and interrupt his line of supplies. Moreover, this arm had to be able to engage enemy forces, especially if the latter appeared to be shaken or wavering, or if a surprise attack was possible, and to undertake pursuits whenever the opportunity arose. Although commentators agreed that these tasks remained vital, they disagreed about how best they could be performed. There had been a foretaste of the controversy in the 1860s. Writing during or in the wake of the American Civil War, MacDougall, Major Henry Havelock and Lieutenant-Colonel George Denison of the Canadian Militia had questioned both the continuing utility and the primacy of shock tactics. Denison, unlike MacDougall, had strongly favoured increased reliance upon mounted infantry, and, after the Franco–Prussian War in which the Prussians had regularly added one or two battalions of *Jägers* (elite infantry units) to each cavalry division, Hamley advocated the formation of a separate corps of mounted infantry. He believed that this force could 'at small cost, produce great results' in guarding advanced posts, manoeuvring on the flanks of an enemy, and executing raids behind the enemy lines. Even the Duke of Cambridge recognised the value of the mounted infantry units in South Africa and Egypt, and, in late 1882, recommended that a full company of mounted infantry should be trained by every battalion.[33]

As this advocacy coincided with debates about the organisation of the cavalry (see Chapter 3), the adequacy of its sword, and the possibility of developing a hybrid form of cavalry, it aroused some anxiety within the arm. After the complaints about the unwieldiness of the 1864 pattern of sword used by the ranks (other than in the Household Cavalry), two lighter patterns were introduced in 1882 but they proved too brittle and tended to bend or break in combat. Another pattern was introduced in 1885, but, as it did not prove any better, a new sword, weighing 2 lb 9 oz (and heavier than the 1864 pattern), was introduced in 1890. In fact, the search for a satisfactory sword had proved doubly frustrating, as the final pattern was optimally designed for neither cutting nor thrusting, although purportedly intended for both.[34] Some junior officers, too, had raised the heresy of abandoning the primacy of charges with the sword and lance. In various lectures and writings, Captain Chenevix Trench, Lieutenant Hamilton and Major Graves advocated a hybrid form of cavalry, equally proficient in mounted and dismounted duties, more thoroughly trained in the use of the carbine, practised in squadrons for scouting and reconnaissance duties, and capable of combining effectively with horse artillery. Many of these views encountered fierce criticisms from senior officers, who queried whether the need for change – infantry firepower – was as compelling as these commentators suggested, or who feared lest their ideas were tantamount to converting the cavalry into mounted infantry (which their advocates firmly denied), or who dreaded any dilution of the emphasis upon shock tactics.[35]

The intensity of the debate reflected confusion partly over terminology, partly over the selective use of historical precedents, and partly over disagreements about the lessons which should be gleaned from Continental practice. Although the terms 'cavalry', 'mounted infantry' and 'mounted rifles' were often used interchangeably, 'mounted infantry' had a precise meaning in the army, namely members of infantry battalions who were temporarily given horses. As Stephen Badsey argues, 'The threat of conversion to Mounted Infantry was . . . a nightmare for even reforming Cavalrymen, who interpreted it to mean the destruction of their regiments by absorption into the Infantry'.[36] As a consequence, the debates often became extremely heated, with protagonists buttressing their claims and counter-claims with examples culled from recent conflicts. If mounted riflemen were often employed, particularly in the western theatre during the American Civil War, there were also numerous examples of charges with sabres by Union and Confederate cavalry. Similarly, if the Prussian cavalry undertook a wide array of tasks in the Franco–Prussian War, including arming themselves with captured Chassepot rifles to combat the *franc-tireurs*, Von Bredow's 'death ride' at Mars-la-Tour (1870) earned lasting renown as a successful cavalry charge. Finally, cavalry reformers and traditionalists quoted liberally from Continental writings in support of their contending theories. By the late 1880s and 1890s traditionalists gained more from this source as the Germans became increasingly committed to shock tactics, even if not as emphatically as the French.[37]

The cavalry, however, never had much to fear from the mounted infantry, as the War Office eschewed any notion of a permanent corps and settled for a relatively cheap expedient. Once mounted infantry training centres were established at Aldershot, the Curragh and Shorncliffe, they were able to instruct 204 officers and 3,670 NCOs and men between February 1888 and December 1892, including many officers from the Militia, Volunteers and colonial forces. After a mere ten weeks' instruction in riding, stable duties, mounted infantry drill and field firing, the soldiers simply returned to their units. On this basis the mounted infantry threatened neither to replace the cavalry nor to challenge their tactical concepts. Indeed, many of those like Wolseley, Henderson and Evelyn Wood who promoted the concept of mounted infantry, did so because they did not believe that cavalry could ever evolve into a perfect hybrid. Although Wood insisted upon better standards of musketry by cavalrymen during his command at Aldershot, reducing the proportion of third-class shots from nearly one half to about a quarter (and on a par with the infantry), he maintained that cavalry 'should never be dismounted to fight' if they could be employed on horseback. Mounted infantry, he argued, would be most useful as an auxiliary force, possibly escorting horse and field artillery.[38]

Far from suffering an eclipse, the cavalry experienced a 'revival' in the 1890s. This may have derived partially from the renewed interest in the American Civil War, and the cavalry's role in that conflict, but also from the impressive displays of Continental cavalrymen in manoeuvres and from the writings of various German authorities. The notion of independent cavalry operations, as expounded in the works of Prince Kraft and Major-General Carl von Schmidt, attracted several British devotees, including Major- (later Lieutenant-) General J.K. Fraser, the Inspector-General of the Cavalry (1890–95). He envisaged cavalries in the next European war operating far in advance, or on the flanks of attacks upon infantry, supported by horse artillery and machine guns. In this respect he accepted, as did General Baker Russell, French, Haig and the more professionally-minded cavalry officers, that the arm had to 'take care' of itself. It had to become more proficient in dismounted duties, take musketry more seriously, practise reconnaissance duties at squadron level, and consider methods of tactical co-operation with machine guns and horse artillery.[39] Some commanding officers tried to implement these ideas, either encouraging the acquisition of machine guns (Lieutenant-Colonel R.S. Liddell even bought one from his own funds for the 10th Hussars) or promoting musketry by inter-service competition or by establishing regimental shooting clubs (as Dundonald did in the 2nd Life Guards).[40]

However, this does not mean that senior cavalry officers had accepted the case for moving towards a hybrid, and were about to abandon the primacy of the massed *arme blanche* charge in favour of squadron-sized actions in a European war. Fraser repeatedly stated that the horse remained the 'first weapon of the cavalry soldier', and that massed cavalry charges, coming up from the horizon 'hull-down', could decisively change the face of battle. Whenever 'the infantry is exhausted', he asserted, 'the sudden appearance of great masses of cavalry upsets the whole arrangement'. He admitted that smokeless powder might reduce the element of surprise but argued, like Captain Maude, that the absence of smoke might actually compound the effects of a massed cavalry charge upon shaken infantry. Fraser's great concern was that the cavalry lacked the men, horses and space in which to practise massed cavalry operations on the Continental model. He agreed with French that 'the real object of manoeuvres is to accustom the cavalry to act together in masses'.[41] Indeed, this precept had not only become a conspicuous feature of German manoeuvres, it had also been embodied in German writings, where the mounted infantry and the notion of a 'hybrid' were dismissed as of 'little use' and the charge was described as 'the life-element of our arm'.[42]

Although cavalrymen debated the merits of various forms of armament, senior cavalry officers had never seriously considered abandoning the use of the sword or lance. They ensured that carbines should be carried on the saddle as a weapon of defence, and, in 1891, required that the lance should be carried by the front ranks of dragoon and dragoon guard regiments as well as by the lancer regiments. Even if the former had trained with the lance since 1817, this change was an imitation of German practice and a clear attempt to enhance the effects of the charge. Moreover, cavalry commanders had eagerly sought the rare opportunities for mounting charges in colonial campaigns, notably the pursuit of the Zulus by the 17th Lancers after Ulundi (4 July 1879), the moonlight charge by the Cavalry Brigade at Kassassin (28 August 1882) and the famous, if extremely costly, charge by the 21st Lancers at Omdurman (2 September 1898). As Winston Churchill, who was attached to the 21st Lancers, recalled,

Everyone expected that we were going to make a charge. That was the one idea that had been in all minds since we started from Cairo. Of course there would be a charge. In those days, before the Boer War, British cavalry had been taught little else.[43]

The *Cavalry Drill Book*, revised by French and Haig in 1896, reiterated the emphasis upon mounted duties. In the last edition issued before the Boer War in 1898, only five pages out of 450 were devoted to 'Dismounted Action', and these duties were contrasted with 'normal mounted action'. After the Boer War, too, French and Haig continued to argue that the *arme blanche* had to have primacy in cavalry tactics. They claimed that it was essential for preserving the morale of the arm, for its ability to counter any European foe armed with lance and sabre, and for its ability to undertake a strategic, offensive role (unlike the more limited, tactical role of the mounted infantry). As Haig asserted, this issue involved 'the very soul of cavalry action', and any removal of the cavalry's power to assume 'the active offensive by mounted action, by depriving it of the *arme blanche*', would withhold from it 'a very considerable advantage without any compensating gain'.[44]

All tactical precepts required practice and inculcation in a systematic manner during peacetime training. Infantry battalions received recruits after they had spent two and a half months in preliminary training at the regimental depot. Thereafter they passed these recruits through a twelve weeks' training of twenty hours per week in drill, gymnastics, marching, musketry and bayonet exercises. In the winter months battalions undertook marches at least once, and usually three times, every week. Between 1 March and 31 October each company was struck off all other duties. It was trained by its own officers in all branches of field service over twenty days and fired off its annual musketry allowance during the summer. At larger camps, like Aldershot, four companies spent four weeks in field duties, and, after battalion drill in May, brigade commanders could request artillery and cavalry assistance for manoeuvres during the summer. Every battalion was inspected on an annual basis, and had to send officers and men on specialised courses on musketry, signalling, field fortifications and mounted infantry duties, and privates for training as infantry pioneers, ambulance men and drivers with the Army Service Corps.

Cavalry training was even more extensive. Recruits spent some six to eight months in preliminary drill, first on foot (gymnastics, fencing and stable work), then in ninety to 120 hours of riding drill, saddling, packing and the use of arms on horseback, and finally in the same musketry course as the foot soldiers. Throughout the winter months cavalrymen were trained in their riding and dismounted duties, and undertook musketry practice in the summer. Each squadron was relieved of all other duties for two three-week courses (one in the winter and one in the summer) to perfect their squadron drill and field duties before the annual inspection in the spring. Regimental drill usually followed squadron drill in June, and, depending upon the proximity of other units and available space, brigade training could follow. Each regiment had to send officers and NCOs on the pioneer course at Chatham, the musketry course at Hythe and to the veterinary and signalling schools at Aldershot. They also sent sergeants and corporals to be trained as riding masters at the riding school at Canterbury.

The field artillery received recruits after eight weeks' drilling on foot, in gymnastics and in physical exercises. Battery officers then trained them in two courses, involving lectures on the theory of firing, drill at a single gun and later in battery, and in how to aim, handle ammunition, mount and dismount guns, load materials, construct gun pits and fire fourteen rounds with a carbine. Officers also instructed 'young soldiers' in stable work and passed prospective drivers through ninety to 120 lessons in riding and driving. During the winter months trained drivers completed recapitulation courses in riding and driving, while gunners trained in sections. In addition batteries and detachments marched out once a week for drill in the open. The annual training for batteries began on 1 March, when men were freed from all other duties for at least twelve consecutive days in 1893 (raised to fourteen days by 1899). Once all batteries had completed their drill, the brigade division undertook its practice in bringing up ammunition, in taking up positions and in collective drill before commencing target practice in May. Northern brigade divisions practised at Morecambe, Irish-based units at Glenbeigh, mountain batteries at Hay in Monmouthshire, some brigade divisions at Shoeburyness, and five brigade divisions utilised the principal range at Okehampton in Devonshire, each firing some 400 to 500 rounds over three weeks. Like the other arms, the field artillery was inspected annually and its batteries sent officers and NCOs to specialist courses on gunnery at Shoeburyness, on signalling at Aldershot and to advanced technical courses at the Artillery College.[45]

Other than in formal courses, training was fundamentally limited, particularly in the infantry, by the shortage of men in the home-based battalions. The losses occasioned by the turnover of men required by short service, and by the annual provision of drafts for the linked battalions overseas, were compounded by the need to employ at least a third of each battalion upon fatigues and other duties on a regular basis. These shortages impaired combined arms exercises, particularly the artillery days instituted by Wood at Aldershot, as the few available infantrymen had to simulate larger units by using flags and markers. The battalions, too, could only expend a limited amount of ammunition per annum (200 rounds per man, of which only forty-one rounds could be employed by the battalion commander as he saw fit, and another 400 rounds for field firing). As much of the musketry was by volley firing at known distances, or at a distance named by section commanders, it hardly prepared soldiers for the independent firing of the Second Boer War. Volley firing, argued Sir Ian Hamilton, demanded an 'exactitude' which 'monopolised every idea of the individual soldier in peace, and in war betrayed its exact position to the watchful enemy'.[46]

Peacetime training was further impaired by the lack of space and facilities. Officers had repeatedly criticised the inadequacies of peacetime training in Britain other than at Aldershot and the Curragh, and even the latter hardly impressed Lord Roberts on his return from India. As he informed Lord Lansdowne in January 1897,

It is only at Aldershot and the Curragh where any number of troops can be collected, and even at those places the ground is too restricted to admit of anything more than ordinary drill instruction. Manoeuvres on an extended scale are out of the question.[47]

Those who had commanded forces at Aldershot thought it quite useful, at least up to the level of brigade training, although soldiers lacked sufficient opportunities to make cover and dig entrenchments, as the ground was also used by the cavalry. Soldiers spent only about one week per year in digging entrenchments, and, if the facilities had shortcomings at Aldershot, they were much worse elsewhere. Colonel Forbes Macbean, who had to train the 1st Battalion, the Gordon Highlanders, for most of the year on the barrack square in Glasgow, reckoned that the four to six weeks spent each year at Barry in musketry and field training was quite inadequate. Sir Evelyn Wood agreed. Although he contended that military training had improved in the 1890s, he admitted that the army had 'no adequate training ground, and the only people who can do field firing practically are those quartered at Aldershot, and that is only 20 battalions . . .'.[48]

If the training of each branch of the service had suffered from the shortages of men and horses and from the lack of space, their collective training had suffered even more from the lack of regular large-scale manoeuvres. These had been held in 1871, 1872 and 1873 but were phased out as an economy and were not resumed until 1898. Wood, as commander of the eastern district and then of Aldershot, resumed smaller manoeuvres in the early 1890s; he also instituted night marches for the infantry, artillery days, and long-distance rides for the cavalry. But it was not until 1898, after the government had purchased 41,000 acres of Salisbury Plain, that the army was able to manoeuvre two army corps against each other. The army had undoubtedly suffered in its combined arms operations, staff work and logistics from the failure to emulate Continental practice and hold such manoeuvres on an annual basis. Its senior officers, too, had not been regularly tested as field commanders of large formations in time of peace.

Many of these shortcomings would be revealed at the manoeuvres of 1898. Although Wolseley praised the performance of the staff, regimental officers, NCOs and other ranks, he noted important failings in the handling of the front-line and support forces. He acknowledged the improvement in the handling of the cavalry, but thought that it had sometimes carried the principle of concentration 'to excess', and that it had 'subordinated' scouting and recon-naissance to a preference for 'fighting formations'. Like Wood, he criticised the repeated tendency of infantry battalions to be caught in quarter column formations where they became exposed to artillery fire. In attacks, too, Wolseley noted that the infantry was often so close that two successive lines could have been hit by the same shrapnel, that soldiers failed to make use of cover, and that the extensions were often premature. He asserted that the artillery changed its targets too frequently and fired at times from excessive range, possibly on account of undulations in the ground. He was particularly critical of the employment of machine guns in batteries and deplored the shortcomings of the supply and transport arrange-ments. He recognised that traction engines had served as an efficient supplement to animal transport but never considered them as a substitute: he simply bemoaned the shortage of horses, particularly for ammunition supply.[49]

If the economies of successive governments were doubtless res-ponsible for many of the imperfections of peacetime training, and for the failure to provide any systematic training for the Reserve, mili-

tary attitudes contributed, too. Brigade training never replaced the
primacy accorded to battery training in the artillery. As many
batteries were quartered in single battery stations, and as majors
jealously guarded their prerogatives, lieutenant-colonels, who had
been brought up in the same tradition, largely contented themselves
with regimental routine. They rarely accompanied their own
batteries to practice, and at camp were often detailed to command a
'detachment' of batteries collected indiscriminately from other
stations. Although Wood's artillery days at Aldershot promoted the
brigade as a tactical unit of action, the brigades were not established
as permanent units with their own staff. The brigade work of the
field artillery remained a palpable weakness at practice and
manoeuvre. Similarly many infantry officers doubted whether they
could follow their drill book's exhortations to develop the intelligence of the rank and file. While some felt constrained by the lack of
training facilities outside Aldershot, others simply doubted that the
majority of their soldiers had the aptitude which could be developed.
Given the quality of the men under their command, these officers
believed that discipline inculcated by drills in the gymnasia and in
company training was of paramount importance. 'The maintenance
of uniformity and good order', argued Lord Roberts, took precedence over the development of the individual.[50]

Finally, the manner in which the army conducted its peacetime
training did not always maximise its value as preparation for war.
Whereas the deployment of troops in manoeuvres and exercises
wearing red coats, bearskins and gold-laced tunics was understandable in 1870, it appeared rather less so in the 1890s. May
described the Aldershot exercises of 1893 in which the soldiers wore
red and blue uniforms, with one side wearing full dress head-dresses:

Guardsmen and Fusiliers were to be seen skirmishing and endeavouring to
hide themselves in red coats and huge busbies, while I think one of the most
imposing sights I have ever seen was the Greys in their red tunics and
immense busbies bestriding great grey horses and charging a line of guns.[51]

By the mid-1890s, soldiers were issued with field service caps but
they continued to train in traditional colours. Officers, even under
Wood's regime at Aldershot, were hardly preoccupied with training;
they hunted for five or six days a week in the winter months, and
sometimes pushed attacks in the field days 'at a rate which verged on
absurdity where there was a doubt about whether the battle would

be over in time for a certain train to London'.[52]

Undoubtedly this training improved the physical endurance, discipline and steadiness of the other ranks (so easing fears that the short service soldier might be lacking in these qualities), but it also preserved some questionable tactics. At Aldershot, the artillery deployed in long straight lines during their exercises without any thought for cover. Cavalry regiments, including those which were proficient in their musketry, devoted the bulk of their winter training to mathematically precise and closely co-ordinated mounted drill. As late as July 1899, some infantry battalions still practised close order battlefield formations, with a final assault launched when 'the battalion formed up in line, dressed by the right within 200 yards of the enemy and then walked forward cheering'.[53] In short, despite the introduction of improved weapons, drill book changes, and the innovations of Wood at Aldershot, the peacetime training of the late Victorian army had significant shortcomings which were only partially alleviated by its extensive experience in colonial warfare.

Notes

1 Forbes, *History of the Army Ordnance Services*, Vol.2, pp.112–16; Col. H.C.B. Rogers, *Weapons of the British Soldier* (Seeley Service; London, 1960), pp.241–7; H. Strachan, *European Armies and the Conduct of War* (Allen & Unwin; London, 1983), pp.112–13; see also C.H. Roads, 'The History of the Introduction of the Percussion Breech-loading Rifle into British Military Service, 1850–70', unpublished Ph.D. thesis (Cambridge University, 1962) and B.A. Temple and I.D. Skennerton, *A Treatise on the British Military Martini: The Martini Henry 1869–c.1900* (Arms & Armour; London, 1983).

2 Col. Lord Cottesloe, 'Notes on the History of the Royal Small Arms Factory, Enfield Lock', *J.S.A.H.R.*, Vol.XII (1933), p.210; I.V. Hogg, *The Illustrated Encyclopaedia of Ammunition* (Quarto; London, 1985), p.47.

3 Brig. O.F.G. Hogg, *The Royal Arsenal: Its Background, Origin, and Subsequent History*, 2 Vols. (Oxford University Press; London, 1963), Vol.2, pp.811–12; Callwell and Headlam, *The History of the Royal Artillery*, Vol.1, pp.168–78; Forbes, *History of the Army Ordnance Services*, Vol.2, pp.126–7.

4 Callwell and Headlam, *The History of the Royal Artillery*, Vol.1, pp.173, 178–80; Forbes, *History of the Army Ordnance Services*, Vol.2, pp.131–2.

5 Callwell and Headlam, *The History of the Royal Artillery*, Vol.1, pp.189–90, 192.

6 R.C. Trebilcock, 'A Special Relationship – Government, Rearmament, and the Cordite Firms', *Economic History Review*, second series,

Vol.19 (1966), pp.364–79; Goodenough and Dalton, *The Army Book for the British Empire*, pp.432–5; on the failure to introduce quick-firing guns, see May, *Changes and Chances of a Soldier's Life*, pp.198–9.

7   Lt.-Col. G.S. Hutchison, *Machine Guns: their History and Tactical Employment* (Macmillan; London, 1938), pp.30, 39, 43 and 47; W.G. Gardner, 'Machine Guns and How to Use Them', *Journal of the RUSI*, Vol.26 (1882), pp.103–14; J. Ellis, *The Social History of the Machine Gun* (Croom Helm; London, 1975), pp.63, 84–5; H.Bailes, 'Technology and Tactics in the British Army, 1866–1900' in R. Haycock and K. Neilson (eds.), *Men Machines and War* (Wilfrid Laurier University Press; Waterloo, Ontario, 1988), pp.43–4.

8   Ellis, *The Social History of the Machine Gun*, p.33; Strachan, *European Armies and the Conduct of War*, pp.113–14; A Lieutenant-Colonel in the British Army, *The British Army* (Sampson Low; London, 1899), hereafter referred to as *The British Army*, pp.141, 147; Capt. F.G. Stone, 'The Maxim Automatic Machine Gun', [*Minutes of the*] *Proceedings of the R[oyal] A[rtillery] I[nstitution]*, Vol.XVI (1889), pp.1–9.

9   Bailes, 'Patterns of Thought in the Late Victorian Army', pp.29–45.

10   Capt. (later Col.) C.B. Brackenbury, 'The Autumn Manoeuvres of England', *Journal of the RUSI*, Vol.16 (1872), pp.222–44 and 'The Latest Development of the Tactics of the Three Arms', *Journal of the RUSI*, Vol.27 (1883), pp.439–65.

11   Col. Lonsdale Hale, comment on *ibid.*, p.459; Capt. F.N. Maude, *Letters on Tactics and Organisation* (G.A. Spooner; Leavenworth, Kansas, 1891), pp.34, 116–36, 227; Maj. C.B. Mayne, *The Late Battles in the Soudan and Modern Tactics: A Reply* (Gale & Polden; London, 1884), pp.17, 33; Maj. F. Clery, *Minor Tactics* (H. King; London, 1875), pp.99–106; Col. W.H. James, comment on Col. Lonsdale Hale, 'The Professional Study of Military History', *Journal of the RUSI*, Vol.41 (1897), p.717; Gen. E.B. Hamley, *Operations of War*, 3rd edition (Blackwood; Edinburgh, 1872), p.425.

12   Col. Lonsdale Hale, 'The Spirit of Tactical Operations of To-day', *Proceedings of the RAI*, Vol.16 (1889), p.459; Luvaas, *The Education of an Army*, pp.150, 158–9, 163; Bailes, 'Patterns of Thought in the Late Victorian Army', pp.32–3 and 'Technology and Tactics in the British Army', p.27.

13   Luvaas, *The Education of An Army*, pp.109–14; Maj.-Gen. P.L. MacDougall, *Modern Infantry Tactics* (E. Stanford; London, 1873), pp.20–1, 29–50 and 'Our System of Infantry Tactics: What is it?', *Nineteenth Century*, Vol.17, (1885), pp.833–46.

14   Luvaas, *The Education of an Army*, pp.175–80; see also J.F. Maurice, *The System of Field Manoeuvres Best Adapted for Enabling our Troops to Meet a Continental Army* (Blackwood; Edinburgh, 1872).

15   Bailes, 'Patterns of Thought in the Late Victorian Army', pp.37–8.

16   Lt. F.V. Greene, *The Russian Army and its Campaigns in Turkey, 1877–78* (W.H. Allen; London, 1880), pp.257–9, 445–9; Capt. G.S. Clarke, 'Plevna', *Professional Papers [of the Corps of Royal Engineers]*, Vol.5 (1881), pp.26–7, 52, 140–2; Mayne, *The Late Battles in the Soudan*

and Modern Tactics, p.33.
17 Capt. H. Brackenbury, *Ashanti War*, 2 Vols. (Blackwood; Edinburgh, 1874), Vol.1, p.367.
18 Col. C.E. Callwell, *Small Wars* (HMSO; London, 1896) reprinted by Greenhill Books, London 1990, p.23.
19 Capt. I.S.M. Hamilton, *The Fighting of the Future* (Kegan Paul; London, 1885), p.18; see also Lt.-Col. R. Harrison, 'The Duties of the Royal Engineers in Time of War' and Col. E.T.H. Hutton, 'Mounted Infantry and its Action in Modern Warfare', *Professional Papers*, Vol.6 (1881), p.256 and Vol.16 (1890), p.37; Sir S. White Baker, 'Experience in Savage Warfare' and Col. J.C. Gawler, 'British Troops and Savage Warfare, with Special Reference to the Kaffir Wars', *Journal of the RUSI*, Vol.17 (1873), pp.904–21 and 922–39.
20 G.F.R. Henderson, *Campaign of Fredericksburg*, 3rd edition (Gale & Polden; London, 1886), pp.129, 144; *The Battle of Spicheren August 6th, 1870, and the Events that Preceded it: A Study in Practical Tactics and War Training* (Gale & Polden; London, 1891), p.265; *The Science of War*, ed. by Col. N. Malcolm (Longmans; London, 1910), pp.130, 132, 134–5, 146–7, 153, 158, 162, 347, 352; Luvaas, *The Education of an Army*, pp.219–20, 230, 232–4; Wolseley, *The Story of a Soldier's Life*, Vol.2, p.122; Col. J.F. Maurice, *War* (Macmillan; London, 1891), p.107.
21 Wolseley comment on Brig.-Gen. J.H.A. Macdonald, 'Infantry Training', *Journal of the RUSI*, Vol.34 (1890), p.647.
22 Maj. G.F.R. Henderson, 'The French Manoeuvres of 1891', *Journal of the RUSI*, Vol.36 (1892), p.873; see also Capt. W. Adye comment on Macdonald, 'Infantry Training', p.644; Col. J.D.P. French, 'Cavalry Manoeuvres', *Journal of the RUSI*, Vol.39 (1895), p.562; Lt.-Col. T.S. Walker and Capt. J.M. Grierson, comments on G. Saunders, 'The Employment of large Cavalry Masses, of Smokeless Powder, and of Movable Fortifications as illustrated by the German Manoeuvres of 1889', *Journal of the RUSI*, Vol.34 (1890), pp.885–6, 888; H. Bailes, 'Technology and Tactics in the British Army', pp.28–9.
23 Lt.-Col. F. Maurice comment on Brackenbury, 'The Latest Development of the Tactics of the Three Arms', p.461; Henderson, *Science of War*, pp.134–5; Bailes, 'Technology and Tactics in the British Army', pp.44–5.
24 Wolseley comment on Macdonald, 'Infantry Training', p.648; Bailes, 'Technology and Tactics in the British Army', p.45.
25 *Infantry Drill* (HMSO; London, 1892), pp.84–6, 99, 103; *Musketry Regulations* (HMSO; London, 1898), pp.82–3; *The British Army*, p.138.
26 *Infantry Drill*, pp.104, 177–9.
27 Maj. A.W. White, 'How far is the Question of Moving Guns in the Field Affected by Modern Improvements?', *Proceedings of the RAI*, Vol.13 (1885), pp.495–504; Capt. H. Brackenbury, *The Tactics of the Three Arms as Modified to Meet the Requirements of the Present Day* (Mitchell; London, 1873), p.15; Lt.-Col. C.H. Owen, *Principles and Practice of Modern Artillery* (John Murray; London, 1871), pp.352–4; Brackenbury, 'The Latest Developments of the Three Arms', pp.448–9.
28 Prince Kraft zu Hohenlohe Ingelfingen, *Letters on Artillery* (Royal

Artillery Institution; Woolwich, 1887), pp.324, 385, 387–8.
   29 Maj. E.S. May, *Field Artillery with other Arms* (Sampson Low; London, 1898), pp.148–9, 162; R.H. Scales, Jr., 'Artillery in Small Wars: The Evolution of British Artillery Doctrine, 1860–1914', unpublished Ph.D. thesis (Duke University, 1976), pp.105, 109–10, 128, 161–2.
   30 Capt. J. Headlam comments on Capt. T.D. Pilcher, 'Artillery from an Infantry Officer's Point of View'; Capt. J.F. Manifold, 'The German Imperial Manoeuvres'; Maj. J.L. Keir, 'Direct and Indirect Fire'; Capt. J. Headlam, 'The German Method of Bringing Guns into Action', *Proceedings of the RAI*, Vols.23 (1896), pp.261–79; 17 (1890), pp.13–23; 24 (1897), pp.231–41; 389–98.
   31 Maj. J.L. Keir, 'A Short Summary of the Cover Question'; Brig.-Gen. C.H. Spragge, 'A Few Plain Remarks on the Positions and Work of Artillery in the Field'; Maj. E.S. May, 'Choice, Occupation and Change of Positions by Field Artillery', *Proceedings of the RAI*, Vols.25 (1898), pp.39–43; 19–28; 24 (1897), pp.375–87.
   32 Maj.-Gen. G.H. Marshall comments on Brevet Lt.-Col. F.B. Elmslie, 'The Possible Effect on Tactics of Recent Improvements in Weapons', *Aldershot Military Society*, Paper 72, 6 February 1899, pp.1–19; *Field Artillery Drill 1896* (HMSO; London, 1896), pp.12, 16, 25, 28; Maj.-Gen. Sir H. Brackenbury, q.1674 evidence appended to the *Elgin Report*, Vol.1, p.79.
   33 Col. P.L. MacDougall, *Modern Warfare as Influenced by Modern Artillery* (London, 1864), pp.15–16, 135–6; Lt.-Col. G.T. Denison, *Modern Cavalry: Its Organisation, Armament, and Employment in War* (T. Bosworth; London, 1868), pp.30–1, 73–5; Maj. H. Havelock, *Three Main Military Questions of the Day* (London, 1867), pp.79–80, 97; Hamley, *Operations of War*, 3rd edition, pp.434–6; Verner, *The Military Life of HRH George Duke of Cambridge*, Vol.2, p.302.
   34 *Reports on Alleged Failures of Cavalry Swords and Pistols at Suakin*, C. 5633 (1889), XVII, pp.3–7; Rogers, *Weapons of the British Soldier*, pp.230–1; Anglesey, *A History of the British Cavalry 1816–1919*, Vol.3, pp.397–8.
   35 Capt. F. Chenevix Trench, 'On the Progress that has been made during recent years in developing the Capabilities of Cavalry', *Journal of the RUSI*, Vol.21 (1877), pp.990–1011; Lt. G. Hamilton, 'Mounted Marksmen, and the Dismounted Service of Cavalry' and comments by Col. Gonne, Viscount Melgund and Capt. Seton, *Journal of the RUSI*, Vol.27 (1883), pp.261–87; Maj. Graves, 'The Functions of Cavalry in Modern War,' Parts I and II and comments by Lt.-Gen. Sir F. Fitzwygram and Gen. Sir Beauchamp Walker, *Journal of the RUSI*, Vol.29 (1885), pp.1–18, 19–43.
   36 Badsey, 'Fire and the Sword', p.94.
   37 J. Luvaas, *The Military Legacy of the Civil War* (University of Chicago Press; Chicago, 1959), p.193; G.J. de Groot, *Douglas Haig, 1861–1928* (Unwin Hyman; London, 1988), p.42–3; Chenevix Trench, 'On the Progress that has been made during recent Years in Developing the Capabilities of Cavalry', pp.991, 994–6, 998; Col. F.N. Maude, 'The Rise, Decay and Revival of the Prussian Cavalry', *Journal of the RUSI*, Vol.38

(1894), pp.20–40.

38 General Sir Evelyn Wood, *Achievements of Cavalry* (G. Bell; London, 1897), pp.241–2, 246, 248 and *From Midshipman to Field-Marshal*, 2 Vols. (Methuen; London, 1906), Vol.2, p.208; Goodenough and Dalton, *The Army Book for the British Empire*, pp.174–7: J. Luvaas, *The Military Legacy of the Civil War*, pp.178, 195.

39 Prince Kraft zu Hohenlohe Ingelfingen, *Letters on Cavalry* (Royal Artillery Institution; Woolwich, 1889), p.96; Maj.-Gen. C. von Schmidt, *Instructions for the Training, Employment and Leading of Cavalry* (HMSO; London, n.d.), pp.186–7; Maj. (later Lt.-Gen.) J.K. Fraser comments on Saunders, 'The Employment of Large Cavalry Masses . . .', p.885 and on French, 'Cavalry Manoeuvres', pp.559–88; D. Haig, 'Dismounted Service', 1892, Haig Mss., NLS, Acc. 3155, No.6a; Gen. Sir B.C. Russell to Wolseley, 19 October 1892, Wolseley Mss.

40 Dundonald, *My Army Life*, p.80; R. Evans, *The Story of the Fifth Royal Inniskilling Dragoon Guards* (Gale & Polden; Aldershot, 1953), p.94; M. Brander, *The 10th Royal Hussars* (Leo Cooper; London, 1969), pp.72–3.

41 Fraser comments on Capt. W.H. James, 'Magazine Rifles, their latest Developments and Effects', *Journal of the RUSI*, Vol.36 (1892), p.943; on Capt. G.E. Benson, 'Smokeless Powder and its probable Effect upon the Tactics of the Future', *Aldershot Military Society*, Paper 45, 23 March 1893, p.16; on Saunders, 'The Employment of Large Cavalry Masses . . .', pp.884–5; on French, 'Cavalry Manoeuvres' and lecturer's remarks, pp.565, 586; Capt. F.N. Maude, 'Cavalry on the Battlefield', *United Service Magazine*, new series, Vol.3 (1891), p.323. Compare with Badsey, 'Fire and Sword', p.118.

42 Schmidt, *Instructions for the Training, Employment and Leading of Cavalry*, p.154; Prince Kraft, *Letters on Cavalry*, pp.45 and 114; Capt. Manifold, 'The German Imperial Manoeuvres', p.22; Capt. J.M. Grierson, 'The German Army', *Professional Papers*, Vol.19 (1893), pp.41–61.

43 Churchill, *My Early Life*, p.187; see also Anglesey, *A History of the British Cavalry 1816 to 1919*, Vol.3, pp.406–7; Goodenough and Dalton, *The Army Book for the British Empire*, p.207; R. Evans, *The Story of the Fifth Royal Inniskilling Dragoon Guards*, p.90.

44 *Cavalry Drill Book* (HMSO; London, 1898), pp.386–91; French, qs.17241 and 17238 and Haig, q.19299 evidence appended to the *Elgin Report*, Vol.2, pp.306 and 403; B.J. Bond, 'Doctrine and Training in the British Cavalry 1870–1914', in M. Howard (ed.), *The Theory and Practice of War* (Cassell; London, 1965), pp.118–19.

45 Goodenough and Dalton, *The Army Book for the British Empire*, pp.152–5, 200, 202–4, 229–30; 427–9; *The British Army*, pp.172–84.

46 Sir I.S.M. Hamilton, q.13941 evidence appended to the *Elgin Report*, Vol.2, p.112; see also *The British Army*, p.176, Sir E. Wood, q.4158, Sir T. Kelly Kenny, qs.4562–3, Lord Methuen, q.14191 and Maj.-Gen. W.F. Gatacre, q.16794 evidence appended to the *Elgin Report*, Vol.1, p.176, 195 and Vol.2, p.121 and 274; Scales, 'Artillery in Small Wars', p.168.

47   Lord Roberts to the Secretary of State for War, 8 January 1897, Roberts Mss., NAM, 7101–23–107, f.85; see also Capt. W. Adye comment on Macdonald, 'Infantry Training', p.643; *The British Army*, p.177.
48   Wood, q.4158, Sir R. Buller, q.15606, Sir H.J.T. Hildyard, qs.15976–7 and 16007, and Col. F. Macbean, qs.19582–5 evidence appended to the *Elgin Report*, Vol.1, p.176, Vol.2, p.221, 240–2, and 415.
49   *Report on the Manoeuvres held in the Neighbourhood of Salisbury in August and September*, C. 1939 (1899), LIII, pp.vii–ix, xii, xvii, 65–78; P. Ventham and D. Fletcher, *Moving the Guns: The Mechanisation of the Royal Artillery 1854–1939* (HMSO; London, 1990), p.6.
50   Lord Roberts, q.10442; see also Lord Methuen, qs.14225–6, Lt.-Gen. Sir A. Hunter, 14597–9 and Maj.-Gen. Sir H.E. Colvile, qs.16998–17000 evidence appended to the *Elgin Report*, Vol.1, p.440, Vol.2, pp.123, 139 and 292; Callwell and Headlam, *The History of the Royal Artillery*, Vol.1, pp.254–5.
51   May, *Changes and Chances of a Soldier's Life*, p.171.
52   Aston, *Memories of a Marine*, p.110; Marling, *Rifleman and Hussar*, pp.172–3.
53   Col. R. Meinertzhagen, *Army Diary 1899–1926* (Oliver & Boyd; London, 1960), entry, 1 July 1899, p.15; Head, *No Great Shakes*, p.66; Evans, *The Story of the Fifth Royal Inniskilling Dragoon Guards*, p.94; Sir C. Warren, q.15852 evidence appended to the *Elgin Report*, Vol.2, p.234.

10

Colonial campaigning

The frequent recurrence of colonial campaigns placed immense demands upon the late Victorian army. They provided an unrivalled experience of war and in the preparations for war, tested the fighting qualities and personal courage of officers and soldiers, and enabled senior officers to display their proficiency in logistics, tactics and battlefield command. Although disasters periodically occurred, triumphs were much more frequent as expeditionary forces adapted to the peculiar demands of small-scale colonial warfare. Undoubtedly the officers and men benefited, as Wolseley claimed, from 'the varied experience, and frequent practice in war' and from 'the sensation of being under fire',[1] but this campaign experience was distinctive inasmuch as it derived from wars which were limited in scope and often very different in form.

Improvisation was a prerequisite in colonial campaigning, partly because the army lacked a General Staff and partly because soldiers had to be sent to an immense diversity of theatres (from 1868 to 1870 military forces saw active service in Abyssinia, the North West Frontier, Manitoba and North Island, New Zealand). British imperialism was largely defensive in this period, reacting to pressures from within or upon her colonies, from economic challenges in Europe and the United States, and from other imperial powers (Russia in central Asia and France in the Mediterranean and tropical Africa). There was certainly not any grand design underpinning the 'forward policies' of Disraeli or the annexations reluctantly contemplated by Lord Salisbury in the 1890s. Although Joseph Chamberlain wished to extend imperial control and develop the tropical estates in Africa, he only entered the Colonial Office in 1895, by which time most of the partitioning of Africa had been completed. Even with his presence in the cabinet, Lord Salisbury did not approve the reconquest of the Sudan until 1898. During 'the scramble for Africa' the flag had not followed trade nor had trade, capital and emigration followed the flag (trade and investment had largely concentrated upon the older, established markets of Europe, the United States and the white-settled colonies, with the only major exception being the goldfields of the Rand, while the vast majority of emigrants had settled outside the Empire).[2]

The direction and coherence of British policy were further complicated by the emergence of two forms of imperialism – the official, policy-making form and the 'new', more populist strand of imperialism. The former, as described by John Gallagher, was still characteristically cautious and reluctant, all too aware of the costs, risks and burdens of protecting the Empire, let alone of extending it. Concerned primarily with protecting and extending Britain's interests, particularly India and the strategic links to India via Cape Colony and the Suez Canal, the responsible politicians and their advisers followed the principle of extending control informally if possible, formally if necessary. After 1888 Lords Salisbury and Rosebery accepted that Britain would have to participate in the scramble for Africa as 'a painful but unavoidable necessity', which arose from the threat of foreign expansion and the spread of trade beyond the bounds of Empire, 'dragging the government into new and irksome commitments'.[3]

Nevertheless, as Freda Harcourt argues, policy was not made in a vacuum; there was an interplay between government and society. Even in the late 1860s and early 1870s, there were pressures from the press, public and Parliament, 'almost wholly middle class in inspiration and execution', which sought action over the prisoners held by King Theodore (the Abyssinian Expedition), slave trading in Zanzibar (Sir Bartle Frere's mission) and the Ashanti invasion of the coastal area of the Gold Coast (the Ashanti War). If these pressures sometimes coincided with the course of official policy-making,[4] they were a factor to be reckoned with by governments of either party. Disraeli clearly sought to exploit these sentiments in the hope of cultivating and rallying patriotic feeling among as broad a swathe of opinion as possible. He believed, too, that Britain had to assert herself and to display some military prowess if she was to retain her military status in an increasingly competitive world. He realised that the source of Britain's military power lay in India, where the Indian taxpayer bore the cost of the Indian Army and of garrisoning approximately 70,000 regular troops – about one-third of the standing army. He duly approved of the practice, which dated back to the Crimean War, of employing Indian troops outside the borders of India for 'imperial purposes' (in Abyssinia, Perak and Afghanistan), and this policy was followed by successive governments (Egypt in 1882, the Sudan in 1885, Mombasa in 1896 and the Sudan again from 1896 to 1899). Disraeli also sent Indian troops to Malta in 1878, so reflecting Britain's power back into Europe during the crisis over the Eastern Question. Directed against Russia, this was a highly popular and dramatic demonstration of Disraeli's belief that Britain was a great imperial power, and that she could behave like one.[5] Finally, the fate of the Empire became inextricably intertwined with notions of national prestige. Salisbury admitted that this had become a restraining influence. Writing to Sir Henry Drummond Wolff in Cairo in 1887, he acknowledged his regret that Britain had ever entered Egypt: 'had we not done so, we could snap our fingers at the world. But the national, or acquisitional feeling has been roused; it has tasted the fleshpots and it will not let them go.'[6] Queen Victoria was even more blunt; in writing to Salisbury about Egypt, she declared that 'giving up what one has is always a bad thing'.[7]

The late Victorian army had one overriding imperial mission, namely the defence of the North West Frontier against the perceived threat of Russian encroachment. This consumed not only the largest proportion of forces stationed overseas, but also shaped the distribution and organisation of the forces in India and required the provision of drafts on an annual basis from the army at home. Had governments expanded the the size of the home army as they embarked upon forward policies in Africa, the Cardwell system might have functioned efficiently; as it was, the home army was effectively sacrificed to the defence of India and the garrisoning of the Empire. The army's only relief lay in the self-governing colonies, where the policy of British withdrawal, begun in the 1860s, was accelerated by Cardwell. Although Britain still had to protect white colonists from dissident Maoris, Fenians and Transkei Xhosa, the policy of encouraging self-reliance proceeded steadily. By 1893, imperial garrisons had been withdrawn from Canada, apart from the naval base at Halifax, Nova Scotia, the five Australian colonies, Tasmania and New Zealand. Garrisons were only retained in southern Africa (Cape Town and Natal), the other 'fortresses' of

Gibraltar, Bermuda and Malta, and the various Crown colonies.

Within this context British forces were engaged in three broad, though not always distinct, types of warfare: campaigns of conquest or annexation, campaigns to suppress an insurrection or lawlessness, and punitive expeditions to avenge a wrong, wipe out an insult, or overthrow a dangerous enemy. Campaigns of conquest invariably took place on foreign soil and involved the overthrowing of a government with an organised military system, even if only one as primitive as Burma's under King Thibaw. Campaigns to crush an insurrection were necessarily internal struggles against guerillas or banditti. Whenever these campaigns involved combating a populace in arms or widespread disaffection they proved the most difficult to conclude successfully. All too often they degenerated (as in the case of the Xhosa and Matabele rebellions) into protracted, indecisive hostilities of many years' duration. Finally, the punitive expeditions were analogous to the wars of conquest, since they were generally conducted on enemy territory. As limited operations, they could be terminated quickly (the Abyssinian Expedition), but, if only partially effective, they might have to be followed by another campaign, culminating in complete annexation (the Ashanti wars of 1874, 1895–96 and 1900). Similarly wars conducted to overthrow a menacing military power (as Frere depicted the Zulus) or to fulfil a political purpose (the Egyptian war of 1882) could result in permanent occupation, even if the British government genuinely wished to withdraw.

Many of these campaigns were first and foremost 'wars against nature'; they involved surmounting difficulties of terrain and climate, frequently over immense distances, and these difficulties, which threatened the health and manoeuvrability of the field forces, were often more formidable than the challenges posed by the enemy. The topographical intelligence was frequently poor and contributed, along with treacherous guides, to the annihilation of Hicks Pasha's force when it marched from the Nile to El Obeid in 1883. Communications were generally indifferent. Railways were rarely available or took an immense amount of time to construct (ten months to construct the 230 miles of track between Wadi Halfa and Abu Hamed in 1897), and all-weather roads permitting the passage of wheeled transport seldom existed. Navigable rivers were sometimes available, and, if usable, enabled columns to dispense with the burden of carrying large quantities of forage. As the forces usually had to travel upstream, and sometimes beyond the reach of steamships, soldiers and their auxiliaries had to become their own transport, rowing and manhandling boats to convey all their supplies, ammunition and equipment. In the Red River Expedition, Wolseley's force spent thirty-nine days traversing 1,370 km of rocky, watery wilderness, and had to master the techniques of white water navigation as they negotiated hazardous rapids, rocky portages and marshy ground. A shortage of water bedevilled several campaigns, particularly those in the Sudan, where the wells fixed the lines of operations through the desert, and in Abyssinia, where Napier's expedition had to carry much of its own water as it moved over 400 miles of largely arid, mountainous terrain. Finally, many of these hazards had to be overcome within fairly limited periods of time. Wolseley had to complete his Ashanti war before the rains thickened the tropical rain forest and decimated his troops with fever; Napier had to reach Magdala before the rains blocked the mountain passes; and, in 1884–85, Wolseley had to try to reach Khartoum before the Mahdi breached the city's defences.

These constraints required not only careful logistical preparations but also considerable flexibility. Commanders had to adapt their transport arrangements and their tactical planning to the local circumstances and, after the Abyssinian campaign, to the expectation that each war should be conducted as economically as possible. When a Select Committee investigated the Abyssinian costs of £8,800,000 (or £5,300,000 more than the original estimate), it attributed the difference to 'the inadequacy of the estimate' and to 'the profuse and enormous expenditure . . .'. When it learnt from Lord Napier that he regarded matters of expense as 'quite out of his province', it recommended that 'a more efficient business training, and something like a business department should be introduced into our military system . . .'.[8] If Wolseley demonstrated that colonial operations could be conducted economically (the Red River Expedition cost less than £1,000,000 and the Ashanti War about £800,000), he still paid close attention to his logistical needs. Indeed, any field commander who had to move his army over a great distance across barren terrain, without the prospect of finding supplies or forage locally, had to cope with the problem of controlling and protecting an immense supply train. He risked, Colonel Callwell observed, seeing his army become 'a mere escort for its food' and so had to establish a protected base for his supplies, with the aim of either operating within range of this base or of pushing his supplies ahead under escort. Irrespective of the procedure employed, the immense logistical difficulties presumed that these wars were conducted with the 'lowest possible strength consistent with safety . . .'.[9] The colonial wars differed radically in the weapons, tactics and military organisations encountered. At one extreme Colonel Arabi's Egyptian army, trained and armed by Europeans, closely resembled a regular army in organisation, if not in the passivity of its tactics. At the other extreme, the primitively armed Ashanti were able to lay ambushes and mount flank attacks, but lacked the discipline and cohesion to survive determined assaults. In between these extremes, the highly disciplined Zulu *impis* were capable of manoeuvring with speed and precision across the veld, but their primitive weaponry and commitment to the offensive ultimately proved their undoing at the battles of Gingindhlovu (2 April 1879) and Ulundi. Better armed, but less mobile and less wedded to the offensive, the Maoris proved resourceful defensive fighters. Their earthen strongholds, known as *pas*, situated on tactically commanding ground, represented a rational response to the superiority of British firepower. At Titokowaru's *pa* (1868), the central stockade was actually a false target which fixed British attention while the Maoris tried to enfilade the attackers from rifle pits on the flanks. However, the Maoris lacked muskets which were capable of rapid, long-range fire; they also suffered from tribal disputes, the lack of a 'warrior class', and could not sustain their military activities for more than a few weeks at a time.[10]

The British encountered great differences in tactics in their various African campaigns, particularly between those employed in the Ninth Kaffir War and those employed in the campaigns in the Sudan. Whereas the Xhosa tribes, the Gaika and Gcaleka, rarely presented a target and usually withdrew before advancing forces, hoping to strike at the rear or flanks of any patrols moving outside the bush, the Mahdists were religious fanatics, who were willing to charge the enemy in mass frontal assaults (albeit in the case of Hicks Pasha after a skilful exercise in harassment and attrition). Although the Xhosa proffered only sporadic, if protracted resistance in the Transkei, the Mahdists achieved some notable successes, not only at El Obeid but also in breaking the British squares at Tamai and Abu Klea, before succumbing to the Anglo–Egyptian firepower at Omdurman. The Boers, finally, presented even more daunting problems. Fine marksmen and highly mobile, they were essentially mounted infantry and, in 1881, confronted forces without adequate cavalry support. They lacked artillery but possessed a serviceable rifle (although the Westley Richards was inferior in range and loading rate to the Martini-Henry). Above all, they were well led and were capable of operating together in comparatively large bodies, even without a permanent military organisation. The Boer commandos 'were merely bodies of determined men, acknowledging certain leaders, drawn together to confront a common danger'.[11] In 1881 they resolutely confronted Colley's forces in three pitched battles on the Transvaal frontier (Laing's Nek, Ingogo and Majuba Hill), precipitating a political capitulation by Britain.

The adaptation required by this multiplicity of different foes, employing different weapons and tactics, did not simply involve the planning of separate operations for separate theatres. Sometimes British forces had to adapt their tactics rapidly as they fought the Xhosa and Zulus or the Zulus and Boers in successive years (the 94th Foot fought all three adversaries). Even in the same campaigns British tactics had to be modified; after the disaster at Isandhlwana, the line formation was replaced by the square, and, in the First Sudanese War and the Gordon Relief Expedition, where squares were regularly employed defensively, attacks were also launched in square formation (El Teb, 29 February 1884) and in open order (Kirbekan, 10 February 1885). Tactical adaptation was essential, as the enemy held the strategic advantage of operating in his own country or over familiar terrain, and could deploy his men much more easily. Enemy forces normally required less food and ammunition than their British counterparts, needed neither a fixed system of supply nor a line of communications, and, in many cases, made little provision for the care of their wounded. Frequently they held the initiative; they could gather promptly, transfer forces rapidly from one part of the theatre to another, and disperse after defeat, so thwarting attempts to follow up a victory in the field. By lacking lines of communication, they did not even possess the most obvious target for retaliatory attacks.

In these circumstances, where strategy and terrain favoured the enemy, the British objective, as Callwell observed, was to fight and not to manoeuvre. The regulars had to assume the offensive strategically, penetrate the enemy's territory, seek him out, and bring him to battle, where superior training, discipline, organisation and firepower should prevail. Occasionally, these advantages did not prove decisive (notably in the First Boer War), and, in some campaigns, the enemy's knowledge of the mountains or rain forests enabled him to minimise the benefits of superior firepower. Normally, though, whenever battle was joined, the tactical conditions favoured the trained and organised force. 'Man for man,' argued Callwell, 'the fanatic or cut-throat, the hardy nomad or the reckless savage may match or be more than a match for the European soldier; in the aggregate irregular warriors fail.'[12]

Although Colonel Callwell's *Small Wars*, written in 1896, was the most systematic and comprehensive study of colonial campaigning, Victorian officers had regularly debated and examined this form of warfare. From the early 1870s onwards they wrote essays and delivered lectures before the Royal United Service Institution and the Royal Artillery Institution upon the lessons of particular wars and the impact of new technologies tested in colonial combat. They heatedly debated the appropriateness of specific tactics, notably the square, and compared the requirements of colonial and regular forms of warfare. The War Office also learned from past experience and sought to expedite overseas expeditions. The centralisation implicit in the administrative reforms of the Cardwell period established the precedent of drawing all the services of supply and transport together into a single department. In 1874 a telegraph service was constructed which enabled a system of contracts to be developed at home and throughout the colonies on uniform procedures. Four years later the first store depot was established at Woolwich, providing a centre in which goods and equipment for overseas service could be sorted, packed and dispatched. More elaborate arrangements were subsequently made as the army began to plan its mobilisation arrangements for home defence. While lighter articles of equipment for serving soldiers and reservists were held at stations, the bulkier items for units (camp equipment, supply wagons, transport wagons, ammunition and many other stores) were pre-positioned at 'places of concentration', and wartime clothing was issued from Pimlico whenever a force was mobilised.[13]

Once assembled and equipped, the expeditionary forces depended upon the Royal Navy for transport, safe passage, and the guarding of its overseas bridgeheads. The two services had evolved these transport arrangements over many years, not least because the army required shipping on an annual, peacetime basis to replace casualties and relieve soldiers at foreign stations. The navy had vessels in its charge, owned by the Indian and home governments, which were specially adapted to carry troops, horses and military carriages. As expeditions usually required additional shipping (sixty-nine vessels were needed to convey the main body of 16,146 troops and 5,487 horses on the Egyptian expedition of 1882), governments had to hire transports and troop freight ships from the merchant marine. Naval support, however, often went beyond the task of sea transport and the disembarkation of supplies.[14] Naval forces proffered assistance by coastal bombardment (Egypt, 1882), by sending boats up rivers to convey troops and supplies and to provide gunnery support (on the Nile, 1885 and 1896–98), by combined operations against pirates (in Perak, 1875–76), and by sending detachments with guns, rockets or machine guns in support of land-based operations (in Abyssinia, Zululand, Egypt and the Sudan). Indeed, Lieutenant Wyatt Rawson, RN, performed the invaluable service of navigating by the stars during Wolseley's night march to Tel-el-Kebir. Yet inter-service co-operation never developed beyond these localised and pragmatic endeavours; at a higher level, joint planning and co-ordinated staff work were conspicuous by their absence.

Expeditionary forces had at the outset to secure their base of operations or, more often, after a seaborne landing, a primary base for the disembarkation of soldiers, horses and equipment and a fortified advance base further inland. The local conditions were seldom ideal. The shallowness of the water at Zula required the construction of two piers of over 300 yards to facilitate the disembarkation of Napier's forces, while the surf and the nature of the beach at Cape Coast Castle delayed the landings prior to the beginning of the Ashanti War (the 2nd Battalion of the Rifle Brigade spent three weeks cooped up in a transport ship off the Gold Coast under a tropical sun awaiting disembarkation). The base commandant had critical responsibilities in choosing the sites for depots, stores and magazines, in making arrangements for hospitals, camping grounds and troop accommodation, and, above all, in making appropriate sanitary provisions, especially if disease was rife or if troops and horses, debilitated by their journey, had to wait in intense heat before their supplies and equipment were unloaded.[15]

Thereafter an expeditionary force had to establish its line of communications. This line of military stations along tracks, rivers and occasionally roads or railways (and sometimes a combination of these) led from the base to the army in the field. Serving as a vital link, it enabled supplies, ammunition, reinforcements and information to be brought to the front, facilitated the return of the sick and wounded to the rear, and, in adversity, furnished a line of retreat. However valuable, the line cramped an expedition's freedom of manoeuvre and required protection whenever it became vulnerable to attack. As the protection usually involved the manning of defensive posts and the provision of flying columns to operate between them, the task often consumed a considerable proportion of the available troops. The proportion could even become the bulk of the expedition when the line passed through hostile country (Napier deployed 7,000 out of his 12,000 regular troops to protect his line of communications in Abyssinia, and 15,000 soldiers guarded the seventeen posts and stations from Kabul to Peshawar in March 1880, leaving a field force of only 12,000). Even in passing through friendly country, there was always the possibility of an enterprising and mobile adversary trying to sever the line (as the Boers endeavoured to do at the Ingogo River on 8 February 1881). On rare occasions, field forces cut themselves loose from their communications (in March 1880 Sir Donald Stewart led his men over the 260 miles from Kandahar to Haider Kel and, some months later, Roberts led the more notable march from Kabul to Kandahar through extremes of climate, dust storms and enemy action to relieve a beleaguered garrison). Generally, commanders dared not risk such ventures, but they appreciated that the dangers would increase as their lines lengthened through hostile country: during his inexorable advance on Omdurman, Kitchener feared that 'if we do not move on the enemy will certainly assume the offensive and with the long line I have to guard an enterprising enemy might give me a good real to do'.[16]

The line of communications structured the deployment and movement of the supplies, ammunition and other impedimenta upon which a regular army depended. These stores were stationed at the base and at intervals along the line of communications, and were often emplaced in advance of the column of troops. The field force would normally consume these supplies before it depleted its movable supplies, namely the personal rations carried by the soldier or horse (usually sufficient for one or two days' consumption), those carried in the regimental and departmental transport, and those transported in the following supply columns. Theoretically the provision of supplies was a calculable proposition, based upon a known force, consuming a fixed amount of food and water per day, and moving at an anticipated rate over a particular distance. The standing orders for the Red River Expedition prescribed that the daily rations of each man in camp would consist of 1 lb of biscuit, or 1 ½ lb of bread, or 1 ½ lb of flour; 1 lb of salt pork or 1 ½ lb of fresh meat; one-third of a pint of beans or a quarter of a pound of preserved potatoes; and one thirty-sixth of an ounce of pepper. One pound of fresh vegetables would also be issued if and when available. The weight of such rations, compounded by the weight of ammunition, camp equipment and medical and engineers' stores, was colossal. In moving a much larger force into Zululand, Lord Chelmsford had to reckon that each battalion would consume over a ton of foodstuffs per day and possibly one and a half tons of firewood. It would also require ninety tents, weighing over 4 tons when dry (or 5 ½ tons when wet), 2 tons of ammunition in the regimental reserve, and another 9 tons of light camping equipment. Overall, Chelmsford had to move some 1,500 tons of equipment, ammunition and rations to keep his four columns supplied for six weeks in the advance on Ulundi.[17]

Logistical planning, though, was never an exact science in colonial warfare, as information about the theatre and its resources or about the enemy and his movements was frequently unreliable. If military circumstances or climatic conditions required a prompt advance, the field force might have to advance before all its stores were disembarked (as in Abyssinia, where only 7,000 out of 35,000 tons of forage were put ashore). Appalling weather conditions could turn roads into quagmires and streams into swollen rivers, slowing the rate of advance and putting men on to half rations, notably in the march to Newcastle in January 1881. Finally, if forces moved at pace and achieved rapid victories, they could outrun their supplies (leaving the Black Watch to exist on forty-eight hours' rations for nine days after Tel-el-Kebir).[18]

These were essentially temporary discomforts and not privations, delays but not disastrous dislocations. If the adequacy of the stores was rarely an issue, the quality was sometimes problematical (the seventy days' supply of flour – 1,868,412 lb – sent to Ismailia in 1882 was found to be bad on arrival, possessing a consistency like 'plaster of Paris'). The packaging of supplies periodically proved troublesome, too. Despite representations after the First Boer War that supplies should not be packaged in quantities larger than 100 lb weight, hay was sent to Ismailia in bales of 240 lb, so slowing the pace of loading and unloading.[19] Transport remained the prime difficulty; it recurrently bedevilled the movement of supplies in the field in spite of the readiness with which British forces adapted to local circumstances. They used bullock carts, elephants and camels in India, wagons drawn by oxen and mules in southern Africa, bearers in west Africa, boats in Perak, and pack animals in mountains and across roadless country. Ideally they preferred railways or canals to haul large quantities of supplies, but, if neither were available, they preferred wheeled transport to pack animals. Whenever pack animals had to be employed, they increased the length of the train and the number of mouths to feed (and, if forage was not available locally, the animals had to carry their own fodder as well, sometimes consuming as much as they carried). Even draft animal requirements could become prodigious (Chelmsford employed 27,000 oxen and 5,000 mules to haul over 2,500 vehicles in Zululand). Purchasing animals in such numbers and hiring their drivers drove up the costs of any campaign, especially if a large proportion of animals died from want of forage or care (of the 36,094 animals landed in Abyssinia, only 7,421 re-embarked after the campaign).[20]

The military persistently complained about the lack of system and organisation in their transport arrangements. Even in the Egyptian campaign, where Wolseley secured his advance base at Kassassin within a week of landing and his victory at Tel-el-Kebir within another sixteen days (13 September 1882), the transport provisions proved controversial. Wolseley brought up 75 tons of supplies per day by boats via the Sweetwater Canal, and larger quantities by rail from 28 August, even 250 tons per day from 6 September onwards. The Railway Company, directed by Major W.A.J. Wallace, RE, the only railway expert available, cleared track, constituted trains, built two short lines from Ismailia station to the wharf, arranged time-tables, and delivered some 9,000 tons of stores to the front in less than a month: an undertaking which has been described as 'a model of what could be achieved in colonial warfare'.[21] Yet the Commissariat complained that the railway had failed to take stores from the wharf (which had to be hauled by horse-drawn trucks to the station) and failed to take various trucks or to load them properly (and Major Wallace admitted that difficulties had occurred in making up trains and in the shunting and marshalling of wagons).

The Commissariat also claimed that difficulties had beset the regimental, divisional and auxiliary transport. The regimental carts, driven by inexperienced soldiers, had proved too few, too heavy, and too prone to break down, so leaving tons of stores abandoned. The general service wagons had proved 'useless, except in the towns', and the divisional transport had arrived too late. Above all the pack mules, intended as auxiliary transport to support the advance from Tel-el-Kebir, had failed lamentably. Of the 2,614 bought, 758 were found to be useless on arrival, 389 arrived too late, and many of the remainder had utterly unreliable drivers. Wolseley ruefully reflected 'that picking up hundreds or thousands of mules did not constitute transport. The drivers whom we obtain are the *canaille* of the Levantine towns, and we really have no authority over them.' Sir Edward Morris, the Commissary-General, was even more blunt:

Drivers, collected any how, under varied or no agreements, on different rates of pay, without clothing, equipment, or regulations; mules, unfit for immediate service, unmarked, unregistered, unshod, without fitted harness or saddles, and in some instances without head-collars, are worse than useless; they are an embarrassment.[22]

The army experienced further problems when Wolseley chose to travel up the Nile and employ camels in his attempt to relieve Gordon. Once his force had reached Korti, he proposed to split it into two columns – one travelling by river, the other by desert. The Desert Column of four camel regiments with supporting units (some 2,000 men, commanded by Sir Herbert Stewart) was to strike out across the Bayuda Desert, bisecting the great bend in the river, and to advance on Khartoum if the city's fall seemed imminent, or to co-operate with the River Column in a longer-term assault on the Mahdists. Using camels to transport themselves and their baggage, the soldiers – all volunteers from different units – were to fight as infantry. The scheme, though imaginative, was fraught with difficulties. Neither the officers nor the men had any knowledge of camels, and, as three of the regiments had to travel from England (other than the mounted infantry based in Egypt), they lacked the time to be trained in how to ride, load, water or feed them. The War Office hardly helped by sending out two farrier sergeants and two shoeing smiths to shoe the camels and two rough-riding sergeants, one of whom had never seen a camel, to instruct in camel-riding. Wolseley's staff ignored the warnings of Major Herbert Kitchener about the treatment and management of camels, and their availability in different parts of Egypt. They failed to buy sufficient camels (over 8,000 were used) or to provide enough forage, and they failed to anticipate that baggage and riding saddles would be difficult to acquire. Stewart's column was short of camels from the outset and, as camel losses mounted rapidly, this slowed his movements across the desert. Ultimately the column, harassed by the Dervishes and attacked in various battles (during which Stewart was killed), reached the Nile but too late to relieve Khartoum. When Buller joined the column to assume command (11 February 1885), he found it in a parlous predicament owing to the plight of the camels. He prudently ignored his orders to take Metemmeh and advance on Berber, preferring to withdraw to Korti along the line of communications, where stores and water were available at prepared positions. Although the complete animal losses were not recorded, the mounted infantry brought back only ninety-five of their original 500 camels, and these miserable specimens fetched about £2 each compared with their original cost of £15.[23]

If the army learnt from these experiences in forming both an Army Service Corps in 1888, and an efficiently organised Egyptian Camel Corps, with officers and men trained in camel management and provided with good-quality Bisharin camels, it developed many of its other support services as a consequence of colonial campaigning (see Chapter 3). Intelligence gathering and analysis were especially important, as British forces required knowledge of enemy armies and tactics and of the topography and climate of particular countries. Although the War Office Intelligence Branch (and later Division) expanded its range of activities during this period, it was always understaffed and underfunded (with an annual budget of about £11,000 at the end of the century). Accordingly, field commanders had to organise their own intelligence-gathering system, but could only do so after a declaration of war or once hostilities appeared imminent in an overseas theatre. They acquired information about enemy forces and their dispositions from a variety of sources, including scouts, spies and local informants (a border agent supplied Chelmsford with extremely detailed information on the Zulu army), but they often lacked accurate information about the terrain (the Zulu maps placed the king's kraal twenty miles from its true position, omitted several rivers, and showed others running in the wrong direction). Hence commanders continued to rely upon reconnaissance parties to ascertain the whereabouts of water holes, passes over mountains, river fords, and camping grounds.[24]

Wolseley paid close attention to his intelligence preparations and wrote sensibly about them. In planning the Red River Expedition he benefited from the advice of a civil engineer, Simon Dawson, on the feasibility of the southern route, and later from the information gathered by the intrepid Captain William Butler, who had scouted ahead of the expedition. In *The Soldier's Pocket Book*, Wolseley emphasised that field commanders should give a high priority to the collection and assessment of intelligence and should make appropriate provisions from the outset of any operations. They should create their own intelligence staffs and require daily reports from the 'head of intelligence' which collated and analysed all the information gleaned from reconnaissance and scouting missions, the interrogation of spies and prisoners, and the interception of telegrams and dispatches. They should be careful, nonetheless, to avoid disseminating this information too widely lest newspaper correspondents learn of it and leak it, carelessly, to the enemy.[25]

Wolseley followed these precepts himself, appointing Buller as his 'head of intelligence' in the Ashanti and Egyptian campaigns. The latter proved more successful in west Africa, where he recruited native spies and interpreters, formed 250 men into a corps of scouts to move ahead of the main force, and gathered remarkably accurate information on the dispositions of the enemy. Conversely, the intelligence estimates of the numbers commanded by Arabi Pasha were greatly exaggerated, which Wolseley attributed to the 'wild people' employed in intelligence collection. For the Nile Expedition, Wolseley appointed Colonel Sir Charles Wilson, Royal Engineers, as the head of the intelligence staff on account of his service in Cairo, the Sinai, and in the Intelligence Branch of the War Office. In addition Wolseley, as president of the Confidential Mobilisation Committee, had access to War Office intelligence papers on the various routes to Khartoum and to the reports of Major Herbert Kitchener, then of the Egyptian Intelligence Department, about possible routes and sources of water for the Desert Column. Although the Desert Column failed to reach Khartoum in time (and Wilson, who succeeded Stewart in command, took much of the blame), the failure could not be ascribed to a lack of accurate intelligence (as in the case of Hicks Pasha). Thereafter Lieutenant Reginald Wingate of the Egyptian Intelligence Department, continued gathering information about the movements and activities of the Khalifa and his army, much of which would be used by Kitchener and his commanders when they prepared for the reconquest of the Sudan.[26]

Foresight and improvisation, in short, were among the requirements of successful field commanders. Even so, their effectiveness often depended upon the political context in which they had to direct operations. The degree of political interference varied considerably from one campaign to another. The sheer distance from Whitehall, and the time taken by a two-way flow of communications, ensured relatively little interference in Abyssinia, the Maori Wars and the Red River Expedition. During the Zulu War, Lord Chelmsford was able to ignore the news of his replacement, even when Wolseley had landed in Natal, and proceeded to restore part of his reputation at Ulundi. Yet governments undoubtedly influenced the course and outcome of some wars; just as the procrastination of Gladstone's government diminished the likelihood of relieving Gordon in Khartoum, so its earlier diplomacy hardly assisted British commanders during the First Boer War. Throughout the conflict Gladstone's government continued its secret negotiations with the Boers, proscribed Colley from advancing into the Transvaal until a reply to truce terms was received, complicated his task by issuing ambiguous instructions, and frustrated Wood in his desire to avenge the defeat at Majuba.[27]

Facing the many difficulties of colonial warfare, commanders had to maximise their advantages of firepower, tactical flexibility, and the disciplined and resilient forces under their command. Firepower was their principal asset, especially if fighting against more numerous enemies, armed predominantly with spears and swords. Hand-to-hand combat generally entailed risks for numerically smaller forces and reduced their ability to inflict heavy casualties. Some regiments, like the Gordon Highlanders, still boasted of their prowess with the bayonet, and their proficiency was demonstrated at Tel-el-Kebir, when Wolseley launched his smaller forces in a remarkable bayonet attack, supported by cavalry and artillery, against a well fortified position. With Highlanders leading the assault on the left, the parapets were scaled, trenches cleared, and the Egyptians and Sudanese put to flight after a short but desperate struggle. Without the element of surprise based upon a pre-dawn attack, following a night march, and exploiting the lax watch of the enemy, this tactic might have proved more costly. As it was, the four regiments of the Highland Brigade bore the brunt of the casualties, although a Royal Marine battalion was actually the worst hit unit. Heavier casualties would befall the Black Watch when ordered to charge at the battle of Tamai (13 March 1884) without the benefit of support or surprise. Feeling deeply aggrieved after General Graham's rebuke for moving too slowly into the attack and for wasting ammunition at El Teb (29 February 1884), the Black Watch drove the Sudanese back, but, on becoming surrounded, had to fight their way back to the square, suffering 'over 100 killed and wounded, nearly all fearful cuts on their knees from two-handed swords . . .'.[28]

If often involved in hand-to-hand combat, and always trained for it, British soldiers had more potent weapons at their disposal. Armed with breech-loaders, machine guns and later repeating rifles, they gained the ability to fight at longer range and to sustain rapid bursts of fire. As their rifles improved in range and rate of firing, and their machine guns became more reliable, they acquired an ever greater advantage over enemies equipped with primitive weapons or partially armed with obsolete muskets or with captured rifles. By the 1890s small British forces found that machine guns were invaluable in helping to quell Matabele revolts, thwart Ghazi attacks in the relief of Chitral, defy Ashanti attacks on Kumasi, and silence the Chinese gunners in the defence of the Peking legations. They also acquired more destructive ammunition after the failure of the 0·303 Mark II bullet to incapacitate some of its victims in the Chitral campaign. Whereas the Indian authorities produced an expanding bullet (and named it after the cantonment where it was developed – Dum Dum), the Royal Laboratory produced a bullet with similar effects – the Mark IV. This was identical to the Mark II save that it had a cylindrical hole, ⅜ inch deep, punched in its point, so ensuring that air would compress in the hole on impact and make the bullet mushroom inside its victim, producing horrific wounds. While the Tirah Expeditionary Force employed the Dum Dum bullet against the Afridis (1897–98), Kitchener's forces used Mark IV ammunition as well as twenty Maxims and forty-four pieces of artillery at Omdurman. Within a few hours the Anglo–Egyptian army had killed some 11,000 Dervishes and suffered only forty-eight fatalities; as Churchill concluded, 'Thus ended the battle of Omdurman – the most signal triumph ever gained by the arms of science over barbarism.'[29]

This firepower, nonetheless, had to be employed effectively.

Although the British periodically fought in their traditional line formation (for example, at Isandhlwana, Kirbekan and Omdurman), they often resurrected the square. Rendered obsolete by modern firearms in European warfare, which had prompted infantry to deploy increasingly in loose skirmishing lines, the square served a multitude of purposes in colonial wars. A less rigid concept than was implied by its name, it simply described a formation which showed a fighting front in all directions. It could be employed offensively or defensively, whether as an order of battle or on the line of march, and at the halt when resting or bivouacking for the night. It could be rigid or compact in form (when facing a fanatical attack), or much more loose and elastic during bush or hill warfare, with the army moving or drawn up in groups or detachments around a central convoy. Advocates of the square, like Wolseley, Chelmsford and Graham, claimed that it had proved useful whenever the numbers of British troops were small and the field force was burdened by baggage and impedimenta. They argued, too, that it had served as a reasonable response to the mobility of irregular warriors, as a means of countering the tactic of envelopment employed in Zululand or of shock charges in the Sudan, and as a prudent precaution when thick bush neutralised the effects of long-range fire. They stressed that the square had protected vital supplies and stores, had enabled field forces to care for their wounded, and had proved supremely flexible as a 'defensive–offensive formation'.[30]

Critics of the square, led by MacDougall, became more vociferous after the Dervishes had broken the British squares at the battles of Tamai and Abu Klea. They asserted that the square presented the narrowest front of fire, lacked mobility, and exposed British troops to loss if the enemy were equipped with rifles and capable of firing them accurately. The square, they argued, was too difficult to manoeuvre over rough terrain, even with strictly drilled troops, that its fire was reduced to a quarter of its strength unless facing tactics of envelopment, and that its rear face was practically useless. They noted (as had the Zulus and Mahdists) that the square had four weak points at its angles, and that, if one of them broke, the result could be extremely dangerous. They feared, above all, that the square was incapable of maximising the effects of British firepower, and that the formation of two squares, as at Tamai, had increased the frontage of fire but only at the risk of causing casualties from 'friendly fire'. In various critiques, MacDougall denounced the massive square as 'an unintelligent and dangerous formation . . . which neutralises all the advantages of superior training and weapons on the part of the soldier, and of superior science on the part of the general'. He affirmed that it betrayed 'a want of confidence' in the British soldier which the latter did not deserve.[31]

Nevertheless, these critics conceded that squares might have to be formed whenever the numbers were extremely small (notably the Desert Column at Abu Klea and Abu Kru) or whenever the field force was awaiting attack (Ulundi). Indeed, their criticisms were essentially theoretical, since field commanders had to adapt their formations to the prevailing circumstances. Fighting in the Sudan, observed Wolseley, permitted 'no half measure': commanders knew that unless they won they died, and so they had to win. They depended entirely upon the resilience, courage and morale of their soldiers, and realised that the latter were likely to fight more effectively if they knew that the wounded would be cared for within the square and not left to their fate on the field of battle. Pragmatism prevailed, and the square remained a tactical option favoured in many colonial conflicts.[32]

Whether the army fought in square, in line or sometimes in column, the maintenance of fire control was essential. Firing by volleys, which had been largely abandoned in European warfare because of more sophisticated weapons and tactics, was still a favoured method of stopping native attacks. In bush warfare, where the main threat came from sniper fire, precautionary volleys were a means of keeping the enemy at a distance. During the Benin Expedition (1897) the advancing columns 'searched' the bush, firing occasional volleys (by a few files and not by sections or companies) and forced the enemy to fire randomly and beyond their effective range. In more open terrain, when forced on to the defensive to meet determined assaults but relatively inaccurate rifle fire, British forces had every incentive to maintain their well regulated fire discipline. Volleys enabled them to conserve ammunition and to withhold fire until the enemy was well within range, so ensuring that their own firing was thoroughly effective. Volleys also served to maintain discipline and cohesion, especially among small, beleaguered forces (as at Rorke's Drift) facing formidable odds. Above all, volley firing could inflict heavy casualties upon an attacking enemy (the Zulus lost over 2,000 dead at Isandhlwana; they fell down, as Corporal Roe remarked, 'in heaps' at Ulundi; and 300 Arabs perished in only five minutes at Abu Kru on 19 January 1885). Steady independent fire often followed or complemented volleys (at Tamai, one square fired independently while the other used volleys); in hill warfare, where the targets were individuals or small groups ensconced among rocks, independent firing was more effective and economical.[33]

Artillery profferred additional fire support, by normally pushing the guns to the front and discharging them in disciplined volleys at close range, often using case shot. As enemy forces rarely possessed large numbers of guns, classical artillery tactics were seldom employed. Artillery duels tended to be short, sharp and decisive, other than at Tel-el-Mahuta (24 August 1882), where the Egyptian gunners armed with Krupp breech-loaders held their ground against British muzzle-loaders, and more seriously at Maiwand, where Ayub Khan deployed his guns in a wide semicircle around the British position and brought converging fire to bear. Enemy artillery was more often quickly silenced, as at the battle of Atbara (8 April 1898), before enemy positions were pounded. Guns were rarely deployed in masses as too many guns were considered an encumbrance, hampering movement and requiring protection. When they were massed at Tel-el-Kebir, they served primarily as a central pivot capable of supporting the infantry division on either flank in case it suffered a reverse. Once the infantry poured into the trenches, the concentration was promptly dispersed. Concentrated fire on specific objectives was also infrequently applied; in many defensive situations, guns were usually dispersed to cover all possible avenues of attack, to counter the tactics of envelopment, and to reinforce the vulnerable corners of squares. Preparatory barrages, though occasionally employed (but without much effect at Laing's Nek, 28 January 1881), were often avoided (notably at Kirbekan and Tel-el-Kebir) lest they demoralised the enemy and put him to flight prematurely. Indeed, Wolseley expressed a widespread view that

The effect of artillery fire is more moral than actual; it kills but very few, but its appalling noise, the way it tears down trees, knocks houses into small pieces, and mutilates the human frame when it does hit, strikes terror into all but the stoutest hearts.[34]

Yet the guns had some material and tactical effect. They inflicted losses upon massed charges in the battles of Khambula (29 March 1879) and Ulundi, and seemingly confirmed the value of direct firing with a clear view of their target at Omdurman. At Kirbekan, they contained the Dervishes while the infantry completed its turning movements, and at Ingogo they kept the Boers at bay, relying upon infantrymen to replace the wounded gunners and man the cannon. The gunners, nonetheless, struggled to meet the twin requirements of firepower and mobility in colonial conditions. Although they sometimes employed draught artillery (notably in Zululand and Egypt), they much preferred light, portable equipment for manoeuvring over difficult and treacherous terrain. Light seven-pounders, carried by bearers, were employed in the Ashanti forests and mule batteries in the march to Kandahar. The 2.5 inch Indian screw guns proved both powerful and manoeuvrable in Egypt and were mounted on camels for service at El Teb, Tamai, and with the Desert Column. They were also used in Burma against wooden stockades, but they had less effect against mud-made buildings. If an expedition planned to destroy forts or bombard buildings, it had to employ heavier guns or howitzers, sometimes borne by elephant or boat. In the Burmese War Sir Harry Prendergast, VC, towed floating batteries of seventy-pounders up the Irrawaddy. Known as 'Mother Carey's chickens' after Colonel Carey, who commanded them, these guns suppressed enemy fire from the two forts which commanded the river and enabled the infantry to take the Gweg-Yaung Kamyo fort with virtually no resistance. Kitchener also bombarded Omdurman, particularly the Mahdi's tomb, with fire from his ten heavily armed gunboats and six 5 inch howitzers, to bring the Khalifa out to battle.[35]

In seeking to maximise the effects of its firepower, a field force required warning of an attack or information about enemy dispositions. Other than in thick bush or in mountainous terrain, this intelligence came primarily from the patrols and reconnaissance missions undertaken by cavalry and mounted riflemen. During colonial conflicts, such as the Zulu War, these tasks were demanding and dangerous: Buller's mounted riflemen continued patrolling for some six months without respite. They regularly moved camp at night and mounted patrols in addition to their daily fatigues, guard duties, vedettes and night pickets. In battle they fought alongside the infantry but performed more specialised missions, too. At the battle of Khambula (29 March 1879), they rode out, dismounted, and began firing at the Zulu right horn from about half a mile, luring it into a premature attack. Once Wood had repulsed this attack, he was able to concentrate his firepower upon the advancing centre and left until the Zulus fell back, whereupon Buller's irregular horsemen engaged in a merciless pursuit, many seizing assegais to ride down the fleeing Zulus. Sir Herbert Stewart also armed his hussars with Arab spears at El Teb, and the 17th Lancers demonstrated the effectiveness of a classical charge against a beaten enemy in the pursuit of the Zulus after Ulundi. The lance, in effect, was still an invaluable weapon in pursuits, and, if the pursuits disintegrated into *mêlées*, the sabre became the primary weapon.

Cavalry units revealed both versatility and tactical weaknesses in colonial warfare. They protected the flanks and rear of Graham's square (or more correctly rectangle) as it moved through eastern Sudan, proffered vital fire support for the hard-pressed infantry at Tamai, and served as mounted infantry in the Desert Column. They demonstrated enormous *élan* in Egypt, routing the Egyptian forces at Kassassin in the moonlight charge of the Household Cavalry, and followed up Tel-el-Kebir with the dash to Cairo under Major-General Drury-Lowe. In battle, however, cavalry forces were generally looking for opportunities to charge, and if they did so without proper reconnaissance and attacked unbroken infantry, danger and difficulties ensued. At El Teb, Stewart repeatedly charged an unbroken enemy over ground covered in many places with high mimosa bush, so letting gaps develop in the ranks from which the Dervishes emerged to cut the hamstrings of the horses and stab their riders. The 10th and 19th Hussars suffered disproportionately heavy casualties and found that their horses were too exhausted to pursue the enemy. Similarly, at Omdurman, the 21st Lancers mounted a gallant but quite reckless and unnecessary charge which killed a mere twenty-three Dervishes at a cost of twenty-one fatalities and fifty wounded out of a total of little more than 300 men, and had 119 horses killed or wounded. Douglas Haig, serving with the Egyptian Cavalry, was furious: the regiment, he noted

was keen to do something and meant to charge something before the show was over. They got their charge, but at what cost? I trust for the sake of the British Cav[alry] that more tactical knowledge exists in the higher ranks of the *average* regiment than we have seen displayed in this one.[36]

Civilian auxiliaries, finally, contributed significantly to all the colonial campaigns. Many were hired locally, others with specialist skills were brought into the theatre of operations. Even if they were sometimes paid more than regular soldiers (like the civilians who

supported the Red River Expedition), they were relatively cheap as a
temporary expedient. They performed a multitude of tasks; Napier
employed some 12,000 civilians (and at one time nearly 15,000
civilians) to support his 12,000 combatants as bearers, cooks, water-
carriers, porters, grass-cutters, sanitary men, and specialists in the
handling of horses, mules, bullocks, beef cattle, camels and elephants. In the Ashanti War of 1873–74 Major Home, the chief
engineer, required 6,000 local labourers to clear a road through
seventy miles of bush, build seven way stations, and construct the
forward base at Prasu. Colley, the chief of staff, reckoned that he
needed 8,500 porters to carry the supplies for the 4,000 combatants,
and to remove the sick and wounded from the front. Friendly natives
served as guides in the bush and as scouts, organised in sections in
1874 and given considerable independence in their movements
ahead of the field force. They gathered information, acted as an outer
line of pickets, and effectively put themselves at considerable risk.
During the Red River Expedition, Wolseley depended heavily upon
the expertise of 800 voyageurs, including some Iroquois Indians,
who were experienced in navigating the inland waterways of
Canada. He even requested that Canadian boatmen should accompany the Nile Expedition, and secured the assistance of 386 voyageurs. They represented the first group from the self-governing
colonies to assist Britain in an overseas war.[37]

Managing these auxiliaries was often troublesome. The military
authorities periodically despaired of the calibre and motivation of
these men, who were not bound by military discipline, sometimes
failed to work at the rate or in the manner expected of them, and, in
some wars, were prone to desert. During the Abyssinian expedition,
Colonel Warden reported that the mule-drivers included 'off-
scourings of the Bombay streets, consisting of broken-down native
tradesmen, discharged Europeans and Eurasians from other departments, and the class termed loafers'. Some 2,100 were discharged in
the first three months of the campaign for 'wanton, barbarous
cruelty' towards their animals, for 'their unwillingness to work or to
bear privations' and for 'extreme' insubordination.[38] Wolseley was
bitterly critical of the 'worthless set' of civilian drivers and 'broken-
down drunkards' who accompanied the Red River Expedition, and
ascribed the defection of some Iroquois Indians to 'the priesthood of
Canada being much opposed to this expedition'.[39] When desertions
threatened to upset the critical timetable for road-building in the

Ashanti campaign, Colley secured the return of the labourers and porters by touring their villages and burning their houses to the ground. The Commissariat despaired of the ill-organised, undisciplined and ill-equipped drivers who supported the Egyptian campaign, dismissing them collectively as 'a mere mob or rabble'. In the construction of his railway, Kitchener detailed an Egyptian infantry battalion to act as an armed guard upon the army of Egyptian and Sudanese navvies, many of them convicts and prisoners of war.[40]

Despite these difficulties, civilian or locally raised auxiliaries were essential, and, in some capaigns, they provided combat support. In the Red River Expedition two battalions of Canadian militiamen, each consisting of twenty-one officers and 350 noncommissioned officers and men, were raised by voluntary enlistment. During the Zulu War Chelmsford met the majority of his scouting needs from 1,000 mounted volunteers and the five troops of the Natal Native Horse. Apart from the Natal Mounted Police, few of these units had any previous training or sense of discipline, but many were committed to fighting Zulus, especially the forty Boers who served under Piet Uys for no monetary reward. Chelmsford also permitted Colonel Durnford to raise the Natal Native Contingent – 7,000 natives organised in seven battalions – but these were poorly armed, ill-equipped and indifferently officered (they were the first unit to crack at Isandhlwana and many of them deserted prior to Rorke's Drift). The Natal Native Horse, though, fought valiantly at Isandhlwana, and the mounted volunteers served resolutely in Wood's column, performing the many duties which were expected of mounted riflemen. In the First Boer War, Colley was reluctant to employ volunteers against the Boers, but he still used the Natal Mounted Police to patrol the border and watch the movements of the enemy. Finally, once the Egyptian army had been reorganised, it provided invaluable support for the conquest of the Sudan. Indeed, the 17,600 Egyptian and Sudanese troops comprised the largest element in Kitchener's army of 25,000 men and their performance at the battle of Atbara impressed their British officers. 'The Gyppie Cavalry,' wrote Haig,

acted *steadily* on the whole, but there was no glorious charging home, as some of the tales I have heard w[oul]d have us believe. Moreover if the Dervish horsemen had *really* come in, I feel sure that few of the Brigade could have escaped.[41]

Even with civilian and/or locally raised support, British forces could not afford to incur excessive levels of casualties. Whenever possible, they had to curb the duration of the hostilities, especially in tropical climates. In non-tropical conditions the losses from sickness or disease were not too severe (there were no sick and only two injured personnel during the Red River Expedition, and battlefield fatalities, bloated by the death toll at Isandhlwana, exceeded the deaths from disease and accidents in the Zulu War). But in Burma and west Africa, the losses from disease and sickness were still considerable (although the West Yorkshire Regiment and the Special Service Corps prevailed over the Ashantis without any combat casualties in 1896, they re-embarked with a sick roll of nearly twenty officers and 200 men). During their service in Egypt and the Sudan from July 1882 to March 1884 the British and Indian forces incurred battlefield casualties (255 killed and 915 wounded, of whom sixty-five died) which were dwarfed by the 871 deaths and the 4,405 invalided home from other causes. Finally, Kitchener's Anglo–Egyptian army suffered 1,500 fatalities, of which only about 15 per cent occurred in battle.[42]

Wolseley realised that preventive measures could mitigate the scale of these losses. In *The Soldier's Pocket Book*, he argued that the health and morale of the soldiers would benefit from better food, clothing and shelter provision on active service. He urged that close attention should be paid to the choice of camp site, the dispersal of tents, personal hygiene, and sanitary arrangements. Officers, he insisted, should ensure that their men received hot meals whenever possible, preserved vegetables in addition to their rations, bread in preference to biscuit, and fresh meat from cattle driven with the line of march instead of salt beef and pork. Above all, he recommended that the rum ration should be abolished, and that field forces should depend upon non-alcoholic beverages. Having followed most of these precepts in the Red River Expedition, he sought to minimise the health risks during the Ashanti War by ordering the advance con- struction of huts every few miles along the line of march as shelter against the sun and rain, by emplacing filters at carefully selected streams, by issuing quinine daily and lime juice four times a week, and by marching the troops at a 'moderate pace'. He also approved the design of a more comfortable grey-coloured tunic and trousers to replace the scarlet and rifle-green uniforms, and a new helmet made of cork and canvas to replace the white helmets of the home-based units. Admittedly, these reforms of diet and clothing took time to be emulated throughout the service. The traditional attachment to the red coat persisted, despite the increasing use of khaki-coloured kit in India and the losses inflicted by the Boer riflemen in 1881. Scarlet was worn by the majority of troops in Egypt until the fighting was over, whereupon 30,000 suits of grey serge were dispatched for use by the garrison which remained. Even after the Colour Committee, chaired by Wolseley, had condemned the 'conspicuousness of white and scarlet' and had recommended the use of neutral colours on active service, some commanders still believed that the sight of scarlet would overawe the natives. Scarlet was worn for the last time in battle at Ginnis (30 December 1885).[43]

However tardily implemented, the reforms of diet and clothing were a sign of a more enlightened attitude towards the welfare of the rank and file on active service. Officers had traditionally recognised that they had to lead by example and to display a calm, determined and conspicuously courageous resolve under fire (Lord Chelmsford and his staff never dismounted during the battle of Ulundi; Major-General William Gatacre led the British forces into battle at Atbara). Some shared the discomforts of campaigning – portering stores on the Red River Expedition, sleeping without any tents at times in Egypt and the Sudan (and suffering as did the men from the attentions of sand-flies, mosquitoes and ants), enduring nights of broken sleep (Wood personally checked his pickets twice nightly throughout the Zulu War), and spending long periods of time in the saddle (Buller ended the Zulu War with suppurating sores on his legs, having spent some six months more often in the saddle than out of it and frequently riding fifty to sixty miles per day). Admittedly, many officers indulged their passion for field sports whenever the opportunities occurred, and often travelled in relative style and comfort (Napier and his staff, numbering thirty-six in all, required 120 followers and 130 mules for tents and baggage, whereas the 800 men of the 33rd Foot had only 132 followers and 221 mules). Yet they shared the risks with their men of some daring tactical operations – divided forces despatched over unfamiliar terrain (to confuse the enemy, entice him into battle, and maximise the chances of at least one line reaching the desired objective), night advances (to enhance surprise and avoid enemy fire), and assaults upon entrenched or uphill positions (and if the latter failed, notably at Laing's Nek and Majuba Hill, officers, carrying swords and wearing insignia of rank and shiny scabbards, suffered as much, and sometimes proportionately even more, than their men).[44]

As reflected in their diaries, letters and memoirs, officers generally shared with their men a sense of innate patriotism, regimental loyalty (which may have motivated some Irish soldiers more than appeals to Queen and Country), and a fierce desire to close with the enemy. Soldiers appeared willing to bear the rigours and privations of campaigning if they could engage the enemy, share in the spoils of war (the looted goods at Magdala, other than items seized 'at the point of sword or bayonet', were auctioned and the prize money distributed among the soldiers), and avenge defeats (a real motivation for those who saw the mutilated corpses at Isandhlwana or were forced to flee at Laing's Nek or Majuba). Baden-Powell shared the bitter disappointment of the men when the Ashantis capitulated without a fight in January 1896. For many weeks, he noted, the ranks had been sustained 'by the one hope' as they struggled 'through the endless, sickly forest . . . literally fighting down leg-weariness and fever' to 'be in it when the fight came off'. He believed that the men, who cursed the 'extra rounds' which they carried back from Kumasi (namely the rounds not used in battle), had only wanted 'to get at the enemy to give him a real good drubbing'.[45]

Neither officers nor men discounted their enemies, and they assessed their fighting qualities frankly. 'The black Soudanese,' wrote Marling, 'fought like blazes' at Tel-el-Kebir, while 'the Gippies ran like hares'. The Dervishes made even more of an impression at El Teb: 'without a doubt', asserted Sergeant Danby of the 18th Hussars, 'these Arabs are the most fierce, brave, daring & unmerciful race of men in the world'.[46] Such assessments were made by soldiers, who possessed a deeply rooted sense of their racial and moral superiority. Colonial victories had come, argued Callwell, by making the 'lower races', who were profoundly 'impressionable', feel 'a moral inferiority throughout'. They were liable to become unnerved by the spectacle of regular columns advancing through their territory, and their morale had repeatedly cracked in the face of 'bold and resolute' attacks, charges by mounted men, and ' a vigorous offensive'. These victories, he added, had to be consolidated by determined pursuits (including the merciless hunting down of the Matabele by Baden-Powell's troops after the action at Umgusa River 6 June 1896). Wolseley, in his more thoughtful writings, ascribed such victories to superior firearms and discipline, but he neither concealed his racialism nor his unbridled confidence in the moral supremacy of a resolute offensive. At the outset of the Ashanti campaign he exhorted his men, 'Soldiers and sailors, remember that the black man holds you in superstitious awe: be cool; fire low, fire slow and charge home.'[47]

These attitudes bred a confidence which disdained any search for cover in the attack. Commanders were willing to employ zeribas and to fight defensively when they had to, but they deprecated any reliance on protection and generally aimed to assume a bold offensive. Wolseley deplored the use of entrenchments lest they depress the attacking spirit of the defending forces; Callwell made similar criticisms of laagers and zeribas. In seeking to maximise their moral effect, commanders were willing to eschew cover and to mount frontal assaults. At the battle of Atbara, after the artillery barrage had ceased, a double line assembled some 1,500 yards long, with the Egyptians on the right and the Cameron Highlanders on the left, supported by columns of Seaforths, Lincolns and Warwicks. As pipers struck up the 'March of the Cameron Men', the drums and fifes began to play and the whole line moved forward 'in slow time and with great deliberation'. The firing line sustained a 'steady independent fire', but, even when the Dervishes began to respond at 200 yards, 'perfect order was maintained' and the slow remorseless advance continued. The attack was a crushing success, achieved at a relatively modest cost of 125 casualties, which largely reflected the inaccuracy of the Dervish firepower.[48] Similarly, at Omdurman, the slaughter produced by Colonel Charles Long's batteries, firing directly into dense masses of Dervishes for three hours from direct fire positions, and the heroic exploits of the 21st Lancers, bolstered confidence in traditional tactics. Achieving victories, using these tactics, hardly prepared the army for operating over battlefields swept by smokeless, magazine rifles. Lyttelton later observed:

Few people have seen two battles in succession in such startling contrast as Omdurman and Colenso. In the first, 50,000 fanatics streamed across the open regardless of cover to certain death, while at Colenso I never saw a Boer all day till the battle was over and it was our men who were the victims.[49]

Prolonged service in small wars had undoubtedly benefited the army in its leadership, organisation, and support services, but these gains were essentially limited. Writing in July 1900, Major Gerald Ellison argued that this service had developed physical and personal qualities which would always be vital in combat, but that it had also produced 'a dangerous narrowing of the intellectual vision'. Commanders, he noted, who had led small armies often failed to develop proper staff arrangements, particularly in major battles. Just as Wolseley was effectively his own chief of staff at Tel-el-Kebir, Kitchener dominated the proceedings at Omdurman, rushing from point to point directing the battle in person. Having built their careers upon imperial service, commanders derived lessons from this experience, and continued to value the qualities of leadership, initiative and improvisation which had proved so valuable in the field. As Ellison asserted, these qualities hardly prepared commanders for the administrative and strategic questions involved in large-scale warfare.[50]

Notes

1   Wolseley, 'The Standing Army of Great Britain', p.346.

2   Durrans, 'A Two-edged Sword: The Liberal Attack on Disraelian Imperialism', pp.267, 275; W. Baumgart, *Imperialism: The Idea and Reality of British and French Colonial Expansion, 1880–1914* (Oxford University Press; Oxford, 1982), pp.66, 178–9; C.J. Lowe, *The Reluctant Imperialists: British Foreign Policy 1878–1902*, 2 Vols. (Routledge & Kegan Paul; London, 1967), Vol.2, pp.58–9, 97–8; Robinson and Gallagher, *Africa and the Victorians*, pp.17, 24, 395–8; J. Gallagher, *The Decline, Revival and Fall of the British Empire* (Cambridge University Press; Cambridge, 1982), pp.6, 14; A.P. Thornton, *The Imperial Idea and its Enemies* (Macmillan; London, 1959), p.6.

3   Gallagher, *The Decline, Revival and Fall of the British Empire*, pp.14–15; Robinson and Gallagher, *Africa and the Victorians*, pp.13, 464–72.

4   N. Rodgers, 'The Abyssinian Expedition of 1867–1868: Disraeli's Imperialism or James Murray's War?' *Historical Journal*, Vol.27 (1984), pp.129–49.

5   F. Harcourt, 'Disraeli's Imperialism, 1866–1868: A Question of Timing', pp.108–9 and 'Gladstone, Monarchism and the New Imperialism, 1868–74', *J.I.C.H.*, Vol.14 (1985), pp.20–51; Thornton, *The Imperial Idea and its Enemies*, p.97; Bond (ed.), *Victorian Military Campaigns*, pp.6–7; Durrans, 'A Two-edged Sword: The Liberal Attack on Disraelian Imperialism', p.269; R. Millman, *Britain and the Eastern Question 1875–1878* (Clarendon Press; Oxford, 1979), p.451.

6   Lord Salisbury to Sir H. Drummond Wolff, 23 February 1887 in Lady Gwendolen Cecil (ed.), *Life of Robert Marquis of Salisbury*, 4 Vols. (Hodder & Stoughton; London, 1921–32), Vol.4, pp.41–2.

7   Victoria to Salisbury, 12 June 1890, in Buckle (ed.), *The Letters of Queen Victoria*, 3rd ser., Vol.1, p.615.

8   *Report from the Select Committee on the Abyssinian Expedition; together with the Proceedings of the Committee, Minutes of Evidence, and Appendix,* hereafter referred to as the *Abyssinian Report,* C. 401 (1870), V, pp.xiv–xv, xxviii–xxix.

9   Callwell, *Small Wars,* pp.44, 57–68; J. Keegan, 'The Ashanti Campaign 1873–4' in Bond (ed.), *Victorian Military Campaigns,* pp.163–98; G.F.G. Stanley, *Toil and Trouble: Military Expeditions to Red River* (Dundurn Press; Toronto, 1989), pp.10, 166–7, 255–6.

10 J. Belich, *The New Zealand Wars and the Victorian Interpretation of Racial Conflict* (Auckland University Press; Auckland, 1986), pp.22, 295–8; Callwell, *Small Wars,* pp.29–30, 32; Lt. R. da Costa Porter, 'Warfare against uncivilised Races; or, How to fight greatly superior Forces of an uncivilised and badly-armed Enemy', *Professional Papers,* Vol.6 (1881), pp.305–60; M.J. Williams, 'The Egyptian Campaign of 1882' in Bond (ed.), *Victorian Military Campaigns,* pp.270–4.

11 Callwell, *Small Wars,* p.31; Morris, *The Washing of the Spears,* pp.256–7, 260–1, 267; A.J. Smithers, *The Kaffir Wars* (Leo Cooper; London, 1973), pp.272–4; Keown-Boyd, *A Good Dusting,* pp.7, 16, 26, 32, 48–53, 224–43; J. Lehmann, *The First Boer War* (Buchan & Enright; London, 1972), pp.108–9; Maj. G. Tylden, 'The British Army and the Transvaal 1875–85', *J.S.A.H.R.,* Vol.30 (1952), pp.159–71.

12 Callwell, *Small Wars,* pp.75, 85–92.

13 Goodenough and Dalton, *The Army Book for the British Empire,* pp.514–16; G. Lawson, q.6884 and E.C. Nepean, q.9146 evidence appended to the *Report from the Select Committee on Commissariat and Transport Services (Egyptian Campaign),* hereafter referred to as the *Egyptian Campaign Report,* C. 285 (1884), X, pp.313 and 427; Bailes, 'Technology and Imperialism', p.90.

14 'Introduction' and Williams, 'The Egyptian Campaign of 1882' in Bond (ed.), *Victorian Military Campaigns,* pp.26–7, 256, 272; Sir J. Adye, q.2804 evidence appended to the *Egyptian Campaign Report,* p.117.

15 Goodenough and Dalton, *The Army Book for the British Empire,* pp.545–7; A. Bryant, *Jackets of Green: A Study of the History, Philosophy, and Character of the Rifle Brigade* (Collins; London, 1972), p.174; Capt. C.E. Callwell, 'Lessons to be learnt from the campaigns in which British forces have been employed since the year 1865', *Journal of the RUSI,* Vol.31 (1887), pp.357–412; B. Bond, 'Mr Gladstone's Invasion of Egypt (1882) – A Revelation of Military Weakness', *Army Quarterly,* Vol.81 (1960), pp.87–92; Col. H. St Clair Wilkins, q.1167 evidence appended to the *Abyssinian Report,* p.82.

16 Sir H. Kitchener to Sir E. Wood, 30 September 1897, Wood Mss., NAM, 6807–234; Callwell, *Small Wars,* pp.115–17, 121; Goodenough and Dalton, *The Army Book for the British Empire,* p.549; D. Bates, *The Abyssinian Difficulty* (Oxford University Press; London, 1979), p.141.

17 Goodenough and Dalton, *The Army Book for the British Empire,* pp.551–3; Stanley, *Toil and Trouble,* pp.88–9; Morris, *The Washing of the Spears,* p.313.

18 Bates, *The Abyssinian Difficulty,* p.216; Lehmann, *The First Boer*

War, pp.140–1; Sir J. Adye, q.2804 evidence appended to the *Egyptian Campaign Report*, p.119; Linklater, *The Black Watch*, p.126; *Abyssinian Report*, p.xix.

19 Sir E. Morris, qs.255–6, 264, 310–13 evidence appended to the *Egyptian Campaign Report*, pp.11, 13.

20 Porter, 'Warfare against uncivilised Races . . .', pp.320–1; Adye, q.2804 evidence appended to the *Egyptian Campaign Report*, p.115; Morris, *The Washing of the Spears*, p.319; *Abyssinian Report*, p.xvii.

21 Adye, q.2804 and Maj. W.A.J. Wallace, report appended to the *Egyptian Campaign Report*, pp.118 and 550; Bailes, 'Technology and Imperialism', p.103.

22 Morris, qs.380, 382–5, 404–5, 408; H.S.E. Reeves, q.2161; Col. R. Harrison, q.5755; and reports by Morris, Reeves and Wallace appended to the *Egyptian Campaign Report*, pp.15–17, 84, 259, 469, 473, and 551; Maurice and Arthur, *The Life of Lord Wolseley*, p.153.

23 Preston (ed.), *In Relief of Gordon*, pp.xxxix–xxxi; Keown-Boyd, *A Good Dusting*, pp.40–1, 43–5, 47, 79, 81; Symons, *England's Pride*, pp.97, 113, 173–7, 260–1; Marling, *Rifleman and Hussar*, pp.125, 129, 131, 149.

24 Fergusson, *British Military Intelligence, 1870–1914*, pp.110, 112, 139; Morris, *The Washing of the Spears*, pp.295–6; Porter, 'Warfare against uncivilised Races . . .', pp.327–8.

25 Stanley, *Toil and Trouble*, pp.86–7, 151–6; Wolseley, *The Soldier's Pocket Book*, 3rd edition, pp.90–4.

26 Keegan, 'The Ashanti Campaign, 1873–4', p.190; Wolseley to Childers, 19 August 1882, in Childers (ed.), *The Life and Correspondence of the Rt Hon. Hugh Culling Childers*, Vol.2, pp.105–7; Fergusson, *British Military Intelligence, 1870–1914*, pp.36–7, 138; Keown-Boyd, *A Good Dusting*, pp.46, 123–4, 146, 180; Symons, *England's Pride*, p.97.

27 Lehmann, *The First Boer War*, pp.129, 230–1, 270, 275, 283–4; Morris, *The Washing of the Spears*, pp.554, 557, 564, 575; Marling, *Rifleman and Hussar*, p.57.

28 *Ibid.*, p.112; Porter, 'Warfare against uncivilised Races . . .', p.339; Williams, 'The Egyptian Campaign of 1882', p.274; Linklater, *The Black Watch*, p.127; Lt.-Col. C. Greenhill Gardyne, *The Life of a Regiment: The History of the Gordon Highlanders*, 3 Vols. (The Medici Society; London, 1903–29), Vol.2, p.248; Hamilton, *Listening for the Drums*, p.120.

29 W. Churchill, *The River War: An Historical Account of the Reconquest of the Soudan* (Nelson; London, 1915), p.372; T.O. Ranger, *Revolt in Southern Rhodesia 1896–7* (Heinemann; London, 1967), p.231; A. Lloyd, *The Drums of Kumasi: The Story of the Ashanti Wars* (Longmans; London, 1964), p.181; P. Fleming, *The Siege at Peking* (Rupert Hart-Davis; London, 1959), pp.198–9; E.M. Spiers, 'The Use of the Dum Dum Bullet in Colonial Warfare', *J.I.C.H.*, Vol.4 (1975), pp.3–14; *Parl. Deb.*, Fourth Ser., Vol.74 (13 July 1899), col.688.

30 Wolseley comments on Lt.-Gen. Sir G. Graham, 'Infantry Fire Tactics: Attack Formations and Squares', *Journal of the RUSI*, Vol.30 (1886), pp.233–74; Lord Chelmsford comments on Maj. C. Cooper King, 'Soudan Warfare', *Journal of the RUSI*, Vol.29 (1885), pp.887–908;

Callwell, *Small Wars*, pp.256–8, 358.

31 MacDougall, 'Our System of Infantry Tactics: what is it?' pp.842–5 and 'The Fall of Khartoum, and its Consequences', *Blackwood's Edinburgh Magazine*, Vol 137 (1885), pp.558–68 (MacDougall's authorship of the *Blackwood's* article is revealed in *The Wellesley Index to Victorian Periodicals 1824–1900* (University Press of Toronto; Toronto, 1966), Vol.1, p.164); Cooper King, 'Soudan Warfare', pp.891, 893–4; Col. Sir L. Graham comments on Graham, 'Infantry Fire Tactics: Attack Formations and Squares', p.267.

32 Wolseley comments on Graham, 'Infantry Fire Tactics: Attack Formations and Squares', pp.272–3; Cooper King, 'Soudan Warfare', p.892; 'The Fall of Khartoum, and its Consequences', p.566; D.R. Headrick, 'The Tools of Imperialism: Technology and the Expansion of European Colonial Empires in the Nineteenth Century', *Journal of Modern History*, Vol.51 (1979), pp.231–63.

33 Callwell, *Small Wars*, pp.371–2, 392–5; Lloyd, *The Drums of Kumasi*, p.180; Graham, 'Infantry Fire Tactics; Attack Formations and Squares', p.271; Symons, *England's Pride*, p.212; Corporal W. Roe, diary, p.66, NAM, 7504–18.

34 Wolseley, *The Soldier's Pocket Book*, 3rd edition, pp.122–3, 282; Callwell, *Small Wars*, pp.429–30 and 'Notes on the Tactics of our Small Wars', *Proceedings of the RAI*, Vol.12 (1882), pp.531–52; Scales, 'Artillery in Small Wars', pp.76–8, 83, 89.

35 *Ibid.*, pp.76–7; Lehmann, *The First Boer War*, pp.166–7; G. Bruce, *The Burma Wars 1824–1886* (Hart-Davis, MacGibbon; London, 1973), pp.156–7; P. Ziegler, *Omdurman* (Collins; London, 1973), pp.93–5: Lloyd, *The Drums of Kumasi*, p.181.

36 Capt. D. Haig to Wood, 7 September 1898, Haig Mss., NLS, Acc. 3155; Callwell, *Small Wars*, p.414; Anglesey, *A History of the British Cavalry 1816 to 1919*, Vol.3, pp.187, 190–2, 200–1, 286–304, 311–17, 378–85; Col. R.S. Liddell, *The Memoirs of the Tenth Royal Hussars (Prince of Wales' Own) Historical and Social* (Longmans; London, 1891), pp.438–9; Col. J. Biddulph, *The Nineteenth and Their Times* (John Murray; London, 1899), pp.242–3.

37 *Abyssinian Report*, p.xviii; Bates, *The Abyssinian Difficulty*, pp.102, 144; Keegan, 'The Ashanti Campaign, 1873–4', pp.184–6; Callwell, *Small Wars*, pp.350–4; Stanley, *Toil and Trouble*, pp.88, 90; Symons, *England's Pride*, pp.106–7.

38 *Abyssinian Report*, p.xviii.

39 'Narrative of the Red River Expedition – Part II. By an Officer of the Expeditionary Force', *Blackwood's Edinburgh Magazine*, Vol.109 (1871), pp.48–73. Dawson blamed the defections upon Wolseley's choice of route, Stanley, *Toil and Trouble*, p.289, n.10.

40 Keegan, 'The Ashanti Campaign, 1873–4', p.186; Morris, qs.527–8 evidence appended to the *Egyptian Campaign Report*, p.21; Keown-Boyd, *A Good Dusting*, p.151.

41 Stanley, *Toil and Trouble*, p.91; Morris, *The Washing of the Spears*, pp.304–10, 376, 403; Lehmann, *The First Boer War*, p.190; Haig to Wood,

12 April 1898, Haig Mss., NLS, Acc.3155, No.6; Keown-Boyd, *A Good Dusting*, p.211.

42   Stanley, *Toil and Trouble*, p.256; *Separate Returns per Regiment, Troop, or Battery, of the Numbers Killed, Died of Disease, or other Casualties among the Troops, British and Native, engaged in the Transkei and Zulu Campaigns in South Africa up to the present Date*, No.190 (1880), XLII; Maj. R. Baden-Powell, *The Downfall of Prempeh: A Diary of Life with the Native Levy in Ashanti 1895–6* (Methuen; London, 1896), p.151; *Return of the Loss of Life during the English Occupation of Egypt in the British Army, from July 1882 to March 1884*, No.97 (1884–85), XLVI; Keown-Boyd, *A Good Dusting*, p.243.

43   Wolseley, *The Soldier's Pocket Book*, 3rd edition, pp.168–9, 181–3, 186–9; Lloyd, *The Drums of Kumasi*, p.88; *Report of the Colour Committee with Appendix*, C. 3536 (1883), XV, p.v; Forbes, *History of the Army Ordnance Services*, Vol.2, p.100.

44   Stanley, *Toil and Trouble*, p.255; Marling, *Rifleman and Hussar*, pp.81, 129; Morris, *The Washing of the Spears*, pp.468, 577–8; Knight, *Brave Men's Blood*, p.176; Bates, *The Abyssinian Difficulty*, p.153; Callwell, *Small Wars*, pp.110–12, 193, 391; Lehmann, *The First Boer War*, pp.151, 153–5; 260; Private M. Tuck, diary, 28 January 1881, Tuck Mss., NAM, 7005–21.

45   Baden-Powell, *The Downfall of Prempeh*, pp.110, 142, 144; Belich, *The New Zealand Wars*, p.23; Bates, *The Abyssinian Difficulty*, p.204; Marling, *Rifleman and Hussar*, p.57; Emery, *Marching over Africa*, pp.70, 113, 181–2.

46   Marling, *Rifleman and Hussar*, pp.83, 103; Sergeant Danby to Adie, 1 March 1884, Danby Mss., NAM, 7003–2.

47   Brackenbury, *The Ashanti War*, Vol.1, p.367; Viscount Wolseley, 'The Negro as a Soldier', *Fortnightly Review*, Vol.50 (1888), pp.689–703; Col. R.S.S. Baden-Powell, *The Matabele Campaign: Being a Narrative of the Campaign in Suppressing the Native Rising in Matabeleland and Mashonaland* (Methuen; London, 1897), p.63; Emery, *Marching over Africa*, p.96; Callwell, *Small Wars*, pp.72, 75–6, 78–80, 109, 406.

48   Churchill, *The River War*, pp.284–301; Capt. T.A. MacKenzie, Lt. J.S. Ewart and Lt. C. Findley, *Historical Records of the Queen's Own Cameron Highlanders*, 6 Vols. (Blackwood; Edinburgh, 1909–52), Vol.1, pp.309–10; C.L. Kingsford, *The Story of the Royal Warwickshire Regiment (Formerly the Sixth Foot)*, (Country Life; London, 1921), pp.109–11; Callwell, *Small Wars*, p.279; Viscount Wolseley, 'An English View of the American Civil War', *North American Review*, No.394 (1889), pp.278–92.

49   Lyttelton, *Eighty Years*, p.212.

50   Maj. G.F. Ellison, 'Considerations influencing the selection of officers for command and the staff', Ellison Mss., NAM, 8704–35, No.30; Haig to Henrietta Haig, 1 April 1898 and Wood to Haig, 25 April 1898, Haig Mss., NLS, Acc. 3155, No.6; Symons, *England's Pride*, p.287; G.H. Cassar, *Kitchener: Architect of Victory* (W. Kimber; London, 1977), pp.89–91.

11

The Second Boer War:
the ultimate test

The Second Boer War proved to be the ultimate challenge for the army reformed by Cardwell, championed by Wolseley, and organised according to the Stanhope criteria. Despite the Boer successes in 1881, the London-based press largely derided the ultimatum from President Paul Kruger which arrived in London on 10 October 1899. Government Ministers were astonished but delighted that the Boers had brought matters to a climax after several months of mounting tension and four years of acrimonious relations. Wolseley was also relieved; since mid-August he had urged the government to reinforce the the garrison of some 12,000 troops in South Africa, and somewhat belatedly, on 8 September, the cabinet resolved to send 10,000 soldiers, mainly from India. As these reinforcements largely reached Natal by early October, and as the cabinet responded to the ultimatum by authorising the despatch of a further army corps of 47,000 men under Sir Redvers Buller, Wolseley exuded confidence. He had confidently predicted that any force sent from Britain would include 'the very ablest soldiers . . . thoroughly equipped for war', and would present 'a very different condition of things from that which existed in the Army sent to the Crimea in 1854'.[1]

The war aroused intense emotions. Within Britain imperial passions were at their height, as barely a year had passed since Omdurman and the Fashoda incident in which French forces had recoiled from a confrontation with Kitchener's army. *The Times* had published 'The Old Issue' by Kipling, which denounced Kruger as 'cruel in the shadow, crafty in the sun' and reminded England of her traditional opposition to tyranny.[2] The majority of the press, Conservative-inclined, firmly supported the war. The Liberal press, like the Liberal Party, was divided. *The Westminster Gazette, The Daily Chronicle,* and *The Daily News,* until it changed hands in January 1901, followed Lord Rosebery and the Liberal Imperialists in support of the war. *The Morning Leader, The Star,* and above all *The Manchester Guardian* endorsed the pro-Boer sentiments of Liberals like Sir William Harcourt, John Morley and David Lloyd George. Anti-war sentiments were voiced, both vigorously and passionately, but had little impact amid the jingoistic clamour. Enormous crowds gathered at the pro-war meetings and cheered the soldiers on their departure for the Cape.

Ministerial spokesmen shared the confidence of Wolseley. George Wyndham, the Parliamentary Under-Secretary of State at the War Office, asserted that 'the Army is more efficient than at any time since Waterloo'.[3] The Ministers and their civil servants revelled in the efficiency of the mobilisation arrangements and the return of 98 per cent of the reservists to the Colours. Sir Ralph Knox, the Permanent Under-Secretary, wrote, 'I peg along cheerily much elated with the success of short service and all our machinery, and the diminution of Forster & Co.'[4] Campbell-Bannerman, though highly critical of the government's diplomacy, commended the preparation of Britain's largest expeditionary force for nearly a century. As he assured the Commons on 20 October 1899, the organisation of the army, 'for which hardly anybody sometimes had a good word to say . . . has completely fulfilled the purpose for which it was created'.[5]

Editors, expecting a prompt and decisive triumph, despatched war correspondents in unprecedented numbers. Veterans like Bennet Burleigh of *The Daily Telegraph* and Melton Prior of *The Illustrated London News* worked alongside the rising stars of the profession, G.W. Steevens of *The Daily Mail* and Angus Hamilton of *The Times.* Dr Arthur Conan Doyle sallied forth as a correspondent and wrote an immensely popular account of the war. Leo Amery, a Fellow of All Souls, went out to cover the Boer perspective for *The Times* in September 1899, but was expelled from the Boer capitals and remained in South Africa as the *de facto* head of the newspaper's team of correspondents, which at one time included twenty journalists. Winston Churchill was hired by *The Morning Post* at £250 a month, with four months' minimum guarantee of employment, all expenses paid, and entire discretion as to movements and opinions – the best terms, he thought, ever offered to a war correspondent from Britain.[6]

The plethora of journalists ensured neither reliable nor accurate reporting. With so many rivals in the field, some reporters sacrificed accuracy for speed. Others preferred fiction to fact; Edgar Wallace, who had gone to South Africa as a medical orderly, joined the staff of *The Daily Mail* and made his name by writing vivid, but largely fictitious, accounts of atrocity stories. Most met the expectations of their editors and readers, with descriptions of the 'dauntless bravery of English officers' and the daring deeds of the 'sweating, swearing, grimy, dirty, fearless and generous Tommy'.[7] They found great difficulty in covering a conflict spread over immense distances and amidst strict censorship. Pressing to the front no longer sufficed, as battles were dominated by long-range rifles and smokeless powder. 'A battle,' wrote J.B. Atkins, had become 'vague, scattered, sometimes even insufferably tedious. . . . After Colenso I spoke to an onlooker who had not the least idea that the British arms had suffered a reverse.'[8] The journalists relied increasingly upon second-hand information and depended upon the military, in many instances, for a line of communications. They failed to reveal many of the scandals of the war, which were exposed by visitors from Britain. Emily Hobhouse, a Quaker, revealed the conditions in the concentration camps, and William Burdett-Coutts, a Member of Parliament, drew attention to the appalling conditions in the military hospitals, in which a large proportion of the 16,168 deaths from wounds or disease occurred. Similarly, some of the most critical reporting of the military operations came from home-based journalists, like Captain William Elliot Cairnes of *The Westminster Gazette*. He not only wrote regularly for the newspaper about the war from November 1899 to April 1901, but he also produced several books on the army, including *An Absent-minded War* (1900), *Social Life in the Army* (1900) and *The Army from Within* (1901). Spiced with pungent, critical and sarcastic asides, these books earned widespread acclaim once the early popularity of the war began to wane.

This reaction took time to set in. The early investments of Mafeking, Kimberley and Ladysmith were perceived as setbacks but hardly disasters. The outnumbered British forces had faced a resourceful, mobile and well armed enemy, equipped with the excellent Mauser 0·276 rifle and guns of the latest design. Buller's army corps was confidently expected to redress the situation and to sweep back the Boers with a direct thrust at Bloemfontein and

Pretoria. Buller, who arrived in Cape Town one day after Sir George White's humiliating reverse at Nicholson's Nek (30 October 1899), chose to split his forces in order to relieve the sieges, before repulsing the Boers and invading their republics. If the strategy proved controversial, the implementation foundered disastrously with the three columns plunging to successive defeats at Stormberg, Magersfontein and Colenso – the infamous 'Black Week' of 10–15 December 1899. The standard of generalship and staff work was cruelly exposed by the appalling reconnaissance in all three battles, the leaving of 561 soldiers behind to be taken prisoner during the retreat from Stormberg, the firing upon the Highlanders in quarter column formation before they could deploy for battle at Magersfontein, and Buller's choice of a frontal assault in broad daylight across an exposed terrain at Colenso. Subordinate officers compounded the disaster at Colenso; Colonel Charles Long advanced precipitately, seeking direct fire positions for his batteries as far forward as possible (effectively well within range of the Boer riflemen), and Major-General Arthur Fitzroy Hart marched his Irish Brigade in close formation (other than its leading battalion of Dublin Fusiliers) into a U shaped loop in the Tugela river, where the brigade came under withering fire from right, left and front.

Although news of the surrenders, the loss of ten guns at Colenso, and the casualties (947 killed, wounded or missing at Magersfontein, and another 1,139 at Colenso)[9] shattered complacency at home, it did not provoke an immediate outburst of indignation and criticism. Editors urged the country to stand firm and encouraged a new rush to the Colours. The War Office called out the whole of the First Class Army Reserve, invited the Militia to come forward, and waived the bar on non-regular troops. The government sought to revive confidence by appointing Roberts as the new commander-in-chief in South Africa, with Kitchener as his chief of staff, but found popular support undermined by Buller's continuing difficulties in Natal. Editorial outrage erupted after the defeat at Spion Kop (24 January 1900), especially as another fiasco followed at Vaal Krantz a fortnight later. Conservative and Liberal papers fulminated upon the incompetence of the military and the failings of 'the system', relieved only by the courage of the soldiers.

The strident criticism was partially defused by the news of belated successes in February. While Buller eventually broke through in Natal, where the terrain was particularly difficult, to relieve Ladysmith (28 February 1900), Roberts transformed the war in the western theatre. Having resolved to strike east from the railway, he amassed a field force of some 40,000 men and 108 guns, reorganised the transport into one central department (a highly controversial move), prepared an elaborate deception strategy for the Boers, and relied upon the mobility of a new cavalry division under French to relieve Kimberley and cut off General Cronje's forces at Paardeberg. Roberts also issued new tactical instructions, 'Notes for Guidance in South African Warfare', to counter the threat from smokeless, magazine rifles and to operate more prudently in South African conditions. These stressed the need for careful reconnaissance before an attack, more use of cover and extended formations by the infantry, the avoidance of positions within range of enemy infantry by the artillery, the use of continuous rather than sporadic bombardments, more marching and better care of their horses by the cavalry, and a delegation of responsibility to battalion and company commanders in the field. The subsequent flank march to Bloemfontein changed 'the whole face of the war', only marred by Kitchener's costly frontal assault at Paardeberg and the failure to prevent the Boer retreat from Poplar Grove (7 March). The capture of Bloemfontein (4 April), the relief of Mafeking (17 May) and the capture of Pretoria (5 June) consummated the offensive of Roberts.[10] The government promptly exploited the divisions in the Liberal ranks by securing a resounding triumph in the 'khaki election'. Equally confident of victory after the advance to Komatipoort, which severed the Boers' last rail link with the outside world, Roberts returned home in November 1900 to receive a hero's welcome, the Garter, an earldom and a grant of £100,000.

The war had only moved into its third phase. Once their main cities had fallen, the Boers retreated to the veld, from which they waged a resourceful guerilla campaign. Unable to engage the Boers in a 'decisive battle', Kitchener settled for a war of attrition. He tried to deny the Boers subsistence and support by continuing and expanding the internment policy begun by Roberts. The burning of Boer farms and the corralling of women and children in concentration camps proved counterproductive at first. It embittered the Boer commandos, relieved them of their family responsibilities, and added to their numbers (as many boys under sixteen years and elderly men above sixty years preferred to take up arms rather than go to the camps). It also diverted soldiers from their combat duties to burn farms, move civilians, and guard the camps. The soldiers had mixed feelings about the task: if some Argyll and Sutherland High-landers cheered as farms were burnt at Rustenberg, and Lieutenant Francis favoured a 'war of extermination . . . against the class of animal who is fighting still', Captains Stewart, Crossman and Bellew all expressed misgivings about farm burning. Even so, they generally accepted it as a regrettable necessity, a method of retaliating against an elusive foe who sniped at their columns and harassed their lines of supply.[11]

The policy steadily expanded in scope. More than forty camps were constructed for whites, holding over 116,000 inmates by the end of the war, and another sixty camps for blacks, containing over 115,000 inmates. Although conditions varied considerably from camp to camp, depending upon the personalities and policies of the superintendents and the facilities available, rations and fuel were often in short supply, the sanitary arrangements unhygienic, and, in some camps, the water insufficient. As the death toll began to mount (eventually some 28,000 Boers died, 22,000 of whom were under sixteen years of age), the conditions were exposed by Emily Hob-house among others. Campbell-Bannerman led the denunciation at home: 'When was a war not a war?' he asked. 'When it is carried on by methods of barbarism in South Africa.'[12]

If such criticism exacerbated political divisions at home, it infuriated Kitchener, members of his staff, and many other officers. As the pro-Boer speeches were widely reported, and their writings circulated in the Boer republics, soldiers feared that they simply boosted Boer morale, prolonged the war, and increased the toll of British casualties. Colonel J. Spencer Ewart, who served on Kit-chener's staff, regarded any expression of support for the Boers as inexcusable: 'how many brave men – how many of my friends – would now be alive, if Campbell-Bannerman, Lloyd George, Stead and Co. had possessed a decent sense of patriotism!'[13] Officers also resented, if not quite so bitterly, the generalised and vituperative criticisms of the press. These critics, they felt, had failed to appreciate the difficulties of the war in South Africa, particularly the demands of a guerilla campaign, the size of the country, and the problems of protecting a railway over 1,000 miles in length. Kitchener aptly summarised these feelings:

It makes the army feel disgusted that the press at home should show delight in running down their work, and criticising from a comfortable arm-chair or railway carriage what is being done.[14]

The mutual recriminations reflected the depth of the frustrations which developed during the conflict. The Boers prolonged the war by exploiting their superior horsemanship, scouting skills and knowledge of the country. Christiaan De Wet and his forces repeatedly eluded capture, and, in the third 'Great De Wet Hunt', the Boer general spent six weeks (27 January 1901 – 11 March 1901) evading the attentions of fifteen columns, totalling 15,000 men, before leading some 2,000 commandos to safety. Kitchener adopted an increasingly methodical policy; he employed the blockhouses (originally erected to protect the railways) linked with barbed wire to divide the land mass into manageable units so that his columns could sweep and net the Boers in a more systematic manner. Although he commanded an army of over 250,000 men, he could employ only about 30 per cent of this number in combat duties (with the remainder either sick, wounded, or employed in passive tasks, patrolling the railway, manning isolated garrisons and blockhouses, guarding depots and coastal towns, and assisting in a myriad of support duties). The 'bags' of captives and confiscations failed to produce any dramatic results, and the Boers persisted with their lightning raids upon British columns or camps (and in one of the last of these, at Tweebosch, 7 March 1902, they captured Lord Methuen). Nevertheless, the process of attrition exacted its toll; by April 1902 the number of armed Boers and rebels had been reduced to about 23,000. Their spirits had fallen, too; when they eventually sought peace, the Boer leaders expressed deep concern about the devastation of their country and the moral and physical welfare of their families. Even if made partly for purposes of propaganda, these admissions testified to the impact of Kitchener's methods.[15]

The war had become increasingly unpopular in Britain. Expected by many to be over by Christmas 1899, it lasted for another twenty-nine months and cost the British taxpayer some £201,000,000. It required the services of 256,340 officers and men from the regular army, 109,048 from the Militia, Yeomanry and Volunteers, 30,633 from the colonies and another 50,000 to 60,000 raised in South Africa. Out of this estimated force of 448,435 officers and men, 5,774 were killed in action and 16,168 died of wounds or disease. Another 22,829 were wounded and 75,430 left South Africa as sick or wounded. Animal wastage was even more prodigious; the War

Office estimated that 400,346 horses, mules and donkeys were 'expended' during the war, and a further 15,960 'lost on the voyage' to South Africa (out of the 669,575 used in the conflict).[16]

If critics agreed that the war had exposed many shortcomings in the army, they disagreed about the various reforms. Dilke, Wilkinson and Arnold-Forster resumed their attacks upon the Cardwell system. Arthur Conan Doyle, in a highly readable account of the war, urged that lessons for 'the modern battle' should be learned from the conflict, and other critics advocated the reform of military tactics, staff work, marksmanship, hospital provision, intelligence collection and many other matters. Leo Amery, as the editor of *The Times History of the War in South Africa*, prepared a particularly influential indictment of the pre-war army, both at the time (the first two volumes appeared in 1900 and 1902 respectively) and in later years. The history was a colossal piece of scholarship, spanning 3,498 pages in six volumes and an index, and appeared over the course of nine years. Amery devoted himself to the task for over five years, and contributed to four of the volumes. He sought to write a serious, substantial and 'frankly critical' account, eschewing any attempt 'to rival the picturesque imaginativeness of Dr. Conan Doyle'. He also endeavoured to make his writing as accurate as possible and so established the practice of circulating drafts and second drafts to senior officers and other sources, often to as many as 100 people, before preparing a final revised version for publication. He derived considerable assistance from Roberts, Kitchener, Hamilton, Wood, Sir George White, Sir Henry Colvile, Henry Wilson, and Altham of the War Office Intelligence Division. Roberts and his staff readily assisted because the history, which acquired a reputation for accuracy and for the 'lucidity' and 'brilliance' of its prose, promoted the cause of army reform. Amery subsequently admitted that his motivations were 'in essence propagandist – to secure the reform of our Army in preparation for coming dangers'.[17]

The *Times* history overshadowed the official history, which was begun under Henderson, continued after his death by Maurice, and was completed in 1910 by the historical section of the Committee of Imperial Defence. Precluded from any discussion of political matters, and required to follow 'a sober, grave style of writing', the official history concentrated upon the minutiae of the campaign and minimised criticism of the military. The *Times* history had much more influence over the way in which future historians would assess the army's performance in the South African War and upon the judgements of some military biographers. In *Goodbye Dolly Gray*, first published in 1959, Rayne Kruger reiterates many of history's criticisms of the pre-war army, of Buller, and of the cavalry's predilection for the *arme blanche*. Julian Symons in *Buller's Campaign* (1963) acknowledges his debt to the *Times* history and asserts that 'Amery's general assessments of military actions seem to need very little amendment'. In a fuller history of the war, *The Great Boer War* (1976), Byron Farwell quotes from the *Times* history on twenty-four occasions and endorses its fierce critique of Buller. Many other historians have echoed these criticisms.[18]

More recent research has amplified, qualified or plainly contradicted some judgements of the *Times* history. In *The Boer War* (1979), based upon a vast array of manuscript material, Thomas Pakenham has sought to redress Amery's bias against Buller and in favour of Roberts. He does not claim that Buller was a *great* general any more than Roberts was, and admits that Buller made 'mistakes'. He rightly emphasises that any assessment of Buller's generalship should recognise the topographical difficulties which he encountered in Natal, the animosities derived from the feud between the rings of Wolseley and Roberts, and the partisanship of Amery, who was responsible for orchestrating a press campaign which resulted in Buller's dismissal from the Aldershot command in 1901. Yet, in seeking to rehabilitate Buller's reputation, he largely relies upon Buller's evidence before the Royal Commission on the South African War headed by Lord Elgin (which other scholars have seen and have not regarded as mitigating their criticisms of Buller's generalship)[19] and some letters written by Buller after the battle of Colenso. He lapses into special pleading over Buller's 'surrender' cable to White – 'If only Buller could have expressed himself more plainly, and less bluntly' – and proffers only a few cursory remarks on Vaal Krantz, where the British forces suffered 333 casualties and had to withdraw again across the Tugela river. As the Vaal Krantz attack was conceived and commanded by Buller, it could not be blamed on any of his subordinates. Finally, Pakenham claims that Buller, in his advance upon Ladysmith, was the 'innovator in countering Boer tactics': 'The proper use of cover, of infantry advancing in rushes, co-ordinated in turn with creeping barrages of artillery: these were the tactics of truly modern war, first evolved by Buller in Natal.'[20]

Undoubtedly the army adapted its tactics and operational skills to the conditions in South Africa. Officers became much more adept at devising, and their men at constructing, field defences; there were general improvements in marksmanship, in the use of cover, and in combined arms operations. At Bergendal (27 August 1900), the 2nd Rifle Brigade and the 1st Inniskilling Fusiliers advanced closely behind a creeping barrage of shrapnel, which largely suppressed the fire from the enemy trenches. Infantry increasingly advanced in open columns, launched attacks in vastly extended formations, and used cover and covering fire as they moved through fire-swept zones. The artillery chose their gun positions with greater care, employed the deliberate method of coming into action, and utilised available cover. Gunners sought to improve their reconnaissance, which had produced ineffective preparatory bombardments (particularly at Magersfontein) and had contributed to their most serious disasters and loss of guns (Colenso, Sannah's Post and Lindley). They latterly organised scouting parties for each battery, equipped with binoculars, telescopes and compasses. These travelled well ahead of the front and flanks and transmitted information by signalling with flags, lamps and heliographs.[21]

Nevertheless, the threat posed by smokeless, long-range, magazine rifles was not new – it had been extensively debated in military circles in Britain in the 1890s. It had also been experienced in the Tirah campaign, where the Afridis had fired upon the expeditionary force with stolen British rifles. Whereas Buller doubted that these weapons had any revolutionary implications – 'when improvements are made in military arms and tactics they almost always follow along the same lines'[22] – others evinced more concern. Colonel Ian Hamilton, a Tirah veteran, came to Ladysmith convinced that his brigade would have to operate in greatly extended formations. Having trained them in this mode, he deployed the 1st Battalion, Devonshire Regiment, at Elandslaagte (21 October 1899) over a front of some 700 yards, with a depth from front to rear of nearly a mile. Roberts also resolved to implement 'radical' changes in tactics and issued his 'Notes for Guidance in South African Warfare' in the wake of Spion Kop. The 'Indian' officers indubitably contributed to the tactical innovations, just as Buller's forces clearly demonstrated more effective fieldcraft and co-ordinated artillery/infantry operations in their assaults upon Cingolo, Monte Cristo, Hlangwane, Inniskilling Hill and finally Pieter's Hill before relieving Ladysmith.[23]

Amery, though, was not primarily concerned with personal criticism of Buller. He regarded the latter as a product of, even the 'typical embodiment of the British military system'. The late Victorian army, he argued, suffered from a deadening peacetime routine, make-believe manoeuvres, and the absence of any scientific study and planning for war. 'As a school of military training,' he asserted, 'the Army was nothing more or less than a gigantic Dotheboys Hall'; as a 'fighting machine', he added, 'it was largely a sham'.[24] Even Lord Roberts, on reading the drafts of volume 2 of the *Times* history, thought that such criticisms erred 'on the side of severity',[25] and several scholars have sought to redress the balance. Howard Bailes, in particular, has argued that the late Victorian army radically improved its organisation, kept abreast of technological changes, developed effective supply and transport services, studied foreign wars, and refined its tactics and methods of training. He rightly lauds the achievements of Sir Evelyn Wood 'as the guiding spirit in the reform of British training', and emphasises the tactical changes adumbrated in the pre-war drill books. The faulty tactics of 1899 and 1900, he claims, 'were not a consequence of the Aldershot teaching of the 1890s. They arose from a failure to act in accordance with it.'[26]

Bailes concedes that the practical application of these ideas may have been at an early stage when the war erupted, but if any officer should have been fully conversant with them it was surely the Officer Commanding the 1st Infantry Brigade at Aldershot (1897–99), namely Major-General Hart. He had his own tactical preferences, however. In commanding the Irish Brigade at Colenso, and in the assault upon Inniskilling Hill (23 February 1900), he kept his men 'well in hand', with the bulk of his forces moving in quarter columns as they marched towards the battle, and sought to push them on in frontal attacks despite considerable losses. If he had failed to grasp the new tactical thinking, he was by no means alone. Wood accepted that several brigade commanders had proved unsatisfactory in South Africa. In his evidence before the Elgin Commission, he deprecated the paucity of Staff College graduates in the pre-war army, the limitations of the training facilities, especially for battalions stationed outside Aldershot, and the standards attained in shooting, outpost duties, reconnoitring, horsemastership and night marching. In short, he recognised, as did Roberts and Hamilton, that the pre-war training had suffered from serious shortcomings, and that these ought to be corrected in post-war reforms.[27]

In the fifth volume of the *Times* history, Erskine Childers presented an extensive critique of the cavalry's performance in South Africa. He deprecated the priority accorded to the *arme blanche* in pre-war training, condemned the arm for its lack of 'inspiration and dashing leadership', and criticised its training and equipment as ill-adapted to South African conditions. He claimed that the arm had failed in its reconnaissance duties, and that 'skilled mounted riflemen can do all that cavalry of the old stamp can do, can do it better, and can do much more besides'.[28] Childers would subsequently write *War and the Arme Blanche* with the co-operation of Roberts and the mounted infantry lobby, and his criticisms closely followed those which Roberts had aired during the war itself. During his eleven months in field command Roberts had dismissed twenty-one senior officers, including eleven of the seventeen cavalry commanders, and he doubted whether any more than one or two of the remaining six were fit to lead a cavalry regiment. He berated the arm for its lack of initiative, failures of reconnaissance, and inadequate horsemastership. He criticised French for his failure to sever the enemy's line of retreat after the action at Poplar Grove, and maintained that 'large bodies' of mounted infantry would produce more satisfactory results.[29]

Stephen Badsey and the Marquess of Anglesey have qualified this critique. Badsey rightly emphasises that the arm suffered from a lack of numbers throughout the conflict. Outnumbered by the Boers, it depended on remounts of variable quality and on supplies of forage and water which were sometimes late in arrival and had to be shared with the mounted infantry and the various bodies of irregular horse. Badsey stresses, too, that the original mounted infantry, like the regular cavalry, had to adapt to South African conditions, and that their pre-war training of ten weeks in a year hardly sufficed to produce good horsemen. The new corps of mounted rifles – Roberts's Horse, Kitchener's Horse and the companies formed from every infantry battalion in South Africa – knew nothing of riding and horses at first and were precipitately thrown into action. Moreover the cavalry, despite its periodic failings against a highly mobile if unconventional adversary, had some successes. It achieved a notable, if solitary, triumph for the *arme blanche* at Elandslaagte, where the 5th Dragoon Guards and the 5th Lancers routed the fleeing Boers; mounted an open-order charge at Klip Drift (15

February 1900), relieved Kimberley, and assisted in the capture of Cronje at Paardeberg (27 February 1900). Its commanders disputed the allegations of failure to capture De Wet and Kruger after Poplar Grove by claiming that the orders from the commander-in-chief's staff were unclear, and that the plan was highly ambitious in view of the debilitated condition of their horses.[30]

More fundamentally, the war appeared to undermine the case for the *arme blanche*. Under Kitchener's command, the cavalry were largely converted into mounted riflemen. They lost their lances, carbines and swords (in all regiments other than those under French's command) and received long-range rifles, which became their principal weapon. They also became more mobile once mounted on the small native South African horses, which were used to living off the rank, dried-up veld grass and occasional handfuls of Indian corn. Kitchener's mobile columns sustained their drives against the Boers and steadily restricted their area of operations, but cavalry commanders disputed whether these tactics could serve as the harbinger of future reforms. They argued that unconventional tactics had to be adopted to counter the Boers, who lacked any regular cavalry. They also maintained that the loss of their swords had been a serious handicap (Haig quoted the remark of Jan Smuts that abandoning the *arme blanche* was the biggest mistake of the war). They stressed that the *arme blanche* had triumphed at Elandslaagte (albeit after the infantry, assisted by the dismounted action of the Imperial Light Horse and the artillery, had compelled the enemy to retreat), and that the threat of the *arme blanche* had compelled the Boers to withdraw at Zand River (10 May 1900). But the Zand River incident merely confirmed that the war had not produced any self-evident lessons, only a range of experiences which could be interpreted to suit the preferences of the interpreter. Whereas French regarded this action as a triumph for the moral force of cold steel, Hamilton decried it as a 'fiasco', since the Boers were able to retreat in good order, without any pursuit by an exhausted cavalry. The Zand River incident, he claimed, had finally eroded his faith in the efficacy of shock tactics.[31]

Less debatable was the need to improve the lamentable standard of horsemastership (the art of looking after horses) displayed in South Africa by experienced horsemen (cavalry, trained mounted infantry and Imperial Yeomanry but not by the field and horse artillery and some irregular bodies of horse, notably Colonel

Michael Rimington's 'Tigers'). Shortcomings in the care and treatment of horses were fully exposed in a relatively long war conducted over an extensive, and often inhospitable, terrain. Many of these failings derived from pre-war training, where cavalrymen knew much more about stable management than about the care of horses in the field. Only by practice in prolonged and regular manoeuvres which simulated war conditions could cavalrymen become more adept at caring for their horses: 'hitherto', admitted Haig, 'there has been too much pampering in peacetime'.[32] Lack of manoeuvres, though, was hardly a sufficient explanation, as it applied equally to the artillery, whose standards of horse care were widely recognised as infinitely superior. As the Marquess of Anglesey indicates, the difference was largely psychological; care of the horse was a prerequisite in artillery training, as it was only by maintaining fit teams of horses that the arm could rapidly deploy its guns in action. Artillerymen, therefore, remained dismounted for as long as possible, while the cavalry soldiers, fearing any reduction to the status of footslogging infantry, preferred to be seen off their horses's backs as little as possible.[33]

The vast number of remounts enabled cavalrymen to indulge these proclivities. The 'softened' muscular condition of many horses on their arrival at the front (after lengthy sea voyages and inadequate periods of time for rest and acclimatisation), and the inadequate feeding which frequently left horses half starved, hardly encouraged better standards of horsemastership. The waste of horseflesh was exacerbated by the conditions experienced on the remount trains in South Africa, the lack of officers and men to accompany these trains and man the feeding stations, the shortages of farriers, shoeing smiths and veterinary officers, and the failure to establish veterinary hospitals until late in the war. Undoubtedly the treatment of horses in South Africa compounded the difficulties of the Remounts Department, headed by Major-General William R. Truman. Occupying a fourth-floor flat in Victoria Street, Truman's tiny staff was normally involved in purchasing about 2,500 horses annually to meet the army's peacetime requirements. Since 1891, it had planned to procure 25,000 horses to support the mobilisation, and replace the wastage in war, of two army corps, a cavalry division and line of communication troops. Underfunded and staffed by men with limited drive and ambition, the department never anticipated how it might meet the expansion required in a large-scale war, and struggled to meet such requirements. It had to rely upon numerous vendors at home and overseas, some of whom were none too scrupulous about the prices and quality of the animals for sale. Examined by a court of inquiry towards the end of the war, the department was largely exonerated of the allegations of corruption, Truman was acquitted of any personal blame, and the department praised for sustaining a supply of horses which exceeded the numerical demands from South Africa. The Elgin Commission, nonetheless, found it incredible that the department had imagined that it could continue buying 'in a leisurely way, through accustomed channels, from recognised dealers' and so meet the demands of mobilisation and wastage of a war involving two army corps.[34]

The supply services generally had to readjust from the constraints of the Stanhope criteria to the emerging requirements of a much larger conflict. Their achievements are briefly acknowledged by Amery in his second volume (written before the Elgin Commission had heard the evidence of Brackenbury) and are more fully reviewed in the second half of his sixth volume. Dr Andrew Page, employing unpublished as well as published sources, amplifies these accounts. The supply services, he argues, were 'on the whole, remarkably successful', and the administration, both in the field and in the War Office, generally overcame the difficulties caused by the scale and duration of the conflict. As Brackenbury revealed, the army had embarked on the war with an appalling lack of reserves and stores (in all categories save rifles, lances, carbines and pistols). Even by mid-December 1899, he had sent out quantities of saddlery, harness, tents, camp equipment and general stores which far exceeded the pre-war stocks. He had to overcome severe shortages in meeting the requests for small arms ammunition and clothing. Out of the authorised stock of 151,000,000 rounds of small arms ammunition held on 31 March 1899, 66,000,000 – the entire stock of Mark IV expanding ammunition – had been declared unserviceable (once it had been found that the bullets tended to strip in hot and dirty barrels). Having sent out 50,000,000 rounds at the outbreak of hostilities, Brackenbury soon received requests for 3,000,000 rounds per week from South Africa at a time when the weekly output from the ordnance factories and trade was only 2,500,000 rounds. He met the demand by nearly emptying the reserves, by sending supplies from colonial stations, and by ensuring that the ordnance factories laid down extra plant and worked incessantly. Similarly he faced considerable difficulties in reclothing all the troops sent out to South Africa when the reserves of clothing did not even meet the peacetime requirements, and when the expansion of the forces and the degree of wear and tear had exceeded all expectations. In a minute, dated 15 December 1899, he requested additional expenditure in excess of £10 million to meet these costs, claiming that 'we are attempting to maintain the largest Empire the world has ever seen with armaments and reserves that would be insufficient for a third class military power'.[35]

Brackenbury also responded to the early criticisms that British guns had been outranged and the artillery humiliated in South Africa. In January 1900 he pressed the cabinet to consider the question of artillery rearmament and promptly gained approval for the appointment of an equipment committee under Sir George Marshall. As senior artillery officers were not required during the guerilla campaign, the committee was constituted on 18 January 1901 and had the advantage of inspecting eighteen batteries of quick-firing field guns, which the government had purchased from the Ehrhardt factories. Roberts claimed that 'The purchase of the German Field Gun has advanced us by 5, if not by 10 years in our knowledge of what Field Guns might do.'[36]

The war itself had not revealed anything about the possibilities of quick-firing artillery (guns which could fire twenty to thirty rounds instead of four to five rounds per minute because their recoil was mechanically absorbed by brakes or buffers). The Boers had not possessed any quick-firing guns, while the only British quick-firers were the Naval guns (the 4·7 inch and the twelve-pounder gun), which were too heavy for field firing purposes. Senior artillery officers simply seized this opportunity to proceed with a rearmament which they had sought before the war, and to incorporate specific refinements based upon their war experience. Marshall wanted only four types of gun, to simplify the process of ammunition supply. He placed a premium upon mobility for the horse artillery (to cope with the extended fronts of modern war), a more powerful shell for the field artillery, and a longer effective range for both (out to 6,000 yards). He favoured developing field batteries of heavy guns, as the 4·7 inch and 5 inch guns had performed better than the field howitzers in South Africa. Like the Boer Creusot 155 mm guns known as 'Long Toms', they had exploited the potential for long-range bombardments over the large, treeless topographical features and in clear climatic conditions. Despite the disappointment of lyddite shells, which tended to bury much of their explosive force within craters in the veld, Marshall favoured retaining field howitzers, as they had proved effective in the more mountainous terrain of Natal. Even so, enhancing the range and not the shell power of the new guns was the main priority derived from the South African experience.[37]

During the war all support arms had to be bolstered by civilian auxiliaries. The Royal Engineers, who had 694 officers and men in South Africa on 1 October 1899, found that they had to deploy nearly 7,000 officers and men in South Africa during the conflict, as well as some 1,500 engineers from the Militia and Volunteers. Deployed in various sections and field companies, they assisted in fortifying besieged towns, road making, bridging rivers, arranging water supplies and blockhouse construction. Specialist sections dealt with telegraphs, laying 18,236 miles of wire and repairing much of the existing 9,395 miles of wire, which the Boers tried to wreck, and so facilitated the 13,575,779 telegraphic transactions during the war. Other sections specialised in balloon reconnaissance, directing artillery fire at Nicholson's Nek and Paardeberg, in erecting telephone links between blockhouses, and in operating the searchlights and traction engines employed in the conflict. Above all, the Engineers under Major Girouard took charge of the railway system, involving 4,628 miles of railway in the British colonies, the Boer republics and the adjacent Portuguese territory. The railway sections, like their telegraph counterparts, relied heavily upon civilian assistance, including native labour and special enlistments from home. They provided invaluable support for Roberts in the three weeks prior to his march on Bloemfontein, moving 27,025 men, 13,590 horses and mules, and 24,168 tons of stores along a single-track railway to different places on the line north of the Orange river.[38]

The Army Service Corps, the Army Ordnance Corps, the Army Pay Corps and the Provost Service all found that their pre-war establishments were hopelessly inadequate to cope with a war of this scale and duration. They had to employ untrained men from other units or large numbers of civilian personnel (indeed, civilian clerks and auxiliaries outnumbered the regulars in the pay and ordnance services and were regarded as vital for the 'success of the supply arrangements locally').[39] The large scale of the operations and the reliance upon mobile columns in the guerilla phase of the war posed problems for each of the services. The military police struggled to contain the looting, straggling and, as the war dragged on, drunkenness among the regular, irregular and colonial forces. They had to guard prisoners of war before they were sent back to base, collect arms from surrendered Boers, protect water holes (lest they were poisoned by the Boers), and keep captured towns in order until local police forces were organised. The ordnance services having provided the stores, camping equipment and ammunition (including shells for fifteen different types of gun) throughout the first year of the conflict, found that it had to meet somewhat different demands thereafter. It had to provide the tentage, bedding and clothing for the concentration camps, supplies for the large columns of mounted infantry (even the gunners either broke up their formations into single gun units or abandoned their guns and became the Royal Artillery Mounted Rifles), and all the equipment to build and furnish the blockhouses and construct the miles of barbed wire and cable connections between them. As the small pay corps, even with civilian assistance, could not perform all its tasks properly in a war of this size, an enormous strain was placed upon the already overworked company captains, who had to pay their men and monitor their company finances. The system, as the Accountant-General admitted, came close to breaking down.[40]

The Army Service Corps encountered a particularly diverse range of problems. Quite apart from the shortage of trained personnel, the quantity of transport was initially deficient and the difficulties of integrating the movement of stores by railway, mule- and ox-drawn wagon were never fully overcome. The ASC personnel were responsible for the ox-drawn supply columns and parks, servicing brigades, divisional and army corps troops, while regimental transport officers moved forward the supplies for fighting and subsistence by mule to regimental units. Roberts feared that this regimental system of transport was too rigid to respond to the conditions of field service in South Africa. Prior to the march on Bloemfontein, he tried to introduce a more centralised system (other than in Natal) in the hope of creating a reserve of transport for use in specific operations. The abrupt withdrawal of the subsistence transport from the regiments and the abolition of supply columns caused delays, confusion and resentment among many regiments. As military opinion was sharply divided over the merits of the change, a reversion to the old system recurred in many areas, and the co-ordination of the different supply services suffered from the absence of an organised staff. Inevitably the Army Service Corps incurred its share of criticism; during heavy and incessant rains the mule- and ox-drawn wagons periodically failed to get through, forcing columns to halt and to curtail the rations for men and horses. Even in good weather, supply columns of ox-drawn wagons, each capable of moving at two miles per hour for a maximum of sixteen miles per day, reduced the mobility of combat forces (in October 1900, French's cavalry division was supported by 155 wagons drawn by 2,480 oxen, which stretched for over four and half miles). In these circumstances, the ASC remained the butt of regimental derision: Lieutenant Henry Jourdain noted in his diary how ASC personnel had shot a native in attempting to kill some oxen.[41] Nevertheless, the Army Service Corps generally kept the army fed, watered, and equipped with all the prerequisites for campaigning under very arduous conditions.

Of all the support departments, none encountered more difficulties than the Royal Army Medical Corps. All its officers and men were fully committed in support of the First Army Corps and in manning the base and stationary hospitals. Thereafter the corps became increasingly dependent upon civilian assistance, and by the end of the war barely a quarter of the 8,500 men who served in South Africa were trained Army Medical Corps men. The 800 army nurses were supported by another 2,300 men supplied by the St John Ambulance Brigade, trained in first aid but not in nursing. In a service described by Major-General Sir H.M. Leslie Rundle as 'overworked, undermanned, and under-orderlied' the principal medical officers had to manage their hospitals while meeting the heavy administrative demands of the army and employing orderlies who were often private soldiers ignorant of their nursing duties. The limitations of the service were frankly exposed by the early outbreaks of typhoid fever. Burdett-Coutts graphically described the conditions in a Bloemfontein field hospital on 28 April 1900:

hundreds of men to my knowledge were lying in the worst stages of typhoid, with only a blanket and a thin waterproof sheet (and not even the latter for many of them) between their aching bodies and the hard ground, with no milk and hardly any medicines . . . without a single nurse amongst them, with only a few private ordinary soldiers to act as 'orderlies' . . . and with only three doctors to attend on 350 patients.[42]

If the outbreaks of typhoid derived from a breakdown of the

army's sanitary arrangements as large bodies of men congregated in camps or besieged towns, and drank from polluted water, the lack of attentive nursing, medical supplies and a proper diet compounded the effects and contributed to the appalling record of hospital fatalities. As Roberts admitted, the medical provisions failed 'to cope' but the shortages of personnel and supplies were more a symptom than a cause of the problem. Fundamentally, medical officers suffered from a lowly status within the army. They lacked a specific remit to advise on sanitary matters and so many were reluctant to voice their opinions on the choice of camp sites from a sanitary perspective. They also had a low priority in the movement of personnel and supplies along the single-track railway. Even the outbreak of typhoid failed to arouse immediate alarm; Roberts regarded the epidemic as an 'inevitability' of war, especially a war of such magnitude. Although he subsequently recognised that sanitation should have been considered more seriously, his fatalism reflected an ambivalence about medical matters which was fairly widespread. Indeed, the War Office had never fully met the corps's concern about its status, leaving the Director-General without a seat on the Army Board and failing to improve the pay of officers significantly or to meet their requests for study leave. It had left the corps overworked and undermanned, neither increasing the strength of the corps in proportion to the growth of the army in the 1890s, nor heeding warnings that the army should take specialist sanitary officers to South Africa.[43]

The failure of the War Office to prepare more effectively (or even as effectively as the Boers had done) for a conflict which had seemed likely for several years rankled deeply among critics in the press and Parliament. Amery was reasonably judicious on this issue, absolving the much-maligned Intelligence Division of any crucial oversights. Despite its paucity of numbers (only eighteen members, compared with over 300 employed by the German General Staff) and a limited budget (about £11,000 a year), it prepared remarkably accurate reports on the numerical strength, armaments and intentions of the Boer republics. If some of its maps were seriously deficient, they were the only maps already in existence, and the Division had been neither authorised nor funded to complete its own surveys (at an estimated cost of £17,000). Once the war began, the collection of tactical intelligence was properly financed, enabling Lieutenant-Colonel Archibald Murray to form the Natal Corps of Guides, composed of

Europeans and natives. The pre-war assessments, though, had concentrated upon quantitative and not qualitative factors; they had not
emphasised that one British soldier, especially at the outbreak of the
war, would not equal one Boer. They had never evaluated the
strengths of the Boers – their mobility, knowledge of the terrain,
excellent use of rifle fire and cover, and powerful motivation. Finally,
in the absence of a General Staff, the intelligence assessments were
simply regarded as information. The Intelligence Division was not
involved in a policy-making or planning process.[44]

Under the reforms of 1895, Wolseley had been charged with the
preparation and maintenance of schemes of offensive and defensive
operations, but he had been preoccupied with his loss of authority as
Commander-in-Chief. On his retirement in November 1900, he protested publicly about civilian interference in the administration of
the army, and prompted an emphatic rebuke from Lord Lansdowne
(see Chapter 2). Although the government stood firm on the principle of civilian control, it could not ignore this protest, as the War
Office had incurred widespread criticism during the war, often from
commentators who agreed with Wolseley. Accordingly it constituted
a committee of inquiry into the administration of the army under the
chairmanship of Clinton Dawkins of the Administrative Reform
Association. The committee began its hearings on 8 January 1901
and presented a report on 9 May, vindicating many of the grievances
which the soldiers had voiced. It asserted that the 'vast system of
minute regulations' by which the War Office governed the army had
destroyed the responsibility of general officers and suppressed individuality and initiative in all ranks. It favoured dividing the work of the
War Office into well defined sections under responsible heads, and
recommended that these sections should be co-ordinated by a permanent board, replacing the present Council and Board. The heads
of all the departments, military and civil, should sit on this board to
prepare the annual estimates, and any member should have the right
to initiate questions for discussion. A complete record of the proceedings and decisions should be kept.[45]

By producing its critical findings so quickly and in the middle of an
increasingly unpopular war, the Dawkins Committee maximised the
likelihood of a favourable response from the government. The latter
made concessions to the soldiers in the War Office memorandum of
12 October and an Order-in-Council of 4 November 1901. Under
the new regulations, the War Office Council and the Army Board

were expanded to include the directors of military intelligence and the medical department, and the council was required to meet more frequently. Members were given more freedom of discussion and their deliberations were to be fully recorded, so precluding any concealment of arguments. The Commander-in-Chief was to remain as the principal adviser of the Secretary of State but assumed 'control' over the Adjutant-General, the Military Secretary and the Director of Mobilisation and Military Intelligence. The amalgamation of the mobilisation subdivision with Intelligence in a new combined department, headed by a lieutenant-general (Sir William Nicholson) reflected a considerable enhancement of status. The new Director was not only a member of the War Office Council, but he also attended the deliberations of the defence committee of the cabinet, and became responsible for

the preparation and maintenance of detailed plans for the military defence of the Empire and for the organisation and mobilisation of the regular and auxiliary forces, the preparation and maintenance of schemes of offensive and defensive operations, and the collection and distribution of information relating to the military geography, resources, etc., of foreign countries and of the British colonies and possessions.[46]

Finally Brodrick sought to capitalise upon the transitory wave of interest in the army to promote reform. A staunch supporter of the Cardwell system, he did not believe that the system had failed, only that it had suffered from a lack of manpower and organisation. He accepted that the Stanhope criteria had proved inadequate, but insisted that 'really our Generals and not W.O. are to blame in this war'.[47] To rectify the deficiencies of command and training, he recommended that six districts should be created in the United Kingdom, in each of which an army corps could muster, train and manoeuvre in its entirety. The first three corps, commanded by officers fit to command them in war, were to be wholly regular in composition, and serve as the new expeditionary force of 120,000 men. The other three corps, composed of regular and auxiliary soldiers, would form the core of the home defence force. To establish these corps, he proposed enrolling an additional 126,500 men, including an extra eighteen battalions of regular troops. In presenting this scheme before the House of Commons on 8 March 1901, he requested an additional £2,000,000 to equip the corps and improve the monetary inducements for the auxiliary forces. He thereby brought the Army Estimates, already bloated by the war, up to £30,030,000, an increase of 50 per cent above their pre-war total.[48]

Gaining funds from Parliament in the midst of a war proved easier than ensuring that men would enlist in sufficient numbers. Blocked by the cabinet from considering the option of compulsory service, Brodrick had to rely upon voluntary enlistments, which were not even producing enough recruits for wartime service. As his scheme depended upon a large increase in post-war recruiting, Brodrick acceded to the demands of Roberts that he should press for improvements in the rates of pay and the terms of service. After a fierce debate in cabinet, with Lord Salisbury and Sir Michael Hicks-Beach, the Chancellor of the Exchequer, deploring any further increase in the military budget, the cabinet agreed that soldiers should be offered a clear 1s a day (if over nineteen years of age) and an initial term of service of three years with the Colours. Thereafter soldiers would have the option of entering the Reserve or of extending their Colours service for an extra 6d a day service pay, subject to character suitability and a second-class standard of shooting (third-class or lower would receive an extra 4d a day). By these measures Brodrick hoped to expand the Reserve rapidly, garrison India with long-service soldiers, and attract more and better recruits (a highly optimistic assumption, as the infantry soldier, even with service pay less daily stoppages, was still earning some two shillings a week less than an agricultural labourer in Caithness, the poorest paid agricultural area in mainland Britain).[49] Brodrick's scheme, in short, was a massive gamble, based on the fear that any delay would risk a return to apathy and fiscal retrenchment in the post-war years. He had proposed reforms before he knew the outcome of the war, or the subsequent deployment of battalions overseas, or the levels of post-war recruiting. Above all, he had risked making erroneous deductions from the problems encountered during the war, and had committed the government to a scheme which, if it proved impracticable (as it did), would not command the confidence of the House. He had ensured that army reform would remain a prominent issue in post-war politics.

In effect, the Second Boer War – the longest, bloodiest and most expensive war fought by the late Victorian army – proved a daunting challenge to the War Office and the army. The Boers proved a tenacious and resourceful adversary, capable of humiliating the army, confounding the pre-war optimism, and shaking the confidence of British imperialism. Admittedly, the army recovered from its early reverses; it adapted tactics and operational procedures to meet the constraints of a war dominated by smokeless, magazine rifles. It ruthlessly countered a highly mobile foe in a protracted guerilla war and ultimately prevailed, precipitating the Boer surrender and the signing of the peace at Vereeniging on 31 May 1902. The War Office, having failed to anticipate that the army would ever become engaged in a war of this type and scale, managed to sustain a force five times larger than expected in a huge and often inhospitable land, some 6,000 miles from home. This was a real achievement, testifying to the improvement in the capacity and organisation of the pre-war army.

The war, nonetheless, had revealed the limitations of the pre-war improvements, namely shortcomings in command and staff work, in aspects of peacetime training and tactical assumptions, and an inability to expand the army efficiently during a prolonged war. If critics differed then, and later, about the lessons which should be learned from this conflict, and about whether they could be applied to wars fought against more conventional enemies over different terrain, they still urged reform. The government and its military advisers, now headed by Lord Roberts, endeavoured to meet these demands, beginning a process which eventually produced an array of administrative reforms, new drill books, an overhaul of peacetime training, and the rearmament of the Royal Artillery. Ultimately this process, once directed by Richard Burdon Haldane and a General Staff, transformed the fighting capacity of the army. The changes found reflection in the preparation, fieldcraft and rifle skills of the British Expeditionary Force of 1914.

Notes

1   Wolseley to Lady Wolseley, 29 September 1899, Wolseley Mss., W/P 28/61; T. Pakenham, *The Boer War* (Weidenfeld & Nicolson; London, 1979), pp.109–11; Wolseley to Lansdowne, 18 and 24 August 1899, PRO, CAB 37/50, ff.52, 56.
2   *The Times*, 2 October 1899, p.7.
3   G. Wyndham to his mother, 6 October 1899, in J.W. McKail and G. Wyndham, *Life and Letters of George Wyndham*, 2 Vols. (Hutchinson; London, 1925), Vol.1, p.361.
4   Knox to Campbell-Bannerman, 2 December 1899, Campbell-Bannerman Mss., B.L. Add. Mss.41,221, f.266.
5   *Parl. Deb.*, Fourth Ser., Vol.77 (20 October 1899), cols.421–2.

6 Churchill, *My Early Life*, p.227; Knightley, *The First Casualty*, pp.66–9.
7 M. Prior, *Campaigns of a War Correspondent* (E. Arnold; London, 1930), p.287; Knightley, *The First Casualty*, p.72.
8 J.B. Atkins, 'The Work and Future of War Correspondents', *Monthly Review*, Vol.4 (1901), pp.84–5.
9 Maj.-Gen. Sir F. Maurice and H.M. Grant, *History of the War in South Africa*, hereafter referred to as the *Official History*, 4 Vols. (Hurst & Blackett; London, 1906–10), Vol.1, pp.301, 329.
10 Lord Roberts, 'Circular Memorandum No.5, Notes for Guidance in South African Warfare', 26 January 1900; Roberts to Lansdowne, 15–17 January 1900, Roberts Mss., NAM, 7101–23–111–1 and 7101–23–117–1; L.S. Amery (ed.), *The Times History of the War in South Africa*, hereafter referred to as *The Times History*, 7 Vols. (Sampson Low; London, 1900–09), Vol.3, pp.369–72, 377, 594–7; D. James, *The Life of Lord Roberts* (Hollis & Carter; London, 1954), pp.280–3, 303; *Official History*, Vol.1, pp.374, 438, 444.
11 Lt. G.S. Crossman, diary, 24 September and 6 October 1900, Crossman Mss., NAM 6306–24–4; Capt. C.E. Stewart, diary, 30 June, and 3 July 1900, Stewart Mss., B[lack] W[atch] A[rchive], item 196; Lt. S.G. Francis, 22 March 1901, Francis Mss., NAM, 7607–49, Capt. R.W.D. Bellew, diary, 25 June 1900, Bellew Mss., NAM, 5707–8; H. Bailes, 'Military Aspects of the War' and F. Pretorius, 'Life on Commando' in Warwick (ed.), *The South African War*, pp.98, 103.
12 *The Times*, 15 June 1901, p.12; S.B. Spies, 'Women and the War' and B. Porter, 'The Pro-Boers in Britain' in Warwick (ed.), *The South African War*, pp.169–70, 172–3, 183–4, 251; S.B. Spies, *Methods of Barbarism? Roberts and Kitchener and Civilians in the Boer Republics, January 1900–May 1902* (Human & Rousseau; Cape Town, 1977), pp.265–8, 285, 290, 292–3.
13 Col. J.S. Ewart, diary, 24 May 1901, Ewart Mss., Scottish Record Office; Crossman, diary, 2 November 1901, Crossman Mss., NAM, 6306–24–4; Capt. J.W.G. Roy, diary, 19 July 1901, Roy Mss., The Worcestershire and Sherwood Foresters Regimental Museum, A/3/48.
14 Kitchener to Brodrick, 6 December 1901, Kitchener Mss., PRO, 30/57/22; Roberts to Wilkinson, 28 September 1900, Wilkinson Mss., 13/14; J.F.C. Fuller to his father, 7 May 1901, Fuller Mss., Liddell Hart Centre for Military Archives, King's College London, IV/3/59; Capt. A.R. Cameron to his father, 21 April 1900, Cameron Mss., BWA, item 186.
15 *The Times History*, Vol.5, pp.67–8, 563, 604–5; Kitchener to Brodrick, 19 and 24 June 1901, Brodrick to Kitchener, 24 June 1901, Confidential Telegrams, M[inistry] o[f] D[efence] Whitehall Library, pp.283–4; Maj.-Gen. E.K.G. Sixsmith, 'Kitchener and the Guerillas in the Boer War', *Army Quarterly*, Vol.104 (1974), pp.203–14.
16 *Elgin Report*, pp.35, 97,
17 L.S. Amery, *My Political Life*, 3 Vols. (Hutchinson; London, 1953–55), Vol.1, p.192; *The Times History*, Vol.2, preface, p.vii; Spiers, *The Army and Society*, pp.241–2; A. Conan Doyle, *The Great Boer War*

(Smith Elder; London, 1900); I.F.W. Beckett, 'Early Historians and the South African War', *Sandhurst Journal of Military Studies*, Issue 1 (1900), pp.15–32.
  18 *Ibid.*, pp.23–7; Bailes, 'Technology and Imperialism', pp.84–5; R. Kruger, *Goodbye Dolly Gray: A History of the Boer War*, 2nd edition (NEL Mentor; London, 1967), pp.61–4, 142, 183, 381–2; J. Symons, *Buller's Campaign* (The Cresset Press; London, 1963), pp.x–xi; B. Farwell, *The Great Boer War* (Allen Lane; London, 1976), pp.136, 138, 166–7, 232; E. Holt, *The Boer War* (Putnam; London, 1958), pp.145, 149–50, 187; E. Belfield, *The Boer War* (Leo Cooper; London, 1975), pp.62, 75.
  19 Bailes, 'Military Aspects of the War', pp.76, 82–90; Scales, 'Artillery in Small Wars', p.214.
  20 Pakenham, *The Boer War*, pp.xvii, 214–15, 239, 307, 344, 370, 457, 613 ns.73, 74, 614 ns.31, 41, 49, 51.
  21 Sir W.F. Gatacre, q.16772, Sir H.J.T. Hildyard, q.15972 and the Hon. Sir F.W. Stopford, q.16635 evidence appended to the *Elgin Report*, Vol.2, pp.273, 238, 267; 'Has the experience of the war in South Africa shown that any change is necessary in the system of Field Artillery fire tactics (in the attack as well as in the defence) in European warfare?' essays by Maj. H.A. Bethell and Capt. N.F. Gordon; and Maj. R. Fitz-Maurice, 'The Artillery Escort', *Proceedings of the RAI*, Vol.29 (1902), pp.136–46, 247–65 and 370–3.
  22 Buller comments on Elmslie, 'The Possible Effect on Tactics of Recent Improvements in Weapons', p.18.
  23 Lt.-Gen. Sir G.S. White, despatch, 2 November 1899, pp.3–9, *South Africa Despatches*, Vol.1, MoD Whitehall Library; Roberts to Lansdowne, 15 December 1899, Roberts Mss., NAM, 7101–23–117–1; E.M. Spiers, 'Reforming the Infantry of the Line 1900–1914', *J.A.S.H.R.*, Vol.LIX (1981), pp.82–94; Maj. A. Hamilton-Gordon, 'Fourteen Days' Howitzer work on Service', *Proceedings of the RAI*, Vol.27 (1900), pp.347–64; *The Times History*, Vol.2, p.184.
  24 *Ibid.*, Vol.2, pp.33, 40 and Vol.3, pp.550–2.
  25 Roberts to Amery, 12 July 1901, Roberts Mss., NAM, 7101–23–122–1.
  26 Bailes, 'Technology and Tactics in the British Army', pp.39, 46 and 'Technology and Imperialism', pp.82–104; Beckett, 'Early Historians and the South African War', p.22.
  27 Bailes, 'Technology and Tactics in the British Army', p.46; Pakenham, *The Boer War*, pp.225, 357–8; Wood, qs.4158, 4161–2, 4176, Roberts, q.10442; Hamilton, q.13941 evidence appended to *Elgin Report*, Vols.1, pp.176–7, 440 and 2, p.112; B.M.Hart-Synnot (ed.), *Letters of Major-General Fitzroy Hart-Synnot* (E. Arnold; London, 1912), pp.298, 319–20; Lt.-Col. H.F.N. Jourdain, *Ranging Memories* (private; Oxford, 1934), pp.100–2.
  28 *The Times History*, Vol.5, pp.xii–xiii, 69–70, 247.
  29 Roberts to Lansdowne, 29 April 1900, Roberts to Akers-Douglas, 29 August 1901 and Roberts to Blackwood, 31 July 1906, Roberts Mss., NAM, 7101–23–117–1, 7101–23–122–2, 7101–23–122–9.

30 Badsey, 'Fire and the Sword', pp.129, 134–5, 139–41, 146–8; Marquess of Anglesey, *A History of the British Cavalry 1816–1919*, Vol.4, pp.136, 149–52; Haig to Henrietta Haig, 12 December 1899 and 16 March 1900, Haig Mss., NLS, Acc. 3155, Vol.6; R.H. Murray, *The History of the VIII King's Royal Irish Hussars*, 2 Vols (W. Heffer; Cambridge, 1928), Vol.2, p.519.

31 Sir I. Hamilton to E. Childers, 30 October 1910, Hamilton Mss., Liddell Hart Centre for Military Archives, King's College London, 7/3/15; French, preface to Gen. F. von Bernhardi, *Cavalry in War and Peace* (Hugh Rees; London, 1910), p.xi; Haig, q.19471 evidence appended to the *Elgin Report*, Vol.2, p.411; Marquess of Anglesey, *A History of the British Cavalry 1816–1919*, Vol.4, pp.60, 236, 276–7, 342; Badsey, 'Fire and the Sword', pp.158–9, 163–4, 166, 170–2.

32 Haig, q.19299 and French, q.17129 evidence appended to the *Elgin Report*, Vol.2, pp.404, 301.

33 Marquess of Anglesey, *A History of the British Cavalry 1816–1919*, Vol.4, pp.363–4.

34 *Elgin Report*, p.98; Marquess of Anglesey, *A History of the British Cavalry 1816–1919*, Vol.4, pp. 280–94, 319–35, 349–54; *Proceedings of a Court of Inquiry . . . on the Administration of the Army Remount Department since January 1899, by the Order of the Commander-in-Chief dated 20th February 1902*, Cd. 993 (1902), LVIII, pp.2, 19–20, 29–31, 33–4.

35 *Elgin Report*, appendix E, pp.278–80; A. Page, 'The Supply Services of the British Army in the South African War 1899–1902', unpublished Ph.D. thesis (University of Oxford, 1976), pp.191–8, 336–7; *The Times History*, Vol.2, p.27 and Vol.6, part II.

36 Roberts to Lansdowne, 16 August 1901, Roberts Mss., NAM, 7101–23–122–2.

37 Brackenbury, qs.1673–5, 1679–80; Marshall, qs.18507, 18510 evidence appended to the *Elgin Report*, Vol.1, pp.79–82, Vol.2, p.360; Callwell and Headlam, *The History of the Royal Artillery*, Vol.2, pp.723; Brackenbury to Roberts, 23 February 1900, Roberts Mss., NAM, 7101–23–11–157; Master General of the Ordnance, 'Minute on History of the Field Gun', Arnold-Forster Mss., B.L. Add. Mss. 50,314, f.21; E.M. Spiers, 'Rearming the Edwardian Artillery', *J.S.A.H.R.*, Vol. LVII (1979), pp.167–76.

38 *Elgin Report*, pp.99–101; Watson, *History of the Corps of Royal Engineers*, Vol.3, pp.84–5, 89, 96–8, 102, 104–9, 125–6.

39 *Elgin Report*, pp.110, 123; Forbes, *A History of the Army Ordnance Services*, Vol.2, p.182; and on the provost service, I am indebted to Gary Sheffield who is currently writing a history of the military police, entitled *The Redcaps*.

40 *Elgin Report*, p.123; Forbes, *A History of the Army Ordnance Services*, Vol.2, pp.183, 187–9; W. Nasson, 'Tommy Atkins in South Africa' in Warwick (ed.), *The South African War*, pp.123–38; R.A.J. Tyler, *Bloody Provost* (Phillimore; London, 1980), pp.211–12.

41 Page, 'The Supply Services of the British Army', pp.339–40, 346–7; *Elgin Report*, pp.110–13; Murray, *The History of the VIII King's Royal*

Irish Hussars, Vol.2, pp.528, 533; Lt. H.F.N. Jourdain, diary, 23 July 1900, Jourdain Mss., NAM, 5603–10, No.3; Fortescue, *The Royal Army Service Corps*, Vol.1, pp.236–9, 243–65; *Lord Methuen*, qs.14322–3 evidence appended to the *Elgin Report*, Vol.2, p.127.

42   *The Times History*, Vol.6, pp.523–4; *Elgin Report* and evidence appended by Sir H.M.L. Rundle, q.17924, pp.102–4 and Vol.2, p.333; *Report of the Royal Commission appointed to consider and report upon the Care and Treatment of the Sick and Wounded during the South African Campaign*, Cd. 453 (1901), XXIX, pp.17–18.

43   *Ibid.*, p.12; Pakenham, *The Boer War*, pp.382–3; *Elgin Report* and evidence appended by Roberts, qs.10485 and 13173–4, pp.106, 109, Vol.1, p.444 and Vol.2, pp.63–4; *Return of Correspondence between the Honourable Member for Ilkeston and the War Department in relation to Medical and Sanitary Arrangements at the Cape*, Cd. 279 (1900), XLIX, pp.2–3.

44   *The Times History*, Vol.2, pp.39–40; *Elgin Report*, pp.128–32; Fergusson, *British Military Intelligence, 1870–1914*, pp.109–15, 149.

45   *Report of the Committee appointed to enquire into War Office Organisation*, Cd. 580 (1901), XL, pp.2, 20–2.

46   'Memorandum on the Present Organisation of the War Office', appendices to the *Elgin Report* (1904), XLII, p.292; Brodrick, qs.21595, 21705 evidence appended to the *Elgin Report*, Vol.2, pp.539, 547–8; Hamer, *The British Army*, pp.179–93.

47   Brodrick to Curzon, 3 January 1900, Curzon Mss., Eur.F.111/10A, India Office Library, f.116.

48   *Parl. Deb.*, Fourth Ser., Vol.90 (8 March 1901), cols.1,052–91.

49   J.H. Clapham, *An Economic History of Modern Britain*, 3 Vols. (Cambridge University Press; London, 1926), Vol.3, pp.98–9; Spiers, *Army and Society*, p.55; Brodrick to Curzon, 15 February 1901, Curzon Mss., Eur.F. 111/10B, f.248; L.J. Satre, 'St. John Brodrick and Army Reform', *Journal of British Studies*, Vol.15 (1976), pp.117–39.

Appendix 1

Secretaries of State for War

Edward T. Cardwell	December 1868 to February 1874
Gathorne Hardy	February 1874 to March 1878
Colonel F.A. Stanley	April 1878 to April 1880
Hugh Childers	April 1880 to December 1882
Marquess of Hartington	December 1882 to June 1885
W.H. Smith	June 1885 to February 1886
Henry Campbell-Bannerman	February 1886 to August 1886
W.H. Smith	August 1886 to January 1887
Edward Stanhope	January 1887 to August 1892
Henry Campbell-Bannerman	August 1892 to June 1895
Lord Lansdowne	June 1895 to November 1900
William St. J. Brodrick	November 1900 to October 1903

Appendix 2

Colonial wars and punitive expeditions, 1869–1902

1863–72	Third Maori War
1870	Red River expedition (Canada)
1871–72 ·	Looshai expedition
1873–74	Second Ashanti War
1874	Duffla expedition (Naga Hills)
1875–76	Perak campaign
1875–76	Race riots (Barbados)
1877–78	Jowakhi campaign
1877–78	Ninth Kaffir War
1878	Dispatch of Indian troops to Malta (Eastern Question)
1879	Zulu War
1878–80	Second Afghan War
1880–81	First Boer War
1882	Egyptian War
1884–85	Bechuanaland Field Force
1884–85	Suakin expedition
1884–85	First Sudan War*
1885	Suppression of Riel's Rebellion (north-west Canada)
1885–89	Third Burma War
1888	Sikkim War
1888	Hazara War (the Black Mountain expedition)
1889–90	Chin-Looshai War
1889–92	Burmese expedition
1891	Samana and Hazara expeditions (North West Frontier)
1891	Manipur expedition (north-east India)
1892	Tambi expedition
1892–93	Chin Hills expedition (north-east India)

1893	Matabeleland revolt
1894	Gambia expedition
1894–95	Waziristan expedition (North West Frontier)
1895	Defence and relief of Chitral (North West Frontier)
1895–96	Third Ashanti War
1896	Matabeleland War
1896–99	Second Sudan War*
1896–97	Bechuanaland expedition
1897	Benin expedition
1897–98	Tochi, Malakand, Buner, Mohmand and Tirah Field Forces (North West Frontier)
1899–1902	Second South African War
1900	Boxer Rebellion
1900	Conquest of Ashanti

Note: The Gordon Relief Expedition was sent out during this war.

Source: B.J. Bond (ed.), *Victorian Military Campaigns*, pp. 310–11; I.F.W. Beckett, *Victoria's Wars* (Shire publications; Aylesbury, 1987), pp.43–66; Captain H.L. Nevill, *Campaigns on the North West Frontier* (John Murray; London, 1912), p.404; *Airey Report*, p.9.

Appendix 3

The Stanhope memorandum

The so-called Stanhope memorandum was a reply by the Secretary of State for War to the proposals of Viscount Wolseley, then Adjutant-General, about the purposes of the army. Stanhope stated that

Her Majesty's Government are not able to concur in the proposed definition of the objects to be provided for, nor can they accept the proposal to aim at forming three Army-Corps of regular troops instead of two. They have examined this subject with care, and are of opinion that a general basis for the requirements of our Army might be more correctly laid down by stating that the objects of our military organisation are –

(a) The effective support of the civil power in all parts of the United Kingdom.
(b) To find the number of men for India which has been fixed by arrangements with the Government of India.
(c) To find garrisons for all our fortresses and coaling stations, at home and abroad, according to a scale now laid down; and to maintain these garrisons at all times at the strength fixed for a peace or war footing.
(d) After providing for these requirements, to be able to mobilise rapidly for home defence two Army-Corps of Regular troops, and one partly composed of Regulars and partly of Militia; and to organise the Auxiliary Forces, not allotted to Army-Corps or garrisons, for the defence of London and for the defensible positions in advance; and for the defence of mercantile ports.
(e) Subject to the foregoing considerations and to their financial obligations, to aim at being able, in case of necessity, to send abroad two complete Army-Corps, with Cavalry Division and Line of Communication. But it will be distinctly understood that the probability of the employment of an Army-Corps in the field in any European war is sufficiently improbable to make it the primary duty of the military authorities to organise our forces efficiently for the defence of this country.

E. Stanhope, minute, 8 December 1888, PRO, WO 33/48, paper A 148A.

Appendix 4

Methodological note

Once tables of officers were obtained from the relevant Army Lists, background information was acquired from the service records of some officers in the PRO, WO 25 and WO 76., from the registers of Sandhurst and Woolwich, and from the standard reference works – *Burke's Peerage, History of Commoners, Landed Gentry*, etc., J. Bateman, *Great Landowners of England*, E. Walford, *County Families of the United Kingdom*, F. Boase, *Modern English Biography*, *The Dictionary of National Biography*, *Who's Who*, *Men of the Time*, *Who was Who*, and *Who's who at the War* (1900). For officers who had won the Victoria Cross, the three volumes entitled *The VC and DSO*, edited by Sir O'Moore Creagh and E.M. Humphris, were consulted. For less famous officers, some information was gleaned from regimental records and museums, obituaries in *The Times*, and the registers of some twenty-five public schools. Information on non-English officers was sought from J.S. Crone, *A Concise Dictionary of Irish Biography*, A. Webb, *A Compendium of Irish Biography*, *The Dictionary of Welsh Biography down to 1940*, and J. Irving, *The Book of Scotsmen*.

The analytical approach sought to compare the social groups within the senior officers in 1868, 1899 and 1914. The approach neither presumed the existence of wholly separate groups within the officer corps nor sought to measure those groups with any statistical precision. It merely recognised that there may have been differences of status and prestige within the regimental mess, and that these differences may have been perceived at the time. It assumed, too, that a paramount concern of the officer gentleman tradition was the maintenance of social standards – not simply the possession of a private income but a pattern of expenditure which met with the approval of brother officers and sustained the customs of the mess.

Of the groups chosen, the possession of a title, prestige and sometimes greater wealth divided the peerage and baronetage from the landed gentry. Where officers in other categories had close connections with the titled aristocracy or the gentry, they have been judged as members of the landed classes. The third group covered self-recruitment within the armed forces, those who entered the army as the sons of serving or retired officers. The fourth and fifth groups comprised traditionally recognised sources of gentility, namely the Church of England and the professions, namely doctors, barristers, surgeons and civil servants (home, diplomatic or Indian Civil Service). The final category included parents who were merchants, teachers, engineers, small farmers or estate managers, among others – groups which were too few or too obscure or too wanting in detail to warrant a separate category. In analysing these groups as well as their rural/urban and regional backgrounds, the aim was not statistical exactness but to gain some idea of the relative proportions involved (Tables 1 and 2 and Appendix 4).

Select bibliography

As material for this book has been drawn from a wide variety of sources, only the more important items are listed here. For a full list of the sources used, and for references *to Parliamentary Debates*, to *Parliamentary Papers*, and to articles or speeches reported in the national or provincial press, readers should consult the notes.

Primary sources

The official papers consulted in the preparation of this book included Cabinet Office and War Office records retained in the Public Record Office. Manuscript collections were:

Army Museums, Ogilby Trust, London
  Wilkinson Papers

Black Watch Archive, Balhousie Castle, Perth
  Cameron Papers (item 186)
  Gordon Papers (item 127)
  Stewart Papers (item 196)

British Library
  Arnold-Forster Papers   (Add. Mss. 50,275–375)
  Balfour Papers   (Add. Mss. 49,683–962)
  Campbell-Bannerman Papers   (Add. Mss. 41,206–52 and
                                 51,512–21)
  Dilke Papers   (Add. Mss. 43,874–967)
  Gladstone Papers   (Add. Mss. 44,086–835)
  Hutton Papers   (Add. Mss. 50,078–113)
  Midleton Papers   (Add. Mss. 50,072–7)

Hove Reference Library
  Wolseley Papers

India Office Library
  Curzon Papers

Kent Record Office
  Stanhope Papers

King's Own Scottish Borderers Regimental Museum
  Haggard Papers KOSB T4/35

Liddell Hart Centre for Military Archives, King's College, London
  Fuller Papers
  Hamilton Papers
  Robertson Papers

Ministry of Defence Whitehall Library
  Confidential Telegrams
  South Africa Despatches

National Army Museum
Anderson Papers	7601–53
Bellew Papers	5707–8
Broadwood Papers	7502–34
Charles Papers	7412–79
Chelmsford Papers	6807–386,
Churcher Papers	7804–53
Crossman Papers	6306–24
Danby Papers	7003–2
Ellison Papers	8704–35
Francis Papers	7607–49
Jourdain Papers	5603–10
Lloyd Papers	7709–43
Longueville Papers	7711–113
Rawlinson Papers	7212–6
Roberts Papers	7101–23
Roe Papers	7504–18
Spraggs Papers	7706–14
Templer Papers	7404–59
Tuck Papers	7005–21
Wood Papers	6807–234

National Library of Scotland
  Blackwood Papers
  Crum Papers
  Haig Papers

Public Record Office
  Ardagh Papers   PRO 30/40
  Buller Papers   WO 132
  Cardwell Papers   PRO 30/48
  Kitchener Papers   PRO 30/57
  Midleton Papers   PRO 30/67
  Roberts Papers   WO 105
  Smith Papers   WO 110
  South African War Papers   WO 108

Queen Mary and Westfield College, University of London
  Lyttelton Papers

Royal Archives, Windsor Castle
  Cambridge Papers

Scottish Record Office
  Ewart Papers

Worcestershire and Sherwood Foresters Regimental Museum
  Roy Papers
  Smith-Dorrien Papers

Military manuals published in various years by HMSO, London

  Cavalry Drill
  Field Artillery Drill
  Infantry Drill
  Manual of Field Artillery Exercises
  Manual of Military Law
  Musketry Regulations
  Queen's Regulations

Published diaries, journals and correspondence

Brett, M.V. (ed.). *Journals and Letters of Reginald Viscount Esher*. 4 Vols. Ivor Nicolson & Watson. London, 1934–35.

Letters of the Rt. Hon. Henry Austin Bruce G.C.B., Lord Aberdeen of Duffryn. 2 Vols. Private. Oxford, 1902.

Buckle, G.E. (ed.). *Letters of Queen Victoria.* 2nd series. 3 Vols. John Murray. London, 1926–28, and 3rd series. 3 Vols. John Murray. London, 1930–32.

Childers, S. *The Life and Correspondence of the Rt. Hon. Hugh C.E. Childers, 1827–1896.* 2 Vols. John Murray. London, 1901.

Emery, F. *Marching Over Africa.* Hodder & Stoughton. London, 1986.

—*The Red Soldier: Letters from the Zulu War.* Hodder & Stoughton. London, 1977.

Fortescue-Brickdale, Sir C. (ed.). *Major-General Sir Henry Hallam Parr: Recollections and Correspondence.* Fisher Unwin. London, 1917.

Hart-Synnot, B.M. (ed.). Letters of Major-General Fitzroy Hart-Synnot. E. Arnold. London, 1912.

Johnson, N.E. (ed.). *The Diary of Gathorne Hardy, later Lord Cranbrook, 1886–1892: Political Selections.* Clarendon Press. Oxford, 1981.

McKail, J.W. and Wyndham, G. *Life and Letters of George Wyndham,* 2 Vols. Hutchinson. London, 1925.

Meinertzhagen, Col. R. *Army Diary 1899–1926.* Oliver & Boyd. London, 1960.

Napier, Lt.-Col. H.D. (ed.). *Letters of Field-Marshal Lord Napier of Magdala.* Simpkin Marshall. London, 1936.

Preston, A. (ed.). *In Relief of Gordon.* Hutchinson London, 1967.

—(ed.). *The South African War Diaries of Sir Garnet Wolseley 1875.* A.A. Balkema. Cape Town, 1971.

Roberts, Field-Marshal Earl. *Letters written during the Indian Mutiny.* Macmillan. London, 1924.

Contemporary works on the army, campaigns and tactics

A British Officer. *Social Life in the British Army.* John Long. London, 1900.

A Lieutenant-Colonel in the British Army. *The British Army.* Sampson Low. London, 1899.

Amery, L.S. *The Times History of the War in South Africa.* 7 Vols. Sampson Low. London, 1900–09.

Arnold-Forster, H.O. *Army Letters 1897–8.* E. Arnold. London,

1898.

Baden-Powell, Maj. R.S.S. *The Downfall of Prempeh: A Diary of Life with the Native Levy in Ashanti 1895–6*. Methuen. London, 1896.

—*The Matabele Campaign: Being a Narrative of the Campaign in Suppressing the Native Rising in Matabeleland and Mashonaland*. Methuen. London, 1897.

Bennett, E.N. *The Downfall of the Dervishes*. Methuen. London, 1898.

Bernhardi, Gen. F. von. *Cavalry in War and Peace*. Hugh Rees. London, 1910.

Brackenbury, Capt. H. *Ashanti War*. 2 Vols. Blackwood. Edinburgh, 1874.

—*The Tactics of the Three Arms as Modified to Meet the Requirements of the Present Day*. Mitchell. London, 1873.

Callwell, Col. C.E. *Small Wars*. HMSO. London, 1896. reprinted by Greenhill Books. London, 1990.

Churchill, W.S. *The River War: An Historical Account of the Reconquest of the Soudan*. Nelson. London, 1915.

Clery, Maj. F. *Minor Tactics*. H. King. London, 1875.

Denison, Lt.-Col. G.T. *Modern Cavalry: Its Organisation, Armament, and Employment in War*. T. Bosworth. London, 1867.

Dilke, Sir C.W. *Army Reform*. Service & Paton. London, 1898.

—and Wilkinson, H.S. *Imperial Defence*. Constable. London, 1892.

Doyle, A. Conan. *The Great Boer War*. Smith, Elder & Co. London, 1900.

Edmondson, R. *Is a Soldier's Life Worth Living?* Twentieth Century Press. London, 1902.

Goodenough, Lt.-Col. W.H. and Dalton, Lt.-Col. J.C. *The Army Book for the British Empire*. HMSO. London, 1893.

Greene, Lt. F.V. *The Russian Army and its Campaigns in Turkey, 1877–78*. W.H. Allen. London, 1880.

Haliburton, Sir A. *A Short Reply to Long Service*. Macmillan. London, 1898.

Hamilton, Capt. I.S.M. *The Fighting of the Future*. Kegan Paul. London, 1885.

Hamley, Gen. E.B. *Operations of War*. 3rd edition. Blackwood. Edinburgh, 1872.

Havelock, Maj. H. *Three Main Military Questions of the Day*. Private. London, 1867.

Henderson, G.F.R. *Campaign of Fredericksburg*. Gale & Polden. London, 1886.

—*The Battle of Spicheren, August 6th, 1870, and the Events that Preceded it: A Study in Practical Tactics and War Training*. Gale & Polden. London, 1891.

—*The Science of War*. ed. Col. N. Malcolm. Longmans. London, 1910.

Ingelfingen, Prince Kraft zu Hohenlohe. *Letters on Artillery*. Royal Artillery Institution. Woolwich, 1887.

—*Letters on Cavalry*. Royal Artillery Institution. Woolwich, 1889.

MacDougall, Maj.-Gen. P.L. *Modern Infantry Tactics*. E. Stanford. London, 1873.

—*Modern Warfare as Influenced by Modern Artillery*. Private. London, 1864.

MacLean, A.H.H. *Public Schools and the War in South Africa*. Stanford. London, 1902.

Maude, Capt. F.N. *Letters on Tactics and Organisation*. G.A. Spooner. Leavenworth, Kansas, 1891.

Maurice, Maj.-Gen. J.F. *Military History of the Campaign of 1882 in Egypt*. HMSO. London, 1887.

Maurice, J.F. *The System of Field Manoeuvres Best Adapted for Enabling our Troops to Meet a Continental Army*. Blackwood. Edinburgh, 1872.

—*War*. Macmillan. London, 1891.

Maurice, J.F. and Grant, M.H. *History of the War in South Africa*. 4 Vols. Hurst & Blackett. London, 1906–10.

May, Maj. E.S. *Field Artillery with other Arms*. Sampson Low. London, 1898.

Mayne, Maj. C.B. *The Late Battles in the Soudan and Modern Tactics: A Reply*. Gale & Polden. London, 1884.

Owen, Lt.-Col. C.H. *Principles and Practice of Modern Artillery*. John Murray. London, 1871.

Sandes, E.W.C. *The Royal Engineers in Egypt and the Sudan*. Institute of Royal Engineers. Chatham, 1937.

Schmidt, Maj.-Gen. C. von. *Instructions for the Training, Employment and Leading of Cavalry*. HMSO. London, n.d.

Sosnosky, T. von. *England's Danger: The Future of British Army Reform*. Chapman & Hall. London, 1901.

Steevens, G.W. *With Kitchener to Khartum*. Blackwood. Edinburgh, 1898.

Wolseley, G.J. *The Soldier's Pocket Book*. 3rd edition. Macmillan.
    London, 1874.
Wood, Gen. H.E. *Achievements of Cavalry*. G. Bell. London, 1897.

Contemporary journals, periodicals and newspapers

Aldershot Military Society
Blackwood's Edinburgh Magazine
The Birmingham Daily Mail
Contemporary Review
The Daily Chronicle
The Daily Mail
The Daily News
The Daily Telegraph
Denbighshire Free Press
Edinburgh Review
Harper's New Monthly Magazine
The Illustrated London News
The Journal of the Royal United Service Institution
The Manchester Guardian
Minutes of the Proceedings of the Royal Artillery Institution
The Monthly Review
The Morning Post
National Review
The Naval and Military Gazette
The Nineteenth Century
North American Review
North British Mail
The Pall Mall Gazette
Professional Papers of the Corps of Royal Engineers
Reynolds's Newspaper
The Saturday Review
The Standard
The Times
The United Service Gazette
United Service Magazine
The Westminster Gazette

Secondary sources

Adye, Gen. Sir J. *Recollections of a Military Life*. Smith, Elder & Co. London, 1895.

—*Soldiers and others I have known*. H. Jenkins. London, 1919.

Ainslie, Gen. C.P. de. *Life as I have found it*. Blackwood. Edinburgh, 1883.

Amery, L.S. *My Political Life*. 3 Vols. Hutchinson. London, 1953–55.

Anglesey, The Marquess of. *A History of the British Cavalry 1816–1919*. 4 Vols. Leo Cooper. London, 1973–86.

Aston, Sir G. *Memories of a Marine*. John Murray. London, 1919.

Atlay, J.B. *Lord Haliburton: a memoir of his public service*. Smith, Elder & Co. London, 1909.

Babington, A. *Military Intervention in Britain*. Routledge. London, 1990.

Bailey, V. (ed.). *Policing and Punishment in Nineteenth Century Britain*. Croom Helm. London, 1981.

Barrow, Gen. Sir G. de S. *The Fire of Life*. Hutchinson. London, 1941.

Barthorp, M. *The British Army on Campaign 1816–1902* (3): *1856–1881*. Osprey Men-at-Arms Series 198. London, 1988.

—*The British Army on Campaign 1816–1902* (4): *1882–1902*. Osprey Men-at-Arms Series 201. London, 1988.

Bates, D. *The Abyssinian Difficulty*. Oxford University Press. London, 1979.

Baumgart, W. *Imperialism: The Idea and Reality of British and French Colonial Expansion, 1880–1914*. Oxford University Press. Oxford, 1982.

Beckett, I.F.W. *Victoria's Wars*. Shire Publications. Aylesbury, 1974.

Beckett, I.F.W. and Gooch, J. (eds.). *Politicians and Defence: Studies in the Formulation of British Defence Policy 1845–1970*. Manchester University Press. Manchester, 1981.

Belfield, E. *The Boer War*. Leo Cooper. London, 1975.

Belich, J. *The New Zealand Wars and the Victorian Interpretation of Racial Conflict*. Auckland University Press. Auckland, 1986.

Best, G. and Wheatcroft, A. (eds.). *War Economy and the Military Mind*. Croom Helm. London, 1976.

Biddulph, Sir R. *Lord Cardwell at the War Office: A History of his*

Administration, 1868–1874. John Murray. London, 1904.

Blake, R. *The Conservative Party from Peel to Churchill.* Eyre & Spottiswoode. London, 1970.

Blatchford, R. *My Life in the Army.* Clarion Press. London, n.d.

Bond, B.J. *The Victorian Army and the Staff College 1854–1914.* Eyre Methuen. London, 1972.

—(ed.). *Victorian Military Campaigns.* Hutchinson. London, 1967.

Bonham Carter, V. *Soldier True: The Life and Times of Field-Marshal Sir William Robertson, 1860–1933.* Muller. London, 1963.

Bowley, A.L. *Wages and Incomes in the United Kingdom since 1860.* Cambridge University Press. Cambridge, 1937.

Brander, M. *The 10th Royal Hussars.* Leo Cooper. London, 1969.

Brereton, J.M. *The British Soldier: A Social History from 1661 to the present day.* The Bodley Head. London, 1986.

—*A History of the Royal Regiment of Wales [24th/41st] 1689–1989.* Regimental Headquarters. Cardiff, 1989.

Brown, L. *Victorian News and Newspapers.* Clarendon Press. Oxford, 1985.

Bruce, A.P.C. *The Purchase System in the British Army, 1660–1871.* Royal Historical Society. London, 1980.

Bruce, G. *The Burma Wars 1824–1886.* Hart-Davis, MacGibbon. London, 1973.

Bryant, A. *Jackets of Green: A Study of the History, Philosophy, and Character of the Rifle Brigade.* Collins. London, 1972.

Burn, W.L. *The Age of Equipoise.* Allen & Unwin. London, 1964.

Callwell, Maj.-Gen. Sir C.E. and Headlam, Maj.-Gen. Sir J. *The History of the Royal Artillery.* 3 Vols. Royal Artillery Institution. London, 1931–40.

Carrington, C. *Rudyard Kipling: His Life and Work.* Penguin. London, 1970.

Cassar, G.H. *Kitchener: Architect of Victory.* W. Kimber. London, 1977.

Cecil, Lady Gwendolen (ed.). *Life of Robert Marquis of Salisbury.* 4 Vols. Hodder & Stoughton. London, 1921–32.

Chancellor, V.E. *History for their Masters: Opinion in the English History Textbook, 1800–1914.* Adams & Dart. London, 1970.

Churchill, W.S. *My Early Life.* Thornton Butterworth. London, 1930.

Clapham, J.H. *An Economic History of Modern Britain.* 3 Vols.

Cambridge University Press. London, 1926.

Clarke, I.F. *Voices Prophesying War 1763–1984*. Oxford University Press. London, 1966.

Connell, J. *Wavell, Soldier and Scholar*. Collins. London, 1964.

Corbett, A.F. *Service through six Reigns*. Private. Norwich, 1953.

Critchley, T. *The Conquest of Violence*. Constable. London, 1970.

Curtis, L.P. *Anglo-Saxons and Celts: A Study of Anti-Irish Prejudice in Victorian England*. New York University Press. New York, 1968.

Dennis, P. and Preston, A. (eds.). *Soldiers as Statesmen*. Croom Helm. London, 1976.

Douglas, R. *The History of the Liberal Party 1895–1970*. Sidgwick & Jackson. London, 1971.

Duminy, A. and Ballard, C. (eds.). *The Anglo–Zulu War: New Perspectives*. University of Natal Press. Pietermaritzburg, 1981.

Dunbabin, J.P.D. *Rural Discontent in Nineteenth Century Britain*. Faber & Faber. London, 1974.

Dundonald, Earl of. *My Army Life*. E. Arnold. London, 1926.

Dunlop, Col. J.K. *The Development of the British Army*. Methuen. London, 1938.

Edmonds, M. (ed.). *The Defence Equation: British Military Systems Policy, Planning and Performance*. Brassey's. London, 1986.

Ellis, J. *The Social History of the Machine Gun*. Croom Helm. London, 1975.

Evans, R. *The Story of the Fifth Royal Inniskilling Dragoon Guards*. Gale & Polden. Aldershot, 1953.

Farwell, B. *For Queen and Country*. Allen Lane. London, 1981.

—*Queen Victoria's Little Wars*. Allen Lane. London, 1973.

—*The Great Boer War*. Allen Lane. London, 1976.

Fergusson, T.G. *British Military Intelligence, 1870–1914: The Development of a Modern Intelligence Organisation*. University Publications of America. Frederick, Maryland, 1984.

Ferrar, Maj. M.L. *A History of the Services of the 19th Regiment, now Alexandra, Princess of Wales's Own (Yorkshire Regiment), from its Formation in 1688 to 1911*. Eden Fisher. London, 1911.

Field, H. John. *Toward a Programme of Imperial Life: The British Empire at the Turn of the Century*. Clio Press. Oxford, 1982.

Finer, S.E. *The Man on Horseback: The Role of the Military in Politics*. Pall Mall Press. London, 1962.

Fleming, P. *The Siege at Peking*. Rupert Hart-Davis. London, 1959.

Foot, M.R.D. (ed.). *War and Society*. P. Elek. London, 1973.

Forbes, Maj.-Gen. A. *A History of the Army Ordnance Services*. 3 Vols. Medici Society. London, 1929.

Forbes, A. *Memories and Studies of War and Peace*. Cassell. London, 1895.

Fortescue, Sir J. *The Royal Army Service Corps: A History of Transport and Supply in the British Army*. 2 Vols. Cambridge University Press. Cambridge, 1930–31.

Fraser, J. *Sixty Years in Uniform*. Stanley Paul. London, 1939.

Fuller, J.F.C. *Memoirs of an Unconventional Soldier*. Nicolson & Watson. London, 1936.

—*The Army in my Time*. Rich & Cowan. London, 1935.

Gallagher, J. *The Decline, Revival and Fall of the British Empire*. Cambridge University Press. Cambridge, 1982.

Gardner, B. *Allenby*. Cassell. London, 1965.

Gardyne, Lt.-Col. C. Greenhill. *The Life of a Regiment: The History of the Gordon Highlanders*. 3 Vols. Medici Society. London, 1903–29.

Gleichen, Lord, *A Guardsman's Memories*. Blackwood. London, 1921.

Godwin-Austen, Brevet-Major A.R. *The Staff and the Staff College*. Constable. London, 1927.

Gooch, J. *The Plans of War*. Routledge & Kegan Paul. London, 1974.

—*The Prospect of War: Studies in British Defence Policy 1847–1942*. Frank Cass. London, 1981.

Gordon, H. *The War Office: Past and Present*. Methuen. London, 1914.

Gough, H. *Soldiering on*. Morrison & Gibb. Edinburgh, 1954.

Grenville Murray, E.C. *Six Months in the Ranks*. Smith, Elder & Co. London, 1881.

Griffith Boscawen, Sir A.S.T. *Fourteen Years in Parliament*. John Murray. London, 1907.

Groot, G.J. de. *Douglas Haig, 1861–1928*. Unwin Hyman. London, 1988.

Gross, J. (ed.). *Rudyard Kipling: the man, his work and his world*. Weidenfeld and Nicolson. London, 1972.

Guttsman, W.L. *The British Political Elite*. MacGibbon & Kee. London, 1965.

Gwynn, S. and Tuckwell, G.M. *The Life of Sir Charles W. Dilke*. 2

Vols. John Murray. London, 1917.

Hall, Sir J. *The Coldstream Guards 1885–1914*. Clarendon Press. Oxford, 1929.

Hamer, W.S. *The British Army: Civil–Military Relations 1885–1905*. Clarendon Press. Oxford, 1970.

Hamilton, Lord G. *Parliamentary Reminiscences and Reflections*. 2 Vols. John Murray. London, 1916–22.

Hamilton, Gen. Sir I. *Listening for the Drums*. Faber & Faber. London, 1944.

Hamilton, I. *Happy Warrior: A Life of General Sir Ian Hamilton*. Cassell. London, 1966.

Hanham, H.J. *Elections and Party Management*. Harvester Press. Hassocks, 1978.

Hardie, F. *The Political Influence of Queen Victoria, 1861–1961*. Oxford University Press. London, 1935.

Harries-Jenkins, G. *The Army in Victorian Society*. Routledge & Kegan Paul. London, 1977.

Haycock, R. and Neilson, K. (eds.). *Men, Machines and War*. Wilfrid Laurier University Press. Waterloo. Ontario, 1988.

Head, Lt.-Col. C.O. *No Great Shakes: An Autobiography*. R. Hale. London, 1943.

Heathcote, A. *The Afghan Wars*. Osprey. London, 1980.

Henderson, D.M. *Highland Soldier: A Social Study of the Highland Regiments, 1820–1920*. John Donald. Edinburgh, 1989.

Hichberger, J.W.M. *Images of the Army: The Military in British Art, 1815–1914*. Manchester University Press. Manchester, 1988.

Hillcourt, W. *Baden-Powell: The Two Lives of a Hero*. Heinemann. London, 1964.

Hodgson, P. *The War Illustrators*. Osprey. London, 1977.

Hogg, I.V. *The Illustrated Encyclopaedia of Ammunition*. Quarto. London, 1985.

Hogg, Brig. O.F.G. *The Royal Arsenal: Its Background, Origins, and Subsequent History*. 2 Vols. Oxford University Press. London, 1963.

Holmes, R. *The Little Field-Marshal: Sir John French*. Jonathan Cape. London, 1981.

Holt, E. *The Boer War*. Putnam. London, 1976.

Howard, M. (ed.). *The Theory and Practice* of War. Cassell. London, 1965.

Hutchison, Lt.-Col. G.S. *Machine Guns: their History and Tactical*

Employment. Macmillan. London, 1938.

Hyndman, H.M. *Further Reminiscences.* Macmillan, London, 1912.

James, D. *The Life of Lord Roberts.* Hollis & Carter. London, 1954.

Johnson, F.A. *Defence by Committee.* Oxford University Press. London, 1960.

Johnson, P. *Front-line Artists.* Cassell. London, 1978.

Jourdain, Lt.-Col. H.F.N. *Ranging Memories.* Private. Oxford, 1934.

Keating, P. *The Working Classes in Victorian Fiction.* Routledge & Kegan Paul. London, 1971.

Kennedy, P. *The Realities behind Diplomacy.* Fontana. London, 1981.

—*The Rise and Fall of British Naval Mastery.* Macmillan. London, 1983.

—*The Rise of Anglo–German Antagonism 1860–1914.* Allen & Unwin. London, 1980.

Keown-Boyd, H. *A Good Dusting.* Leo Cooper. London, 1986.

Kingsford, C.L. *The Story of the Royal Warwickshire Regiment (Formerly the Sixth Foot).* Country Life. London, 1921.

Knight, I. *Brave Men's Blood: The Epic of the Zulu War, 1879.* Guild Publishing. London, 1990.

Knightley, P. *The First Casualty: The War Correspondent as Hero, Propagandist, and Myth Maker from the Crimea to Vietnam.* André Deutsch. London, 1975.

Knollys, H. (ed.). *Life of General Sir Hope Grant.* 2 Vols. Blackwood. London, 1884.

Koch, H.W. (ed.). *The Origins of the First World War: Great Power Rivalry and German War Aims.* Macmillan. London, 1972.

Kruger, R. *Goodbye Dolly Gray: A History of the Boer War.* Nel Mentor. London, 1967.

Langer, W.L. *The Diplomacy of Imperialism 1890–1912.* Alfred Knopf. New York, 1951.

Lee, J.M. *Social Leaders and Public Persons.* Clarendon Press. Oxford, 1963.

Lehmann, J. *All Sir Garnet: A Life of Field-Marshal Lord Wolseley.* Jonathan Cape. London, 1964.

—*The First Boer War.* Buchan & Enright. London, 1972.

Linklater, E. and A. *The Black Watch: The History of the Royal Highland Regiment.* Barrie & Jenkins. London, 1977.

Lloyd, A. *The Drums of Kumasi: The Story of the Ashanti Wars.* Longmans. London, 1964.

Low, R. and Manwell, R. *The History of the British Film.* Allen & Unwin. London, 1948.

Lowe, C.J. *The Reluctant Imperialists: British Foreign Policy 1878–1902.* 2 Vols. Routledge & Kegan Paul. London, 1967.

Luvaas, J. *The Education of an Army: British Military Thought, 1815–1940.* Cassell. London, 1964.

—*The Military Legacy of the Civil War.* University of Chicago Press. Chicago, 1959.

Lyons, F.S.L. *Ireland since the Famine.* Fontana. London, 1975.

Lyttelton, Gen. Sir N. *Eighty Years Soldiering, Politics, Games.* Hodder & Stoughton. London, 1927.

Macbride, Maud Gonne, *A Servant of the Queen.* Victor Gollancz. London, 1974.

MacDonald, Brig.-Gen. J.H.A. *Fifty Years of It.* Blackwood. Edinburgh, 1909.

McHugh, P. *Prostitution and Victorian Social Reform.* Croom Helm. London, 1980.

MacKenzie, J.M. (ed.). *Imperialism and Popular Culture.* Manchester University Press. Manchester, 1986.

—*Propaganda and Empire: The manipulation of British public opinion 1880–1960.* Manchester University Press. Manchester, 1984.

MacKenzie, Capt. T.A., Ewart, Lt. J.S. and Findley, Lt. C. *Historical Records of the Queen's Own Cameron Highlanders.* 6 Vols. Blackwood. Edinburgh, 1909–32.

Magnus, P. *Kitchener: Portrait of an Imperialist.* John Murray. London, 1975.

Malmesbury, Susan, Countess of. *The Life of Major-General Sir John Ardagh.* John Murray. London, 1909.

Marling, Col. Sir P. *Rifleman and Hussar: An Autobiography.* John Murray. London, 1931.

Mason, P. *A Matter of Honour: An Account of the Indian Army, its officers and men.* Jonathan Cape. London, 1974.

—*Kipling: the Glass, the Shadow and the Fire.* Jonathan Cape. London, 1975.

Matthew, H.C.G. *The Liberal Imperialists.* Oxford University Press. Oxford, 1973.

Maurice, Sir F. and Arthur, Sir G. *The Life of Lord Wolseley.*

Heinemann. London, 1924.

Maxwell. L. *The Ashanti Ring: Sir Garnet Wolseley's Campaigns 1870–1882*. Leo Cooper. London, 1985.

May, Maj.-Gen. Sir E. *Changes and Chances of a Soldier's Life*. Philip Allan. London, 1925.

Menzies, Sgt. J. *Reminiscences of an old Soldier*. Crawford & McCabe. Edinburgh, 1883.

Millman, R. *Britain and the Eastern Question 1875–1878*. Clarendon Press. Oxford, 1979.

Montgomery-Cuninghame, Col. Sir T. *Dusty Measure: A Record of Troubled Times*. John Murray. London, 1939.

Morris, D.R. *The Washing of the Spears*. Sphere. London, 1986.

Murray, R.H. *The History of the VIII King's Royal Irish Hussars*. 2 Vols. Heffer. Cambridge, 1928.

Newton, Lord. *Lord Lansdowne: A Biography*. Macmillan. London, 1929.

Nutting, A. *Gordon Martyr and Misfit*. Constable. London, 1966.

Pakenham, T. *The Boer War*. Weidenfeld & Nicolson. London, 1979.

Pelling, H. *Social Geography of British Elections 1885–1910*. Macmillan. London, 1967.

Pomeroy, Maj. the Hon. R.L. *The Story of a Regiment of Horse: being the Regimental History from 1685 to 1922 of the 5th Princess Charlotte of Wales' Dragoon Guards*. 2 Vols. Blackwood. Edinburgh, 1924.

Porter, W. and Watson, C.M. *History of the Corps of Royal Engineers*. 3 Vols. Longmans. London, 1889–1915.

Price, R. *An Imperial War and the British Working Class*. Routledge & Kegan Paul. London, 1972.

Prior, M. *Campaigns of a War Correspondent*. E. Arnold. London, 1930.

Ranger, T.O. *Revolt in Southern Rhodesia 1896–7*. Heinemann. London, 1967.

Regimental Historical Records Committee. *The Royal Inniskilling Fusiliers*. Constable. London, 1928.

Repington, Lt.-Col. C. à Court. *Vestigia*. Constable, London, 1919.

Robertson, N. *Crowned Harp*. Allen Figgis. Dublin, 1960.

Robertson, Field-Marshal Sir W. *From Private to Field-Marshal*. Constable. London, 1921.

Robinson, R. and Gallagher, J. with Denny, A. *Africa and the*

Victorians: The Official Mind of Imperialism. Macmillan. London, 1961.

Rogers, Col. H.C.B. *Weapons of the British Soldier*. Seeley Service. London, 1960.

St Aubyn, G. *The Royal George*. Constable. London, 1963.

Schurman, D. *The Education of a Navy: The Development of British Naval Strategic Thought, 1867–1914*. Cassell. London, 1965.

Seymour-Smith, M. *Rudyard Kipling*. Queen Anne Press. London, 1989.

Simon, B. and Bradley, I. (eds.). *The Victorian Public School*. Gill & Macmillan. London, 1975.

Skelley, A.R. *The Victorian Army at Home*. Croom Helm. London, 1977.

Skennerton, I.D. *A Treatise on the British Military Martini: The Martini Henry 1869–c 1900*. Arms & Armour. London, 1983.

Smith, P.T. *Policing Victorian London: Political Policing, Public Order, and the London Metropolitan Police*. Greenwood Press. Westport, Connecticut, 1985.

Smith-Dorrien, Sir H. *Memories of Forty-eight Years' Service*. John Murray. London, 1925.

Smithers, A.J. *The Kaffir Wars*. Leo Cooper. London, 1973.

Smyth, Brig. the Rt. Hon. Sir J. *In this Sign Conquer*. A.R. Mowbray. London, 1968.

—*Sandhurst: The History of the Royal Military Academy, Woolwich, the Royal Military College, Sandhurst, and the Royal Military Academy Sandhurst 1741–1961*. Weidenfeld & Nicolson. London, 1961.

Spiers, E.M. *The Army and Society 1815–1914*. Longman. London, 1980.

Spies, S.B. *Methods of Barbarism? Roberts and Kitchener and Civilians in the Boer Republics January 1900–May 1902*. Human & Rousseau. Cape Town, 1977.

Springhall, J.O. *Youth, Empire and Society: British Youth Movements, 1883–1930*. Croom Helm. London, 1977.

Stanley, G.F.G. *Toil and Trouble: Military Expeditions to Red River* Dundurn Press. Toronto, 1989.

Steedman, C. *Policing the Victorian Community: the formation of English provincial police forces, 1856–80*. Routledge. London, 1984.

Steiner, Z.S. *Britain and the Origins of the First World War*.

Macmillan. London, 1977.

Strachan, H. *European Armies and the Conduct of War.* Allen & Unwin. London, 1983.

—*Wellington's Legacy: The Reform of the British Army 1830–54.* Manchester University Press. Manchester, 1984.

Summers, A. *Angels and Citizens: British Women as Military Nurses 1854–1914.* Routledge & Kegan Paul. London, 1988.

Symons, J. *Buller's Campaign.* The Cresset Press. London, 1963.

—*England's Pride: The Story of the Gordon Relief Expedition.* H. Hamilton. London, 1965.

Thomas, H. *Sandhurst.* Hutchinson. London, 1961.

Thompson, F.M.L. *English Landed Society in the Nineteenth Century.* Routledge & Kegan Paul. London, 1963.

Trench, C. Chenevix. *Charley Gordon: An Eminent Victorian Reassessed.* Allen Lane. London, 1978.

Trustram, M. *Women of the Regiment: Marriage and the Victorian army.* Cambridge University Press. Cambridge, 1984.

Tyler, R.A.J. *Bloody Provost.* Phillimore. London, 1980.

Usherwood, P. and Spencer-Smith, J. *Lady Butler: Battle Artist 1846–1933.* Alan Sutton. Gloucester, 1987.

Vagts, A. *A History of Militarism.* Norton. New York, 1937.

Vaughan Knight, A. *The History of the Office of the Provost Marshal and the Corps of Military Police.* Gale & Polden. Aldershot, 1943.

Ventham, P. and Fletcher, D. *Moving the Guns: The Mechanisation of the Royal Artillery, 1854–1939.* HMSO. London, 1990.

Verner, Col. W. *The Military Life of H.R.H. George Duke of Cambridge.* 2 Vols. John Murray. London, 1905.

Vicinus, M. (ed.). *Suffer and be Still.* Indiana University Press. Bloomington, 1973.

Walkowitz, J.R. *Prostitution and Victorian Society.* Cambridge University Press. Cambridge, 1980.

Ward, T.H. (ed.). *The Reign of Queen Victoria.* 2 Vols. Smith, Elder & Co. London, 1887.

Warwick, P. (ed.). *The South African War: The Anglo–Boer War 1899–1902.* Longman. London, 1980.

Wavell, Gen. Sir A. *Allenby: A Study in Greatness.* Harrap. London, 1940.

—*Soldiers and Soldiering.* Jonathan Cape. London, 1953.

Wheeler, O. *The War Office Past and Present.* Methuen. London,

1914.

White, T. De Vere. *The Anglo–Irish*. Victor Gollancz. London, 1972.

Wilkinson-Latham, R. *From Our Special Correspondent: Victorian War Correspondents and their Campaigns*. Hodder & Stoughton. London, 1979.

Willcocks, Brig. Gen. Sir J. *From Kabul to Kumassi: Twenty-four Years of Soldiering and Sport*. John Murray. London, 1904.

Wilson, J. *CB: A Life of Sir Henry Campbell-Bannerman*. Constable. London, 1973.

Wolseley, Field-Marshal Viscount. *The Story of a Soldier's Life*. 2 Vols. Constable. London, 1903.

Wood, Gen. Sir H.E. *From Midshipman to Field-Marshal*. 2 Vols. Methuen. London, 1906.

Wyndham, H. *The Queen's Service*. Heinemann. London, 1899.

Younghusband, Sir G.T. *Soldier's Memories in War and Peace*. H. Jenkins. London, 1917.

Ziegler, P. *Omdurman*. Collins. London, 1973.

Unpublished dissertations

Badsey, S.D. 'Fire and Sword: The British Army and the *Arme Blanche* Controversy 1871–1921'. Unpublished Ph.D. dissertation. University of Cambridge 1981.

Bond, B.J. 'The Introduction and Operation of Short Service and Localisation in the British Army, 1868–1892'. Unpublished M.A. dissertation. University of London 1962.

Moon, H.R. 'The Invasion of the United Kingdom: Public Controversy and Official Planning 1888–1918'. 2 Vols. Unpublished Ph.D. dissertation. University of London 1968.

Moses, N.H. 'Edward Cardwell's Abolition of the Purchase System in the British Army 1868–1874: A Study in Administrative and Legislative Processes'. Unpublished Ph.D. dissertation. University of London 1969.

Muenger, E.A. 'The British Army in Ireland, 1886–1914'. Unpublished Ph.D. dissertation. University of Michigan 1981.

Page, A. 'The Supply Services of the British Army in the South African War 1899–1902'. Unpublished Ph.D. dissertation. University of Oxford 1976.

Scales, Jr., R.H. 'Artillery in Small Wars: The Evolution of British

Artillery Doctrine 1860–1914'. Unpublished Ph.D. dissertation. Duke University 1976.

Spiers, E.M. 'The Reform of the Front-line Forces of the Regular Army in the United Kingdom, 1895–1914'. Unpublished Ph.D. dissertation. University of Edinburgh 1974.

Stearn, R.T. 'War Images and Image Makers in the Victorian Era: Aspects of the British Visual and Written Portrayal of War *c.* 1886–1906'. Unpublished Ph.D. dissertation. King's College, London 1987.

Articles

Anderson, O. 'The Growth of Christian Militarism in mid-Victorian Britain'. *English Historical Review.* 86. January 1971.

Bailes, H. 'Patterns of Thought in the Late Victorian Army'. *Journal of Strategic Studies.* 4, no.1. March 1981.

—'Technology and Imperialism: a case study of the Victorian Army in Africa'. *Victorian Studies.* 24. 1980.

Beckett, I.F.W. 'Edward Stanhope at the War Office, 1887–92'. *Journal of Strategic Studies.* 5, no.2. June 1982.

—'Early Historians and the South African War'. *Sandhurst Journal of Military Studies.* I. 1990.

—'The Stanhope Memorandum of 1888: a Reinterpretation'. *Bulletin of the Institute of Historical Research.* LVII, no.136. November 1984.

Blanco, R.L. 'The Attempted Control of Venereal Disease in the Army of Mid-Victorian England', *Journal of the Society for Army Historical Research.* 45. 1967.

—'Attempts to Abolish Branding and Flogging in the Army of Victorian England before 1881'. *Journal of the Society for Army Historical Research.* 46. 1968.

Bond, B. 'Mr Gladstone's Invasion of Egypt (1882): A Revelation of Military Weakness'. *Army Quarterly and Defence Journal.* 81. 1960.

—'Recruiting the Victorian Army 1870–92'. *Victorian Studies.* 5. 1961.

—'The Effect of the Cardwell Reforms on Army Organisation 1874–1904'. *Journal of the Royal United Service Institution.* 105. 1960.

—'The Retirement of the Duke of Cambridge'. *Journal of the Royal*

United Service Institution. 106. 1961.

Burroughs, P. 'John Robert Seeley and British Imperial History'. *Journal of Imperial and Commonwealth History*. 1. 1972–73.

Cottesloe, Col. Lord. 'Notes on the History of the Royal Small Arms Factory, Enfield Lock'. *Journal of the Society for Army Historical Research*. 12. 1933.

Cowling, M. 'Lytton, the Cabinet, and the Russians'. *English Historical Review*. 76. 1961.

Cunningham, H. 'Jingoism in 1877–78'. *Victorian Studies*. 14. 1971.

—'The Language of Patriotism, 1750–1914'. *History Workshop*. 12. 1981.

Dunae, P.A. 'Boys' Literature and the Idea of Empire, 1870–1914'. *Victorian Studies*. 24. 1980.

Durrans, P.J. 'A Two-edged Sword: the Liberal Attack on Disraelian Imperialism'. *Journal of Imperial and Commonwealth History*. 10. 1982.

Ellison, G. 'From here and there: reminiscences'. *Lancashire Lad*. 12. 1934.

Gallagher, T.F. 'British Military Thinking and the Coming of the Franco–Prussian War'. *Military Affairs*. 39. 1975.

—'Cardwellian Mysteries: The Fate of the British Army Regulation Bill, 1871'. *Historical Journal*. 18. 1975.

Harcourt, F. 'Disraeli's Imperialism, 1866–1868: A Question of Timing'. *Historical Journal*. 23. 1980.

—'Gladstone, Monarchism and the New Imperialism, 1868–74'. *Journal of Imperial and Commonwealth History*. 14. 1985.

Hawkins, R. 'An Army on Police Work, 1881–2'. *Irish Sword*. XI. 1973.

Headrick, D.R. 'The Tools of Imperialism: Technology and the Expansion of European Colonial Empires in the Nineteenth Century'. *Journal of Modern History*. 51. 1979.

Hill, R. 'The Gordon Literature'. *Durham University Journal*. XLVII. June 1955.

Howard, M. 'Empire, Race and War'. *History Today*. 31. December 1981.

—'Soldiers in Politics'. *Encounter*. 19. September 1962.

Johnson, D.H. 'The Death of Gordon: A Victorian Myth'. *Journal of Imperial and Commonwealth History*. 10. 1982.

Koss, S. 'Weslyanism and Empire'. *Historical Journal*. 18. 1975.

Maitland, Maj. D.D. 'The Care of the Soldier's Family'. *Royal Army Medical Corps Journal*. 1950.

Mangan, J.A. 'Images of Empire in the late Victorian Public School'. *Journal of Educational Administration and History*. 12. January 1980.

Otley, C.B. 'The Educational Background of British Army Officers'. *Sociology*. 7. 1973.

—'The Social Origins of British Army Officers'. *Sociological Review*. 18. 1970.

Preston, A. 'Frustrated Great Gamesmanship: Sir Garnet Wolseley's Plans for War against Russia, 1873–1880'. *International History Review*. 2. 1980.

—'Wolseley, the Khartoum Relief Expedition and the Defence of India, 1885–1900'. *Journal of Imperial and Commonwealth History*. 6. 1978.

Richter, D. 'The Role of Mob Riot in Victorian Elections, 1865–1885', *Victorian Studies*. 15, no.1. September 1971.

Rodgers, N. 'The Abyssinian Expedition of 1867–1868: Disraeli's Imperialism or James Murray's War?' *Historical Journal*. 27. 1984.

Semple, A.J. 'The Fenian Infiltration of the British Army'. *Journal of the Society for Army Historical Research*. 52. 1974.

Sixsmith, E.K.G. 'Kitchener and the Guerillas in the Boer War'. *Army Quarterly and Defence Journal*. 104. 1974.

Smith, F.B. 'Ethics and Disease in the later Nineteenth Century: the Contagious Diseases Acts'. *Historical Studies*. 15. October 1971.

Spiers, E.M. 'Rearming the Edwardian Artillery', *Journal of the Society for Army Historical Research*. 57. 1979.

—'Reforming the Infantry of the Line, 1900–1914'. *Journal of the Society for Army Historical Research*. 59. 1981.

—'The Use of the Dum Dum Bullet in Colonial Warfare'. *Journal of Imperial and Commonwealth History*. 4. 1975.

Springhall, J. 'Rise and Fall of Henty's Empire'. *Times Literary Supplement*. 3 October 1968.

Stearn, R.T. 'Archibald Forbes and the British Army'. *Soldiers of the Queen*. 61. June 1990.

—'G.W. Steevens and the Message of Empire'. *Journal of Imperial and Commonwealth History*. 17. 1989.

—'War and the Media in the 19th Century: Victorian Military Artists and the Image of War, 1870–1914'. *Journal of the Royal*

United Services Institute for Defence Studies. 131. 1986.

Stuart-Smith, J. 'Military Law: its History, Administration and Practice'. *Law Quarterly Review.* 85. 1969.

Summers, A. 'Militarism in Britain before the Great War'. *History Workshop.* 2. 1976.

Trebilcock, R.C. 'A Special Relationship – Government, Rearmament, and the Cordite Firms'. *Economic History Review.* Second series. 19. 1966.

Tucker, A.V. 'Army and Society in England 1870–1900: A Reassessment of the Cardwell Reforms'. *Journal of British Studies.* 2. 1963.

Tylden, Maj. G. 'The British Army and the Transvaal 1875–85'. *Journal of the Society for Army Historical Research.* 30. 1952.

Index